TANGO LESSONS

TANGO *LESSONS*

MOVEMENT, SOUND,
IMAGE, AND TEXT
IN CONTEMPORARY
PRACTICE

MARILYN G. MILLER, EDITOR

Duke University Press ⋮ Durham and London ⋮ 2014

Library of Congress Cataloging-in-Publication Data
Tango lessons : movement, sound, image, and text
in contemporary practice / Marilyn G. Miller, ed.
pages cm
Includes bibliographical references and index.
ISBN 978-0-8223-5549-6 (cloth : alk. paper)
ISBN 978-0-8223-5566-3 (pbk. : alk. paper)
1. Tango (Dance) — Social aspects — History. 2. Tangos —
History and criticism. I. Miller, Marilyn Grace, 1961–
GV1796.T3T3369 2013
793.3'3 — dc23   2013025657

Duke University Press gratefully acknowledges the support
of Tulane University, which provided funds toward the
publication of this book.

FOR EDUARDO

CONTENTS

ACKNOWLEDGMENTS

A great many colleagues and fellow *tangueros* in Argentina, Uruguay, the United States, and elsewhere were extraordinarily gracious in sharing their time, knowledge, resources, and personal histories during the gestation of this edited volume. In addition to the contributors and translators whose formidable knowledge and hard work is represented in these pages, I would like to acknowledge and thank the Academia Porteña de Lunfardo, the Academia del Tango, Carlos Alonso, the Ateneo Popular de La Boca, Carlos Barea, Liliana Barela, Salvador Batalla, Florencia Bazzano, Marcos Blum, Eduardo Bucich, Juan Carlos Cáceres, Carlos Cañás, Giselle Casares, Juan Carlos Copes, Edgardo Cozarinsky, Arlene Dávila, Claudia DeBrito, Horacio de Dios, Lea Dolinsky, Estudio DNI Tango, Luis Feldman, Horacio Ferrer, Paula Ferrio, Jorge Firpo, Sebastián Freire, Fundación Kónex, Florencia Garramuño, Omar Gasparini, Diego Goldberg, Adriana Groisman, Fermín Hontou (Ombú), Daniel Kaplan, the Latin American Library at Tulane University, Hernán Lombardi, Jorge López, Marcos López, Alfredo Lucadamo, Cristian MacEntyre, Acho Manzi, Deborah Miller, Gabriela Miró, Ben Molar, Alberto Mosquera Montana, Gustavo Mozzi, Jorge Muscia, the Museo de la Ciudad, Curry O'Day, Marcelo Héctor Oliveri, Shannon Payne, Albert Paz and Valerie Hart, Marta Porto, Lydia Pugliese, Olga Reni, Walter Romero, Fernando Saavedra Faget, Alejandro Saderman, Marino Santa María, Gustavo Santaolalla, Walter Santoro, Marcia Schwartz, Claudio Segovia, Carlos Semino, Aldo Sessa, Luis Sessa, Gabriel Soria, Martín Soubiate, Rodrigo Spagnuolo, Rafael Squirru, Manuel Surribá, Julie M. Taylor, Cristina Torrallardona, Ignacio Varchausky, Rubén Vela, Leo Vinci, Manrique Zago, and all my colleagues and students at Tulane, with whom and from whom I learn so much.

Four figures who nurtured my *metejón* with the tango by providing an unending supply of information, friendship, and inspiration throughout the process deserve special mention. Oscar Conde indulged my curiosity and questions from start to finish with patience, wisdom, and good humor. Fernando Rosenberg, a cosmopolitan *porteño* par excellence, recommended people, places, classes, and resources that were exactly right. Hermenegildo Sábat accompanied the project with his art, vision, ear for jazz, and reminisces of New Orleans. Gregorio Traub, the oracle of Barracas, offered privileged information on the histories of tango and Buenos Aires from a massive memory bank that he keeps in his head.

Research and assembly of this book was made infinitely richer and sweeter when Eduardo Alvelo stepped in as the project's *guitarrista de Gardel*, its essential accompanist. A great many of the contacts and interviews with hallowed figures of *rioplatense* cultural history were secured through his intervention. This is very much his book, too.

Many thanks to Valerie Millholland, Miriam Angress, Susan Albury, and everyone else at Duke University Press who helped see the book through to publication.

Research for this edited volume was supported by several generous grants from the Stone Center for Latin American Studies and the School of Liberal Arts at Tulane University.

MARILYN G. MILLER

The tango is an infinite possibility.
— popular saying

The Tango Continuum

For more than a century, an eclectic array of students, scholars, and fans have debated the origins, meanings, and relevance of the tango. Where did it originate? Who invented it, and who has composed, sung, played, or danced it best? How did it develop into what we know today as tango, and how should it be performed and preserved in our own times? Why is it called *tango* in the first place?[1] The scholars convened in this edited volume address the fields of music and dance but explore tango's vitality in language, literary critique, film, and art as well, concluding that tango is alive and flourishing in all these venues, in some cases to a degree perhaps never before seen. For some, this heightened interest and enthusiasm signals a resurgence, for others a continuation, and yet for still others a rupture with hallowed traditions. However one understands its recent history, tango praxis today constitutes a hub of rich, diverse, and multifarious activity in contexts both local and global.

Questions about tango's present state in relation to its storied history are not new. In an essay published in 1926, the Argentine writer Jorge Luis Borges distinguished between a "contemporary" picturesque tango and a more genuine "primordial" tango built of "pure insolence, pure shamelessness, pure happiness in bravery" (*On Argentina* 43). Such categorizations, resting on the tensions between tradition and innovation, authenticity and creativity, still generate impassioned debate. Attesting to tango's deep resonance in the twenty-first century, the twenty-four members of UNESCO's Intangible Heritage Committee named the music and dance forms of the *tango rioplatense* a world cultural heritage in 2009.[2]

As scholars and students who find ourselves in its thrall, we are witnesses to tango's vitality and complexity. Though we take into account its many historical trajectories, here we focus principally on its current resonance and power. In addition to its relevance as dance or music or literature, tango presents a useful tool for studying global cultural flows and their interactions. Indeed, there are few popular cultural forms so thoroughly interdisciplinary as the tango.[3] In tango, "musical and nonmusical materials [are apt] to comment on, criticize, or reinterpret each other as well as to repeat each other" (Kramer, *Music as Cultural Practice* 14).[4] Nonetheless, scholarly investigations from different disciplines have rarely acknowledged this multivalence. As dancers, listeners, and participants in other practices of the form, we use this edited volume to make a case for tango as a vast repository of local experience, wide-ranging knowledge, and global significance. Inspired by the luminaries who have contributed to its rise to international fame in the last century, we offer fresh perspectives on tango's vigor and continuing appeal for new generations of aficionados.

The backstory to tango's unlimited possibilities can be found in the parallel and complementary processes of local development and transnational circulation. Within this story, scholars refer to varied influences in the forms and styles that contributed to its basic structure (*candombe*, milonga, *milongón*, habanera, *tango andaluz*, etc.), in the home cultures of those elements (Spain, Uruguay, Cuba, Africa, Italy, the Argentine pampas, specific Buenos Aires neighborhoods, etc.), and in the colorful characters who implemented them, such as immigrants from Europe, people of African descent, *compadritos* (pimps), and *payadores* (street poets), among others. These myriad musical and kinetic practices conjoined and coalesced as tango rioplatense in Buenos Aires and across the Río de la Plata in Montevideo about 1880.[5] The initial attractions were the dance and the rhythms driving it, rhythms so infectious that twenty-first-century tango still retains a movement repertoire based on the same holy trinity of milonga, *vals* (waltz), and tango proper.[6]

Of its three principal rhythms, milonga offers a key to understanding tango's history as well as its contemporary practices. Milonga harkens back to the late nineteenth century and a brash, rules-bashing dance style (*canyengue*) that developed from African diasporic elements and aligns tango with other popular American forms such as jazz and Cuban son (see Thompson; Salinas Rodríguez).[7] Aníbal Ford describes the milonga, popularized in rural zones and Buenos Aires's *suburbios* or marginal neighborhoods, as a "slow, conversational, boastful, rebellious, at times reflexive and at times laudatory form of expression" (39).[8] Robert Farris Thompson calls it simply the "conscience of tango" (12). "Like blues next to jazz, or *son montuno* with salsa," milonga "keeps tango honest, being close to the roots" (Thompson 12).[9]

While musicologists, cultural historians, and writers, including Borges, discuss the specific role of milonga in tango's evolution, most agree on its hybrid lineage, which displays traces of the habanera rhythm popularized throughout the Americas. The dance historian Sergio Pujol cites a comment in an edition of the magazine *Caras y Caretas*, published in 1903, that documents this process over a century ago: "The sleepy and steady habaneras easily won over the lazy *compadrito*, who was already enjoying the lubricious back-and-forth of the milonga, and the latter and the former fusing together engendered the plebian tango, whose baby steps are practiced today on the sidewalks of the *conventillos* to the beat of a street piano" (qtd. in Pujol 29).[10] Whatever the exact ingredients and their order of aggregation to the tango mix, the movement synthesis described above would soon be complemented by increasingly elaborate instrumental and vocal accompaniment. The strains of the bandoneon, a small accordion-like instrument imported by German immigrants but adapted to the hybrid strains of the tango, ultimately came to define the characteristic tango sound.

Born in Brothels

In its earliest manifestations as a form that was danced and played in the brothels of Buenos Aires, the tango was jovial and ribald (G. Varela, *Mal de tango* 45). Even before the introduction of the *tango canción* with Carlos Gardel and other vocalists, to which we will return, tango lyrics exhibited characteristics of verbal daring and signifying.[11] From 1870 on, periodicals published in rioplatense black communities contain curious references to "los tangos negros, como terribles, significando bonitos, gratos de escuchar" (black tangos as terrible, meaning pretty, pleasant to listen to) (Carretero 63). The earliest fans, who were overwhelmingly male and immigrant (Pujol 27), often danced to songs with titillating titles such as "Echale aceite a la manija" (Grease the handle), "Ponela, sacala y volvémela a poner" (Put it in, take it out, and put it in for me again), "Tocámelo que me gusta" (Touch it, I like that), "Mordeme la oreja izquierda" (Bite my left ear), "El fierrazo" (The orgasm), "Tomame el pulso" (Take my pulse), and "Dos sin sacar" (Two without withdrawing) (G. Varela, *Mal de tango* 46), all tunes for which accompanying lyrics arguably would have been superfluous.[12] Early twentieth-century songwriters such as Angel Villoldo, famous today for such "standards" as

"El choclo" and "La morocha," also penned eyebrow-raising titles such as "Chiflala, que va a venir," a masterpiece of double entendre that could mean "Whistle at her, she'll come" or, alternately, "Blow her, she'll come."[13] The "juicy" quality of these lyrics resonates with long-held assumptions about tango as an activity intimately tied to sex, as a form of physical contact bound by the conventions of heteronormativity and subject to (and of) a long history of male dominance. Such titles serve as prophesies of the charged gender dynamics of the dance as it develops throughout the twentieth and twenty-first century. Many such song titles confirm that early tango and sex were often companion activities: "True, men and women descended from Kongo, Andalusia and Italy met and created a new dance in rough neighborhoods. Some danced for sex; some danced for art; some danced to show off their bodies. New steps could hardly have emerged, however, had the best not been dancing for dance. In a city in motion, bravura moves were the crest of all change" (Thompson 221).

It is out of this dynamic atmosphere of experimentation, paradoxically, that tango's "classic" style and markers would begin to take shape. The canyengue style would cede to a more upright, less closely danced *tango de salon*. Tango dancers would move from the marginal bordellos and *piringundines* (early twentieth-century dives) to the dance halls and glossy cabarets of city centers. Street musicians playing under the iconic *farol* or streetlamp would move inside to integrate *orquestas típicas* and even concert ensembles.[14] But first, early twentieth-century tango needed an image makeover.

Transatlantic Traffic

Although Buenos Aires and Montevideo provided an ideal growing medium for tango as dance, music, and text, it was transnational and transatlantic circulation that converted it into a global sensation. One of the earliest and most celebrated of tango's travels was its appearance in Paris in the second decade of the twentieth century. Upper-class Argentines who regularly traveled to the City of Light to polish and display their European family pedigrees discovered that the same dance still associated with marginal figures and houses of ill repute in Buenos Aires had unexpectedly become a sensation in the French capital. What's more, dance skills could trump an illustrious surname to open the doors to Parisian high society.

Acceptance by French society was an essential key to tango's reevaluation in Buenos Aires, which had by then been dubbed the so-called Paris of Latin

America. Word spread that even the Princess Bonaparte had taken classes at one of the Parisian dance academies specializing in tango (Gasió 18–19), proving to *porteños* that this dance of ruffians and rapscallions had become, rather shockingly, the dance of royalty.[15] Still, the transformation of tango's reputation from savage to civilized by virtue of the French connection was perhaps less sudden and wholesale than might first appear.[16] In October 1913 the Algerian-born Jean Richepin gave a lecture at the Institute of France that served as a teaser for his stage show *Le Tango*, which opened two months later in a Paris theater house. By presenting tango in an elite academic context and an opulent stage show, Richepin celebrated tango in both empirical and aesthetic terms. The same year the newspaper *La Razón* published a report by the Society of French Medicine affirming that, "from the point of view of physical education, [tango] offers, beyond all other [dances] of the last twenty years, the advantage of making the body and arms work more, forcing the flexions and alternative extensions of the musculature of the lateral region of the torso, the extensions of the muscles of the chest region . . . [and] the extensions of the lumbar group and the lateral abdominals" (qtd. in G. Varela, *Mal de tango* 68). In other words, the dance previously dismissed as a social ill was now espoused as a cure. Its turn in the salons and parlors of Paris (as well as in London and other European metropoles) converted the tango into something *infectious* in an entirely different way.

Richepin's sumptuous production fascinated theatergoers and sparked a revolution in Parisian style trends as well, but not without a backlash.[17] Cardinal Amette, the scandalized archbishop of Paris, prohibited the faithful from dancing tango, directing priests to include a phrase in confession manuals that claimed the imported dance was of a lascivious nature and offensive to morals (Gasió 43).[18] The publicity generated by events such as Richepin's lecture and stage show, combined with the church's prohibition, ultimately unleashed a media frenzy around all things tango, inspiring a host of new trends in Paris and beyond: clothing designed to be more danceable, a specific color and dessert labeled "tango," a men's haircut *a la argentina*, a spate of tango-themed dinners in London (Fuentes 290), and a series of drawings by Xavier Sager based on Richepin's show (Gasió 39). The Parisian media lamented, "we have to put up with it everywhere, in every detail of life" (qtd. in Gasió 44).[19]

Upon its return to the Río de la Plata after taking Paris by storm, tango's popularity exploded. We can see its progressive repurposing as an icon of national culture in the way song lyrics take center stage in poetry, narrative, advertising, and everyday language. That process itself is documented in the tango "Como se pasa la vida" (How life goes on), composed by Manuel Romero with words by Alberto Novion:

> Cuando el tango se inventó
> era nada más que un baile . . .
> Pero ahora es una canción
> y de las más populares . . .
> Todo el mundo canta el tango
>
> [When the tango was invented
> it was nothing but a dance . . .
> but now it is a song,
> and one of the most popular sorts . . .
> Everybody's singing the tango] (Collier 69)

Song titles reveal shifts as well, as tongue-in-cheek numbers make way for loftier sentiments and local pride in themes such as "Viva la patria" (Long live the homeland) (G. Varela, *Mal de tango* 67). So thorough was this process that by the 1920s, tango had become the central component of Argentine popular entertainment in cabarets, cafés, dance halls, and theaters and could be heard on the radio and sound recordings as well (Collier 69). Soon, it would occupy a central role in cinema and television.

The status and cultural value of tango would from then on reside in the interstices of the primitive and the modern, the popular and the cultured (Garramuño 106). Despite lingering associations with the underclass, the verses of renowned lyricists Homero Manzi, Enrique Discépolo, Cátulo Castillo, and Enrique Cadícamo were early on categorized and canonized as "poetry" and printed in Buenos Aires literary magazines such as *Sur*.[20] We can see this graphically illustrated in the work of *vanguardista* artists who used tango to tell the story of modernization while often retaining traditional or nostalgic elements (Garramuño 133). In "Picturing Tango," chapter 3 in this edited volume, I invite readers on a virtual tour of tango's representation in art from the early twentieth century to the twenty-first century, revealing how painters and other visual artists helped build a local aesthetic informed by cosmopolitan values, an aesthetic in which tango plays a key role.

Art of Walking, Art of Talking

If its Parisian success created broad acceptance and increased transnational circulation during the so-called golden age of tango from about 1935 to 1950, tango has in the twenty-first century become even more popular, even with competition from a host of other music and dance. Despite preservationist efforts by traditionalists, tango as music, dance, text, and language has exhibited an extraordinary elasticity and is now more accessible to international audiences than ever before, though perhaps not with the same widespread access across social classes that characterized earlier periods in Argentina (see, for example, Dávila). Tango has successively absorbed influences from jazz, rock, hip-hop, and other musical and dance styles. In October 2007 it was the focus of a globalization conference convened at Harvard University by the cultural critic Homi Bhabha titled "Tango! Dance the World Around: Global Transformations of Latin American Culture." Participants examined globalization, gender issues, urban development, and performance history to move beyond the idea of tango as "simply" music or dance.[21]

However global or diverse it becomes, though, tango retains a core mystery; despite commonplace, even hackneyed associations with the past and its attendant nostalgias, something of the uncanny—both verbal and corporeal, both on and off the stage—still accompanies us as we watch, listen to, and participate in tango performances in Buenos Aires, Montevideo, Paris, Portland, and beyond. New articulations invite us to see tango as abundance rather than as loss and lament. The renowned Argentine poet Juan Gelman, himself an avid dancer from the age of fifteen, attributes the paradox of the binaries dispossession/marginalization and connection/pleasure to the notion of the *danceable dialogue*. While acknowledging Borges's characterization of the tango as a way of walking, as an *arte de caminar*, he himself saw it as a way of making conversation, as an *arte de conversar*.[22] Tango's ability to serve both as a vehicle of communication and the subject of a musical, kinetic, or poetic conversation marks it as a perpetually renewable resource. This elemental connection between dance partners or the members of a musical collective is emphasized and respected by proponents of all tango styles—including fans of so-called *nuevo tango*, in which the classic embrace may be opened or relaxed and the standard tango musical signature questioned but never completely abandoned. The connections grafted in the three-minute duration of a standard tango are the source of the release and fulfillment we experience in its embrace.

The quintessential characteristic of tango dance performance resides in the pursuit of a communion between two or more bodies in a single dynamic structure, using an improvised form (Dínzel 9, 13).[23] Juan Carlos Copes, considered one of the best *milongueros* ever to grace both a dance floor and a theater stage, explains that together, dance partners create a unique body with one head and four legs, a body that exhibits its combined passions with the hope that the orchestra will never reach the final "tchan-tchan," the two-note rhythmic resolution characteristic of the tango (12). Rodolfo Dínzel, recognized as an expert *bailarín* and theorist of tango movement, notes that "one plus one in the tango isn't two, but one" (9).[24]

Until the twenty-first century, tango dancers generally advocated the formula of a male leader and a female follower, in which the sought after communion of "one plus one equals one" did not erase problematic gender relationships. Works by such scholars as Estela Dos Santos, Julie Taylor, Donna Guy, and Anahí Viladrich acknowledge the male privilege and dominance that have characterized dance practices, but they also show how "women have been historically able to defy conventional gender stereotypes both through lyrics and performance" (Viladrich, "Neither Virgins nor Whores" 274). These specialists reveal that within a form created, manipulated, and dominated by men, tango contains a zone—a *tolerance house*, to use an old term associated with the brothels themselves—in which women were allowed to sing, dance, compose, and perform (Dos Santos, *Las Cantantes* 2225).[25]

Nonetheless, female dance partners went unnamed alongside their male counterparts on theater marquees, women composers assumed male pseudonyms to improve their chances of publication or circulation, and singers practiced "female transvestism" by interpreting tangos whose lyrics were written for male vocalists (see Viladrich, "Neither Virgins nor Whores"). Further, actresses who eschewed performing in seedy bars brought tango to life in radio dramas, and iconic figures such as Tita Merello challenged gender expectations and rejected prevailing standards of female beauty. All of these women harnessed diverse resources and talents to challenge and spurn the male dominance at the heart of the industry throughout the twentieth century. In the twenty-first century, as Carolyn Merritt's chapter in this collection shows, women are taking on increasingly important roles in expanding global tango dance circuits. Their explorations and innovations as teachers, dancers, choreographers, and musicians enable us to broadly rethink gender roles in tango today.

From the Feet to the Eyes, Ears, and Mouth

Milongueros still dance in couples, seeking creativity and connectivity within the context of the *pareja*, however that duo is constituted. But tango dancers in the twenty-first century hear the accompanying soundtrack differently. Contemporary dancers are often oblivious to the rich textual legacy of song lyrics, poems, and a tango-influenced popular vocabulary that constituted another aspect of the danceable dialogue referred to by Gelman, who himself granted tango a central role in his literary endeavors. In his chapter in this edited volume, Oscar Conde analyzes the contemporary legacies of *lunfardo*, a popular argot of Buenos Aires that dates back to the late nineteenth century, when it developed among immigrants and native-born inhabitants in the tenements and outlying areas of the city. He shows how lunfardo retains a semantic richness fertilized by successive waves of cultural influences from the Argentine pampas, other national regions, as well as from Spain, Italy, Eastern Europe, Africa, and elsewhere. Remarkably, many words that figured in the first lunfardo dictionary from 1894, such as *mina* (young woman), *guita* (money), and *bulín* (den, love nest), are still in common usage in the Río de la Plata region.[26] In a story that parallels that of the tango itself, lunfardo is typified by uncertain and disputed origins and by a muddied process of consolidation in a laboratory of everyday practices of a mestizo, working-class population.[27] After its early circulation among mostly poor and "fringe" groups situated along the *orillas* or outskirts of the modernizing city, songwriters and poets appropriated both tango and lunfardo and validated them as central tenets of local cultural identity.

However, whereas tango dance and instrumental music translated well to foreign publics, lunfardo terms and the tango lyrics that incorporated them remained indecipherable to all but local listeners. Consequently, lunfardo has been sometimes exploited by Argentine lyricists and poets keen on accentuating privileged local knowledge and proving their "authenticity"; it was simultaneously rejected by thinkers more interested in the cosmopolitan features of local culture.[28] For songwriters and poets such as Cátulo Castillo, Homero Expósito, Enrique Santos Discépolo, Enrique Cadícamo, and Celedonio Flores, though, lunfardo terms were like keywords or shorthand in the enunciation of a criollo poetics that sought legitimacy not through copying imported styles and tastes but through the elevation of a "locally owned and operated" vocabulary.

These histories of tango reflect volatile dynamics of the couple, the neighborhood, the nation, and the canon in uneven and uneasy formation. The early twentieth-century Argentine novelist Roberto Arlt believed tango was the escape valve for the pain of the city; the famous left-leaning composer and orchestra director Osvaldo Pugliese called it a register of neighborhood complaints; the contemporary political figure Susana Rinaldi deemed it the protest song that expresses the pain of a people (Horvath 22). These associations with release, free expression, and boundary crossing between genres, genders, social groups, and zones of the city take us back to tango's early associations with carnival (see, for example, Chasteen 63–70). Carnival provoked the illusion that happiness was possible and egalitarian, illusions that extended onto the tango dance floor (Pujol 58). Even as it underwent a process of *adecentamiento* or gentrification that placed new value on glamour, high society style, and more socially condoned behaviors, tango continued to offer the allure of temporary release from the everyday constrictions of rank and class.

Descriptions of tango as an escape valve highlight its propensity for lament, complaint, or confrontation and frustrate the characterization of sentimentality that typically accompanies the stock images of tango in its globalized forms. They show how tango can function as a predictable performance of standardized elements as well as an outlet for local expressivity.[29] For most fans of tango as a textual form, songwriters the likes of Discépolo and Manzi remain its true poets and privileged mouthpieces. Manzi brilliantly combined erudite and popular elements, synthesizing the two predominant schools of expression represented by the left-leaning, working-class Boedo group on the one hand and the more refined, cosmopolitan aesthetic of the Florida group on the other.[30] In 2007, when Argentina celebrated the hundredth anniversary of Manzi's birth, the artist Hermenegildo Sábat created a triptych portrait of the beloved lyricist with the heading "Manzi Somos Todos" (We are all Manzi). In fact, Manzi and many other great twentieth-century lyricists are still so revered that the youngest and most innovative performers of today's tango continue to interpret their songs and sample their voices in electronic remixes. As Esteban Buch and Morgan Luker show in their chapters in this edited volume, "new" tango music is as much about recycling, recombining, and repurposing as it is about innovation.[31]

Tango's Intersecting Histories

Besides providing a rich account of itself, the tango rioplatense also gives us a tool with which we can plumb a whole host of other related histories.[32] For example, if the most important events tied to tango's emergence were the construction of the new port of Buenos Aires in 1870, the end of the war with Paraguay in 1871, and the federalization of Buenos Aires in 1880 (Nogués 198), then work on tango will lead us to a broader knowledge of the Atlantic world's maritime and port histories, South American military history, and nineteenth-century political histories. With tango, we can also examine the labor and economic history that attracted millions of Italians, Spaniards, Poles, and Russians to the Río de la Plata region in the early twentieth century to work in slaughterhouses and other burgeoning industries, an influx that in turn increased prostitution, petty crime, urban overcrowding, and impoverished living conditions so often associated with the early development of the music (see Castro, *The Argentine Tango*). Or, we might investigate how growth in the film industry and international travel and tourism subsequently spread tango's fame to vast new publics.[33]

Tango history also intersects with African and Jewish diasporas in the region in surprising ways. George Reid Andrews, Gustavo Goldman, Robert Farris Thompson, and Juan Carlos Cáceres all make a case for the key contributions of Afro-Uruguayans and Afro-Argentines to tango.[34] Julio Nudler and José Judkovski have similarly shown how tango bisects twentieth-century Jewish history, both in the Southern Cone and in Europe. Tango was very popular in Berlin, Vienna, and other European cultural capitals by the 1930s, and these scholars note that Jews imprisoned in concentration camps in Germany, Poland, and elsewhere composed many tangos, including some in Yiddish (Judkovski 19).[35] Many Jews who emigrated to Argentina (including a long list of classically trained violinists) found in tango a performance environment in which they rubbed elbows with composers and musicians from a wide variety of immigrant backgrounds. Together, these "new" Argentines and Uruguayans explored common themes of uprooting, nostalgia, insecurity, dispossession, and despair, but they also faced the danger of contagion or dilution of religious particularity in the process of assimilating to their intensely hybrid environments (Nudler 13–14).

Tango carries the freight of memory and identity in the saga of Argentine exile as well. Antonio Gómez's chapter examines *Tangos, the Exile of Gardel* and *The Pavements of Saturn*, two films that portray the Argentine exile community in Paris during their home country's dictatorship from 1976 to 1983. In both pictures tango accompanies the protagonists as they navigate the conditions of political repression and exile and as they discover that their efforts must conform to French audiences' preexisting notion of tango's meaning and function. Ultimately, the story of Argentine and Uruguayan exiles seeking refuge from a brutal dictatorship—a story the protagonists attempt to tell in part through tango—is thwarted, even repressed, by European patrons more interested in entertainment than historical experience.[36] In another chapter focused on film, Fernando Rosenberg shows how recent tango-themed film documentaries frustrate a reading of internal Argentine history that is seamless, linear, or straightforward. The works he takes up reveal unsettled boundaries between daily life and filmic artifice and between "the real" in quotidian experience and its cinematic evocation.

In his chapter on shifts in Borges's ideas concerning tango and milonga, Alejandro Susti demonstrates that while we may never resolve the controversies over tango's origins or "true" nature, such debates compel us to consider competing understandings of national and regional history and aesthetics. Susti shows how in his essay "A History of the Tango," published in 1955, Borges modified his earlier, stricter posture regarding the form's provenance. After reexamining the assertions of the Uruguayan cultural historian Vicente Rossi, who argued for its African antecedents (by way of the Afro-Uruguayan candombe), and of the Argentine musicologist Carlos Vega, who just as adamantly affirmed its Spanish roots,[37] Borges conceded that these and other histories might all have their merits (*On Argentina* 101). Beyond a few "essential facts," such as its emergence in the brothels south of Buenos Aires around 1880 or 1890, the truth about the tango, Borges concluded, depended on who was asking and answering the question (*On Argentina* 102).[38]

Great Moments around the Globe

By the third decade of the twentieth century, the previously disreputable dance of the underclass had been proudly rechristened as a marker of Argentine national character. Growing numbers of porteños from many social classes danced and listened to tango, and tango's early triumph in Paris, London, and elsewhere in Europe created a foothold for its ongoing transcontinental circulation. The increased travel of Argentine tango performers and teachers to metropolitan centers in North America, Europe, Asia, and elsewhere in Latin America;[39] tango's incursions in radio broadcasting;[40] the production, sale, and distribution of recorded music in several formats (records, CDs, digital formats, etc.); the portrayal of tango in film, on television, and in visual culture;[41] and the diffusion of textual materials touching on tango in history, literature, anthropology, sociology, and other disciplines all represent important details of this colossal circulation history. Within this epic account, certain performers, performances, and productions stand out.[42] Confessing beforehand to gross oversimplification, we suggest four "great moments" that have overtly determined tango's global recognition and international popularity: Carlos Gardel's creation of the tango canción in 1917 and the heralding of tango's so-called golden age; the rise of nuevo tango with the unique style of the bandoneonist Astor Piazzolla in the 1950s, directed primarily at audiences of listeners rather than dancers; the "rebirth" of the international tango stage show with Claudia Segovia's opulent production of *Tango Argentino* in Paris in 1983; and finally, beginning in 2000, tango's irruption in the "world music" arena with recordings by Gotan Project, Bajofondo, and other electronic tango musicians.

The most sacred of these stories for older generations of tango enthusiasts is that of the inimitable (though frequently imitated) Carlos Gardel (ca. 1890–1935), whose disputed origins, like those of tango and lunfardo, are still hotly debated three quarters of a century after his death. Uruguayans, Argentines, and the French all claim him as their own, and his birth date and birth place remain matters of fiery contention, despite the "proofs" that have been presented all around.[43] Simon Collier, the first researcher to publish a biography of Gardel in English (1986), identifies the singer as Latin America's first and perhaps greatest entertainment superstar (xi). More than the tale of a remarkable voice, his was also an immigrant success story, imbued with the good fortune of belonging to an era and a place with a rich tradition of popular music that would soon be disseminated to a global audience. Privileged heir to a host of song styles from the Argentine provinces as well as from immigrants from Spain, Italy, and elsewhere, Gardel also learned from the payadores, dueling masters of verbal and musical improvisation who began to disappear just as he was coming of age.[44]

In August 1925, while performing with José Razzanno, Gardel was invited to sing for Edward, Prince of Wales, who was visiting Argentina. That concert proved Gardel's abilities to win over an international, celebrity-studded audience and inaugurated a transnational tour with stage and film performances in France, the United States, and Latin America. From Paris, Gardel wrote to Razzano that seventy thousand of his records had been sold in three months, an incredible figure for that era (Collier 111–12). By 1931 he was making his first feature film, *Luces de Buenos Aires* (Lights of Buenos Aires), accompanied by the great Julio de Caro and his orchestra. De Caro famously postponed a gig at Buckingham Palace for King George V in order to film with Gardel (Collier 181). Audiences were so taken with *Luces* that they forced projectionists to rewind and replay the segment in which Gardel sang his own composition "Tomo y obligo" (Collier 183). The public reaction was even more deafening when Paramount Pictures released the New York–shot *Cuesta abajo* in 1934. A Buenos Aires film house reported "delirious public applause" and audiences' insistence that Gardel's singing scenes be replayed over and over (Collier 226).

Thanks to these huge successes, by the mid-1930s Gardel had come to epitomize many of the supreme values of porteño society: friendship, courage, virility, and the capacity for seduction (Mascia 243). These qualities of "Gardelism" outlived "the songbird" himself, and for decades Gardel was a household name in Argentina and other parts of Latin America, as well as in France and the United States. Colombians joke that they may not know where Gardel was born, but they definitely know where he died: the plane crash that cut short his life in Medellín in 1935 converted the international star into a character more tragic and heroic than any he had embodied in his film and stage performances. When Gardel died, it was "almost as if the voice of Buenos Aires itself had been cut off," a reporter for *Crítica* wrote (qtd. in Collier 272). Radio stations in Buenos Aires agreed to not broadcast a single note of tango, whether of Gardel or his interpreters, for an entire week (Ulanovsky et al. 98), and desolate fans in several cities committed or contemplated suicide (Collier 273–74).

After this period of mourning, Gardel's voice returned to the airwaves, and today we can hear him intone such beloved favorites as "El día que me quieras" (The day that you love me), "Volver" (Return), and "Mi Buenos Aires querido" (My beloved Buenos Aires) on the radio as well as on sound recordings and digital downloads. His aural presence is complemented by a strong visual imprint: Gardel has a subway stop named after him in his old barrio, a statuesque final resting place in Buenos Aires's Chacarita Cemetery to which the faithful still flock, and a face so famous its recognition quotient in Latin America is second only to that of a later revolutionary named Ernesto "Che" Guevara. The Uruguayan photographer José María Silva's famous portraits of "Carlitos" adorn millions of walls and businesses (see Del Barco) and grace the covers of newspapers and magazines designed to attract his nostalgic fans. Gardel still grins out at us in beloved caricatures by Hermengildo Sábat and in huge, Warhol-hued street murals by the contemporary artist Marino Santa María.[45]

Despite the time that has lapsed, Gardel and his version of tango have stayed the test of time, in and beyond Argentina. In 2011 the United States Postal Service included him in a stamp series commemorating Latin music legends along with Tito Puente, Carmen Miranda, Celia Cruz, and Selena. In Argentina his philatelic fame had already spread via postage stamps created by the artists Carlos Alonso, Hermenegildo Sábat, and Aldo Severi. His devotees maintain that through the combined miracles of high fidelity sound recordings and the fidelity of his fans, "cada día canta mejor" (every day he sings better). Indeed, it does seem that Gardel's enduring appeal remains unmatched in the vocal history of the genre. Something in Gardel's style and persona still satisfies our need for an expressivity so broad that it can encompass joy, pain, longing, and hope, all in the same full-throated notes.[46]

The Piazzolla Phenomenon

On the set of the New York–shot *El día que me quieras* (1935), Gardel met a thirteen-year-old extra named Astor Piazzolla (1921–92). Piazzolla's father Vicente had moved the family from Argentina to Manhattan a few years earlier, but he remained a great fan of Gardel and tango. When Astor was eight, his father had given him a bandoneon, wagering (rather presciently, it turns out) that his son would go far with the instrument (Fischerman and Gilbert 27).[47] Astor studied classical and popular musical styles with various teachers, took bandoneon lessons with Andrés D'Aquila, and made his first recording at age eleven (Kuri 20).

The young Piazzolla demonstrated his skills for the great singer, and Gardel invited him to join the crew on its upcoming Latin American tour.[48] Vicente insisted his son was too young to go, saving the budding bandoneonist from the tragic fate of Gardel and the others; Piazzolla later joked that if his father had agreed to the tour, he would be playing a heavenly harp instead of a *fuelle*.[49] That fortuitous missed opportunity nonetheless planted a seed. In 1937 Astor returned to an Argentina in which tango reigned supreme and where hundreds of orquestas típicas—ensembles composed of piano, bandoneon, bass, guitar, flute, violin, and sometimes other string instruments—played in nightclubs, cabarets, and dance halls throughout Buenos Aires and beyond. Piazzolla sat in with several of these groups, most notably with that of the revered composer and director Aníbal Troilo or "Pichuco," considered by many the best bandoneon player of all time.[50] He was simultaneously studying piano and composing with classical musicians such as the pianist Arthur Rubinstein (then living in Buenos Aires) and the Argentine composer Alberto Ginastera. By day Piazzolla was scoring his own compositions inspired by the works of Stravinsky, Bartok, and Ravel, while by night he was seeing how well his talents on the bandoneon stood up to the demands of the porteño public for *música popular*.

In 1953 Piazzolla's *Buenos Aires Symphony* won a contest that allowed him to study in Paris with the acclaimed composition teacher Nadia Boulanger. Boulanger, concerned that an emotive core was missing from his symphonic works, reportedly quizzed Piazzolla on his personal life and creative endeavors, finally uncovering the "dirty secret" of his bandoneon playing in the nocturnal haunts of the Argentine capital. Legend has it that when he began playing his tango composition "Triunfal," Boulanger stopped him after just a few bars, took his hands and said, "Don't ever abandon that. That is your music. Here is Piazzolla" (Fischerman and Gilbert 120). As with Gardel decades earlier, the French connection allowed Piazzolla and other Argentines to approach tango differently, to see it not as an unrefined cultural product directed at an unsophisticated mass public but as a legitimate arena for creative inquiry, skills development, and musical performance of the highest order.[51] In Paris tango was time and again redefined as cosmopolitan and transnational, and its reception there enabled and ennobled new levels of experimentation.

In fact, Piazzolla's immigrant experiences in New York (where he modified George Gershwin and Bach for the bandoneon) and Paris (resonating in the early 1950s with the hard bop and cool jazz sounds of the likes of Art Farmer, Sonny Clark, and Miles Davis) were crucial to the subsequent integration of "foreign" matter in his tradition-bending tango compositions. These borrowings were considered heresy by many tango purists, some of whom would heckle Piazzolla at his performances by shouting "¡Ahora tóquese un tango, maestro!" (Now play a tango, maestro!). But the incorporation of jazz and classical styles would also garner the composer and musician worldwide acclaim among a new kind of fan, one more prone to appreciative listening than to dance floor derring-do. With compositions featuring bold, new harmonic and melodic structures, arrangements that included instruments previously unassociated with the tango such as saxophone and electric guitar, and a signature style of playing standing up, with one foot propped on a stool or chair to help support his bandoneon, Piazzolla singlehandedly inaugurated the first coming of nuevo tango or *tango nuevo*, a term that at that moment referred to musical innovation and would later describe radical changes in tango dance as well. Though he would remain "misunderstood" by many, especially his fellow Argentines (see Fischerman and Gilbert), Piazzolla is currently the best-known tango composer on the planet.[52] Dancers of canyengue, milonguero, and tango de salón styles may still choose to sit out the Piazzolla pieces as "undanceable," but such works, described as "baroque" and "avant-garde" and praised for their contrapuntal qualities, have found a more receptive audience in a new generation of dancers trained in the more open, improvisational, and musically diverse environment of nuevo. Renditions of his works by classical musicians and ensembles such as the cellist Yo-Yo Ma and the Kronos Quartet have also helped fulfill Piazzolla's wish to be considered a "serious" musician. Undoubtedly, the Piazzolla sound, which can be heard in a broad array of projects, is a central reason for Argentine tango's continuing influence.[53]

Lives and Deaths of the Tango

Before outlining two final "great moments" in global tango history that bring us current with its contemporary prominence and manifold practice, we step to the side to recognize the understudied Ben Molar. In 1966 the Buenos Aires man-about-tango mounted an energetic campaign to contest the notion that tango had become antiquated or moribund, a vanquished competitor in the global circuits of popular music. True, the golden age of tango was by then over, as was the heyday of the orquestas típicas. Some historians date this decline to 1955, when a military coup ended the first presidency of General Juan Perón. Perón's ousters were less sympathetic to Argentina's popular classes and considered the beloved música popular to be subversive and dangerous. They blacklisted or imprisoned many tango musicians, instituted new curfews, and placed new restrictions on free assembly, all measures that reduced the circulation of tango musicians in Buenos Aires's prime performance venues (Gift 77). Attendance in the dance halls also plummeted (Horvath 159).

Other reasons for the *decadencia* of the tango in the late 1950s included the rise of U.S.-based recording houses with which local labels simply couldn't compete, and most importantly, the soaring popularity of other dance rhythms from North and Latin America. Sergio Pujol marks 1952 as the year of the mambo, 1953 as the year of the cha-cha-chá, and 1957 as the moment when the twelve-year-old singer Roberto Sánchez perfectly imitated Elvis Presley, launching his ascent to worldwide fame as "Sandro" (Pujol 235–57).

A column published in 1956 in the newspaper *La Razón* asked "¿Qué pasa con el tango?" (What's going on with the tango?) and bemoaned the fact that popular preferences were tending ever more to "North American rhythms" (qtd. in Horvath 159).

Molar, however, was undaunted, and he set out to prove that tango not only remained an essential element of local culture but indeed constituted the very pulse of the country and region's expressive identity. That pulse, he argued, could be heard in the music and its lyrics, and it could be *seen* in the paintings, drawings, and engravings of the country's most celebrated artists. Against enormous odds, Molar managed to convene fourteen each of Argentina's renowned poets, composers, and painters to collaborate on a long-play record he titled *14 con el tango* (14 with the tango). By including fourteen full-color reproductions of commissioned artworks in the packaging of the LP, as well as the full text of all the lyrics alongside comments by the featured authors, Molar combined the auditory and textual experiences of tango with a visual feast of images. His ideologically, generationally, and aesthetically diverse list of contributors represented a veritable Who's Who of literary, musical, and art world names, including authors Jorge Luis Borges, Ernesto Sábato, Manuel Mujica Lainéz, and León Benarós; musicians Juan D'Arienzo, Alfredo De Angelis, Lucio DeMare, Sebastián Piana, Aníbal Troilo, and Astor Piazzolla; and painters Héctor Basaldúa, Carlos Cañás, Carlos Alonso, Raúl Soldi, and Carlos Torrallardona.[54] If tango's deep and wide influence today—in language patterns and gender relations; in the local and national economy; in theater, television, radio, and other media; in art and popular art; in musical performances ranging from the classical concert hall to electronica; and in the highly stylized choreography of elaborate stage shows as well as in the *ganchos* and *volcadas* of the hipster nuevo tango set—seems ubiquitous, Mr. Molar deserves credit for his vision of its interdisciplinary value a half century ago. His project was one of the chief inspirations for the book readers now hold in their hands.

Once More, with Feeling, in Paris

Despite the dogged defense of the tango by ambitious custodians such as Ben Molar, from the 1960s on political and economic factors increasingly conspired to push tango from center stage ever further to the margins of rioplatense cultural life. Perhaps tango never "died" or disappeared, as many lamented, but its popularity definitely waned, both at home in Argentina and Uruguay and abroad. By the 1980s only a fraction of the earlier masses of milongueros and musicians were performing the dance or music in Buenos Aires and Montevideo. So it was a risky, daring proposition when the choreographer Claudio Segovia and the designer Héctor Orezzolli teamed up to stage *Tango Argentino* in Paris in 1983. Responding to a request from the director of the Parisian Chatelet Theater to create a completely original stage show, Segovia returned to Buenos Aires and rounded up the best dancers, musicians, and singers he could find (Falcoff).

While Segovia considered enlisting Piazzolla in the project, the role of music director ultimately went to the great pianist, composer, and arranger Horacio Salgán; he was joined by a host of gifted musicians and singers, including the Sexteto Mayor, Roberto Goyeneche, Raúl Lavié, Elba Berón, Jovita Luna, and María Graña. The impressive list of dancers included Juan Carlos Copes (who choreographed the show) and María Nieves, Carlos and María Rivarola, Gloria and Eduardo Arquimbau, Pablo Verón, Nélida and Nelson, and Miguel Zotto and Milena Plebs. With this fantastic pool of talent, Segovia staged a general rehearsal in Buenos Aires in anticipation of the Paris engagement. The response of the Argentine spectators at that rehearsal was tepid, Segovia recalled. Why do a tango show when there were so many other things happening in the music scene? porteños wondered. Why sign these musicians, singers, and dancers, who were noticeably older and plumper than in the glory days of tango? Was this the best Buenos Aires had to offer a Paris audience?

Upon their arrival in France, the tide turned in a very decisive way for Segovia and Orezzolli. Since advance ticket sales were flat, the theater's director insisted the cast perform for an audience of reporters. Segovia and company obliged, and the opening night of *Tango Argentino* met with rave reviews in *Liberation, Le Matin,* and *Le Monde* the next morning. Many Argentines then living in Paris were part of the delirious public, and at least one told Segovia, teary-eyed, "I spent thirty years hating the tango, and in reality life is a tango" (Falcoff). Almost immediately, the performers had a contract for the Festival of Venice and other tour dates in France and Italy; the show later traveled to Canada and then hit Broadway in 1985, where it met with even more thunderous applause (see Ferrer, *El tango* 418).[55]

The reception of *Tango Argentino* was so ecstatic that the show spawned a slew of imitators and avatars: *Forever Tango, Tango Inferno, Tango Fire,* and so on, with many of them working with members of the original crew. However spectacular, such performances arguably have been unable to surpass (or equal, some would say) the Segovia-Orezzolli show. What these shows have accomplished, nonetheless, is to place tango back on center stage, where rapt spectators are once again transported and delighted by a heady (and footy) mix of instrumental music, dance, and song. If twenty-first-century fans can find milongas in such distant sites as Verona or Alaska or even in Buenos Aires (where the production arrived ten years after its Paris debut), then much of the credit undoubtedly must go to Segovia's initial staging of *Tango Argentino*.[56]

Nuevo Tango Redux

Tango in the twenty-first century contains all of the political, geographic, economic, and cultural shapings of a century and is yet still new. As a dance, it continues to expand exponentially, thanks to increased travel by dance instructors from Argentina to more cities worldwide and by dance students to classes and workshops in Europe, the United States, and elsewhere.[57] Tango enthusiasts can find classes or milongas in many, if not most, of the major cities of Europe, Asia, Africa, the Americas, and Australia. The United States boasts the greatest number of cities with regular social dance venues, with more than two hundred from Akron to Ypsilanti. And in the mecca of Buenos Aires, foreigners now often outnumber the locals in many milongas and *prácticas*.

Newcomers enter this phenomenon on the heels of an evolution of music and dance forms that began in the 1990s and has been variously labeled nuevo tango, tango nuevo, neotango, electronic, alternative, or fusion tango—labels that themselves have been rejected by the key players we might identify as the architects of this evolution. These labels have only a tangential relationship with the nuevo tango musical style of Piazzolla, but they do allude to the emphasis on innovation and improvisation at the core of these new performative styles. Gustavo Naveira, one of the contemporary dance instructors most associated with nuevo, clarifies that for him, at least, "tango nuevo is everything that has happened with the tango since the 1980s . . . Tango nuevo is not one more style; it is simply that tango dancing is growing, improving, developing, enriching itself, and in that sense we are moving toward a new dimension in tango dancing. . . . We have learned, and we have developed our knowledge. The result of this is a dance of greater possibilities, and also of a much more artistic quality" (qtd. in Gift 82).[58] Traditionalists warn that a lack of respect for time-honored codes will produce a dance display that may be athletically impressive but risks being devoid of *argentinidad* or even tango. For its proponents, though, nuevo offers the chance to incorporate new music, revamp dance styles, experiment with the embrace, reconfigure the standard male-female lead-follower roles, and in short, rethink the dance in terms of the physics and logics of human movement, as well as "un sentimiento que se baila" (a feeling that is danced).

In her chapter in this edited volume, the anthropologist Carolyn Merritt examines how notions and experiences of gender and sexuality intersect in this contested field of Argentine contemporary dance and music practice. New generations of dancers ask to what extent they can "queer" tango while still retaining its historical, aesthetic, and social integrity—even as all of these are simultaneously being questioned. Merritt contends that the emergence of a new generation of practitioners with access to ever more venues in an increasingly fluid and interconnected global community signals the liberation of the dance from the hold of place and tradition, while still respecting tango's historic propensity for experimentation and hybrid incorporations.

Similar questions inform the rapidly growing presence of music styles in the global arena classified as nuevo or electronic tango. In his analysis of the phenomenal success of the Parisian-based collective Gotan Project, the musicologist Esteban Buch argues that in quantitative terms, at least, Gotan's massive appeal has no equal in the history of tango recordings or performance. With sales numbering in the millions (with the recordings figuring prominently in both the world music and dance/electronic charts), and viewings of their videos on YouTube approaching or topping the seven-figure mark, the members of Gotan have become the best-known tango musicians in the world—if you consider their music to be tango, of course.

Buch examines how tango's nomadic tendencies, already in evidence a century ago, have expanded due to the capacities of twenty-first-century "technological crossover," in which the strains of the bandoneon, tango's signature instrument, are now joined—or replaced by—digital sounds created on a computer. He maintains that while the group incorporates unorthodox elements, a respect for tango's long history and canons can be seen in Gotan's integration of classic tango musicians such as bandoneonistas Niní Flores and Facundo Torres and pianist and arranger Gustavo Beytelmann, as well as in the inclusion of "straight" tango numbers in concert performances and recordings. In fact, their recordings reference a surprising number of revered tango personalities from Gardel to Piazzolla and cite key events in Argentine cultural and sociopolitical history.[59] For example, in *Tango 3.0*, released in 2010, they lay musical tracks over a recording of the Argentine author Julio Cortázar (who also relocated to Paris and produced many of his most important works there) reading excerpts from his novel *Rayuela*.[60] For traditionalists, the radical modification and repackaging of the beloved tango genre for sale to a massive world music market unaware of its tangled national and transnational social histories threaten to strip the music of everything but perhaps a lingering *tangotude*. But Buch avows that such products attract new generations of listeners and spectators to social and aesthetic histories they might otherwise ignore. Thus, the musical result of Gotan Project's experimentations can be at one and the same time—like tango itself—a lesson in the new and the historical, a "sexy combination of chillout programming and authentic tango."[61]

As Morgan Luker demonstrates in his chapter on contemporary efforts to re-create tango as música popular, the same tension between preservation and renovation is equally at play in contemporary versions of "classic" tango. While the members of Astillero and other contemporary groups may reject the radical changes of the electronic sector, they ultimately must engage with the same history of globalization in their efforts to reactivate tango as a música popular produced for and through a locally based social collective. This reactivation impulse, itself fueled by sociopolitical crises in Argentina since 2000, has generated substantial activity around the preservation of tango as an all-access genre bridging old and new. Musicians emulate and re-create the sounds of revered masters from yesteryear; composers and arrangers archive and update musical scores and other documentation from earlier periods; young players stage live performances for new audiences of listeners and milongueros too young to have witnessed tango's social power prior to 1955. But, as Luker notes, Astillero and other musicians committed to tango as música popular circulate in the same global context as their fellow electronic musicians and may find a more responsive audience in Berlin than in Buenos Aires.

The New Language of Tango

The Golden Globe and Grammy–winning composer, musician, and film music producer Gustavo Santaolalla is perhaps best known for his work on the film soundtracks of *Brokeback Mountain*, *The Motorcycle Diaries*, *Amores Perros*, and *Babel*. But Santaolalla is also a central figure in twenty-first-century tango. His self-confessed obsession with the question of rioplatense identity led him to experiment early on with tango and many other local folk music from his home country, including those he found and recorded on a road trip that extended from the northern tip of Argentina to its southern-most city. Those recordings formed the basis of the groundbreaking *De Ushuaia a la Quiaca*, produced with the fellow Argentine rocker León Gieco and recently rereleased in a twentieth-anniversary edition.

In 2002 Santaolalla teamed up with veteran musicians from Argentina and Uruguay to create the Bajofondo Tango Club. While their earliest work was mostly electronic, by the time he and his colleagues produced *Mar Dulce* in 2008, they had dropped the "Tango Club" to become just Bajofondo and con-sidered themselves principally a rock band.[62] The resulting electronic dance music fuses Latin alternative rock, tango, and milonga in a style that is unde-niably contemporary. Santaolalla's hybrid efforts include a collaboration with the Puerto Rican reggaetón stars Calle 13, another with the Spanish rapper Mala Rodríguez, and yet another down-tempo joint effort with the alterna-tive rocker Elvis Costello. "With Bajofondo," says Santaolalla, "we don't like the label 'electronic tango' because we try to make a contemporary music of Río de la Plata. . . . Obviously, if you want to do music that comes from there or represents that part of the world, tango is going to be part of it—but, in our case, so is rock 'n' roll, electronica and hip hop. Hopefully a new language [results], not pure tango."[63]

Whereas Bajofondo brings tango to a global audience of mostly younger listeners, Santaolalla's tradition-honoring *Café de los maestros* offers a lushly produced aural and visual archive of tango as the exquisite and unique ex-pression of a generation that will soon pass away.[64] That effort brought to-gether singers, musicians, and arrangers from the so-called golden age of tango to record in the studio, perform on the stage of the Teatro Colón in Buenos Aires, and later star in an award-winning documentary of the same name in 2008. A two-CD box set titled *Café de los maestros*, produced by Santaolalla and Gustavo Mozzi and mixed and mastered by Aníbal Kerpel, was released in 2005. Although the audio-visual synergy of *Café de los mae-stros* has led some to compare it to the recording and film versions of Cuba's *Buena Vista Social Club*, Santaolalla has said he sees it more as an outgrowth of his road trip research decades ago. In any case the ambidextrous producer has managed to simultaneously master—literally and metaphorically—the soundtracks of tango as innovation and as preservation.

Santaolalla's varied engagements are just one notable example of the myr-iad ways in which the tango rioplatense lives on, appreciated by ever-larger local and global audiences. Like the vocalist and songwriter Carlos Gardel, the instrumentalist and composer Astor Piazzolla, the stage show director Claudio Segovia, and his fellow musicians and electronic wizards in Gotan Project, Santaolalla embodies a metejón (obsession or love affair) with the tango that acknowledges previous masters, responds to contemporary desires, and paves the way for new renovators and innovators inspired by an ever-vaster treasure trove of sensorial pleasures. This is a metejón the writers in this volume all share. What new worlds of tango now stretch out before us? What hidden gem of its inexhaustible history will we find in a library or dusty bookstore? What new sound will catch our ear? What movement will we master to help us translate its complexity and mystery to the dance floor? What difficulties and disappointments will it express and ease? How will tango connect us with neighbors and cultural kin near and far? And who will be the next singer, player, dancer, poet, painter, or philosopher to school us in its many lessons, its infinite possibilities?

Notes

1. On the origins of the term *tango*, see Salas, *El tango*; Gobello's "Tango, vocablo controvertido" in *La historia del tango*; and Megenney.

2. The adjective *rioplatense* refers to tango's origins and development in both Argentina and Uruguay, especially in the principal port cities of Buenos Aires and Montevideo located on the Río de la Plata or River Plate. A glossary at the end of this edited volume provides brief definitions of tango-related terms.

3. As Ramón Pelinski notes in *El tango nómade*, "transethnic and transtechnical, transregistered bricoleur, the nomad tango is reluctant to let itself be restricted by the typologizing and philologizing procedures of traditional musicology; its semantic possibilities and its compositional strategies are open on all horizons" (33).

4. See also Kramer, "Dangerous Liaisons."

5. See, for example, Rivera. A defense of tango's Cuban roots is offered by Ortiz Nuevo and Nuñez. Daniel Vidart includes a lengthy discussion of northern and southern Italian influences in the tango in *El tango y su mundo*.

6. There are many variations and combinations of milonga, *vals*, and tango, but the three basic rhythms are still distinguishable for musicians and dancers; in the traditional milonga (dance event in a salon or hall), each *tanda* or set of three to five songs is devoted to one of the three rhythms. More recently, DJs have begun to add tandas of *nuevo tango* or other musics not identifiable as tango.

7. "'Canyengue' is the term often used to describe the first dance recognized as 'tango.' Canyengue first appeared in the slums at the outskirts of Buenos Aires around the turn of the 20th century and is considered to have lost its popularity by the late 1930s, when 'tango de salon' primarily replaced it as the predominant manner of social tango dancing" (Tango Voice, "Canyengue, Candombe and Tango Orillero: Extinct or Nonexistent Tango Styles?," *Tango Voice* (blog), accessed May 3, 2012, http://tangovoice.word

press.com/2010/03/19/canyengue-candombe-and-tango-orillero-extinct-or-non-existent
-tango-styles/). *Tango Voice* also offers an excellent summary in English of the kinetic
characteristics of this style.

8. "La milonga en sus formas primigenias rurales y suburbanas había ido desarrollando
en pulperías, almacenes, fogones de milicos, comités, una forma de expresión lenta, con-
versada, jactanciosa, rebelde, a veces reflexiva, a veces homenajeadora" (Ford 39).

9. Thompson provides additional etymological and formal details: "Milonga, spirited
and strong, emerged in Argentina in the 1870s. It was not a mere precursor to tango
but a tradition in its own right, with its own sound, its own mode of action. Derived
from Kimbundu and Ki-Kongo words meaning, respectively, 'argument' and 'moving
lines of dancers,' milonga furthered a tradition of aesthetic dueling: pugnacity as poetry,
battling as dance. It was, in short, African-influenced 'carving contests' on a scale turned
heroic" (121).

10. A *conventillo* is a tenement or boarding house, associated with the throngs of immigrants who arrived in Buenos Aires from Europe and elsewhere at the end of the nineteenth and beginning of the twentieth centuries.

11. A definition of *signifyin(g)* from a glossary of terms related to the blues identifies it
as "the act of using secret or double meanings of words to either communicate multiple
meanings to different audiences, or to trick them" (PBS, "Blues Glossary," *The Blues*,
accessed July 1, 2013, at http://www.pbs.org/theblues/classroom/glossary.html).

12. Pujol notes that in this era, tango, like sex in the Victorian era, is what's *not* said,
what appears in print only by error (51).

13. Villoldo even wrote and performed some of his tunes under the pseudonym Lope
de la Verga, a play on the name of the famous Spanish Golden Age dramatist Lope de
Vega that made use of the slang term for penis, *verga* (or dick) (G. Varela, *Mal de tango*
47). It's likely that Villoldo was influenced by the "challenge songs" of Afro-Argentines
such as Gabino Ezeiza (Thompson 26). While Thompson has surprisingly little to say
about Villoldo's more off-color work and its possible relationship to black precedents or
influences, he notes the "electro-obscenities" included in Villoldo's "La bicicleta," which
"cuts the pretensions of modernism down to size" (29). Thompson provides a translation
(albeit partial) of a particularly amusing section of that tango:

El teléfono, el micrófono,
El tan sin rival fonógrafo,
El pampirulintintófano,
Y el nuevo cinematógrafo
El biógrafo, el caustígrafo
El pajalacaflunchincófano,
El chincatapunchincógrafo
...
[The microphone,
The telephone
The panpirilintintophone
Plus cinematography

Biography, caustography,
Pajalacafluchinography,
Not to mention chingatapuchinography]. (29)

Villoldo's tongue-twisting mockery of the wonders of modern technology bears witness to the discomforts and discontent modernization produced in turn-of-the-century Buenos Aires. See, for example, Sarlo, *Una modernidad periférica*.

14. An excellent source on the *orquestas típicas*, and indeed on the instrumentalization of tango from its inception to the 1960s, is Sierra.

15. This is likely a reference to Princess Marie Bonaparte (1882–1962), the same figure who would gain fame for her psychoanalytical and sexual research, her professional and personal relationship with Sigmund Freud, and her role in facilitating the latter's escape from Nazi Germany. See Bertin.

16. The perceived need for civilization in the face of barbarism was the primary cultural "problem" of the Southern Cone region and arguably of all of Latin America in the nineteenth century; Sarmiento's midcentury treatise on that tension (*Facundo: Civilization and Barbarism*) predates the emergence of tango but also predicts its complicated tale of rejection and ultimate incorporation by the guardians of national and regional culture. Carlos Fuentes includes tango in his broader discussion of Latin American civilizing campaigns (289–90).

17. In a review published in the magazine *Mundial* (directed by the famed *modernista* poet Rubén Darío) in 1914, Enrique Gómez Carillo concluded that the show elevated the tango beyond the superficial and the sentimental and constituted "a profound moral study" (qtd. in Gasió 32).

18. When his students stopped attending his classes due to the archbishop's ecclesiastical admonition, a prominent dance teacher named Stilson sued the church for twenty thousand francs in damages and won. The religious authorities were forced to concede that they didn't in fact condemn the tango itself, only certain ways of dancing it (Gasió 43–44). Nonetheless, many Argentines, including the writer Leopoldo Lugones, maintained their abhorrence of the form, despite its popularity in Paris. "Cualquiera entiende el prejuicio moral que comporta el adjetivo argentino pegado a esa innoble y bastarda danza, con la cual canta sus folias de licencia la canalla mestiza de nuestro suburbio descaracterizado" (Anyone can see the moral prejudice that the Argentine adjective carries when tied to this ignoble and bastard dance, with which the half breed low life sings his licentious exploits), claimed Lugones (qtd. in Gasió 19).

19. For many younger Argentines, tango's appeal and relevance were long ago surpassed by those of rock, *rock nacional, cumbia,* and, more recently, reggaetón. In point of fact, these seemingly unlike genres often intersect. See, for example, Plaza on the interactions of tango and rock and Gallego on the relationship of tango and cumbia.

20. While each of these writers is emblematic in his own way, Cadícamo's biography is an especially resonant example of the profoundly interdisciplinary nature of twentieth-century Argentine tango. Born in 1900, Cadícamo registered over 1,200 songs before his death in December 1999. He was a favorite composer of Carlos Gardel, who between 1925 and 1933 recorded twenty-three of his compositions. He authored several volumes

of poetry (*Canciones grises*, 1926; *La luna del bajo fondo*, 1940; and *Viento que lleva y trae*, 1945), as well as *El debut de Gardel en París, La historia del tango en París*, several texts for theater and film, and his own memoirs. In a preface to a photo-essay on tango by the acclaimed Argentine photographer Aldo Sessa (1999), Cadícamo reflects on the African origins of tango dance and the synthetic nature of tango lyrics: writing a tango involves "reducing the plot of a three-act play that lasts two hours, with a beginning, a middle, and an end, to just three minutes, which is the time it takes to play a tango; that is to say, one minute per act." In that essay, Cadícamo also attributed tango's appearance to its black roots, whether from Guinea, Angola, or elsewhere in Africa and it was then brought to Argentina by Portuguese slave traders (Sessa 7).

21. It turns out that Bhabha himself was exposed to tango growing up in Bombay, where his father was an avid listener as well as an accomplished dancer. See Gewurtz.

22. See Gelman's autobiographical text titled "Semblanza."

23. Heightened attention to improvisation within the space of the tango embrace, unique among other popular dances of the Americas, is already much in evidence in the earliest existing motion picture recordings of the form, including Luis José Moglia Barth's film *¡Tango!*, released in 1933. That landmark picture (which helped initiate the film industry in Argentina) enlisted a host of popular performers such as Libertad Lamarque, Tita Merello, Pepe Arias, and Azucena Maizani, all already familiar to Argentines from live stage acts, earlier silent films, or their participation in radio broadcasts of telenovelas and musical programs (Falicov 11–12). The legendary figure José Ovidio "Benito" Bianquet, better known as "El Cachafaz," also appeared briefly. The basic structure of the embrace, the mechanics of dissociation, and other elements of the tango movement vocabulary performed by the dancers in that film can still be witnessed in tango dance today. Despite its early production date, *Tango*—like Borges's 1926 essay—represents tango from an earlier era. A clip of the film can be viewed on Youtube (http://www.youtube.com/watch?v=5Yv9V-3APpc, accessed May 3, 2012). Carmencita Calderón, El Cachafaz's partner in the film, looks almost as spry dancing at age ninety-six (http://www.youtube.com/watch?v=-kX5j_WJY-c&feature=related, accessed May 3, 2012) and was still dancing on the occasion of her hundredth birthday (http://www.youtube.com/watch?v=AuLVZnEpg4E&feature=related, accessed May 3, 2012). Dínzel recognizes tango's "mechanics of dissociation," in which the activity of the body from the waist down is distinct from that of the body from the waist up, as the principal proof of its African antecedents (10).

24. The Dínzels' fame has extended to the White House, where they danced during the Reagan administration (Ferrer and del Priore, *Inventario del tango*, vol. 2: 291).

25. Viladrich uses a translated fragment of Dos Santos's text as the epigraph of her "Neither Virgins Nor Whores."

26. An online Lunfardo-English dictionary can be found at http://www.freelang.net/dictionary/lunfardo.php, accessed May 3, 2012.

27. For a discussion of tango's problematic relationship to other mestizo cultural discourses in Latin America, see M. Miller, "Tango in Black and White," in *Rise and Fall of the Cosmic Race*.

28. Borges regretted the studious crassness of tango lyrics and poems too heavily laced

with *lunfardo* (*On Argentina* 72), and he generally avoided the local vocabulary in his own references to tango in such masterpieces as the poem "The Mythical Founding of Buenos Aires," published in 1929:

> El primer organito salvaba el horizonte
> con su achacoso porte, su habanera y su gringo.
> El corralón seguro ya opinaba YRIGOYEN,
> Algún piano mandaba tangos de Saborido.
>
> [The first barrel organ teetered over the horizon
> with its clumsy progress, its *habaneras*, its wop.
> The cart-shed wall was unanimous for YRIGOYEN.
> Some piano was banging out tangos by Saborido]. (*Selected Poems* 48–49)

Enrique Saborido (1877–1941) was a Uruguayan-born musician, dancer, and composer. A celebrated figure of the "vieja guardia," his composition "La morocha" (just one of his many successes) sold two hundred and eighty thousand copies after it was recorded in 1905. He also became a much sought after dance instructor in Paris. Hipólito Yrigoyen (1852–1933) was twice elected president of Argentina (1916–1922 and 1928–1930), and Borges is apparently referencing the period leading up to his first term. Known as the "president of the poor," Yrigoyen instituted social reforms, including universal suffrage for all male voters. In 1930 he was deposed in a military coup.

29. In 2004 a reporter for the Buenos Aires daily newspaper *La Nación* asked the renowned Mexican author Carlos Fuentes (1928–2012) what his adolescence in Buenos Aires had contributed to his literary voice. "A great deal," Fuentes responded, "it was here that I read Borges for the first time. I frequented the Ateneo bookstore; I followed the orchestra of Aníbal Troilo and I learned the lyrics of the tango, which is another way to learn Spanish" (Reynoso).

30. Despite being frequently identified with the second of these groups, Borges considered the antagonism between the two a pseudopolemic, and in 1928 he published his essay "La inútil discusión de Boedo y Florida" [The useless argument about Boedo and Florida] in *La Prensa*. See Salvador.

31. The tango-inflected verbal expression that appeared on song sheets and in literary magazines from the 1920s on soon found many echoes in scripts for radio, theater, and film performances, and poets and songwriters became cultural provocateurs and entrepreneurs of the first order. Along with his work as a songwriter, filmmaker, screenwriter, political militant, and labor activist, Manzi, for example, also created the record label Aula with the idea of protecting songwriters' intellectual rights, founded the journal *Micrófono*, and participated in the formation of the political party Forja. And while Manzi is a notorious example of this cross-pollination of forms and fields, he is just one of many such stories in tango past or present. When he set about researching his father's participation in tango history, Acho Manzi discovered that "it wasn't only lyrics of popular songs that appeared during that period. Every time I opened a file, there appeared scripts for films that were never filmed, librettos for radio programs, and works for the theatre" (11). See Ford; Romero; and Salas, *Homero Manzi y su tiempo*.

32. Two interesting examples of this phenomenon are Fernando Ayala's film *El canto cuenta su historia* [The song tells its story], released in 1976, which features tango within a broader song history in Argentina, and Humberto Ríos's film *El tango es una historia* [The tango is a history], released in 1983, with performances by Astor Piazzolla and Osvaldo Pugliese.

33. *El tango en la Economía de la Ciudad de Buenos Aires* (2007), published by Argentina's Ministry of Production, examines tango's economic impact in such fields as tourism, the online music industry, tango instruction, public policy, and copyright matters.

34. Another part of this African diasporic history is the relationship between early tango and early African American jazz. A key figure in this story is the black pianist Harold Phillips, who was active as a performer and composer of cakewalk, tango, and other styles in Buenos Aires and Montevideo from about 1900 until 1913, when he left for Europe. A postcard sent from the continent after German forces advanced into Belgium reported that he had been accused of espionage, imprisoned, and shot there (Nogués 200–201).

35. What is less well known is that other Jews at the Janowska camp were forced by an ss officer to accompany marches, tortures, tomb excavations, or executions by playing or singing "Plegaria," a composition of 1929 by the Argentine composer Eduardo Bianco that became known as "The Tango of Death" (Judkovski 26; Nudler 27–28). The Jews integrating that orchestra were apparently murdered by the ss before Janowska was liberated (Nudler 28). Nudler notes that Bianco had played the tango for Hitler and Goebbels in 1939. In an interview Bianco noted that he had even earlier played "Plegaria" for King Alfonso XIII of Spain, a great fan of the tango to whom the composition is dedicated. It was apparently part of his repertoire for the seventeen months he performed in various other courts, where he was praised by Stalin, among others. Bianco was giving concerts in Germany when war broke out, and though he sought to leave the war-torn region, he was arrested at Innsbruck. The fear of being constantly watched reportedly produced heart problems so severe that Bianco was hospitalized in Magdeburg (see "Eduardo Bianco," http://www.todotango.com/spanish/creadores/ebianco .asp, accessed May 3, 2012). Nudler nonetheless aligns him with fascist forces in Italy and notes that Enrique Cadícamo accused Bianco of working for the Gestapo (Nudler 30). The "Tango of Death" anecdotes from the camps likely informed the writing of the Jewish poet Paul Celan, whose "Tangoul mortii" [Tango of death] was penned in German in 1944 (Nudler 27). The lyrics to Bianco's "Plegaria" can be found at http://www .todotango.com/spanish/las_obras/Tema.aspx?id=UUPUSyhwUOM=, accessed May 3, 2012. There are reportedly two other compositions that bear the name "Tango de la muerte" as well as a film and *sainete* (short theater piece), see http://www.todotango .com/spanish/biblioteca/CRONICAS/el_tango_de_la_muerte.asp, accessed May 3, 2012.

36. Despite these difficulties, *Tangos. El exilio de Gardel* "reinstalls the tango-dance in the audiovisual field of contemporary culture," Pujol asserts (340).

37. Rossi's *Cosas de negros* is considered a groundbreaking if controversial argument for the African origins of the tango, an argument sustained by contemporary historians and musicians such as Goldman, Thompson, and Cáceres. The opinions of Carlos

Vega, considered the forefather of musicology in Argentina, are summarized by Kohan, "Carlos Vega y la teoría hispanista del origin del tango."

38. Borges pointed out that, by the middle of the twentieth century, cinema had propagated yet another compelling if not entirely accurate story of the tango, and "this 'from rags to riches' *Bildungsroman* is by now a sort of incontestable or proverbial truth" (*On Argentina* 101).

39. See, for example, Viladrich's work on the presence of "tango immigrant" communities in New York ("Tango Immigrants in New York City"; "From Shrinks to Urban Shamans"). For a general history of tango in the United States, see Groppa.

40. An excellent source on radio history in Buenos Aires is Ulanovsky et al. One of the highlights of this broadcast history was the Glostora Tango Club program, a daily show from El Mundo Radio recorded before a live audience that first broadcast in 1946 (1940, according to Ulanovsky et al. 142) and continued on the air for more than two decades.

41. See, for example, P. Ochoa.

42. On tango in literature, see Rossner; Orgambide. Antoniotti and Sebastián adopt a broader cultural studies approach. Azzi's *Antropología del tango* offers one of the earliest incursions from that discipline; Taylor's *Paper Tangos* provides an innovative anthropological engagement that addresses psychosocial aspects as well. On tango as social history, Carretero is a good resource.

43. Gardel claimed, on different occasions, to have been born in all three places (Monsalve 102).

44. Both Gardel and Razzanno reportedly met the great *payador* Gabino Ezeiza in early twentieth-century political committee meetings in the San Telmo neighborhood, according to a website dedicated to the history of the payador Gabino Ezeiza: http://www.ensantelmo.com.ar/Cultura/Mitos%20y%20Bohemia/gezeiza.htm, accessed July 1, 2013.

45. Santa María's work can be viewed at http://www.marinosantamaria.com/, accessed May 3, 2012. I touch on Marcos López's photographic homage to (or parody of) Gardel's beloved image in my chapter on tango art in this edited volume.

46. A Buenos Aires–based all-tango radio station that frequently plays Gardel can be streamed at http://www.la2x4.gov.ar/, accessed May 3, 2012.

47. After moving the family from Argentina to Manhattan in search of economic opportunities, Piazzolla Sr. worked as a barber to the Sicilian mob in New York, the same cohort immortalized by Herbert Asbury in *The Gangs of New York* and by Borges in *Historia universal de la infamia* (Fischerman and Gilbert 26).

48. Gardel reportedly claimed that the young Piazzolla played bandoneon "like a Gallego," that is, like a Spaniard or other foreigner, calling attention to a formation taking place outside the Argentine tradition. See Fischerman and Gilbert 12.

49. *Fuelle* or bellows is a lunfardo term for the bandoneon.

50. Piazzolla also arranged tangos for Troilo's orchestra, but Troilo reportedly would go back and edit the arrangements, fearing they were "too advanced" and would scare away the dancers (Pessinis and Kuri).

51. Fischerman and Gilbert question the influence of these private classes with Boulanger on Piazzolla's development, noting that the anecdote presents us with a

"recurring fantasy amongst musicians in the popular tradition, who at the same time reject and envy the mannerisms of the academic musician"; they point to a parallel narrative in the memoirs of George Gershwin (121).

52. Though he wrote an estimated three thousand works and recorded some five hundred of them, Piazzolla is most revered for pioneering compositions such as "Adios Nonino," written in 1959 to commemorate the death of his father, and "Libertango," written in 1974 and considered the quintessential example of Piazzolla's particular musical language.

53. The operetta *María de Buenos Aires* written on a libretto of the poet Horacio Ferrer, the soundtrack of the film *Tangos. The Exile of Gardel* studied in this edited volume, and a landmark LP recording in 1965 of poems by Borges interpreted by Piazzolla and the vocalist Edmundo Rivero are just a few examples.

54. For a full list of contributors, see "Ben Molar and His Master piece: *14 con el tango*," *Todo Tango*, http://www.todotango.com/english/biblioteca/cronicas/14_con_el _tango.asp, accessed May 3, 2012. I study the art segment of Molar's project at more length in my chapter in this edited volume.

55. A line in the show's original program sums up Segovia's dual understanding of tango's role on and off the stage: "The tango resembles, reassembles all of life." Segovia further clarifies, "I try to reflect on the stage a life that actually exists, and that at the same time should come together as a scenic entity . . . I look for purity, for roots, but with artists who have dominion of the stage, who won't get stage fright, who can give their all" (Falcoff). Whereas other Argentines had moved on by the 1980s, setting aside tango for other genres, Segovia forged ahead, convinced that a show conceived with a genuine love for popular culture would be read by audiences as a love story of sorts. For his efforts, he was credited with the second worldwide success of tango, some seventy years after it had originally taken Paris by storm.

56. Segovia's singular achievement was further recognized in the return of *Tango Argentino* to the Argentine capital in February of 2011, this time under the auspices of the Ministry of Culture and in the context of La ciudad al aire libre, cultura para respirar [The open-air city, breathable culture]. On a stage erected near the city's famous obelisk, experienced fans and curious newcomers could watch some of those same dancers from the show staged in 1983, including Copes, María Nieves, Carlos and María Rivarola, Gloria and Eduardo Arquimbau, Pablo Verón, and Miguel Ángel Zotto, and they could listen to interpretations of classic tangos by artists such as María Graña, Walter Ríos, Raúl Lavié, and Pablo Agri. All told, Segovia brought seventy musicians and dancers to (or back to) the stage, and some fifteen thousand fans enjoyed that free performance. A series of photos and videos of the event are collected at Sophie, "Claudio Segovia's Argentine Tango," *2xTango*, accessed May 3, 2012, http://www.2xtango.com/?p=8959& lang=en.

57. One of the Argentines who saw Segovia's original production in 1983 was the writer and filmmaker Edgardo Cozarinsky, then living in Paris. In 2007 Cozarinsky published *Milongas*, a memoir of his milonga-hopping in Europe and elsewhere that confirmed the far-reaching influence of *Tango Argentino* as well as the migration of tango back to the main stages and dance halls of global affections.

58. Though he rejects the moniker *tango nuevo*, Naveira is considered, along with Pablo Verón and Fabián Salas, a founder of the movement that bears that label. See Merritt's chapter in this edited volume.

59. Gotan Project's collaboration with the veteran New Orleans musician Dr. John on "Tango Square" evokes Congo Square, where slave populations were permitted to meet, drum, sing, and dance in pre–Civil War New Orleans, and it pays homage to the shared African parentage of jazz and tango. Ned Sublette argues that New Orleans is the site of the first documented use of the term *tango*—almost a century before it appears in any Argentine or Uruguayan reference (123).

60. Cortázar evokes the seedy milongas of the 1940s in his short story "Las puertas del cielo," but *Rayuela* is his best-known novel. See Savigliano, "Nocturnal Ethnographies," for an analysis of Cortázar's tango story.

61. See Tad Hendrickson's editorial review for Amazon.com, http://www.amazon .com/Revancha-Del-Tango-Bonus-CD/dp/B00008NRL8, accessed May 3, 2012.

62. Bajofondo is composed of Santaolalla on guitar, percussion, and vocals; Juan Campodónico on programming, beats, samples, and guitar; Luciano Supervielle on piano, keyboards, and scratch; Javier Casalla on violin; Martín Ferrés on bandoneon; Gabriel Casacuberta on upright bass and electric bass; Adrián Sosa on drums; and Verónica Loza as vj and on vocals.

63. See the "Bio" under the "General Info" category at http://www.myspace.com/bajo fondomardulce, accessed May 3, 2012.

64. In fact, several of the "maestros" profiled in *Café de los maestros* had died by the time of the film's debut, or they have since passed away.

CHAPTER ONE

Lunfardo in Tango

A Way of Speaking That Defines a Way of Being

OSCAR CONDE

Translated by Kurt Hofer

Tango has demonstrated a singular originality and vitality during its many decades of existence. It presents us with a wide range of perspectives in both its musical and choreographic aspects, and we should not fail to take into account its very rich history as a poetics and a literary history as well. Even before the emergence of that period of tango history known as *tango canción*, initiated in 1917 with the appearance of "Mi noche triste" (Gobello, *Letras de tango,* 24),[1] tango lyrics had already begun to make use of *lunfardo*, the distinct vocabulary of the popular classes of the Río de la Plata region, to achieve an enhanced level of expressivity.[2] Thanks to the particularly strong bond between lunfardo and tango lyrics, especially in the 1920s and 1930s, the popularity of the form increased, and tango music and dance were ultimately complemented by a new element: poetry.[3] This was by no means the only use of lunfardo in a literary context: it has also been used in comic sketches, in the grotesque and other forms of popular theater,[4] in *costumbrista* journalism that focused on local and regional customs, in comic strips, in rock lyrics, and even in the works of some of Argentina's most canonical authors, such as Leopoldo Marechal, Ernesto Sábato, Julio Cortázar, and Manuel Puig. Nonetheless, the connection between tango and lunfardo remains readily apparent today due to the role of the former in disseminating the latter, the latter being initially circumscribed to the lower classes.

The aim of this chapter is first to show how lunfardo has occupied a privileged space in tango, even if a few of its principal lyricists (such as Homero

Manzi and Alfredo Le Pera) made infrequent use of its unique vocabulary in their compositions. I then take up the relationship of tango and lunfardo, a relationship that we could credit, without risk of overstatement, with the continuing presence of tango language in the everyday experience of people living in the Río de la Plata region.

Tango is in all of its aspects a product of hybridization, constituted through a diverse constellation of musical, instrumental, and choreographic syncretisms throughout its long history. The resulting phenomenon has proved appealing over a long period to a variety of academics in fields such as anthropology, sociology, philosophy, psychology, and linguistics. Even if such a model results in the oversimplification of certain elements of this history, it is only through the adoption of an integrationist approach to tango that any of the aforementioned fields do not become the single axis of our analysis but rather are reconfigured with the aim of providing a broad, multidimensional vision of the form. Tango is without doubt a product of complexity.[5] A series of distinct elements, all of them necessary to the process, had to come together and work in conjunction with one another to enable its emergence and development as a cultural matrix. It is for this very reason not only appropriate but also advisable that we study tango as a phenomenon of transcultural symbiosis.

While the preservation and study of tango strengthens the regeneration of the dance's singularities and constitutes a kind of return to origins and to questions of regional identity in Argentina and Uruguay, tango has at the same time become part of an indubitably transnational culture in which it has been identified as unique within "planetary folklore" (an expression coined by Morin). This status is evident in its extensive popularization in academies and dance halls throughout Europe and the Americas as well as in movies, plays, and other diverse contexts and venues.

In its early stages, however, tango was rarely seen for what it truly was: a genuine creation of the popular classes, a product of hybridization and of the waves of immigrants who arrived in the port of Buenos Aires between the end of the nineteenth and the beginning of the twentieth centuries. Contrary to what has been said time and time again, tango was not solely the creation of a marginalized segment of the population. Its history is a singular parable that stretches from the inner reaches of the lower classes to academic studies and intellectual circles, from humble cafés and popular dances of the masses to the opulent halls of the Teatro Colón, Buenos Aires's renowned opera house. Once the dance had been legitimated abroad in Paris in 1913, the Argentine upper classes adopted tango both as music and choreography, but as Eduardo

Romano has pointed out, "they never swallowed the vulgarity and crassness of its lyrics" (Romano 126; nunca deglutieron el vulgarismo y la cursilería de sus letras). Nonetheless, tango lyrics in the Río de la Plata region have accompanied the common man or woman for many decades: they have provided comfort in the face of disgrace, company in moments of solitude, and an opportunity to ponder the caprices of one's destiny. No one can doubt that a corpus numbering more than thirty thousand tango lyrics provides a series of images that together constitute an extensive history of sentiment—and of private life in general—of Buenos Aires and other Argentine and Uruguayan cities during most of the twentieth century.

If anything defines the tango as a genre, both with respect to its musical roots and in terms of its poetic origins, it is hybridity. In the first case, as is now common knowledge, the earliest forms of tango developed from the confluence of various black rhythms: the habanera, the Andalusian tango, and the milonga. Blas Matamoro summarized the contribution of each of these genres in the following way: "Just as the *habanera* was lyrical and *candombe* danceable, we can say that the *milonga* was a lyrical genre that became a dance by incorporating some of the elements of the candombe's choreography overlaid onto the rhythmic scheme of the habanera. This formula attempts to resolve the question of defining the tango *porteño* [identified with the port cities of Buenos Aires and Montevideo], starting with its necessarily hybrid character" (Matamoro, "Orígenes musicales" 89).[6] So it was in the territory of dance that tango came into its own.[7] The discursive construction of the identity of inhabitants of the Río de la Plata region, which had begun within the practice of listening to forms of music born of hybridization, at that point still more cheerful than nostalgic, continued to insinuate itself within the bodies of dancers and ultimately became consolidated in the voice of the region's poets.

The immediate antecedent of the tango lyric was the lyric of the *cuplé español*, a short and light-hearted song form that female singers from Spain known as *tonadilleras* spread through the theaters of Buenos Aires in the late nineteenth and early twentieth centuries, although other literary influences also left their mark, such as those of the payadores (a kind of rural folk poet and musician) and the *canción criolla* on the one hand, as well as brothel songs (*canciones prostibularias*) and pimp poetry (*poesía rufianesca*) on the other.

Many of the tango lyrics of Ángel Villodo and Alfredo Gobbi, like the popular *cuplés* of the time, began with the introduction of a character: "Yo soy... [I am . . .]." Perhaps the most memorable example is Villodo's "La

Morocha" (The dark-haired woman) (1905), which might be considered less a tango then a creolized cuplé:

> Yo soy la morocha,
> La más agraciada,
> la más renombrada
> de esta población. (Gobello, *Letras de tango*, 7)

> [I am the dark-haired woman,
> the most graceful,
> the most renowned,
> of the whole community.][8]

This first generation of musicians took the tango to Paris, where they enjoyed an incredible level of success. But in those years (between 1907 and 1913), the tango lyric remained unchanged and, far from constituting a collective representation of *porteño* life, reflected a limited construction of rather amoral archetypes, such as that of the *compadrito* who is not only presented as an accomplished dancer but also as a successful *cafishio* or pimp.

It was a guitarist by the name of Pascual Contursi (1888–1932), who sang and played at the Moulin Rouge cabaret in Montevideo, who unexpectedly inaugurated what we recognize today as tango song (tango canción), when he began to add lyrics to diverse forms of instrumental tango. This turn of events is very clearly evident in Francisco Canaro's "Matasano," which he debuted in 1914. The first stanza mimics the tone of Villoldo's cuplés, but the spirit of the second and third stanzas is considerably different:

> Yo he nacido en Buenos Aires
> y mi techo ha sido el cielo.
> Fue mi único consuelo
> la madre que me dio el ser.
> Desde entonces mi destino
> me arrastra en el padecer.
> Y por eso es que en la cara
> llevo eterna la alegría,
> pero dentro de mi pecho
> llevo escondido un dolor. (Gobello, *Letras de tango*, 21)

> [I was born in Buenos Aires
> and my roof has been the sky.

My only consolation
was the mother who gave me birth.
Since then my destiny
has dragged me through tribulation.
That is the reason that in my face
I show eternal happiness,
but in my chest
I bear concealed pain.]

Pain enters tango in these lyrics that Contursi wrote for Canaro's composition, and there it will remain, forever branding tango with the quality of affliction. As Gobello has written, the text of this particular tango "is very representative because in these lyrics the tango of the *compadrito* and the sentimental tango are fused" (Gobello, *Letras de tango* 3; es muy representativa porque en ella se funden el tango compadrito y el tango sentimental), to which he later adds that it was in fact Contursi who "converted into an intimate confession of the *porteño* what had previously been the bragging style of the *compadritos*" (Gobello, *Letras de tango* 4; convirtió en una íntima confesión del porteño lo que solo era alarde de compadritos).

In other words, suffering began to appear with Contursi. The poet has distanced himself from the happy nature of the cuplé, pains and laments have appeared, and with them a whole series of material and formal characteristics that denote the decisive influence of the melancholy-laden themes of the canción criolla and the lines of the poet Evaristo Carriego (1883–1912). Contursi, the first lyricist of tango canción, thus fathered two innovations that definitively changed the literary structure of sung tango: the insertion of the second person, that is to say, of the apostrophe ("*Percanta,* que me *amuraste* / muchacha, que me abandonaste" [You, my love, who deceived me / you, the girl that abandoned me]), and the incorporation of a plot line—that is, the transition from pure description to the actual telling of a story. These novel elements appeared in the now-classic "Mi noche triste" (My sad night), a song frequently associated with the introduction of lyrics into what had been primarily instrumental dance music. These lyrics—like several others Contursi composed for tango pieces then in vogue—were added to the instrumental tango "Lita" by Samuel Castriota, probably in the year 1915, although the song wasn't recorded by Carlos Gardel until two years later.[9] The song begins:

Percanta que me *amuraste*
en lo mejor de mi vida,

dejándome el alma herida
y espina en el corazón,
sabiendo que te quería,
que vos eras mi alegría
y mi sueño abrasador.
Para mí ya no hay consuelo
y por eso *me encurdelo*[10]
pa' olvidarme de tu amor. (Gobello, *Letras de tango*, 24)

[Woman, you who abandoned me
in the prime of my life
leaving me with a wounded soul
and thorns in my heart
knowing that I loved you
that you were my happiness
and the dream that embraced me.
There's no consolation for me
and for this reason I get drunk
to forget about your love.]

This is the radiography of a loser. From this point forward, a primary foundation existed upon which the whole superstructure of the literary system of tango would be built. Contursi's importance derives from his having re-created a sensibility rooted in characters who are willing to paint themselves as failures, to be sentimentalists, characters who represent the other face of Villoldo's arrogant and triumphant compadritos. When the legendary singer Carlos Gardel first became familiar with "Mi noche triste" in 1917, he immediately wanted to record it, and the success he achieved with this tango would forever change the trajectory of his career. This would ultimately be of decisive importance to the history of tango; Contursi, consciously or not, gave shape to the genre of tango canción, and Gardel would literally invent the way in which that genre would be interpreted. From that moment on, tango would never be the same.[11]

Beginning in 1915, a series of traits began to take form that would come to characterize the school known as the Guardia Nueva or New Guard.[12] The great composers and poets who were beginning to appear started to create a tango that was *meant to be listened to* more than to be danced to, as had been the case up until that point. This did not spell the end of the dance itself, but rather a growing perception of tango as a triangular form. Now, the public would be faced with three possibilities: tango as music to listen to, tango as music to dance to, or tango as a lyric narration to follow. Obviously, these options could also be combined. So it is that, beginning in the 1920s, tango stopped being the music of the gritty outskirts alone and became the impetus of an entire industry with a mass audience, an industry that soon became materialized in records, sheet music, radio shows, plays, concerts, and dances.

Osvaldo Pelletieri has lucidly explained exactly how the literary system of the tango lyric took shape:

> Since that era marked as the first generation—Pascual Contursi, Celedonio Flores, José González Castillo—tango poets invariably worked with materials that the highbrow literary system had discarded and replaced with others.
>
> The creation of these marginal artists consisted in proposing and solidifying a change of functions produced within the canonical text of "high" poetry. The case of modernism is paradigmatic: it is known that by the end of the first decade of the twentieth century, this movement as well as Carriego's sentimental poetry "spoke" very little to the highly educated sectors reading poetry at the time.
>
> Nonetheless, Contursi and Flores included their work in tango within Carriego's intertextual model and converted the poet's texts in true generators of new texts, constituting the tango category, fixing its norms to such a degree that Carriego continued to serve as a model until well into the decade of the 1950s. (10)[13]

Pelletieri then goes on to conclude that "Carriego's poetry already contained a near totality of the elements necessary to construct a literary system. All that was lacking was the definitive creation of a common literary language, the achievement of the union of poetry and music and the subsequent securing of an audience for this new invention" (11).[14]

This creation of a common literary language happened with "Milonguita" (1920, with lyrics by Samuel Linnig and music by Enrique Delfino), which, within the history of tango, should hold a place at least as important as that of "Mi noche triste" for having contributed a definitive structure. Beginning with this work, the linearity of Contursi's and Flores's earliest lyrics is henceforth modified, and what emerges is a pattern of three movements composed of two longer stanzas of a narrative-evocative character, a shorter refrain meant to exhort or prompt reflection between the two stanzas, and a refrain often repeated at the end of the song.[15]

Lunfardo, a popular vocabulary born of the encounter between immigrants and criollos (native-born Latin Americans) in the *conventillos* (tenements) and suburbs of the city, appeared in the majority of the lyrics from the early period of the tango canción. Indeed, it is almost a commonplace to say that lunfardo constitutes, with its contribution of a rich lexical imagination full of shadings, a true stamp of identity. A stamp that, on the one hand, distinguishes Argentines from other Latin Americans with whom they share a common language and, on the other, strengthens the sense of belonging to a culture in which the "popular" (language, culture, and popular arts) has never been a mere condiment but rather an essential ingredient.

Nonetheless, lunfardo was for decades considered—erroneously, in my opinion—a criminal lexicon. The fact that the term *lunfardo* originally meant "thief" led to misguided conclusions by those who first began studying the phenomenon, who assumed the vocabulary was the sole domain of delinquents or the prison system. Policemen such as Benigno Lugones and José Álvarez, as well as the prison guard Luis Contreras Villamayor, mistakenly ascribed to lunfardo a delinquent character.[16] Like many of his successors, Dellepiane, author of the first lunfardo vocabulary, took the argot as a model and labeled something as *lunfardo* that in reality extended well beyond the prison sector; ultimately, he and others compiled a lexicon used not just by criminals but by an extremely broad segment of the *populus minutus,* of which criminals were naturally a part. Lunfardo never has been, nor is it today for that matter, a technolect or professional slang.[17] From its origins, lunfardo has signified much more than this, not only in terms of the lexical fields it combines but also for the high level of dissemination it has enjoyed, first among the lower classes and later in porteño society at large.

Lunfardo is not a lexicon of thieves because in its very origins the words that constituted it exceeded the semantic field of the criminal. What direct relationship do such words as *mufa* (upset), *morfi* (food), *vento* (money), *pucho* (cigarette), *gomía* (friend), or *descangayado* (deteriorated) have with thievery? But such a misguided perception is very prevalent. It is not uncommon to hear many of the cultured elite refer to lunfardo as a vocabulary that pertains to the world of crime or even, to be more precise, a vocabulary of the prisons. It is one thing to acknowledge that technical terms related to criminal activity or the prison environment have entered the popular mainstream by way of poems published in pamphlets or magazines or through tango or milonga lyrics, but it is something else altogether to consider these as quintessential lunfardo terms. Obviously, every profession has its own slang or technolect.

Those policemen mentioned earlier, who at the end of the nineteenth century tried to find in Buenos Aires forms of expression characteristic of thieves, weren't able to see (and were not able to discern, since they were not linguists) a crucial factor: the words that constituted these early lexicons went well beyond the criminal technolect in question.

Lunfardo is simply a popular lexical repertoire, that is, a vocabulary whose origins can be linked to the Argentine capital, although at present it can be found all over Argentina and even beyond the country's borders. Almost every country in the world has a similar vocabulary: in France it's the *argot*, in Brazil the *gíria*, in the United States *slang*, in Peru *jeringa*, in Colombia *parlache*. And these examples are not merely examples of criminal jargon, as Teruggi has correctly observed: "I reject the notion that argots are by nature associated with criminality, considering them instead forms of popular speech. With this interpretation we naturally broaden the concept of lunfardo, which presents itself as an argot born in Buenos Aires that has since become a national argot. . . . I realize there has been an initial confusion in the characterization of argots, which can be found in the tendency of the upper classes to identify poverty with criminal lifestyles" (2).[18]

All these argots are lexical repertoires created by communities at the margins of standard language, but comprised of voices and expressions that pertain to this same language. Lunfardo, when compared with these other argots, is, however, a unique linguistic phenomenon. Because, while it is entirely true that many lunfardisms are terms taken from Spanish but invested with different meanings[19]—such as *empaquetar* (to pack), which in lunfardo might signify "to deceive or betray," *azotea* (roof) becoming a human head, or *alpiste* (birdseed), now meaning an alcoholic beverage—what distinguishes lunfardo from these argots is the extraordinary quantity of vocabularies taken from languages other than Spanish. An already classic example is the habitual citation of lunfardisms of Italianate origin such as *laburar* (to work), *biaba* (a hit or a slap), *fiaca* (laziness), *yuta* (police), and so on. But there are also more than a few lunfardisms taken from the language of the Gypsies of Spain known as *caló*, such as *gil* (idiot), *chorear* (to steal), or *pirobar* (to fornicate), as well as from various African terms brought to the Americas by the slave trade, such as *fulo* (angry), *marimba* (a beating), or *quilombo* (brothel or disorder), and even words of Lusophone origin—such as *chumbo* (revolver) or *tamangos* (shoes). Lunfardo also includes anglicisms, such as *espiche* (speech), and even the occasional word derived from Polish, such as *papirusa* (a beautiful woman). What's more, lunfardo received a significant contribution to its lexicon from words of indigenous origin, such as those deriving from Quichua, such as *pucho* (cigarette butt), *cache* (in bad taste), or *cancha* (skill); from Nahuatl, as in *camote* (courtship or amorous infatuation); and finally from Guaraní, *matete* (disorder).

Within lunfardo there exists the so-called *vesre* or syllabic inversion, which consists (in its canonical form) of the taking of the last syllable of a lunfardo or Castilian based word and replacing it in the front of the word, in taking the penultimate syllable of the word and replacing it in the position of the second syllable, and so on, thus inverting the order of syllables sequentially such as with the word *zabeca,* vesre for *cabeza* (head), or *bolonqui,* vesre for *quilombo* (a mess). This anagrammatic process, which owes its name to the inversion of the Spanish term *revés* (backward), might have served originally to obscure the meaning of the word in question or simply to enrich it by adding a ludic, skeptical, or teasing dimension. Many uses of vesre are rather obvious, the original words from which they are derived being easily deduced, but some cases constitute a specialization and exception to the aforementioned role of sequential syllable inversion. Such is the case with the word *trompa* replacing *patrón* (boss or master), *tordo* replacing *doctor* (physician or lawyer), or *orre* for *reo* (low life), *dorima* replacing *marido* (husband), and *ispa* for *país* (nation or country). But *jermu* does not just mean simply *mujer* (woman) but rather wife, and *cañemu* does not mean *muñeca* (doll) but instead skill or ability. Furthermore, many cases of vesre have irregular conjugations: *viorsi* for *baño* (bathroom) is the irregular vesre conjugation of *servicio* (restroom), *bramaje* is the conjugation of *hembraje* (a slang term meaning a large group of women), *dolobu* is derived from *boludo* (a frequently used Argentine word that means idiot or dumbass), and the word *lompa* comes from *pantalón* (pants or pant leg).[20]

Involuntary changes to words due to mutations or phonetic variations also find their way into the lunfardo vocabulary. An example of the former would be the word *espamento,* sometimes seen as *aspamento,* both of which are variations of the Spanish *aspaviento* (an excessive display of emotion). An example of phonetic variations might be *chacar* (from *shacar* meaning to rob) and *cafisio* (from cafishio or pimp). Other modifications are augmentatives (*piolón,* from *piola,* sharp or astute) and, of course, diminutives (*pulastrín* from *pulastro,* a term used for a male homosexual).

What we know of lunfardo today was until the middle of the twentieth century a universe completely unknown outside police and penitentiary circles, one that was meticulously ignored by linguists and academics. This all changed in 1953 when José Gobello, who wasn't a professional linguist but a journalist by vocation, first approached lunfardo from a more scientific point of view and published his first study *Lunfardía*. Few studies of lunfardo from a linguistic perspective exist. The oldest, such as those by Antonio Dellepiane in 1894 and by Luis Contreras Villamayor in 1915, were undertaken primarily from the perspective of positivist criminology, and they were thus subject to the priorities of the disciplinary system. Excluding the studies by Gobello (*El lunfardo* 1989, *Aproximación al lunfardo* 1996) and Teruggi (1974), only three linguists to date have attempted a scientific characterization of lunfardo: Beatriz Lavandera (1976), Beatriz Fontanella de Weinberg (1983), and Susana Mátorell de Laconi (*Salta lunfa* 2000, "El lunfardo" 2002a, "Hacia una definicíon" 2002b). All three share the same stance regarding the origins of lunfardo: that it was born as a slang of criminals or the penitentiary system or of both simultaneously. However, they do not provide concrete reasons, instead basing their positions on the accounts given by Benigno Lugones, Drago, and Dellepiane, without reflecting on the vocabulary's many enigmas both in the field of semantics and in its lexical corpus, which, if it were purely the language of thieves, would be limited to a technical vocabulary of theft, having no reason to include words pertaining to daily life and other semantic fields that do not refer directly or indirectly to criminal activity.[21]

According to Gobello's thesis, to which I subscribe, the origins of lunfardo lie in the everyday speech of the *compadrito*, that is, of the young criollo of the popular classes, who by virtue of a ludic affinity began to appropriate many of the terms brought to Buenos Aires by immigrants—especially the Italians —at the end of the nineteenth century, subsequently incorporating these terms into his own speech, generally adopting the terms phonetically.[22] In doing so the intention was not to create a kind of slang but rather a transgressive language that was both attractive and festive for the criollo population (Gobello, *El lunfardo* 13). But the diffusion of these terms, and thus of a literary language, was achieved by journalists, playwrights, and tango lyricists.

Just as we recognize in Argentine literature the poetry of the gaucho (the cowboy of the Argentine pampas) and a genre of lunfardesque poetry,[23] we can also affirm that each of these subgenres has given rise to gauchesque or lunfardesque language, respectively. The latter, in as much as it is a literary language, was cultivated initially by poets such as Felipe Fernández (*Yacaré*), Dante A. Linyera, Carlos de la Púa, and Celedonio Flores, then by others such as Alcides Gandolfi Herrero, José Pagano, and Julián Centeya, and later, by a generation that included, among others, Nira Etchenique and Daniel Giribaldi. *Poesía lunfardesca* to this day claims some big names, such as those of Luis Alposta, Orlando Mario Punzi, Luis Ricardo Furlan, and Roberto Selles.[24] To get an idea of this lunfardesque language, a citation of a very short poem from *La crencha engrasada*, the legendary book by Carlos de la Púa, published in 1928, should suffice. It is titled "Amasijo habitual" (Habitual beating):

> La durmió de un *cachote, gargajeó de colmiyo,*
> se arregló la *melena,* y *pitándose* un *faso*
> salió de la *atorranta* pieza del *conventiyo . . .*
> y silbando bajito *rumbió pal escolaso.*[25]

> [He knocked her out with one blow, he spit out the side of his mouth
> he fixed his hair and, smoking a cigarette
> he left the miserable room in the tenement
> and whistling quietly, headed toward the casino.]

As the quantity of italicized lunfardo terms in the original language demonstrates, de la Púa is one of the poets who has taken the lunfardo vocabulary to its possible limits, with compositions that are truly impossible to understand for the uninitiated, such as the lunfardo-laden poem "Línea No. 9," also included in *La crencha engrasada.* But this, as we will see, is an extreme case.

Lunfardo has also enjoyed generalized usage both in the Argentine theater of the first thirty or forty years of the twentieth century—especially in comic sketches—and in *costumbrista* works and journalistic and popular literature. In fact the earliest compositions of tango canción circulated this way, as they were included as sung interludes to accompany comic sketches. But besides becoming generalized as a specific spoken vocabulary of the Río de la Plata region, and despite its use in multiple literary genres, lunfardo has, apart from this, configured itself in the popular imaginary as a distinctive element of tango lyrics.

I argue that even though there are many tango lyrics that do not contain a single lunfardo term, we should still consider lunfardo an essential element of tango poetics, since it claims the tango lyric as a terrain unto itself. According to Mario Teruggi, one of the scholars who has best articulated the relationship between tango and lunfardo:

> one finds an entire spectrum, which goes from those tangos that aspire to express themselves exclusively in lunfardisms to those that offer a Castilian poetry. . . . Undeniably, tango has been a fundamental agent in the

divulgation of lunfardo as well as in its preservation. Little known lunfard-isms, such as *acamalar, fané, chiqué,* and other similar terms are normally made known—and their meanings guessed or intuited by the context—via the lyrics of tango. Save for a few exceptions, lyricists have in the majority of cases lent authority to their lyrics with commonplace lunfardisms, that is, they have made few contributions themselves as creators; all in all, the influence of lyricists has been fundamental in fixing set terms and expressions. (152)[26]

When lunfardo was incorporated into tango canción with the help of Contursi, three decades had already passed since it had begun to multiply exponentially in anonymous milongas, in pimp poetry (poesía rufianesca), and in the verses of anonymous or unknown neighborhood poets known as *arrabaleros.* A large portion of this material has been preserved thanks to the efforts of the German anthropologist Robert Lehmann-Nitsche (1872–1938). Under the pseudonym of Victor Borde, he published a book in 1923 that, reedited in Spanish in 1981, bears the title *Textos eróticos del Río de la Plata* (Erotic texts of the Río de la Plata).[27] The work is an anthology of anonymous materials that primarily falls under the category of the obscene, of poems concerning brothels and the eschatological, sexual relations, refrains, sayings, stories, and riddles. One section in which lunfardo flourishes is that of so-called epic poems (*poesías épicas*), some of whose titles make direct reference to the pseudo-epic actions treated within their pages: *El Gran cojedor* (The big fucker), *La Vida del canfinflero* (The life of the pimp), and *Aventuras de una atorranta* (Adventures of a hooker). The connection here between the "epic" and the vulgar is a long-standing one: texts with vulgar content are common in Western popular culture, beginning with the pornographic iconography of ancient Greece and the explicit graffiti found on the walls of Pompeii. In terms of a more recent context, one should keep in mind as well that brothels were extremely plentiful in early twentieth-century Buenos Aires and its outskirts, where recent waves of male immigrants from Europe had skewed the balance between the sexes in the urban population.

During the thirty years he lived in Argentina, Lehmann-Nitsche compiled a large number of pamphlets that contain the texts of *payadas* (improvised songs), popular poems (many of them anonymous), knockoffs of well-known tangos, and also prose texts. Grouped under the name Biblioteca Criolla (Creole library), the texts were acquired by the Iberoamerican Institute of Berlin after the German scholar's death.[28] Some of the tangos included in this collection already bear the evidence of lunfardisms in their titles: "El otario"

(The gullible one), "El tango de la patota" (Gang tango), "La catrera" (The bed), "Los vichadores" (The spies), "El cachafaz" (The cocky one), and "El chamuyo" (The heart-to-heart chat).

There are other interesting incorporations of lunfardisms, some more than a century old. In 1902 Quesada cites the lyrics of one of the songs that at the time could be heard in the streets of Buenos Aires: "Somos los *bacanes guapos* / de las *minas* más *nuevitas*, / que no usamos florecitas / como usan los *cajetillas*" (We are the slick sugar daddies / of the youngest girls, / we don't put flowers [in our lapels] / like the youths of the upper class) (161). Evaristo Carriego (1883–1912), an admirer of Rubén Darío and creator of a poetic sensibility that influenced numerous tango lyricists, utilized lunfardo very little. Nonetheless, the September 26, 1912, issue of a detective magazine called *L.C.* includes five *décima* poems in which Carriego does in fact use lunfardo. In these poems the first-person narrator bemoans an unfortunate turn of fate that has culminated with his wife abandoning him: "Hoy *se* me *espiantó* la *mina*. / ¡Y si viera con qué *gato*" (Today my woman walked out on me. / And if you could only see the bum she left with!) (Soler Cañas, 196).

With the advent of tango canción in 1917, Contursi initiated a new phase for a genre whose musical and choreographic elements had already undergone significant evolution. One of the principal instruments of this evolution was of course lunfardo, which salvaged tango canción from the destiny of caricature to which the *sainete* seemed to have condemned it. Contursi's measured use of lunfardo in his lyrics (between four and eight lunfardisms in each text) reveals the lyricist's will to make his language meaningful and, at the same time, reflect the speech of his audiences. An exaggerated dependence on lunfardo-derived words, besides making his texts hermetic, would also have detracted from their verisimilitude, as is the case with various poems by Carlos de la Púa and with some of the tangos of Alfredo Marino ("El Ciruja," 1926) and Eduardo Escariz Méndez ("Barajando," 1929), both of which contain nearly thirty lunfardo-based expressions, making them extremely difficult to understand.

Defined in such a way, the tango lyric assumes its place in relation to canonical poetry of the first half of the twentieth century. Negating erudite language and letting lunfardo take its course, while in the process legitimating it, tango simultaneously defined, affirmed, and transformed itself into the ideal venue for the growth and expansion of lunfardo expressivity, an expressivity enabled by the performances of singers and songwriters, the advent of the phonograph, and, a few years later, the pervasive presence of the radio. Together, tango and lunfardo, both the offspring of immigration, won popular favor by feeding off of one another.

The expansion of tango also helped to popularize lunfardo. As Palermo and Mantovani realized, "the success of tango didn't just contribute to the consecration of the lunfardo vocabulary of the Argentines, but also incentivized its use by lyricists in tango itself—the lyricists and poets of tango picked up, refined and created lunfardo terms" (77).[29] In another sense the use of lunfardo invested the poetics of tango with an innovative character that permitted it to differentiate itself from other vocal genres of its day. These innovations of the tango lyric in preestablished language are, according to Carlos Mina, those that permit the tango to "carry forth the gargantuan task of making it acceptable to the masses" (105).

Hardly a year had passed since Gardel's recording of "Mi noche triste" in 1917 when other tangos began to incorporate lunfardo vocabulary. Florencio Iriarte, some time after penning his compadrito dialogues, wrote "El cafiso" (circa 1918), a tango with musical accompaniment by Juan Canavese, which begins: "Ya me tiene más *robreca* / que *canfli* sin *ventolina* / y *palpito* que la *mina* / *la liga* por la *buseca*" (He's already got me more pissed off / than a pimp without money / and I get the feeling that the woman / gets beatings for food) (Gobello, *Letras de tango*, 33). Over half of the lyrics produced in the 1920s and 1930s contain at least three or four lunfardisms and in some cases as many as ten. Lunfardo therefore became one of the most powerful vehicles in the consolidation and characterization of a tango poetics. In many cases its use is deliberate and responds to confessed intentions. Celedonio Flores (1896–1947), probably one of the more decisive influences in the use of lunfardo among lyricists, consciously postulates a poetics destined for the common man at the beginning of his sonnet "Musa rea" (Low-class muse):

No tengo el *berretín* de ser un bardo,
chamuyador letrao, ni de *spamento*.
Yo escribo humildemente lo que siento
y pa' escribir mejor, ¡lo hago *en lunfardo*! (Flores, *Antología poética* 76)

[I'm not obsessed with being a poet
a lettered author or a scene-maker
I humbly write what I feel
and to write better, I do it with lunfardo!]

Keeping in mind his audience, Flores chooses a register distanced from that of the written poetry of his time, one in which lunfardo plays a central role: his tangos describe a universe of common characters from a modest social and economic background, who typically expressed themselves through the medium of a lunfardo vocabulary. Such is the case, for instance, in "Mano a mano" (Hand to hand, 1920), in which the narrator of the poem compares the past and the present of the woman who left him:

> Se dio el juego de *remanye* cuando vos, pobre *percanta*,
> *gambeteabas* la pobreza en la casa de pensión.
> Hoy sos toda una *bacana*, la vida te ríe y canta,
> los *morlacos* del *otario* los *tirás a la marchanta*
> como juega el gato *maula* con el mísero ratón.
> (Gobello, *Letras de tango* 54)

> [The game was up when you, poor girl,
> eluded the poverty of the boarding house.
> Now you're loaded, life smiles on you and sings,
> you toss around the bills of the idiot (who supports you)
> just as the wicked cat plays with the unfortunate rat.]

Several poets made good use of lunfardo terms in memorable tango lyrics. José de Grandis (1888–1932) uses just the right dose in "Amurado" (published in 1927, with music by Pedro Maffia and Pedro Laurenz):

> *Campaneo* a mi *catrera* y la encuentro desolada;
> sólo tengo de recuerdo el cuadrito que está allí,
> *pilchas* viejas, unas flores y mi alma atormentada;
> eso es todo lo que queda desde que se fue de aquí.

> Una tarde mas tristona que la pena que me aqueja,
> arregló su *bagayito* y *amurado* me dejó. (Gobello, *Letras de tango* 85)

> [I take a look at my bed and find it's empty;
> the only memory I have is the little picture that's there,
> old clothes, some flowers and my tormented soul;
> that's all that remains since she took off.

> On an afternoon sadder than the pain that afflicts me,
> she packed her few belongings and left me abandoned.]

In a completely different tone, Fernando Ochoa made humorous use of the lunfardo lexicon in "Pipistrela" (published in 1933, with music by Juan Canaro), the story of a young woman from the neighborhood who refuses the courtship of a young man of her same social class in the hopes of seducing a man with deeper pockets:

Yo quisiera tener mucho *vento*
pa' comprarme un sombrero y zapatos,
añaparme algún *coso* del centro,
pa' dejar esta *manga* de *patos* . . . (Gobello, *Letras de tango* 378)

[I'd like to have lots of money
so I could buy myself a hat and shoes,
to trap some guy from downtown,
so I could leave behind this bunch of losers . . .]

Enrique Santos Discépolo (1901–1951) and Enrique Cadícamo (1900–1999) both used a great deal of lunfardo in the early phases of their work. Tangos like "Qué vachaché" (1926), "Chorra" (1928), and the dark "Yira . . . yira" by the former and "Che, papusa, oí" (1927), "Anclao en París" (1931), and "El que atrasó el reloj" (1933) by the latter are eloquent testimonies to the incorporation of the local vocabulary. Cadícamo, for example, has left an absolutely magisterial example of his handling of lunfardo in the poem "Eya se reía," whose point of departure is "Ella" by the German romantic Heinrich Heine, a poem that would eventually be put to music by Juan Cedrón. It begins:

Eya era una hermosa *nami* del arroyo,
él era un *troesma* pa' usar la ganzúa.
Por eso es que cuando de *afanar* volvía,
ella en la *catrera* contenta reía,
contenta de *echarse* un *dorima* tan *púa*.
    (Cadícamo, *La luna del bajo fondo* 60–61)

[She was a pretty girl from the gutter,
he was a master at picking locks.
That's why when he returned from stealing,
she would lie in bed content and laughing,
content at having such a sharp husband.]

Several other tango authors composed in lunfardo, especially in the 1920s: Manuel Romero (1891–1954) with "El taita del arrabal" (1922), Enrique Dizeo

(1893–1980) with "Pan Comido" (1926), Francisco Martino (1884–1938) with "Soy una fiera," Alberto Ballesteros (1892–1931) with "¡Qué papa estar en presidio!," Francisco Lomuto with "Cachadora" (1928), and Eduardo Escariz Méndez (1888–1957) with "La Cornetita" (1929), to name just a few examples from the dozens in existence. Admittedly, though, several of the most important tango lyricists did not use lunfardo to a large extent. This is often said of the legendary Homero Manzi (1907–1951) and Cátulo Castillo (1906–1975). But in both artists' oeuvres, we can, in fact, find exceptions. In Manzi's case I can mention the tangos "Basurita" (1925) and "Triste paica" (1929), and in the case of Castillo the extraordinary "Desencuentro" (1961), written deliberately in the style of Enrique Santos Discépolo. On the other hand, Alfredo Le Pera (1900–1935) and José María Contursi (1911–1972) stayed away from lunfardo in nearly all their compositions. During the phase of poetic renovation of tango undertaken in the 1960s, other voices such as Eladia Blázquez (1931–2005), Horacio Ferrer (1933), Héctor Negro (1934), Chico Novarro (1933), and Cacho Castaño (1942) entered into dialogue with the aforementioned lyricists, occasionally incorporating lunfardo as well.

Without a doubt tango is a unique creation with an extraordinary musical richness and, thanks to its plurality of forms and styles, an equally rich and broad range of aesthetic varieties. But the advent of music accompanied by lyrics—especially in the case of those lyrics with great poetic value—greatly multiplied its possibilities. There are even cases of musically impoverished tangos that have persevered thanks to their lyrics (and vice versa). Tango lyrics reflect a series of shared understandings or complicities with which a kind of social character is determined. According to María Susana Azzi,

> For those who listen to them and know them by memory, tango lyrics provide a tradition that concerns who they are, what their neighborhood, their city, and their past signify, what they should expect out of life, and how many of life's frustrations are waiting for them around the corner. The mailbox, the grocery store, the streetlamp, and the moon are not just part of an urban geographical description but rather acquire an emotional significance that ends up being transcendental for a great portion of the neighborhood's inhabitants: this significance is the vital force of the past and the interpersonal relations that give them their personal and cultural identity.... The culture of tango has organized, through its lyrics and music, a kind of way of feeling for immigrants and Argentines alike. ("La inmigración y las letras de tango en la Argentina" 88)[30]

The social representations portrayed in tango poetry have permitted the inhabitants of Buenos Aires and other cities of the Río de la Plata region to establish a common vision of the world. For decades, tango lyrics comprised a symbolic universe and even a value system within the moral order. In a much-cited article in his book *Evaristo Carriego*, the author Jorge Luis Borges foresaw the endurance of the tango lyric, to the point of predicting that the lyrics associated with tango dance numbers would outlast the poetry of many of those figures sanctioned by the literary establishment: "Uneven in quality, as they conspicuously proceed from hundreds and thousands of diversely inspired or merely industrious pens, the lyrics of the tango, after half a century, now constitute an almost impenetrable *corpus poeticum* which historians of Argentine literature will read or, in any case, defend.... By 1990, the suspicion or certainty may arise that the true poetry of our time is not found in Banchs's *La urna* [The urn] or Mastronardi's *Luz de provincia* [Provincial light], but rather those imperfect pieces conserved in the songbook *El alma que canta* [The soul that sings]" (*On Argentina* 106).[31] These words would prove to be prophetic. Enrique Banchs and Carlos Mastronardi are two Argentine poets who have been for the most part forgotten, but dozens of tango lyrics still endure in the porteño memory. The reasons for their lasting imprint in the popular Argentine imaginary should be sought not only in their quality as poetic works but also in their connection to the social context, the latter being the condition of possibility of all legitimate symbolic production.

In much of the world tango is valued for its music, and even more so for the visual delight of its dance, but for Argentines—or at least, for the inhabitants of Buenos Aires—tango lyrics provide a veritable mirror in which they can examine themselves, a refuge in which they find comfort and counsel. What underlies tango lyrics is a complete, deeply rooted system of values shared by the majority of the inhabitants of the Río de la Plata region, especially between 1920 and 1960. But even for those who did not live in that period and for whom the underlying value system has lost its currency, many tango lyrics still resonate with the unquestioned force of truth.

The image of a worldview unto itself, the tango offered the inhabitants of various Argentine cities a way to interpret or give voice to their experiences during most of the twentieth century. It is still common to appeal to the corpus of tango lyrics to express truisms legitimized by the Argentine social imaginary. So it is that such oft-repeated and accepted phrases as "la fama es puro cuento" (fame is a tall tale) (from "Mi vieja viola," published in 1932 by Osvaldo Frías-Humberto Correa), that "amores de estudiante flores de un día son" (the love affairs of a student are flowers that bloom for only a day) (from "Amores de estudiante," published in 1934 by Alfredo Le Pera-Mario Batistella), or that "la vida es una herida absurda" (life is an absurd wound) (from "La última curda," published in 1956 by Cátulo Castillo) still represent a deep vein of popular wisdom. These are all now *endoxa*, anonymous and indisputable opinions that permit the construction of diverse collective representations that continue into the present. Many Argentines also seek in tango lyrics formulas that will explain life's vicissitudes or describe someone's way of being or acting. And many of these phrases contain lunfardisms, such as when, for example, one speaks of the "*berretines* de *bacana* que tenías en la mente" (the fantasies of wealth you had stuck in your head) (from "Margot," published in 1919 by Celedonio Flores), or when one complains that "lo que más *bronca* me da es haber sido tan *gil*!" (What upsets me most is having been such an idiot!) ("Chorra," published in 1928), or when one expresses how well they know someone by saying "pero si sos más *manyada* que el tango 'La Cumparsita'" (But I know you better than the tango standard "La Cumparsita"] (from "Tortazos," published in 1933 by Enrique Maroni).[32] In this same vein it is commonly known and often repeated that "cualquier *cacatúa* sueña con la *pinta* de Carlos Gardel" (any old loudmouth dreams of being like Carlos Gardel) (from "Corrientes y Esmeralda," published in 1934 by Celedonio Flores) and that "el que no llora no mama y el que no *afana* es un *gil*" (he who doesn't cry doesn't nurse and he who doesn't steal is an idiot), just as "el que *liga* y *se embalurda se deschava* sin pensar" (he who surrenders and talks too much exposes himself without thinking) (from "Pa' que sepan cómo soy," published in 1951 by Norberto Aroldi).

Besides its prevalence in tango, songwriters also incorporated lunfardo in other musical genres such as rock and *cumbia villera,* both of which became very popular in Buenos Aires in later years. Nonetheless, lunfardo has never disappeared from the lyrics of contemporary tango, such as those by Acho Estol and Alfredo "El Tape" Rubín. In fact, in recent years lunfardisms have also made their way into the texts of so-called electronic tango (*tango electrónico*). Such is the case in "Mi confesión" (My confession), which the hip-hop group Koxmoz recorded with Gotán Project (*Lunático,* 2006), in which one finds these lines rapped by Apolo Novax:

Apuesto *a pleno*, pero *de callado*,
cada uno *en la suya*, yo ando *rayado*.
. . .
Escuchame bien. . . . No es *chamuyo*, es amor.

[I bet big, but quietly,
everybody in their own business, I'm feeling hooked.

. . .

Listen to me well. . . . It's not just talk, it's love.]

Lines to which Chili Parker responds: "Los más hábiles dejamos pasar los *abriles*, / inmóviles para no quedar como *giles*" (The smartest of us let the years go by, / unmoved, so we don't look like idiots). In the same way, in "Ya no me duele" by Bajofondo (*Mar Dulce*, 2007), performed by Fernando Santullo, one hears the following lines:

Laburo por *chirolas*, no quiero seguir y decido salir de la cola.
Y aunque el lomo no puede, y aunque las *gambas* casi no quieren,
doy una vuelta a ver si todavía llueve.

. . .

Chiflo bajo, me *pateo* el hormigón
mientras pienso, *calentón*, que *me rajo* del *laburo*
y que *me rajo* con razón.

[I work for pocket change, I don't wanna go on like this so I get out
   of the line.
And even if my back can't take it, and even if my legs almost don't
   want to,
I take a walk to see if it's still raining.

. . .

Whistling low, I walk through the concrete jungle
while I think, steamin,' that I'm leaving this job
and that I am right to leave.]

I hope to have shown in the course of this chapter the subtle yet effective way in which lunfardo has been organically incorporated into tango lyrics, constituting across time one of the essential characteristics of this poetic and sung form of expression. The lunfardo vocabulary has persisted in popular memory thanks to the popularity of tango and thanks to the continued performance of tango texts that offer interpretive keys, timeless maxims, and life lessons for contemporary experience. In the symbiosis of tango and lunfardo, a distinct and vital symbolic order is revealed that is utterly unique to the Río de la Plata region.

Notes

1. *Tango canción* or tango song, a genre in and of itself, should not be confused with *tango cantado* (sung tango) or *tango con letra* (tango with lyrics). Even though the genre was basically an instrumental one in its first decades of existence, there are several tangos from this period that have lyrics, such as "Justicia criolla" (1897, music by Antonio Reynoso and lyrics by Ezequiel Soria), "El Porteñito" (1903) and "La Morocha" (1905)—both with lyrics and music by Ángel Villoldo—"El taita" (1907, music by Alfredo Gobbi and lyrics by Silverio Manco), and "Don Juan" (1914, music by Ernesto Ponzio and lyrics by Ricardo Podestá). As Gobello and Oliveri point out, "en lo que atañe al tango como canción debe señalarse que si bien los primitivos tangos tuvieron letrillas improvisadas o compuestas más o menos improvisadamente por autores que, como Ángel G. Villoldo, no atribuían importancia alguna a su labor poética, el nacimiento del llamado tango-canción debe fijarse hacia 1915, cuando Pascual Contursi comenzó a cantar en Montevideo sus propias letras, compuestas sobre músicas ya divulgadas" (Gobello and Oliveri 339–40; in what concerns tango as song it should be pointed out that even if primitive tangos had improvised lyrics or were composed more or less in an extemporaneous fashion by authors who, like Ángel G. Villoldo, attributed no importance whatsoever to their poetic labor, the birth of the so-called tango song should be set about 1915, when Pascual Contursi began to sing his own lyrics in Montevideo, composed to music that had already been in circulation).

Tango song (tango canción), defined as having plot-driven lyrics, is one of the definitive elements of the Guardia Nueva (Ferrer, *El tango* 33; Salas, *El tango* 93–94). The fact that "Mi Noche Triste" is considered the genre's first examples essentially is due to the fact that it was the first tango recorded by Carlos Gardel (Morena 31–32; Barsky and Barsky 241–43), who for the next five or six years—until his own success provoked the emergence of new singers and songwriters—would be one of the sole singers working in the genre. Tango canción presupposes a specific kind of performance (which in large part was Gardel's creation), a level of specialization on the part of the lyricists, and, in its content, the narration of a story (Matamoro, *El tango* 43).

In fact, 1917 is so widely held to be the year that marks the appearance of tango canción that in 2007 Carlos Mina published a work in which he analyzes the relationship between tango lyrics and the process of social integration in the Río de la Plata region during the first half of the twentieth century titled *Tango: La mezcla milagrosa (1917–1956)* [Tango: The miraculous mixture (1917–1956)]. The dates in parentheses, which account for the birth and expiration of tango song as a genre, coincide with the recordings of "Mi Noche Triste" in 1917 and "La última curda" (lyrics by Cátulo Castillo and music by Aníbal Troilo) in 1956. It is certainly debatable whether tango song was brought to a close with "La última curda" or not—some of us think that the genre lived on into the 1960s, and for others, the genre has survived to this day—but few dispute the year 1917 as the birth of tango canción.

2. I in no way consider *lunfardo* to be merely a vocabulary of thieves, as many authors continue to believe. The reasons for this and the characterization of this linguistic phenomenon that concerns me here will be treated in the following pages.

3. I'm using the word *poetry* in this context to refer specifically to tango lyrics. I do

not subscribe to the distinction commonly made between the textual genres of poetry on the one hand and song lyrics ("letra de canción") on the other. In so doing I am not overlooking the fact that, in the case of the latter, music itself qualitatively modifies literary expressivity, yet the attempts to demonstrate that the tango lyric constitutes a genre that is different from poetry always stand on dubious grounds of critical evaluation contingent on the subjectivity of the beholder and based on categorizations of supposedly distinct characteristics that are not just difficult but in fact impossible to gauge. When or by what stylistic means does a lyricist become a poet? I wrote as much in the prologue to my study *Poéticas del rock*: "Si aceptamos que las canciones son literatura—una literatura surgida a partir de una lógica musical, por así decirlo—, pues entonces, ¿qué otra cosa podrían ser sino poesía?" (Conde, *Poéticas del rock* 15; If we accept that songs are a form of literature—a form of literature that arose via a musical logic, as it were—then, what exactly would they be if not poetry?).

4. Popular theater of the Río de la Plata region enjoyed an apogee starting in 1886, when *Juan Moreyra* was included in the circus performances of the brothers José and Jerónimo Podestá. In the following decades two genres in particular began to flourish, first the *gauchesco* and later the *sainete* (a brief comedic drama that is realist in nature), both of which were influenced in large part by the genre known as *chico español*. In the mid-1920s Armando Discépolo gives shape to what would be known as the *grotesco criollo*, whose structure can be traced back to the productions of the Italian Luigi Pirandello. This Creole or native grotesque is defined as a short piece that is tragicomic in nature, wherein the author portrays some deformation of reality that reveals an epochal crisis in which society questions the established system of values. Regionalist journalism (*periodismo costumbrista*) flowered in the form of illustrated magazines in the first three decades of the twentieth century. The numerous authors who utilized this genre—including such standouts as Félix Lima, Juan Francisco Palermo, Máximo Teodoro Sáenz (Last Reason), Roberto Arlt, Luis Alfredo Sciutto (Diego Lucero), and Miguel Ángel Bavio Esquiú (Juan Mondiola)—captured in their chronicles (*crónicas*), etchings, and newspaper columns the customs and modes of self-expression of the commoner. The comic sketch (*historieta*) was, for a good part of the last century, a genre of broad popular appeal in Argentina, in which many authors such as Divito, Calé, and Lino Palacio made consistent use of lunfardo.

5. If one accepts that "la complejidad es efectivamente el tejido de eventos, acciones, interacciones, retroacciones, determinaciones, azares, que constituyen nuestro mundo fenoménico" (Morin, Ciurana, and Motta 40; complexity is effectively the fabric of events, actions, interactions, retroactions, determinations, and chance occurrences that constitute our phenomenological world), then the tango phenomenon turns out to be an ideal field or object of study in which to explore this notion of complexity.

6. "Así como la habanera fue lírica y el candombe, bailable, podemos decir que la milonga fue un género lírico que se convirtió en baile aceptando algunos elementos coreográficos del candombe sobre el esquema rítmico de la habanera. Esta fórmula intenta resolver la definición del tango porteño, partiendo de su necesario carácter híbrido."

7. In the second half of the nineteenth century, the milonga came to be known in the Río de la Plata region as the *habanera con quebrada y corte* (the habanera with breaks and

steps). In the "academies" or dance halls that in 1870 began to multiply in the peripheral neighborhoods of Buenos Aires and Montevideo, as well as in the "waitress cafés" (*cafés de camareras*)—de facto brothels—*compadritos* improvised audacious and Africanized movements, imitating them from the choreography of the *candombe* dance genre, taking note of the dance's steps and conventional figures. These innovations obliged musicians to adapt the habanera rhythm to this new and to a certain degree unexpected choreography. In this way a new musical genre was born that in just a few years would be recognized around the world with the name *tango*, a word that up until the final years of the nineteenth century meant nothing other then a *way to dance* the extant genres of the polka, the mazurka, and the milonga.

8. All translations of lyrics, unless otherwise noted, are the translator's and/or editor's.

9. Contursi repeated the process with "Ivette," "Flor de Fango" (Flower from the mud), and "Si supieras" (If you only knew), the last written to the music of "La Cumparsita."

10. In lunfardo, "I get drunk" (*me emborracho* in standard Spanish).

11. Although Contursi is considered the first of the lyricists of tango canción, in 1914 Celedonio Flores (1896–1947) won a competition held by the newspaper *Ultima Hora* (Last hour) with his poem "Por la Pinta," which in 1919 would at Gardel's insistence become known as the tango "Margot." In this sense both poets deserve to be recognized as precursors.

12. The establishment of the *orquesta típica* configuration (an orchestra designed for performing live tango in dance halls and other venues) allowed for a systematization of the solo role of each instrument, ultimately consolidating itself with the adoption of orchestration. This contributed to an impoverishment of tango dance. At this moment the inventiveness of the dance's choreography suffered in an inverse relationship to musical and poetic inventiveness.

13. "Desde la época de la denominada primera generación—Pascual Contursi, Celedonio Flores, José González Castillo—los poetas del tango trabajaron invariablemente con procedimientos que el sistema literario culto había desechado y reemplazado por otros.

"La creación de estos artistas marginales consistió en proponer y concretar un cambio de funciones que producían dentro del texto canónico de la denominada poesía culta. El caso del modernismo es paradigmático: es sabido que este movimiento y la poesía sentimental de Carriego ya le decían muy poco, a fines de la década del diez, a los sectores cultos que leían poesía.

"Sin embargo, Contursi y Flores incluyeron su obra tanguística dentro de la intertextualidad de Carriego y convirtieron los textos del poeta de Palermo en verdaderos generadores de nuevos textos, constituyendo la convención tanguera, fijando sus normas, de modo que Carriego continuó siendo el modelo hasta muy avanzada la década del cincuenta."

14. "Ya estaban presentes en la poesía de Carriego la casi totalidad de los elementos necesarios para constituir un sistema literario. Sólo faltaba la creación definitiva de una lengua literaria común, lograr la unión de la poesía y la música y que esta invención encontrara un público."

15. This results musically in the following type of structure: *A b A b*, although according to the lyrics the structure is actually *A b C b*. Sometimes the fourth stanza is new and

sometimes it is a variant of the second, resulting in the following rhyme scheme: A b C d. It is important to remember that many instrumental tangos already possessed this structure, which derived from a modality initiated in "El entrerriano" (1897) by Rosendo Mendizabal (Selles 44). See Gobello, "Gardel en la evolución del tango" 37–41.

16. This can be confirmed by consulting Lugones, "Los beduinos urbanos" and "Los caballeros de industria." Both articles by Lugones were reproduced with updated language in Gobello, *Vieja y nueva lunfardía* 101–17.

17. At most, one could say that lunfardo approached, in its origins, something akin to a sociolect, that is, an aggregate body of language forms (constituted as systematic variations) used by a part of the linguistic community of Buenos Aires and its surrounding areas: the popular classes, the inhabitants of the suburbs who, as has been reiterated over and over, do not constitute a geographical category but rather a social category.

18. "Descarto la teoría de que los argots son de naturaleza delictiva, considerándolos, en cambio, hablas populares. Con esta interpretación se amplía naturalmente el concepto de lunfardo, que se presenta como un argot nacido en Buenos Aires que está deviniendo en argot nacional. . . . Entiendo que ha habido una confusión inicial en la caracterización de los argots, que arranca en la tendencia de las clases superiores a identificar pobreza con mal vivir."

19. This concerns instances of construction of meaning or re-lexicalizations, which can be created by restriction or expansion of meaning or by its displacement, as is the case with metaphors, metonymies, or synecdoches.

20. Of course, anagrammatic word play is not exclusive to lunfardo. In French argot *verlan* is used and is in fact identical to *verse* and derives its name from the inversion of the same term in French, à l'envers, meaning "backward" or "in reverse."

21. Both Lavandera and Fontanella recognize the same two chronological phases in which lunfardo was designated first as a criminal technolect (between the last quarter of the nineteenth century and the first quarter of the twentieth) and then as a *porteño* colloquial repertoire. Lavandera continues to refer to the vocabulary of the second phase as lunfardo, while Fontanella de Weinberg decides at this point to refer to it as "*continuous post-lunfardo,*" erroneously assimilating, in my opinion, the vocabulary into the category of other "post-criollo" continuities. For her part, Martorell ("Hacia una definición del lunfardo") refers to the first phase as historic lunfardo or primitive lunfardo and, like Lavandera, opts for the term *lunfardo* to name the "general" lexical repertoire spoken in Buenos Aires from approximately 1930 onward. From Martorell's point of view, lunfardo is still recognizable in a third stage (virtually superimposed onto the second), which is characterized by a lexical repertoire that absorbs words from various domains, to the extent that many lunfardisms become indistinguishable from Argentinisms.

22. Gobello puts it this way: "Si en cuanto léxico el lunfardo es un producto directo de la inmigración, en cuanto lenguaje–manera de expresarse–resulta, entonces, una creación literaria basada en los elementos léxicos inmigrados característicos del habla del compadrito" (Gobello, *El lunfardo* 14): If as a lexicon, lunfardo is a direct product of immigration, then as a language—a way of expressing oneself—it ends up being a literary creation based in immigrant lexical elements derived from the speech of the compadrito.

23. Despite what is perhaps a lack of thematic and formal renovation that might have kept the genre at the forefront of literary production, gauchesque poetry still conserves a certain vitality to this day within a relatively small circuit of people.

24. Concerning this topic, see Furlan, *La poesía lunfarda* and *Esquema de la poesía lunfardesca*.

25. *Amasijo* can be translated to standard Spanish as *paliza* (a hit or a slap). Both in this quotation and the preceding examples, lunfardo words appear in italics.

26. "Se cuenta con toda una gama, que va del tango que aspira a expresarse casi exclusivamente con lunfardismos hasta aquél que ofrece una poesía castellana. . . . Es indudable que el tango ha sido uno de los agentes fundamentales en la divulgación del lunfardo y también en su preservación. Lunfardismos poco usuales, como *acamalar, fané, chiqué* y similares son normalmente conocidos–y sus significados adivinados intuitivamente o por el contexto–a través de letras tangueras. Salvo excepciones, los letristas se han valido en la mayoría de los casos de lunfardismos comunes, o sea que han hecho pocas contribuciones como creadores; con todo, su influencia ha sido fundamental para la fijación de términos y expresiones."

27. A more literal rendering in Spanish of the German title (*Texte aus den La Plata-Gebieten in volkstümlichen Spanish und Rotwelsch*) would be Textos de la zona de la Plata español popular y lunfardo (Popular and lunfardo texts from the Spanish River Plate region). In the original title there is no reference to the book's erotic content, and instead the emphasis is placed on the fact that these testimonies were written in *volkstümlichen* Spanish ("in popular Spanish") and *Rotwelsch* (lunfardo). The sexual nature of these texts is nonetheless implied by the first edition of the work, which was edited as the eighth volume of a collection bearing the title *Anuarios para pesquisas folklóricas e investigaciones de la historia del desarrollo de la moral sexual* (Annual publication for the study of folklore and the investigation of the history of the evolution of sexual morality).

28. According to Adolfo Prieto, who had access to this material, the Biblioteca Criolla contains 950 pamphlets (80). In addition to the book by Prieto, important information pertaining to so-called *literatura del cordel* (cheaply produced publications for a popular market) that is virtually unobtainable in Argentina can be found by consulting the following articles published in three consecutive numbers of the magazine *Cuadernos* of the Instituto Nacional de Antropología y Pensamiento Latinoamericano: Olga Fernández Latour de Botas, "Poesía popular impresa de la colección Lehmann-Nitsche," parts I, II, and III, *Cuadernos*, nos. 5–7 (1967–1972): 207–40, 179–226, 281–325. In addition some of these same pamphlets were compiled in the work of Guido and Redy de Guido.

29. "El éxito del tango no solamente contribuyó a consagrar el vocabulario lunfardo entre los argentinos, sino que además incentivó su uso, por los letristas, en el propio tango–los letristas y poetas tangueros recogieron, refinaron, crearon términos lunfardos."

30. "Las letras otorgan a quienes las escuchan y saben de memoria una tradición sobre quiénes son, qué significan el barrio, la ciudad y el pasado, qué han de esperar de la vida y cuántas frustraciones les esperan al doblar la esquina. El buzón, el almacén, el farol y la luna no son solo parte de una descripción geográfica urbana sino que adquieren un significado emocional que resulta trascendente para un muchacho de barrio: es la fuerza vital del pasado y de relaciones interpersonales que le dan identidad personal y

cultural. . . . La cultura del tango, a través de sus letras y música ha organizado la forma de sentir de inmigrantes y argentinos."

31. *El alma que canta* (The soul that sings) is the name of a popular weekly magazine, published from 1916 until 1960, in which the era's most popular lyrics were printed, most of them tango lyrics. We should note that this essay did not appear in the first edition of *Evaristo Carriego*, which dates back to 1930, but was added by Borges to the 1955 edition.

32. Editor's note: "La cumparsita" is arguably the best-known and most iconic tango worldwide and is traditionally the last number played in the milonga (social dance in a hall or salon), signaling the end of the event.

CHAPTER TWO

Borges, Tango, and Milonga

ALEJANDRO SUSTI

*Translated by Katharina Keppel
and Marilyn G. Miller*

Tango que fuiste feliz,
como yo también lo he sido,
según me cuenta el recuerdo;
el recuerdo fue el olvido.

[Tango, you who were happy,
as I also have been,
the way my memory tells it;
memory was forgetting.]
—"Alguien le dice al tango"
   (Someone says to the tango),
   Jorge Luis Borges

This chapter suggests a new reading of the relationship between the work of
the twentieth-century Argentine author Jorge Luis Borges and two genres
of Argentine popular music, the tango and the milonga.[1] As is well known,
Borges produced a series of texts, in poetry, fiction, and essay form, in which
he postulates a very particular vision of the tango, one that changes over time
and, for better or for worse, has occupied a privileged place in subsequent histories of the tango up to the present moment. Unquestionably, any study of
this relationship in our own time should take into account the creation of a
complex universe of imaginaries fundamental for understanding the entire
oeuvre of this author. In this sense Borges's approach to the tango was guided
from the start more by the necessity of establishing a historical relationship

with the form than by the search for materials or supplies that would permit the creation of a mythical or imaginary past.

At the same time, the establishment of a relationship between these two discursive events, Borges and the tango, prompts a reconsideration of the relationships between what we understand as *the literary*—which is inscribed within a system that privileges certain mechanisms of production and artistic reception—and so-called *mass culture*, whose mechanisms of production and consumption obey the ever-greater influence of technology in art and daily life, an influence that is most evident since the advent of photography and, later on, cinema.[2] In this sense we should not lose sight of the attraction certain expressions of popular culture, such as tango, milonga, *lunfardo*, the *sainete*, and popular poetry, had on Borges and other authors and intellectuals. Such influences should be understood within the context of the new relationships that emerged from a society subject to a whole series of structural transformations that were not only social but also economic and cultural.[3] These popular expressions became, to a certain extent, the venues for an imaginary that survived the repercussions of the major changes of the era and, at the same time, operated as instruments of adaptation for those social subjects whose cultural identities were threatened by these same changes.

While the formulation of these initial coordinates can help us better understand the nature of the dialogue I hope to establish, my intention, nonetheless, is not to apply a mechanical model of analysis in an attempt to justify the results of the contact and interaction between these two discursive instances. Any use of categories such as *the literary* or *the popular* must acknowledge that these categories ultimately respond to a particular way of understanding historical phenomena. In our own day it's evident that the boundaries that only a few years ago clearly separated the terrain of the literary from that of the popular have been toppled, prompting the rearticulation of methods and analytical tools taken from diverse disciplines such as literature and anthropology. Clearly, the classification of an author's work as *literary* runs the risk of leaving aside elements that fall outside the a priori conceptualization of what the critic judges should constitute *literature*. Borges's works—and here we're referring to the author's fictionalization of his own person in his texts as well as to a subject constructed by and in a critical tradition and consecrated within that tradition's canon[4]—provide an exemplary case of what we might call "atypicality."[5] Thus, the equation Borges = literature, and its immediate confrontation with what we might define as the popular, become provisional categories of analysis whose purpose is justified to the extent that they historically reconstruct a relationship that was established very early on. To relate these two categories implies the task of restoration as well as the questioning of our very tools of analysis.

The Tango: "A Long Civic Poem"

In my analysis of the dialogue between Borges and the tango, I take as my point of departure citations from two separate essays by the Argentine author that in a certain way anticipate the outcome of the encounter between these two discourses. In his text on the Spanish Golden Age poet and dramatist Francisco de Quevedo in *Other Inquisitions*, Borges writes that the Spanish author "is less a man than a vast and complex literature" (42); later in "A History of the Tango," first published in the 1955 edition of *Evaristo Carriego*, Borges refers to the tango this way: "At the end of the eighteenth century, Wolf wrote that the *Iliad* was a series of songs and rhapsodies before it became an epic; this knowledge may allow for the prophesy that, in time, tango lyrics will form a *long civic poem*, or will suggest to some ambitious person the writing of that poem" (108; emphasis added).[6] Reading these two citations together serves to create an analogy with the two discourses that interest me here: Borges, like Quevedo, is a "vast and complex literature," just as the lyrics of the tango are a "long civic poem." Despite announcing the possibility of an "ambitious person" who could write an epic poem composed of tango lyrics, Borges erases the image of the author hiding behind the texts; he chooses to focus not on the author but on the text, a text that is transmittable throughout time, beyond the moment of its initial contingency.[7]

This analogy suggests an encounter between two discursive instances whose positions are diametrically opposed. In his relationship with the tango or the milonga, Borges demonstrates a fascination with the limit or, perhaps more precisely, with the "margins" (*orillas*)—not only topographic but also symbolic—those territories that are not part of the "center" of a preestablished artistic or literary canon. In Borges's approach to the margins, there is an intention to incorporate the liminal space into the center. However, this operation requires the understanding of certain modes of production of this liminal discourse. In the author's work, this operation takes place in different stages and its development depends on a key point; at the end of this process, which encompasses his earliest discussions on the origin of the tango through to the penning of his own milonga poems, we see that the incorporation of the tango never crystallizes into a final product. Moreover, it becomes clear that Borges is not merely attempting the assimilation of discursive margins or peripheries into the center but also a mutual exchange between the two realms. We might say that the canon becomes "marginalized" in the texts that emerge out of this contact (particularly in the case of the milongas, which I will discuss later) and, with it, the image of the writer as well, who becomes an "other," an "I" who is different from the one that exists in the texts that do not include this contact.

The analogy *Borges = tango* that I am proposing admittedly has its limitations. First, while Borges negates contingency and assumes a projective perspective, the two discourses I am referring to, "Borges as literature" and "the tango as poem," emerge in the same historical period (with slight chronological differences). That is, the dialogue between both texts itself is the product of a concrete contingency: the period of the formation of what Beatriz Sarlo elaborates in *Una modernidad periférica* as the modernity of Buenos Aires. More significantly, during the 1920s and 1930s, Borges is immersed in the task of recognizing and establishing the basis of what will be called a national Argentine literature (Farías; Sarlo, *Una modernidad periférica* and *Jorge Luis Borges*). It is within this context that Borges tries to incorporate the tango in his own work, an operation that ultimately will imply the construction of a mythology that, as we will see, responds to an appropriation based on very personal and specific valorizations of the tango.

It is also important to take into account the nature of what we call *literature*, which is related here to Borges's development as a writer. As Sarlo points out, Borges "wrote at [a] meeting of roads"; diverse literatures, both foreign and Argentine, converge in his work, and it is precisely this crossroad and the reordering in which it is situated that "allows him to invent a strategy for Argentinian literature" (*Jorge Luis Borges* 5). In the specific case of tango lyrics, and with those of the milonga, this strategy consists of rooting them in the *payada*, a manifestation of popular poetry that culminates in one of the founding texts of Argentine literature, *Martín Fierro*. Interestingly, the type of literature that Borges prefers as a reader of tango and as a creator of milongas shines through his own education as a writer and reader of other literatures. In terms of his milongas, Borges explicitly recognizes his debt to the payada tradition. Borges declares, "in my milongas . . . I have done my respectful best to imitate the joyous courage of Hilario Ascasubi and the old-time street ballads [*coplas*] of the different neighborhoods of Buenos Aires" (qtd. in Cara-Walker 284).[8]

It should be noted that the second part of my proposed analogy, "the tango as poem," supposes the arbitrary separation of at least two of the original and constitutive elements of the tango: music and dance. If one considers the tango a text or narrative that establishes a relation to other literary texts, then all elements that shape the tango must be taken into account. The corpus of tango lyrics, that extensive "poem" that Borges presumes to be immortal, is subject to interpretation on the part of the musicians and dance couples who perform the pieces. Music is implicitly present in those texts by Borges structured around tango. We must also keep in mind that the tango was originally instrumental, and in its earliest form it was played and danced, not sung. Clearly, the tango did not originate with the goal of capturing the attention of its listeners through its lyrics but rather through the aspects of music and dance, a detail that doesn't escape Borges in *Evaristo Carriego*.

Despite these limitations, the analogy proves nonetheless useful. Throughout his work Borges returns time and again to the idea of the civic (and I would add, popular) poem of tangos and milongas. He persistently shows his interest in cultivating a poetics of the tango and milonga, even if his approach differs significantly from that of other authors who develop a tango poetics.

A "Tearful Aesthetic"

While the term *tearful aesthetic* (*lacrimosa estética*) does not specifically refer to tango lyrics but instead to one of the weaknesses Borges identifies in the poetry of Carriego, the author also tends to apply it to the character of tango lyrics, especially those that pertain to the so-called golden age of tango from 1917 to 1943.[9] In the following fragments, Borges divides the evolution of the tango into two eras, a division he shares with most tango historians:

> The first milongas and tangos might have been foolish, or at least slipshod, but they were heroic and happy. The later tango is resentful, deplores with sentimental excess one's miseries, and celebrates shamelessly the misfortunes of others. (*Jorge Luis Borges: Selected Non-Fictions* 400)[10]

> The contemporary tango, made totally out of picturesque and worked-over lunfardo, is one thing, and quite another the old tangos made of pure insolence, pure shamelessness, pure happiness in bravery. Those were the genuine voice of the *compadrito*: the new ones (music and lyrics) are the fictions of those incredulous about comradeship, those who explain things and create disillusion. The primordial tangos—"The Cabaret," "The Mustang," "The Argentine Apache," "A Night of Fun," and "Hotel Victoria"—testify to the ribald bravery of the *arrabal*. (*On Argentina* 43)[11]

The "primordial tangos" Borges refers to in the latter citation belong to the so-called era of the Old Guard, which covers the final years of the nineteenth and the first years of the twentieth century, 1895–1917.[12] The tangos of this era might have lyrics or not, but such lyrics inevitably served to make the melody of the tango easier to remember. The lyrics could be replaced while keeping the same melodic base, as tends to happen with many folkloric songs that survive to this day.

The dominant protagonist in this form of tango was the *compadre*, a character who in turn was distinguished from the compadrito and the *malevo* (see the glossary). The tango of this period emphasized dance, a trait that separated it from tango song *(tango canción)* that appeared around 1917. Donald Castro in "Popular Culture as a Source for the Historian" explains that through dance, the criollo or native-born inhabitant practiced the art of the "cachada," of ridiculing those who tried to imitate him. In general the target of this mockery was the poor immigrant who tried to imitate the criollo by assuming a new identity and thus integrating his new environment. The challenge implicit in the dance often resulted in knife duels, a fact that Borges himself includes in one of his milongas titled "Alguien le dice al tango" (Someone says to the tango):

> Tango que he visto bailar
> contra un ocaso amarillo
> por quienes eran capaces
> de otro baile, el del cuchillo.
> (Gobello and Bossio, *Tangos, letras y letristas* 3: 34)

> [Tango that I have seen danced
> Against a yellow sunset
> By those who were capable
> Of another dance, that of the knife.][13]

Regarding the linguistic aspect of the tangos, Daniel Vidart in *Teoría del tango* points out that the lyrics of the tangos of the Old Guard were written in the language of the slum and not in lunfardo. This characteristic has been described by Borges in *El idioma de los argentinos* (*The Language of the Argentines*), published in 1928: "The first tangos, the old, wonderful tangos, never had *lunfardo* lyrics: This use of lunfardo is merely an affectation that novelty-seeking, contemporary simplemindedness makes obligatory, and which fills tangos with phony secrets and false emphases.... The soul of the *orillas* combined with a vocabulary that belonged to everyone: That was the substance of the snappy *milonga*; international banality and an underworld vocabulary are what we have in today's tango" (*On Argentina* 82).[14] Vicente Rossi, cited by Vidart, also describes this language: "The language of the riverfront slum dweller (*orillero*) springs from his particular ingenuity; always graphic with exact allusions, metaphorical, of onomatopoeic simplicity, brutally ironic and always innovative, because the *orillero* is a tireless renovator of his picturesque vocabulary" (*Teoría del tango* 28).[15] Despite the distinctions drawn by Vidart, Borges, and Rossi, there doesn't seem to be a way of demonstrating any appreciable difference between "marginal" language (*lenguaje orillero*), "slum" language (*lenguaje arrabalero*), and lunfardo.

From the musical point of view, the tangos mentioned by Borges in *El tamaño de mi esperanza* (The extent of my hope) also have other particularities. According to José Gobello, Vicente Greco, the author of "El flete" and "El cuzquito," is responsible for creating the first *orquesta típica* (typical orchestra), which includes for the first time "two instruments that until then had been ignored by the academies: the piano and the bandoneon" (*Crónica general del tango* 58). The inclusion of the sound of the bandoneon to replace the flute signals to a certain extent the Italianization of the tango—despite the German origin of the instrument. For some critics, the bandoneon, with its sad and melancholic sound, represents the entry and predominance of the sentiment of uprooting felt by the Italian immigrant in the tango.[16] Initially, Borges opposes the Italianization of the tango, but later he accepts it in *Evaristo Carriego*. Nonetheless, despite this change of mind, in his essay "A History of the Tango" there is no mention of what he considers Italian beyond the last names of early native-born composers such as Bevilacqua, Greco, or de Bassi (*On Argentina* 108).

The musical critique that Borges outlines also coincides with the previously mentioned division regarding the evolution of the tango: "the old tango, as music, immediately transmits that joy of combat which Greek and German poets, long ago, tried to express in words. Certain composers today strive for that heroic tone and sometimes conceive competent *milongas* about the Batería slums or the Barrio del Alto, but their labors—with deliberately old-fashioned lyrics and music—are exercises in nostalgia for what once was, laments for what is now lost, intrinsically sad even when their melody is joyful" (*On Argentina* 104).[17] Borges finds some clues regarding the origins of the tango in the use of certain instruments. For him, the tango does not originate from the common people, since it is played with expensive instruments such as the piano, the flute, and the violin. Borges does not think that the guitar, which he identifies as being characteristic of the milonga, was used in early tango (Sorrentino 9–10).

The sources on which Borges bases this judgment are, as he himself points out, works on the origins of the tango by Vicente Rossi, Carlos Vega, and Carlos Muzzio Sáenz. However, the methods these authors use to treat the subject differ considerably from each other. For Borges, Rossi's work, for example, suffers from chronological imprecision and a discontinuity in terms of development. Among other theories, Borges agrees with Rossi's statements in relation to the black influence in the formation of the tango: "I must say I subscribe to all their conclusions—as well as to others" (*Jorge Luis Borges: Selected Non-Fictions* 394).[18] Nevertheless, Castro observes that there is an important disagreement between Rossi, Borges, and the critic Julio Mafud regarding the origin of the milonga, a genre practiced by urban *payadores* and a direct precursor of the tango: "The critical element in their counter argument is the specific geographic origin of the tango ingredient in milonga. Rossi suggests strongly that it came from Brazil via Montevideo and was essentially a Black cultural contribution to the tango mix. Borges and Mafud present the argument that, while the milonga may have been part of the tango mix, it was from the Argentine creole (mestizo) and was different from the Black milonga" ("Popular Culture as a Source for the Historian" 73). The disagreement between Rossi and Borges regarding the origin of the milonga shows Borges's eagerness to situate the tango in a purely Creole environment, a characteristic that we have already highlighted in his stance on the subsequent Italianization of the tango. One could say that Borges maintains a purist position regarding the tango and the milonga, a position he assumes not only as it concerns the origins of the tango but also its later manifestations. Finally, in terms of the tango's rhythmic structure, Borges points to the change it suffers in its evolution after the era of the Old Guard, an aspect also noted by Gobello, who refers to the "slowing down of the tempo in the execution of the tango, reflected in the move from 2/4 time to 4/8 time" (*Crónica general del tango* 193; refrenamiento de la velocidad en la ejecución del tango que se refleja en el paso del compás de 2 por 4 al 4 por 8).

Milonga: *Para las seis cuerdas*

According to Rossi, the tango emerges from one of the variants of the milonga, the dance milonga. This latter form existed alongside the song milonga, a genre that Borges himself includes in his book of poems *Para las seis cuerdas* (1965).[19] In the prologue the narrator announces to the reader: "In the modest case of my milongas, the reader should supply the missing music to the image of a man who is humming in the doorway or in a storefront, accompanying himself with a guitar. The hand lingers on the strings and words tell less than the chords" (*Obra poética* 281). [20] Borges leaves it up to the reader to provide the music that should accompany his verses. However, when one of his readers takes over the task of musicalizing the verses of four of his milongas—as happens with the work of the famous bandoneonist Astor Piazzolla—Borges's reaction to the result is rather harsh: "I don't want anything to do with that man . . . he does not feel the Creoleness [*lo criollo*]" (Salas, *Borges* 266). Piazzolla, on the other hand, confirms the care with which he addressed the task, as noted and remarked on by Gobello: "'Jacinto Chiclana' has the air of a guitar milonga, that is, an improvised milonga; 'Alguien le dice al tango' can be considered melodically and harmonically to belong to the style of '41; 'A Nicanor Paredes,' given its dramatic content, I have composed over the eight-count beat of the Gregorian chants, solving the melodic part without artificial modernisms, everything very simple, deeply emotional and honest; 'El títere' can be defined as a prototype of the light rhythm from the beginning of the century, humorous and fraternal [*compadrón*]" (Gobello and Bossio, *Tangos, letras y letristas* 3: 30).[21] We should clarify that for the text of "Alguien le dice al tango," Piazzolla composed a tango and not a milonga (Gobello and Bossio, *Tangos, letras y letristas* 3: 30).

According to Piazzolla's comments and Borges's musical preferences as espoused in previous writings, in at least two of the four musicalized milongas, the composer sticks to the canon that historically rules the tango and the milonga. Because of its improvised character, "Jacinto Chiclana" is adapted to the tradition of urban payadores at the end of the nineteenth and the beginning of the twentieth century. "El títere" (The puppet), on the other hand, is linked to those "primordial" tangos that Borges mentions in *El tamaño de mi esperanza*. In only one of the milongas does Piazzolla diverge from Borges's manifest tastes in tango: "Alguien le dice al tango" is situated in the tradition of the golden age tango that Borges deplored because of its "tearful aesthetic." Now that we know the positions of the writer and the musician, the question is: What does it mean for Borges to "feel the Creoleness [*sentir lo criollo*]" or not?

To respond to this question, it might be useful to take up a position first suggested by Ricardo Ostuni. For this critic, there is an implicit connection between the pride that Borges exhibited many times in relation to his "creole ancestry" (*prosapia criolla*) and the nature of the feats attempted by the characters of the primitive tangos. For Ostuni, the Borges of *El tamaño de mi esperanza* "intuits an epic in the primitive tangos, a sort of heroic drama whose characters, though marginal, nonetheless had their brush with the great feats of their ancestors" (28; intuía una épica en los Tangos primitivos, una suerte de gesta bravía cuyos personajes, aunque orilleros, en algo rozaban las valerosas hazañas de sus mayores). Along these lines, we could assume that for Borges, "the Creole"—at least in terms of his praise for the milonga as opposed to the later tango of the era of the Old Guard—responds to a desire to trace a genealogy that could be defined as "mythic," in which the autobiographical element comes together with a so-called tango epic. The tango epic or "long civic poem" referred to earlier constitutes a kind of narrative archetype located in a remote past in which history gives way to myth and in which its protagonists—the compadritos—embody virtues such as valor and bravery. These characters are modeled in such a way that they never express the weaknesses of the troubled and remorseful beings who will appear in the later tango lyrics of the golden age. Taking these elements into account, one might conclude that Borges, by way of a subtle intellectual operation, produces a tango chronology or, more precisely, a tango mythology in which not only is the history of the genre reconfigured and resignified but also in which the tango in fact reinvents itself. Through the simulacrum of a voice authorized by its own descent from this valiant race, Borges reformulates his own genealogy, creating a common parentage with the compadritos and their heroic deeds.

Musicalization and Instrumentalization in the Milonga

Given the title of his book of milongas published in 1965, *Para las seis cuerdas* (For the six strings), the reader can anticipate that Borges envisions simple instrumentation with one single guitar, such as in Rossi's description: "The simple-hearted payada of the pastoral hearth, a romance unique to those natives healthy in body and soul, became the milonga of the urban hearths and hovels of the city. This is why the milonga is the payada of the townspeople. It consists of octosyllabic verses that are recited in a not unpleasant tone tinged with suitable guitar accompaniment, filling the hold measures between one stanza and the next, usually marked by three different notes, while the *milonguero* catches his breath or looks for inspiration" (124–25).[22]

Apparently, Borges didn't like Piazzolla's musicalizations because of his use of instruments such as the bandoneon, the piano, and the violin to interpret some of the writer's milongas, a use that for him presented an imbalance with what he hoped to represent textually and in the interpretation of those texts musically. The implicit agreement between Rossi's observations and the way in which Borges conceives the musical execution of the milongas reveals the link between the milonguero and the payador. It becomes clear that

Borges's concept of Creoleness is already announced in the payador, and that his transformation coincides with the displacement of this figure to the margins (orillas) of the city. Perhaps this is why Borges sees little relation between the later tango that derives from the dance milonga (and even less of one in Piazzolla's musicalizations of his milongas) and the tradition of popular Creole poetry that developed in the payada and later in the milonga. Once more Borges clearly establishes the origin of the tango and its instrumentation in the brothels of the red light district: "The primitive instrumentation of its earliest orchestras—piano, flute, violin, and later the concertina—confirms, with its extravagance, the evidence that the tango did not arise from the riverbank slums, where, as everyone knows, the six strings of the guitar were sufficient" (*Jorge Luis Borges: Selected Non-Fictions* 395).[23] In musical terms the Creole signifies for Borges a return to the simple sound of the guitar as played in alleys and doorways, postulating a lone melody and lacking a defined song, a feature shared by the payada and the milonga. As Rossi notes, "indeed, one performs the payada and the milonga singing, but it's not quite a song, it's more like a tone which, associated with the guitar, gives the imagination time and a rest for inspiration" (130; Ciertamente que se paya y se milonguea cantando, pero no es precisamente un canto, es una tonada que asociada a la guitarra da a la imajinacion [*sic*] tiempo y alivio a la inspiración).

So it is that in the milonga that Borges cultivates, there is what we might call a "double silence" that excludes the sound of other accompanying instruments, in particular the aforementioned orchestra, and the sound of the voice, understood as another instrument performing a melody that is added to the lyrics. The voice in this case gathers the verses and interprets them without actually singing them. From a historical perspective, the milonga crafted by Borges can be considered an archetype or a reconstruction that does not necessarily coincide with the original model. This reconstruction also includes the incorporation of stories of compadritos (the Ibarra brothers, Juan Muraña, and so on) that Borges claims to have heard from different sources and references to bygone urban spaces, such as Maldonado, mentioned by Carriego himself. This archetypal milonga, or the mythical milonga referred to above, probably did not exist in terms of these themes and this treatment until Borges gave shape to it. With it, he displays his knowledge of how this type of discourse is formed, but in addition he reinvents it. The creation of this archetypal milonga, or "mythic" milonga, to use an expression that Borges employs in his well-known poem "Fundación mítica de Buenos Aires" (Mythical founding of

Buenos Aires), is established in a passage of another poem significantly titled "El tango," published after the milonga poems in *El otro, el mismo* (1965):

> Una mitología de puñales
> Lentamente se anula en el olvido;
> Una canción de gesta se ha perdido
> En sórdidas noticias policiales. (*Obra poética* 204)

> A mythology of knife thrusts
> Slowly dying in oblivion:
> A chanson de geste lost
> In sordid police reports. (*A Personal Anthology* 159)

Borges reconstructs this "mythology of knives" in his milongas, where it simultaneously signifies oblivion and memory, "the impossible memory of having died while fighting." This creation, or re-creation, of a milonga archetype implies a recovery of the musical genre but also, and most importantly, the incorporation of certain procedures that are characteristic of popular poetry translated into Argentine literature through the milonga, as shown analogically in the case of the payada in the gauchesque literary genre. In this way Borges plots an attempt to incorporate a kind of milonga poetics into literature, which is itself a product of what he himself defines as the literary, a definition that depends on atypicality and that responds to a constant reformulation of the limits that separate it from the popular.

Borges in the History of Tango

The next step in the study of the relationship between Borges and the tango consists of an inversion of the terms in this relationship: How important is Borges to the history of tango? More specifically, what role do *tangueros*, and especially lyricists, assign to the venerated author as a composer of tango lyrics? Opinions vary considerably. For Enrique Cadícamo, one of the most famous tango authors and poets, the answer is decisive. When asked by Clark M. Zlotchew, "What position does Jorge Luis Borges occupy in the history of the tango?" Cadícamo responded:

> EC: Borges? In the history of tango: none. In the history of Argentine literature, he has a brilliant place; he is taken as the literary mainspring of this country. I don't know, to what degree, but that's the way it is, isn't it? . . . Borges can be thought of as an intellectual,

but not as a poet of Argentine roots. . . . Borges, in his literature, uses foreign turns of phrase which we have read in all the European classics.

CMZ: I ask because he has written quite a few milongas.

EC: Yes, well, but without managing to give them the substance, without being able to make concrete the substance of Buenos Aires, the humble neighborhoods of Buenos Aires. (Zlotchew, "Tango from the Inside" 138)

Cadícamo also emphatically points to the differences between the writer of popular musical lyrics and the poet, although without explicitly referring to the case of Borges: "You know, there are important, illustrious poets here who can be found in anthologies as great poets, but who have never been able to write any tango lyrics. The reason is that they don't have that contact with the atmosphere, the environment, of the tango, which is so difficult to capture" ("Tango from the Inside" 136). Another testimony regarding Borges's possible influence on the authors of tango lyrics appears in the interview conducted by Zlotchew with José Gobello ("Tango, Lunfardo and the Popular Culture of Buenos Aires"). The central topic of that exchange is the poetic value of tango texts. Gobello recognizes a Borgesian influence in some lyricists (Homero Manzi and Catulo Castillo), an influence evident not in the themes they treated—such as the mythification of the neighborhood thug (malevo) and of other marginal characters, which are present in Borges—but rather in the devices they use in their lyrics. According to Gobello, the Borgesian mythification of the malevo has an antecedent in Eduardo Gutiérrez, to whose style Borges will add a poetic personality (Zlotchew, "Tango, Lunfardo and the Popular Culture of Buenos Aires" 275). This detail is noted by Borges himself in the prologue to *Cuaderno San Martín* (1929): "The two pieces of 'Muertes de Buenos Aires's [Deaths of Buenos Aires]—titles I owe to Eduardo Gutiérrez—unpardonably exaggerate the working class connotation of the Chacarita neighborhood and the elite connotation of the Recoleta neighborhood" (*Obra poética* 87; Las dos piezas de "Muertes de Buenos Aires"—título que debo a Eduardo Gutiérrez—imperdonablemente exageran la connotación plebeya de la Chacarita y la connotación patricia de La Recoleta).

According to Gobello, the direct influence of Borges in the work of lyricists such as Homero Manzi consists of the use of particular literary devices such as enumeration, which are present in Borges's early poetry collections.

We can add to this the nostalgic element found in some of Manzi's lyrics, such as "Sur"—a title that, in turn, Borges had used for one of his poems from *Fervor de Buenos Aires* (1923) to evoke the topography of the margins of the city. For Manzi, the "south" is:

San Juan y Boedo antiguo, y todo el cielo;
Pompeya y más allá la inundación;
tu melena de novia en el recuerdo
y tu nombre flotando en el adiós.
La esquina del herrero, barro y pampa,
tu casa, tu vereda y el zanjón
y un perfume de yuyos y de alfalfa
que me llena de nuevo el corazón.

Sur,
paredón y después,
Sur,
una luz de almacén
Ya nunca me verás como me vieras
recostado en la vidriera
y esperándote . . . (Gobello and Bossio, *Tangos, letras y letristas* 1: 145)

[Ancient San Juan and Boedo and the entire sky,
Pompeya and beyond, the swampland,
In my memory, the long hair you had when we were together,
and your name floating in our goodbye . . .
The blacksmith corner, mud and pampa,
your house, your pavement, and the ditch
and a smell of weeds and alfalfa
that fills my heart all over again.

South . . . a thick wall and then. . . .
South . . . the light of a grocery store . . .
You will never see me again like you used to,
leaning against the shop window,
and waiting for you . . .][24]

When asked about Borges's prejudices regarding the tango of the Guardia Vieja, Gobello responds by pointing to Borges's inattention to the phenomenon of immigration, a phenomenon that for Gobello finds its expression in tango. Borges only "stays with the *compadrito*, with the knife-fighter. He is very sensitive to these things" (qtd. in Zlotchew, "Tango, Lunfardo and the Popular Culture of Buenos Aires" 283).

Although Cadícamo and Gobello measure Borges's influence on tango differently, their positions coincide in pointing out the arbitrariness of his judgments concerning the form. For Cadícamo, Borges remains completely oblivious to the development of the tango and his influence on it is null. He emphasizes the division between tango literature and poetics and suggests that there are few writers who successfully engage in both. Even when Borges, in the attempt to write a "mythology of tango" tied to a remote and archetypical past, creates lyrics not for tango but for milongas, Cadícamo considers the project a failure. For him, Borges is incapable of inscribing himself in a tango poetics, and by extension a milonga poetics, because such a poetics has "a great deal to do with people, with popular sentiment" (qtd. in Zlotchew, "Tango from the Inside" 132). In this aspect he seems to coincide with Gobello, who affirms that tango lyricists "have to write things that people like, that people understand" (qtd. in Zlotchew, "Tango, Lunfardo and the Popular Culture of Buenos Aires" 277). Both opinions emphasize the "popular" or the inclusion of the "other" in tanguero or milonguero texts—in this case the listener or the public of the tango. This inclusion refers not only to referential components that are shared by the lyricist and the listener but also to the inclusion of the "other's" sensibility, a fact that implies, to some extent, the depersonalization of the lyricist in his work.

The project of rewriting that Borges takes on in the elaboration of his milongas involves a personal component that differs substantially from the anonymous or pseudo-anonymous character of the original payadas and milongas.[25] The lyrical "I" never disappears from the texts of Borges's milongas, as can be seen in the "Milonga de Jacinto Chiclana":

> Me acuerdo. Fue en Balvanera,
> En una noche lejana
> Que alguien dejó caer el nombre
> De un tal Jacinto Chiclana.
> . . .
> Quién sabe por qué razón
> Me anda buscando ese nombre;
> Me gustaría saber
> Cómo habrá sido aquel hombre. (*Obra poética* 287)

[I remember. It was in Balvanera,
On a night long ago
When someone let drop the name
Of a certain Jacinto Chiclana.

. . .

Who knows for what reason
That name comes looking for me
I'd like to know
What that man would have been like.][26]

Borges himself, when commenting on Manzi's famous tango "Sur," brandishes certain arguments that eventually can be applied to his own milonga poems and can help to explain their lack of acceptance by other tango lyricists:

The tango "Sur," yes. It has a nice opening line: "Southside, an alley and then . . ." At the same time, there are some phrases that obviously don't ring true, that betray, I won't say the man of letters, but certainly the pseudo-man of letters. For example, in a tango I believe is his there is a mention of "the wind of the outer limits." This is a phrase that no neighborhood tough would have used. In the first place, because the idea of the wind of the outer limits is a phony idea and, in the second place, because the slum dweller doesn't boast of living in the outer limits. . . ." The stars and the wind of the outer limits whisper her name": you can plainly see it was written by someone from the affluent downtown area, who has sentimental ideas concerning the compadre and is totally unfamiliar with the songs of the people, which never would have contained such lyrics. (qtd. in Sorrentino 104)

In the milonga "Alguien le dice al tango," though, Borges uses the same devices he criticizes in Manzi and even adds others that erase the character of verisimilitude he demands from this lyricist:

Tango que fuiste la dicha
de ser hombre y ser valiente.
Tango que fuiste feliz,
como yo también lo he sido

. . .

Yo habré muerto y seguirás
orillando nuestra vida. (*Obra poética* 34)

[Tango, you who were the happiness
Of being a man and being brave.
Tango, you who were happy,
Like I also have been

. . .

I will have died and you will go on
margining our lives.][27]

Borges invents a tango man and imagines his acts with equally obscure words, such as *orillar* (the verb form of *margin*). In this marvelous act of invention or reinvention of a "tango that was," there is no concern with verisimilitude in the creation of the milonga or tango text, or of the words pronounced by an urban payador accompanied by his guitar. It is in this sense that the Borgesian project differs substantially from the original milongas. Nevertheless, later on Borges shows more concern for authenticity and takes more care with the coherence that the milonga genre demands, a development that will prompt him to omit "Alguien le dice al tango" from the second edition of the book and successive volumes of his *Obra poética*.[28]

Once the milongas from *Para las seis cuerdas* are integrated into the rest of Borges's poetic works, the writer seems to be convinced that this volume is not a book of poems in itself, or that it does not fit into the category of lyrical texts. This lack of adaptation can also be perceived in the little attention the book has received from the critics.[29] In the prologue to the collection *Elogio de la sombra* (In praise of darkness), published in 1969, immediately following the milonga book, Borges notes, rather disturbingly, "this is my fifth book of verse."[30] This affirmation would indicate that his milongas occupy an autonomous space in his poetic work, a space in which the poet tries to become the "other," not the lyrical "I" of his previous books but rather what we could call a payador "I," who sits down to intone texts in which he includes stories and characters known by his "public," which is also an imaginary construction of this "other" Borges.

Borges's project of incorporating a milonga poetics into the literary canon or, inversely, of moving the canon toward the margins, has awakened little understanding or empathy from the tango historians cited in this study or from literary critics and the reading public in general. This response can be interpreted in various ways. It indicates the difficulty Borges must have experienced in trying to erase the contingency of being "Borges, the writer" who presents himself before a public (*his* public), a contingency that probably is more attractive to the reader than the reconstruction of a discourse pronounced or intoned by an urban payador from the margins of Buenos Aires almost a century later. A series of obstacles emerge from within this context: first, the milongas do not fit the lyrical definition established by the literary tradition the reader venerates. Second, another canon exists that unfolds from the evolution of Borges as a poet and that also influences the reception of his texts. Finally, we have that canon established according to a milonga poetics that rules the production of lyrics and whose guidelines must be observed. The judgments of Borges's efforts by Cadícamo constitute an example of this type of canon.

In this way the displacement intended by Borges in his milonga poetics—in which an alternate "I" is moved toward the limits (*las orillas*), and the poetic discourse is marginalized or takes on popular elements—operates in a terrain in which the writer runs the risk of being isolated. However, this transgression, if it can be called that, does not constitute a full rupture with the previously mentioned canons, whether the lyrical, the "Borgesian," or the milonga canon. As we have already seen, Borges introduces certain lyrical notes in his milongas, a trait that not only restores his own "poetic voice," recognizable in all his poetic works, but also the genre as such. In this way we can recognize an exchange in which the poet both gives and takes in this dialogue between texts or discourses that come from different latitudes. The resulting heterogeneity—lyrical, milonguera, and, finally, entirely personal—is proof of Borges's efforts to enrich and develop the "long civic poem" that in 1955 he had divined would become immortal.

Notes

1. It is important to clarify that even though they were two separate genres historically, the milonga is one aspect of tango in a practical sense, since it is one of the three rhythms that is played and danced within the tango repertoire. For this reason, the distinction between the two that Borges proposes is somewhat arbitrary. In order to better explain the origin and multiplicty of the meanings associated with the term *milonga*, Mónica Fumagalli goes back to the testimony of Ventura Lynch, who in 1883 documented the milonga as a popular dance par excellence: "This encounter . . . we called milonga; as a consequence, to say 'let's milonga' could mean interchangably to sing or to dance or both at the same time. The new and temtpting dance could not elude the baptismal oil of the environment in which it was created and was called Milonga, incorporating a fully developed criollismo" (A la reunión entonces se le llamó milonga; en consecuencia, decir vamos a milonguear, indistintamente podía significar cantar o bailar o ambas cosas a la vez. El tentador y nuevo baile no pudo eludir el óleo bautismal del ambiente en que se creaba y se llamó Milonga, incorporándose al criollismo neto) (62).

2. As is well known, the bibliography on this topic is abundant. I refer readers to the classic essay by Walter Benjamin, "The Work of Art in the Age of Mechanical Reproduction," as well as the chapter titled "La impronta estética del mundo moderno" in Jiménez.

3. To better understand the historic, cultural, and political panorama of Argentina from the end of the nineteenth cnetury through the beginning of the twentieth, and its relationship with intellectuals of the time, see Fumagalli.

4. On the notion of *canon* and its distinct types, see Harris, who uses the framework of Alistair Fowler for distinguishing up to six different types of canons. Even though these distinctions do not operate systematically due to overlapping, one in particular seems to apply particularly well in the case of Borges: the so-called critical canon, which, according to Harris, "se construye con aquellas obras, o partes de obras, que son tratadas por los artículos y libros de crítica de forma reiterada" (is constructed with those works, or parts of works, that are repeatedly taken up in books and articles of criticism) (42).

5. Regarding this atypicality, I acknowledge the work of Sarlo, *Jorge Luis Borges*.

6. Borges added several new chapters to the second edition of *Evaristo Carriego* (first published in 1930), the last of which is titled "Historia del tango" (A history of the tango).

7. As regards the writing of that hypothetical "long civic poem" suggested by Borges, the author's desire would in fact become a concrete reality. On this point I refer to an electronic conversation with Oscar Conde in which he noted: "Borges was asking for a *Martín Fierro* for the city, that is, an epic poem whose protagonist was not a gaucho but a *compadre*: 'I hope that this volume will serve as a stimulus for someone to write that authentic poem that will do with the compadre what *Martín Fierro* did with the gaucho'" ("Historia del tango" 161). What is remarkable is that this poem was written. Although it can't be proved, its author possibly 'was inspired' upon reading this stimulating request by Borges made in *La Nación* in 1952, because in 1954 Miguel D. Etchebarne published a long poem titled *Juan Nadie: Vida y muerte de un Compadre* (Buenos Aires: Editorial Alpe). We can surmise that in 1955, when Borges published the second edition of *Evaristo Carriego*, he wasn't aware of the existence of Etchebarne's book, since a year later, when he formed part of the jury for the Premio Nacional de Literatura in the poetry category, corresponding to the three-year period 1953–1956, Borges read the work and was fascinated by it. Lastly, the back cover of the 1995 edition (Buenos Aires: Ediciones Iniciales), cites Borges's comments in this regard: 'there is a poem that I would like to bring to your attention, which I had the honor of giving an award in a national literary competition. Unfortunately, I could only get a third place award for the author. Cervantes said that in competitions, the second prize was first, because the first is always given for reasons apart from literary concerns. But I wasn't even able to get this second-first prize for Miguel D. Etchebarne, but only third, and the book was titled *Juan Nadie: Vida y Muerte de un Compadre*. That book sought to be for the compadre the book that I had prophesied years earlier, but naturally, it is easy to prophesy a book and very difficult to write it, a book that would do for the compadre what Hernández had done for the gaucho. And I would like for you all to remember the name of this book: *Juan Nadie*, the name of its author, and that you order it unsuccessfully in the bookstores of Buenos Aires, which never obtain any book—but at least I have done my part in this useless task' (from the conference 'Poesía y arrabal,' delivered in the Paraninfo of the University of Antioquía,

Colombia. Published in the *Revista Universidad de Antioquía* 53, no. 203 (January–March 1986): np."

8. Cara-Walker also includes the testimony of critic José Gobello, who observes that "in those lyrics [of Borges's tangos and milongas] a payador-like tone is displayed. I think that the compadritos would have written them just like Borges, had they not been illiterate" (284). While Gobello's criteria are debatable, the citation illustrates the tone Borges preferred in the tangos he listened to and the milongas he wrote.

9. I follow the chronology suggested by Donald Castro (1986), who focuses on the tango's diffusion after World War I. Another key event was the success of the first tango song (*tango canción*), which appeared in 1917: "In 1917 Pascual Contursi wrote the first tango which was designed to be sung and not just danced. This tango "Mi noche triste" [My sad night] began the new era for the tango, one in which the tango moved 'from the feet to the mouth.' This is the origin of the tango-canción" (Castro, "Popular Culture as a Source for the Historian" 45).

10. "La milonga y el tango de los orígenes podían ser tontos o, a lo menos, atolondrados, pero eran valerosos y alegres; el tango posterior es un resentido que deplora con lujo sentimental las desdichas propias y festeja con diabólica desvergüenza las desdichas ajenas" (Borges, *Prosa completa*, vol. 1, *Evaristo Carriego* 95–96).

11. "Una cosa es el tango actual, hecho a fuerza de pintoresquismo y de trabajosa jerga lunfarda, y otra fueron los tangos viejos, hechos de puro descaro, de pura sinvergüencería, de pura felicidad del valor. Aquéllos fueron la voz genuina del compadrito: éstos (música y letra) son la ficción de los incrédulos de la compadrada . . . Los tangos primordiales: El caburé, El cuzquito, El flete, El apache argentino, Una noche de garufa y Hotel Victoria aún atestiguan la valentía chocarrera del arrabal" (Borges, *El tamaño de mi esperanza* 29–30).

12. Castro observes that "the Argentine tango in its stages of development prior to World War I (La guardia vieja [The Old Guard], 1895–1917) was very much an example of the 'human condition' in that it was the dance and musical vehicle of the urban poor, the socially unacceptable, the disenfranchised, and the disinherited of the Argentine littoral. After World War I, the tango was changed. While it still had some elements of its earlier form, it became more a vehicle of those who were recognized as being socially acceptable, the middle and upper classes" ("Popular Culture as a Source for the Historian: The Tango in its Era of La Guardia Vieja," 70).

13. Editor's translation.

14. "Los primeros tangos, los antiguos tangos dichosos, nunca sobrellevaron letra lunfarda: afectación que la novelera tilinguería actual hace obligatoria y que los llena de secreteo y de falso énfasis . . . Alma orillera y vocabulario de todos, hubo en la vivaracha milonga: cursilería internacional y vocabulario forajido hay en el tango" (Borges and Clemente, *El idioma de los argentinos* 21).

15. "El lenguaje del orillero es de su particular inventiva; siempre gráfico, exacto en la alusión; metafórico y onomatopéyico meritísimo, siempre inclemente en la ironía; siempre novedoso porque ese orillero es un incansable renovador de su pintoresco léxico."

16. Regarding the influence of the Italian immigrant, Castro notes that "even in his own creation, the tango, creole ascendency was gone. The musical instrument most equated with the tango is the bandoneon. It became associated intimately with the tango

after 1899 and primarily was due to Italian influences (notwithstanding the fact that the bandoneon is German in origin). With the introduction of the plaintive tone of the bandoneon, the tango becomes sad and loses its earlier joyfulness associated with the flute" ("Popular Culture as a Source for the Historian" 82).

17. "El tango antiguo como música, suele directamente trasmitir esa belicosa alegría cuya expresión verbal ensayaron, en edades remotas, rapsodas griegos y germánicos. Ciertos compositores actuales buscan ese tono valiente y elaboran, a veces con felicidad, milongas de la Batería o del Barrio del Alto, pero en sus trabajos, de letra y música estudiosamente anticuadas, son ejercicios de lo que fue, llantos por lo perdido, esencialmente tristes aunque la tonada sea alegre" (Borges, *Prosa completa*, vol. 1, *Evaristo Carriego* 92).

18. "Nada me cuesta declarar que subscribo a todas sus conclusiones, y aún a cualquier otra" (Borges, *Prosa completa*, vol. 1, *Evaristo Carriego* 89).

19. While a literal translation of this book of poems is "for the six strings," it has also been rendered as simply "for guitar."

20. "En el modesto caso de mis milongas, el lector debe suplir la música ausente por la imagen de un hombre que canturrea, en el umbral de su zaguán o en un almacén, acompañándose con la guitarra. La mano se demora en las cuerdas y las palabras cuentan menos que los acordes."

21. "'Jacinto Chiclana' tiene el aire de la milonga guitarrera, o sea el tipo de milonga improvisada; 'Alguien le dice al tango' puede considerarse melódica y armónicamente dentro del estilo del 41; 'A Nicanor Paredes,' por su contenido, dramático, la he compuesto sobre 8 compases de canto gregoriano, resolviendo la parte melódica sin modernismos artificiales, todo muy simple, muy sentido y sincero; 'El Títere' puede definirse como el prototipo del ritmo ligero, jocoso y compadrón de principio de siglo."

22. "La Payada injenua [*sic*] de los fogones pastoriles, únicamente romance de los nativos sanos de cuerpo y alma, se convirtió en la Milonga de los fogones y de los tugurios ciudadanos. Por eso la Milonga es la payada pueblera. Son versos octosílabos, que se recitan con cierta tonada no desagradable matizada con intervenciones adecuadas de guitarra, llenando los compases de espera entre una estrofa y otra, un punteado característico de tres tonos, mientras el milonguero resuella o se inspira."

23. The original text uses the term *bandoneón* rather than *concertina*: "El instrumental primitivo de las orquestas—piano, flauta, violín, después bandoneón—confirma, por el costo, ese testimonio; es una prueba de que el tango no surgió de las orillas, que se bastaron siempre, nadie lo ignora, con las seis cuerdas de la guitarra" (Borges, *Prosa completa*, vol. 1, *Evaristo Carriego* 90).

24. Editor's note: Tango lyrics are notoriously difficult to render adequately in other languages. This English translation of "Sur" comes from Tanguito, Argentine Tango Academy in London, available at http://www.tanguito.co.uk/tango-culture/tango-lyrics /tango-lyrics-sur/ (accessed May 22, 2012). The website includes this additional context for the translation:

> The South of Argentina is a physical and imaginative frontier that defined the nation. This spatial and temporal frontier, which evolved over time, illustrates divisions not only between the urban and rural worlds but also between modernity and past.

Sur is an elegy for a lost love, framed in the landmarks of Boedo and Pompeya, in the South of Buenos Aires. Sur describes a physical trip south of Buenos Aires and at the same time, an imaginary trip into the past, and laments both the end of a love story and changes in the barrio.

The thick wall described in the song not only marks the division between the end of the city and the beginning of the countryside, it also represents a before and an after, and is coloured by the bitterness of lost love.

25. Cara-Walker highlights an important trait in Borges's milongas, their "conversational" character: "They involve a multiplicity of social voices which thrive on irony, on a tongue in cheek delivery, on a suggestive, understated, and allusive kind of speech which recalls (or implies at least) a previous utterance, a simultaneous aside, or a dialogue" (285). My reading of this trait, however, does not annul the lyric tone of the milonga poems.

26. Editor's note: This milonga is not included in Alexander Coleman's compilation *Selected Poems: Jorge Luis Borges*. I offer here my own translation.

27. Editor's translation.

28. This omission is noted by Gobello and Bossio 30; and Cara-Walker 292.

29. Cara-Walker observes that "not only have the milongas remained quietly ignored even by scholars who treat traditional elements in Borges' work, they are conspicuously absent from the text and indices of books dedicated to the author's comprehensive works" (280).

30. Borges does not appear to include in this list the volume *El hacedor* (1960), which contained poems in verse and prose. The chronological order of the four collections previous to *Para las seis cuerdas* is *Fervor de Buenos Aires* (1923), *Luna de enfrente* (1925), *Cuaderno San Martín* (1929), and *El otro, el mismo* (1964).

CHAPTER THREE

Picturing Tango

MARILYN G. MILLER

The voluminous story line of tango in visual culture stretches from its earliest appearances in sheet music and other ephemera through to a staggering variety of twentieth- and twenty-first-century works that range from the abstract to the hyperrealist and from classical to kitsch. The representative artists from Argentina and Uruguay whose works I analyze in this chapter portray tango as a complex social drama of intense encounters between bodies, instruments, voices, movements, and styles.[1] By following this trail of images, we discover that despite the proliferation of clichés and stereotypes that threaten to color our collective imagining of tango, such works offer us an extraordinarily rich and multifaceted set of tools with which to track aesthetic and social histories.[2]

The relationship between *tango* and *art* has been a rocky one from the start. Representations of tango by renowned masters such as Pedro Figari, Carlos Torrallardona, Héctor Basaldúa, Carlos Alonso, Aldo Severi, Marcia Schvartz, Hermenegildo Sábat, Aldo Sessa, and many others hang in prestigious museums and private collections.[3] In Buenos Aires, long known as Tango City, both the National Academy of Tango and the Academia Porteña de Lunfardo (a smaller institution devoted to the study of the city's unique tango-related vocabulary) collect, house, and display artwork related to tango; the first dedicates space to four exhibits a year of works in this vein.[4] Some of the same grand halls in which tango is danced, such as the famed Salón Canning in the Palermo neighborhood of Buenos Aires, also display tango-themed art. At the same time, hundreds, perhaps even thousands, of artists and artisans laboring in a myriad of media offer more serialized versions of tango to the throngs of consumers trolling the tourist markets of

Caminito, La Boca, San Telmo, Recoleta, Palermo Soho, Florida Street, and other zones of the Argentine capital and elsewhere.[5]

Whether or not such works constitute *art* is a fraught question, especially given the long and colorful history of tango as a popular form created by and for immigrants, pimps, prostitutes, autodidacts, and anarchists. Even if local critics and theorists have long rejected rigid distinctions between so-called high and low art, visual depictions of tango are often judged a priori to be crude souvenirs rather than art. Its associations with gritty, grimy urban life and the visceral experiences of petty criminals and the working class in Buenos Aires and Montevideo—or simply with the mundane, the commonplace, and the unoriginal—have frequently condemned tango as a topic unworthy of serious aesthetic contemplation, whether in sound, kinetic, or visual culture.

In some cases the art establishment has rejected the very notion of *tango art*. In 2003 Jorge Glusberg, then director of Argentina's Museo Nacional de Bellas Artes, refused to mount an exhibit of tango-themed pieces, claiming that such material was not art (Horvath 27). Similarly, a tango mural painted in 2004 as an homage to the twentieth-century painter Carlos Torrallardona was defaced with graffiti in 2008 that also declared "Esto no es arte" (This is not art) (figure 3.1).[6] While the lines between art and kitsch, the authentic and the crass, and the artful and the merely useful are always subjective and inherently contentious, we can anticipate that on our journey through a century of tango art history we will encounter a veritable minefield around such distinctions.

This Is (Not) Art?

Admittedly, few of the images associated with the form in the earliest stages of tango's history, from about 1880 to 1920, would have concerned art critics. Just as the lettered classes in Argentina and Uruguay eschewed tango itself before its triumph in Paris, so also did they dismiss the earliest expressions of it in visual culture. The illustrations that graced the sheet music that began to proliferate in the first decades of the twentieth century have only recently been collected in handsome, full-color volumes and exhibited in museum galleries.[7]

Art connoisseurs of the early days of tango also looked askance at the *filete*, a decorating tradition that developed parallel to tango and often incorporated it thematically (figure 3.2). In her essay on the master *fileteadores* of Buenos Aires, María Estenssoro traces the uncertain origins of this painting style, which first appeared on horse-drawn wagons and grocers' carts in

Figure 3.1. Street mural in homage to Carlos Torrallardona, 700 block of Paraná, Buenos Aires, with graffiti in lower right corner that reads "Esto no es arte" (This is not art). Author photo.

the late nineteenth and early twentieth centuries. Characterized by colorful arabesques, Gothic inscriptions, religious figures, floral and fruit themes, ribbons, banners, and references to national icons (gauchos, the flag, tango, Carlos Gardel, and so on), early filete paintings were almost always anonymous and designed for public consumption, if not entirely classifiable as "advertising."[8] Given the intellectual prejudices dividing *arts* from *crafts* until the last quarter of the twentieth century, porteños mostly dismissed filete as "only a bad copy of Sicilian cart paintings brought to Argentina by the Italians" (Estenssoro 157, 161).

Today, Argentines revere the form and consider it as fundamentally porteño as the city's famous music and dance. Tango and filete complement each other in new ways as dancers—usually women—have master fileteadores paint their bodies in preparation for performances. Those who specialize in the form, including Jorge Muscia, to whom I will return, Luis Zors, Martiniano Arce, Elvio Gervasi, and Mariano Capiello, profess allegiance to the early masters and their themes, but they also apply those traditional styles to tennis shoes, cars, commercial vehicles, and even the covers of laptop

Figure 3.2. *Filete* decoration with elements of the Argentine flag and the bust of Gardel on the back of a bus, Buenos Aires. Author photo.

computers. Mirroring ongoing debates concerning the aesthetic value of tango itself, filete references a mythical past but also offers the artist or artisan space to express originality and innovation.

Tango and Social Realism

The "official" incorporation of tango in local art production dates to 1917, when the printmakers and other artists known as the Artistas del Pueblo (Artists of the people) initiated "the first sustained and organized movement of Social Realism" in Latin America (P. Frank, *Los Artistas del Pueblo* 18), including tango among their themes. Informed by currents of humanitarian anarchism, Adolfo Bellocq, José Arato, Guillermo Facio Hebequer, and Abraham Vigo honed a social realist aesthetic with which to expose the despicable working conditions and dire quotidian circumstances of the urban poor, many of them recent immigrants. With close ties to the writers of the leftist Boedo literary group, the Artistas del Pueblo presented tango as a Pandora's box of release and recreation that could lead to personal ruin for those in its thrall. Their works express suspicion of tango as a panacea for social ills and a distraction from collective action for social change. The collaboration of the *grabador* (engraver) Adolfo Bellocq and the author Manuel Gálvez on the dark novel *Historia de arrabal* (Slum story), published in 1922, exemplifies this tendency.[9]

Historia de arrabal portrays in word and image the rapid industrialization and capitalist expansion of Buenos Aires in the first part of the twentieth century, as poor immigrants streamed into the port city and sought survival amid an underpaid labor market and overcrowded housing.[10] Gálvez's representation of the precarious situation of young women is especially poignant. His story charts the descent of his tragic protagonist Rosalinda into a life of prostitution and homicide, casting tango as the irresistible suitor of her downfall. In Bellocq's zinc-relief illustration on page sixty-six of the novel, couples dance tango in the patio area of a cheap boarding house (figure 3.3). In the accompanying text the still unsullied Rosalinda is roughly pulled into the dance scene by the *malevo* or thug El Chino, who will progress from tango partner to jealous lover and finally sadistic pimp.[11] In the tango embrace of El Chino, the transfixed Rosalinda dances and dances, with "no awareness of anything, except that this man had claimed her as his own and dominated her, and she could do nothing but obey him" (Gálvez 67; Y ya no tuvo conciencia de nada, sino de que ese hombre la había hecho suya y la dominaba y de que ella no podía sino obedecerle [translations are the author's, unless otherwise noted]).

Bellocq's illustration emphasizes the sensual, sinuous elements of the dance, and the closed or semi-closed eyes of all the figures (including the musicians) allude to tango's power to enrapture its participants.[12] A *farol* in the upper right sector of the print casts a virtual half-light on the scene, outlining the voluptuous curves of the women but allowing the male dancers to remain shadowed. The beams of a doorway or window in the center of the background suggest a cross and thus, by implication, Rosalinda and other women's "sacrifice" of their bodies to the tango—a sacrifice that is ultimately doomed.

Tango in Black, White, and Color

Not all early twentieth-century artists considered tango's influence to be quite so malevolent. The upbeat, festive nature of social dance dominates the representation of tango and its predecessor *candombe* in the works of the Uruguayan painter Pedro Figari (1861–1938). Perhaps the most recognizable and most copied practitioner of tango art of all time, Figari was also the first

Figure 3.3. Adolfo Bellocq, *Tango Dance*, zinc-relief book illustration for Manuel Galvéz, *Historia de Arrabal* 66.

to exhibit and sell such works in the context of fine art.[13] The late-blooming Figari reportedly left over four thousand works to posterity, works so popular and valuable that his own descendants reportedly have been swindled into accepting carefully executed copies of his distinctive style.[14] A prominent lawyer, journalist, philosopher, and poet in the first five decades of his life, Figari became a visual artist at age fifty-five, moving first to Buenos Aires and then to Paris. His three-volume primer *Arte, estética, ideal* (Art, aesthetics, ideals, 1912) preceded Figari's first major show in Buenos Aires by a decade, revealing him to be an art theorist and administrator before his incursions in painting.

Critics deemed Figari's exhibit at the Galería Müller in Buenos Aires in 1921 a flop, given that he sold only one painting.[15] But Figari's second Buenos Aires exhibit in 1923—the same year Borges published his groundbreaking book of poetry *Fervor de Buenos Aires*—made history. Manuel J. Güiraldes, the father of Ricardo Güiraldes (author of the classic *Don Segundo Sombra*, 1926), endorsed Figari, and a group of influential writers and artists who would later create a literary stir with the cultural magazines *Prisma*, *Inicial*, *Proa*, *Valoraciones*, and, most importantly, *Martín Fierro* feted him in the press (Figari, *Figari* 9). The notable camaraderie enjoyed by the *martinfierrista* writers and artists would characterize the production of tango as an interdisciplinary form from that point forward.[16] Observers commented on the criollo or localist tendencies in Figari's work and celebrated its innovative use of color and humorous undertones (see Lacalle 10–11).[17]

As both a visual artist and theorist, Figari urged a turn away from *wealth as culture*, in which culture was the exclusive domain of the upper classes, and toward *culture as wealth*, in which the middle and lower classes could also enjoy the "riches" of aesthetic production (Glusberg and Kalenberg 24). He dismissed as "arbitrary" the traditional distinctions between belles arts (music, literature, dance, sculpture, architecture, painting, and poetry) and the "useful" or applied arts of ceramics, furniture, ironwork, stained glass, and so on (Glusberg and Kalenberg 34). This rejection of the old, mutually exclusive definitions of high art and popular art endeared him to the members of the *Martín Fierro* group as well as to Alfonso Reyes, Ángel Rama, and Marta Traba, all of whom later wrote interdisciplinary studies of his work.

Figari and his son Juan Carlos moved to Paris in 1925. The visitors who passed through their studio there included James Joyce, Pablo Picasso, Le Corbusier, Pierre Bonnard, and Oswaldo de Andrade. In Paris the painter also met the Cuban writer Alejo Carpentier, who in 1928 wrote "Pedro Figari y el clasicismo latinoamericano" (Pedro Figari and Latin American classicism).[18] Carpentier quotes the artist as saying, "in my paintings, I haven't tried to solve this or that problem of métier, I have only wanted to leave on the canvas a series of past and present aspects of South American life, so that they will serve as a document for the great painter who will come later" (20; En mis cuadros no he intentado resolver tal o cual problema de *métier*. Sólo he querido fijar en el lienzo una serie de aspectos pasados o actuales de la vida suramericana, para que sirvan de documentos al gran pintor que vendrá después). The Cuban author calls particular attention to Figari's focus on black subjects and notes parallels between the Uruguayan's vision of Montevideo and his own experience of Havana.[19]

The inclusion of Afro-Uruguayan subjects surprised many of Figari's fans and critics, especially since earlier artists had ignored that sector of the population.[20] This "new" subject matter provoked both curiosity and debate; Figari defended himself by stating: "I want to refer to man and in order to better do so, I take the Negro as my example, bearing in mind that we white men carry a black man, a very black man, within us—the same one who frequently suggests things that otherwise could not be suggested to a white man without incurring irreverence" (Figari, *Intimate Recollections* 14–15). Whatever the mixture of desire and fear at the base of these comments, they reflect a more explicit identification with Afro-Uruguayans than ever before. Angel Kalenberg writes that "Figari saw in the black all the force of the rhythm which in North America produced jazz and in South America, the candombe" (Glusberg and Kalenberg 51; Figari vio en el negro toda la fuerza del ritmo que, al norte de América produjo el jazz y, en América del Sur, el Candombe). The Uruguayan artist Luis Camnitzer counters that Figari should be understood as a contradictory figure, on the one hand espousing forward-thinking ideas on art and arts education and on the other failing to see how his own work was limited by European traditions and neocolonial ideas (139). If Figari "stereotyped black culture through a paternalistic caricature of innocence, vitality, and happiness" (Camnitzer 143), he nonetheless invested Afro-Uruguayan subjects with cultural value and, for the first time, deemed them worthy of inclusion in national and regional artistic endeavors.

While the subjects of Figari's candombe series are always Afro-Uruguayans, his tangos feature both black and white subjects.[21] Figari populated *El tango* (figure 3.4) with an entirely black cast and wrote on the reverse of the image, "El tango (echa a perder aún a los negros)" (The tango [spoils even black people]). The painting *En la calle* (figure 3.5) features a white or at least noticeably *whiter* cast of characters. Despite some differences in size and coloration, both works feature pairs of dancers in the standard tango embrace, seated bandoneonists who face the viewer, and a background doorway to help frame the "stage" of the dance scene.[22] Both also correspond to Kalenberg's description of Figari's work as a "treatise on gestures" that emphasizes profiles and high-contrast color schemes designed to "excite the retina" (Glusberg and Kalenberg 54–55, 62). The dress of the female spectators, and the fan held by the figure situated in the doorway that repeats into the background of *En la calle*, suggest the entryway to a bordello; the woman sitting in the window of *El tango* may have the same function. While neither work may clarify Figari's comment regarding the relationship between blackness and tango, both situate the dance in a context of familiarity and pleasure. Together, they document tango's appeal for a racially diverse population and situate Figari as a founding member of a growing field of tango art.

Tango Squared

While Figari's winsome paintings on hardboard constitute efforts to mitigate the "loss" of a bygone cultural landscape, the works of the Argentine-born Emilio Pettoruti (1892–1971), Figari's contemporary, represent the entrée of tango into abstract art. From virtually the same historical juncture, one artist looks back and the other forward. With such artists as Diego Rivera (Mexico), Amelia Peláez (Cuba), Joaquín Torres-García (Uruguay), and fellow Argentines Norah Borges and Xul Solar, Pettoruti helped constitute Latin American modern art, occasionally addressing the tango in that new field.[23] Critics frequently associate his works with cubist and futurist vanguards, but Pettorutti resisted being rigidly categorized in either movement (Sullivan and Perazza 52). Together, the works of Figari and Pettorutti exemplify the tug-of-war that characterizes the representation of tango in the Río de la Plata then and now, visual and otherwise: on the one hand it triggers nostalgia and provides a repository for the past, while on the other it negotiates the urgent needs of the present.

Pettoruti's works contrast not only with Figari's postimpressionist evocations but also with those of the Artistas del Pueblo, whose emphasis on Marxist social concerns he countered with an insistence on formal modernism and invention.[24] Just three years after Figari's first important exhibit in the Argentine capital, Pettoruti's works were displayed at the city's Witcomb Gallery, following the painter's return from more than a decade in Italy. The conservative critics of the Argentine art establishment decried his bold, semi-abstract style. Pettorutti's friend Xul Solar defended the work in the pages of the influential journal *Martín Fierro*, also initiated that year, contributing to a debate that soon converted the exhibit into an art event of "almost mythic proportions" (Sullivan and Perazzo 20, 90).

Xul Solar's defense of his friend hinted at his own vanguard tendencies, in which tango played a minor role as well. Pettoruti wrote that his painting *Bailarines* (Dancers), completed in 1920, was in fact conceived "while Xul Solar danced a tango in one of those New Empire-style mansions that we used to frequent in Florence" (cited in Sullivan and Perazzo 170). Painted in oil on canvas, *Bailarines* conceptualizes a dancing couple in highly abstract terms, setting the pair against a diamond-patterned floor, illuminated by a

Figure 3.4. Pedro Figari, *El tango*, oil on hardboard. Used by permission of Fernando Saavedra Faget.

Figure 3.5. Pedro Figari, *En la calle* (On the street). Used by permission of Fernando Saavedra Faget.

light source that casts an angular shadow and creates additional triangular and rectangular shapes as it is refracted from the tile floor. As Sullivan notes, *Bailarines* was "among the first examples in which Pettoruti refers directly to a specifically Argentine form of music and dance." It was also the first of Pettoruti's paintings to hang in a museum (Sullivan and Perazzo 78, 170).

As tango's fame was spreading rapidly throughout Europe and the Southern Cone through music and dance, Pettoruti was translating its musicality and movement into the geometric and chromatic intensity of modernism. The emphasis on musical and theatrical themes that typified much of his work from the 1920s finds one of its maximum expressions in the painting *La canción del pueblo* (The song of the people), completed in 1927 (figure 3.6).[25] Skyscrapers flank a trio of musicians anchored from behind by a building and skyline centrally divided between light and dark. Susan Verdi Webster has noticed that the bandoneon most explicitly references tango in *La canción del pueblo*. But the piece's title and visual portrayal of the people's "song" (with the motif of balance between light and dark repeated in the vocalists' open mouths) also reference tango, this time within a diurnal futurist plane entirely void of the patina of the past.[26]

Staging Tango

The young Argentine painter Héctor Basaldúa was deeply impressed with Pedro Figari's exhibit of 1921, but decades would pass before he would create his own tango-themed works. Like Figari and Pettoruti, Basaldúa spent many years in Europe, hoping to establish himself as a painter. He progressively took on other projects such as book illustration and stage design that didn't necessarily earn him fame as a painter but did make him "one of the most complete, profound and sensitive artists of his generation" (Whitelow 11). An illustrator of works by well-known authors such as Jorge Luis Borges, Silvina Ocampo, Manuel Mujica Láinez, and Ricardo Güiraldes, Basaldúa also worked for some thirty years in stage direction at Buenos Aires' opulent Teatro Colón. He first designed opera sets there in 1921, returned in 1931 after spending several years in Paris, and then functioned as the hall's head designer from 1933 to 1952 (Basaldúa 40–41).

Fellow artist Horacio Butler considered it a mistake for Basaldúa to work in these other exhausting labors, rather than in front of an easel in a quiet studio (Whitelow 11). But the worlds of the stage spectacle and painter's studio ultimately were mutually enriching for Basaldúa. His sketches for stage productions at the Colón exhibit an atypical attention to detail and painterly

Figure 3.6. Emilio Pettoruti, *La canción del pueblo* (The song of the people), 1927, oil on wood, 76 × 64 cm. Reproduced in the itemized catalog *Pettoruti*, edited in 1995 by Fundación Pettoruti, label number 253. All rights reserved Fundación Pettoruti—www.Pettoruti .com. Used by permission of Colección Malba, Fundación Pettoruti.

depth, and many of his paintings capture the drama of the theater.[27] We find a good example of Basaldúa's stage designer penchant for lighting, actor place- ment, and choreography in his painting of 1956 *Salón de tango* (Tango hall) (figure 3.7).[28] Basaldúa orients the couple at the center of the work so that the spectator sees both their faces, as on a stage. The other figures frame the couple, directing the viewer's gaze toward their intimacy in the midst of the visually "noisy" social gathering. *Salón de tango* portrays the milonga as a space not just for making, hearing, or dancing to music but also as a place to see and be seen, to watch and judge other dancers, and to experience and provoke curiosity and desire. The use of deep orange hues in both the fore- ground and background unify and warm the scene, and diffuse lighting and gradations of detail in the figures' features and postures add to the nocturnal, stage-lit atmosphere.

Carlos Torrallardona's grand columns, balconies, spotlights, and heavy curtains also connect tango on the theater stage to its practice in more inti- mate spaces. His oil painting on hardboard *El espíritu del tango* (The spirit of the tango) (figure 3.8), completed in 1978, steers us back to the bordello as a historical staging ground of tango. A semi-naked woman in the foreground

Figure 3.7. Héctor Basaldúa, *Salón de tango*, 1956. Used by permission of Fundación Kónex.

Figure 3.8. Carlos Torrallardona, *El espíritu del tango* (The spirit of the tango), 1978. Used by permission of Fundación Kónex.

of the painting seems to return and challenge the viewer's gaze, suggesting both an invitation and a provocation. Couples dancing close together on a "hot" floor of intense reds hint at tango's continuing connections to the *arrabal* and the brothel, despite its increasing identification with the glamour and grandeur of the stage. Also known for his portrayals of Buenos Aires's *boliches* and pool halls, Torrallardona's paintings capture or recapture tango's nocturnal sensuality in a period when the social practice of the milonga was on the wane.

Fourteen Painters, Writers, and Poets with the Tango

Both Basaldúa and Torrallardona contributed to the impressive assemblage of writers, musicians, and artists that Ben Molar brought together for his multimedia phenomenon *14 con el tango* (14 with the tango) in 1966. As noted in the introduction to this edited volume, those who purchased the LP could listen to tangos composed by eminent musicians, read lyrics written by recognized poets, and view a portable gallery of fourteen works painted by Basaldúa, Torrallardona, and a dozen others reproduced on paper and included in the record jacket. According to Molar, when the record was released, the original paintings were also displayed in a series of store windows along Avenida Santa Fe, one of Buenos Aires's famous pedestrian boulevards.

While some of the artists of *14 con el tango* addressed the tango and the city of Buenos Aires explicitly in their compositions, others interpreted their commission in more abstract terms. Basaldúa's portrait of a *compadrito* references early tango lyrics that portray these urban players but not the dance or music directly. The only explicit mention of tango in Torrallardona's contribution is a tiny image of a dancing couple that adorns one wall of the pool hall he depicted.[29] Works by these two artists and the dozen other collaborators make it clear that by the mid-1960s one could "be with" the tango in a variety of ways and visibly evoke it using a wide range of styles and media. They also demonstrated the ever-deeper cross-pollination and enrichment of music, poetry, and image, despite growing fears of the encroachments of rock and pop in contributing to tango's demise.

Of the fourteen who contributed to Molar's multi-genre effort, Carlos Cañás and Carlos Alonso were the only two artists still living as this chapter was completed. Molar chose Cañás to illustrate "Milonga de Albornoz" written by Jorge Luis Borges.[30] Its protagonist is the sauntering, milonga-whistling Alejo Albornoz, a dupe who doesn't know that three knives await him on a street in the gritty south side of town. The text begins by invoking the past and the compadrito's dark fate: "Alguien ya contó los días" (Someone already counted the days). Albornoz, and by extension the tango, are victims of time's march, even as they are retrieved and remembered in Borges's self-reflexive song-poem, which ends with this stanza:

> Pienso que le gustaría
> saber que hoy anda su historia
> en una milonga. El tiempo
> es olvido y es memoria.

> [I think that he would like
> to know that his story
> continues today in a milonga. Time
> is oblivion and memory.][31]

Cañás's accompanying painting also displays temporal ambiguity. Dominated chromatically by grays and blues and composed almost entirely of straight edges, *Milonga de Albornoz* (figure 3.9) situates the emblematic figure of the compadrito or urban tough within a semi-abstract, coolish frame. The single two-story building of the background suggests a *conventillo*, rather than Pettorutti's skyscrapers. The piece evokes milonga, and by extension tango, as suspended somewhere between the archaic and the contemporary.

Despite the pressures felt by Ben Molar and his fellow guardians in the face of the rapid growth of rock, their collective effort proved that tango still provided a wide open space for reflection and innovation, spacious enough to accommodate nostalgic treatments as well as new realisms, abstractions, expressionisms, caricature, and populisms. If for the Borges of "Milonga de Albornoz" tango's primary appeal resided in its connection to the past, other artists simultaneously affirmed its relevance to the present.[32] To make the case for tango's continuing vitality in the period ahead, artists working in both of those schools would have to warily negotiate tango's growing global success and ever more prevalent stereotyping.

Gains and Losses

The painter and illustrator Carlos Alonso (b. 1929) tells a story of running into fellow artist Felipe de la Fuente (1912–2000) on the street one day, disheveled and at wits' end. De la Fuente had agreed to produce several hundred tango-themed canvases for a string of Japanese hotels, but after completing the first few dozen, he saw that this jackpot was in fact a road to creative

Figure 3.9. Carlos Cañás, *Milonga de Albornoz*. Used by permission of Carlos Cañás.

ruin and complained to Alonso that he would go mad if he had to fulfill the contract. For Alonso, de la Fuente's cautionary tale reveals the dark side of tango's success as a commodity in a global market. How does an artist avoid aesthetic debasement when tango images and objects are being reproduced cheaply the world over? Alonso answers that question in graphic, unsettling ways in his art, resolute and incorruptible in avoiding the trap of predictability and straitjacketing, especially as that trap concerns tango.

Art historians have mostly ignored the few references to tango in Alonso's works, however, focusing instead on two major tendencies: the relationships his oeuvre establishes with those of other writers and artists and his attention to political concerns. Examples of the first of these characteristics include Alonso's illustrations for the second half of *Don Quixote*, which converse with Cervantes's text as well as with the drawings of Salvador Dalí, who illustrated the first part; his rendering of Ernesto "Che" Guevara's cadaver as a response to Rembrandt's "The Anatomy Lesson";[33] and his portraits of Vincent Van Gogh and the Argentine artist Lino Spilimbergo, one of his teachers.[34] Though tango doesn't appear in those works, it constitutes an important presence in other works in which Alonso addresses harsh topics such as political repression, censorship, and torture, especially as they relate to Argentine national history.

Defined as a social realist early on, Alonso participated in politically charged efforts such as the exhibit *El Che Vive* (The Che lives, 1968), which was closed down by the police, and *Malvenido Rockfeller* (Unwelcome Rockfeller), in which he and his counterparts decried the visit of the North American millionaire to Argentina in 1969. In 1976 Alonso's show *El Ganado y lo Perdido* (The cattle and the lost) opened at the Art Gallery in Buenos Aires within a month of the start of the Process of National Reorganization that marked Argentina's descent into military dictatorship. The title is a provocative play on words, as *el ganado* means cattle, but a change of the article converts the term to *lo ganado*, which means "what's gained or earned." In his tally of gains and losses, Alonso questions "the dehumanization of our society" (*Carlos Alonso* 14). *El Ganado y lo Perdido* drew a markedly different crowd from the usual gallery-hopping set, and the show received bomb threats from members of the political right (*Carlos Alonso* 13). That same year Alonso went into exile in Italy, and soon after, his daughter Paloma, who had remained in Argentina, was "disappeared" by the dictatorship.

While aesthetically impressive, tango-themed works by Alonso from that exile period and after are also important as a record of the artist's negotiations of the injustice, personal loss, and displacement experienced by so many Argentines in the second half of the twentieth century.[35] The paintings *Gran tango* (1975) and *Tango* (1978) portray tango in its intersections with political life and national history and in its figurative sense as an important happening or encounter. In *Gran tango*, rendered in mixed media on paper, he places several couples in the context of a butcher shop, where they dance among a string of sausages, a slab of ribs, organ meats, and several menacing empty hooks (figure 3.10). Dominant reds represent blood as visceral, eschatological. One woman's hand pulls a hunk of meat into the embrace of her dance partner; one man's hand digs into his partner's bare back as if he were cutting flesh. The feet of the dancers float unanchored above the floor; Alonso enhances our sensation of ungroundedness by incorporating legs and feet on a slightly higher plane on both flanks of the work. The men in the picture are all fully dressed, while the women are naked except for shoes and skimpy or translucent underclothing. Rather than beauty or allure, the state of undress of the women suggests an obscene breach of privacy. The horrifying image of

Figure 3.10. Carlos Alonso, *Gran tango*, 1975, mixed media on paper. Used by permission of Carlos Alonso.

Gran tango establishes irony with the piece's title and strips away the veneer of tango as a picturesque, flirtatious dance.

Gran tango does more than associate the social dynamic of a milonga with a "meat market" in which flesh is displayed for purchase. The work belongs to Alonso's large-scale project *Hay que comer* (One has to eat), certain pieces of which were banned by the Argentine government in the 1970s. In *Hay que comer*, exhibited in an expanded version in Buenos Aires in 2004, Alonso recounts the country's *historia carnívora*, in which revenues from cattle and beef contributed to huge personal fortunes and Argentina's emergence as the richest country in Latin America and one of the dozen richest in the world. The early twentieth century became known as the era of the *vacas gordas* or fatted calves (see Hora), and meat is perhaps more closely tied to Argentina's capitalist development and expansion in export markets than any other product— unless that product is tango. By superimposing the two commodities, Alonso disturbs the viewer and his or her tidy versions of history. He blurs the lines between butcher and *bailarín*, between human and animal flesh, and between Argentine national identity as defined by its alluring music and dance or by the horrific actions of its authoritarian governments (see Viñas, untitled).

Alonso's painting *Tango* from 1978 (reproduced in Alonso, *Carlos Alonso* 125) further upsets conventions, forcing us to once again move beyond the generalities and commonplaces around the term *tango*. On a very large canvas, an almost life-sized woman wearing only underclothing and a pair of red heels straddles a supine man, fully dressed—including his fedora—except for his shoes and socks, which are visible next to the mattress.[36] A nightstand or cabinet in the upper right-hand corner reveals to us that the couple's heads are pointing down toward the foot of the bed, their feet up. While the position of the couple and their state of undress evoke an encounter that is fleeting, maybe even clandestine, the skewed perspective positions both the illustrator and the implicit viewer as voyeurs of this intimate scene. Each partner clasps only his or her own hands, rather than the hand or body of the other, and their hidden faces appear turned away from each other. Alonso thus stands the tango on its head (almost literally), calling into question such sacred cows as the "tango embrace" and the "tango connection." Also intriguing is what the painting might say about gender relations vis-à-vis the tango, as the woman's position on top also defies a predictable rendering of her supposed role as a passive or pliable "follower."

When Alonso returned to Argentina after the restoration of democracy in the early 1980s, he found Buenos Aires to be a city scarred by the dictatorship in which he "had the sensation that there were too many assassins and too many torturers running loose, too much worry and sadness, too much crisis" (Alonso, *Carlos Alonso* 14). Soon after, he went to live in the province of Córdoba, where he concentrated on painting landscapes, explaining that his experiences had caused a "rupture with the image" provoked by his disillusion with humankind. Still, Alonso never lost his faith in art itself. In the frontispiece to his autobiography in images, published in 2003, he declared: "I still believe in art, and above all, in its incorruptible memory, not sentimental but capable of fixing the wounds that reality leaves in us; I don't believe that art can resolve any of the problems of the world, a maxim that is used when ambiguity invades figurative art and banality is consecrated by public utility; world states try to sterilize misery and terror for us, but it's with this terrorized love that that we can begin to build our paintings."[37] Ever wary of the temptations of "public utility" and the banal sentimentality that so frequently results when artists succumb to such temptations, Alonso implicitly urges artists, art viewers, and even *tangueros* to reject facile representations built on nostalgia and instead engage fully with the political verities of our times, however painful.

The Idea of the Tango

Following the end of dictatorship and the restoration of democracy in Argentina and Uruguay in the 1980s, the role of tango and tango art began to shift to reflect new levels of economic and cultural flow at the global level. Many of the region's most revered artists chose not to return from exile in Europe and elsewhere, instead creating *rioplatense* art from outside the region's borders. Films such as *Tangos: El exilio de Gardel* (treated elsewhere in this edited volume), released in 1985, demonstrate how creative energies related to the tango both flourished and were subject to pigeonholing in the contexts of such exiles and displacements. In 1986 Claudio Segovia brought dozens of top dancers and musicians from Buenos Aires to Paris, where he was then living, to stage the hugely popular *Tango Argentino* (see the introduction to this edited volume). For the playbill and other promotional materials for the show, he chose an upscale image from a vintage German dance poster that, though it took liberties with traditional tango form (by reversing the embrace), recalled the glamour and grandeur of the tango of yesteryear (figure 3.11).[38] Mixing antique elements such as this one with new choreography and production values, *Tango Argentino* jumpstarted a renaissance that attracted new generations to tango dance, music, and art in the international market. As had happened nearly a century earlier, tango practice would be energized and expanded by this international exposure, and by the end of the twentieth century, its significance in all these venues once again began to rise dramatically.

In 2002, a German gallery displayed sixty paintings, drawings, sculptures, and works in mixed media under the title *Die Tango-Idee* (The idea of the tango), giving an international audience access to some of the latest works in visual culture representing tango. The Montevidean painter Virginia Patrone and her daughter Laura Spagnuolo conceived the project with a foreign public in mind. The twelve artists' base of Montevideo, rather than Buenos Aires, allied them geographically and culturally with tango but also suggested a certain distance from the ever-more pervasive stereotyping that characterized the form in Buenos Aires. "Everyone knows what the tango is, just like everyone thinks it is Argentine," explains Patrone. "The exhibit didn't have to do with the tango, but with the idea of the tango."[39] The show catalog described the resurgence that occurred in Uruguayan art circles following the end of that country's military dictatorship (1973–1985) (39). Dubbed the "Generation of the '80s," the young artists working in the postdictatorship

Figure 3.11. Playbill image from the stage show *Tango Argentino*. Used by permission of Claudio Segovia.

period became known for their dialogue with such European forms as German neoexpressionism and the Italian transavant-garde, their interrogation of the events of the recent past, and their often violent use of color. Now, they were applying those tendencies to fresh representations of the tango rioplatense and its history in both Montevideo and Buenos Aires.

Like the artists of *14 con el tango*, the twelve contributors to *Die Tango-Idee*—most of them infants or children when Molar's project had debuted almost four decades earlier—chose to interpret tango freely, providing predominantly abstract pieces for the exhibit. Painting, drawing, and sculpture were taken "not as dogmas but as porous elements that allow for the reunion of multiple vectors with which contemporary art harbors and responds to the experience of the present" (39). After its debut in Munich, *Die Tango-Idee* traveled back to Montevideo and then to Frankfurt, Berlin, Vienna, Paris, Madrid, and Barcelona during a two-year period.

Like so many other Uruguayans and Argentines far from their home countries, Patrone recounts how she had a chance reencounter with the tango well into her artistic trajectory that struck a deep emotional chord, despite earlier indifference to it. One day, in a rented car in the outskirts of Paris, her eyes filled with tears as she listened to a fragment of tango on the radio. That emotion ultimately triggered a renewed interest in the classic tangos of

Carlos Gardel and his era, and Patrone began to reconsider what the tango represented for her immigrant grandparents and the history of her birthplace: "And I found many images in the lyrics of those tangos heard over and over again. More than in the lyrics themselves, I found poetry in what remains when you join lyrics, music, and voice. That evocation has poetic resonances." Patrone was interested in tango's masculinist tendencies, its discourse of machismo, and the schematic representations of women contained in its lyrics. "There is a disadvantage, a lack of features in the woman of tango lyrics; she doesn't have a voice," she explains. Thus, in her own work, Patrone determined to use tango as a place to search for "a representation of the feminine from the feminine."[40] In the Uruguayan painter's intensely colored works, curvy female figures cease to be solely danceable objects, partners, or followers of their male counterparts: in one canvas, they dance together, embracing each other; in others they stand alone in a self-embrace. In a piece she reworked after its original inclusion in *Die Tango-Idee*, Patrone expands her focus by incorporating allusions to Japanese literature, Zen Buddhism, and the art of kabuki, noting that Japan has had a privileged relationship with the tango. The title of *Sumo tango* is playfully polyvalent, since *sumo* is both a Spanish adjective for "maximum" and a style of Japanese wrestling in which the idea is to topple the opponent (figure 3.12). A face with Asian features, implicitly that of a female wrestler, is suspended on the back of the woman dancer who looks out at the viewer from the tango embrace. Besides contesting another stereotype of the sumo wrestler as invariably male, she suggests exceptional physical and metaphysical strength. *Sumo tango* thus redefines the *tanguera* as equal or superior to her male counterpart.

Other contemporary artists also acknowledge the power of old lyrics in their new works. The Argentine artist Marcia Schvartz's project *El alma que pinta* (The soul that paints) reinterprets classic tango texts by placing women at the center of the situations those lyrics dramatize. Like Alonso, Schvartz avoids benign sentimentality and directly addresses personal and collective pain and loss. Not only do Schvartz's works in *El alma que pinta* revisit well-known tango lyrics but also the project as a whole recalls *El alma que canta* (The soul that sings), an early twentieth-century publication dedicated to tango lyrics and news. The catalog of *El alma que pinta* imitates aspects of the early journal, including an antique typeface and sepia-toned paper, the latter of which mimics Schvartz's predilection for using charcoal on burlap. Each of the images is accompanied by a title or other fragment from an emblematic tango such as *Tinta roja* (Red ink), *Arrabalera* (Low-class woman), *María, Mi*

Figure 3.12.
Virginia Patrone,
Sumo tango. Used
by permission of
Virginia Patrone.

noche triste (My sad night), and *Volver* (Return). Along with vintage elements, Schvartz includes modern or even postmodern elements such as distortion, intense contrasts, a sordid or macabre quality, and comic book-like splashes of red or shocking pink.

Because Schvartz worked with a model who closely resembles her, many have assumed that the female figures in the canvases of *El alma que pinta* are autobiographical. She stresses that they came out of a collective effort: "I can't listen to tangos alone because I cry and they are very connected to having lived outside the country" (qtd. in Isola). As Schvartz and her model worked together chatting and listening to tangos, the painter honed in on the specific problems of women. "I really liked working on stereotypes, but that wasn't the only thing," Schvartz clarifies, "I think that once I go back and look at these paintings, they are speaking to me about more than just the tango. They are women who suffer, who get drunk, who bleed" (qtd. in Isola).

Schvartz's *Tabernero* (figure 3.13) treats the historic associations of tango with alcohol and the effects of its abuse on body and soul, but it substitutes a female protagonist for the masculine voice of the original lyrics. The pathos-driven words in the composition of the same title, written by Raúl Costa Oliveri in 1927 and popularized by Carlos Gardel, include the following stanza:

Todos los que son borrachos
no es por el gusto de serlo,
sólo Dios conoce el alma
que palpita en cada ebrio.
¿No ves mi copa vacía?
¡Echa vino, tabernero!,
que tengo el alma contenta,
con tu maldito veneno . . .

[Not all who are drunks
are that way because they like it,
only God knows the soul
that beats in every drunkard.
Don't you see my empty glass?
Give me some wine, barman!
My soul is content
with your accursed venom.][41]

Schvartz inscribes some of those lyrics directly into the work, using a deep
red tint and wet, splotchy writing that suggests a text written in blood. "There
is a lot of alcohol in my paintings because there was a lot in my life. When
we were in exile in Barcelona, we drank a lot and I have friends who died
alcoholics. I can also relate blood with wine, and by putting them together,
the rather neglected zone of menopause also jumps out," Schvartz explains
(qtd. in Isola).

The text of the incorporated lyric frames a woman clad in a black slip and
hose, stretched out across an orange-red swath on the floor, who pours a
stream that repeats the same bloodlike "font" of the script as it travels from
bottle to wine glass. An old telephone, several LPs, and a pair of spiky heels
anchor the lower left sector of the painting, the records perhaps symbolizing
the auditory pleasures of the tango and the shoes its kinetic appeal. Schvartz
notably modifies the original lyrics (included in full alongside the reproduction of the work in the exhibit catalog) by changing the speaker's request to
the barman to keep refilling his glass with "bloody venom" ("Sigue llenando
mi copa con tu maldito veneno") to the first-person confession "I keep filling
my glass with your accursed venom" ("Sigo llenando mi copa con tu maldito
veneno"). The switch in subject adds a foreboding overlay, suggesting an addiction on the part of the female protagonist that goes beyond mere alcohol,
perhaps to a relationship that is itself both pleasurable and poisonous. Once

Figure 3.13. Marcia Schvartz, *Tabernero*, 2004, mixed media. Used by permission of Marcia Schvartz.

again, tango's elasticity in expressing pain or pleasure, rhapsody or ruin, is on display.

What Remains

Contemporary artists face more pressures than ever before from international consumers keen on purchasing visual representations of tango that follow the picturesque formulas of the tourist guidebooks. Artists today must negotiate the allure and pitfalls of tango art *for export* and participate in the polemics regarding origins, originality, authenticity, historic relevance, and aesthetic quality. Much of contemporary tango art exploits these debates, treating the icons and emblems of tango with irony or parody. Five recent examples of tango art exemplify these ongoing engagements. Works by the fileteador Jorge Muscia, the abstract painter Cristian Mac Entyre, the post-realist painter Daniel Kaplan, the photographer Marcos López, and the caricaturist Hermenegildo Sábat make it abundantly clear that like tango music and dance, the field of tango art continues to expand and diversify.

In *San Pugliese* (figure 3.14) Jorge Muscia uses the "vintage" filete style discussed at the beginning of this chapter to create a postmodern, hagiographic invocation of the composer and pianist Oswaldo Pugliese, a venerated "saint" of the tango pantheon whose arrangements and recordings remain popular

Figure 3.14. Jorge Muscia, *San Pugliese*. Used by permission of Jorge Muscia.

with today's tangueros. The blue and white of the Argentine flag are imposed over Pugliese's keyboard, and a legend across the top of the image, flanked by two large ears, implores, "Protect us from whoever doesn't listen." In a nod to the popular tradition of repeating "Pugliese, Pugliese, Pugliese" to ward off bad luck, readers of *Tangauta* magazine, where the image was published, were encouraged to cut out their *San Pugliese* and affix it to a votive candle or use it as a talisman. This popular or pop appropriation of the filete might seem trite to art critics and disrespectful to music purists, but Muscia's *San Pugliese* does pay homage to both the decorative tradition of the filete and to Pugliese, who, as a dedicated communist, is the historical figure that most closely aligns tango music and performance to socialist aims.

Cristian Mac Entyre's painting *Dinámica de baile 2* (Dance dynamic 2) (Figure 3.15) recalls the highly geometric work of Emilio Pettoruti, but it displays a more pronounced interest in movement. The monochromatic intensity of the couple, the absence of facial features, the repeating lines of the foreground image, and the overall diagonality of the work all intensify the dynamism referred to in the title. Mac Entyre acknowledges the influence of the early twentieth-century surrealist and Dadaist artist Marcel Duchamp: "His

Figure 3.15.
Cristian Mac Entyre,
Dinámica de Baile 2,
2003, mixed media.
Used by permission of
Cristian Mac Entyre.

manner of capturing an entire movement sequence and transmitting it on the canvas always attracted me," Mac Entyre explained. The work from 2003 resembles Duchamp's *Nude Descending a Staircase No. 2* from 1912 and references other early twentieth-century futurists Mac Entyre was studying when he painted *Dinámica*: "The superimposition of images helps me to conceptualize rhythm. It also enables one to freeze the action in its point of greatest expressive tension."[42] Despite this attention to *vanguardista* traditions from decades earlier, Mac Entyre's interest in tango is informed by local, lived elements, beginning with the Barracas neighborhood where he grew up and still lives. His influences range from Kandinsky and Jimi Hendrix to Eduardo Mac Entyre, the artist's father, famous for his own participation in Argentina's pop, abstract, and cubist art movements.[43]

Although he studied with Carlos Cañás (of *14 con el tango*) at age seventeen, Daniel Kaplan's interest in tango developed much later when he began to frequent milongas in Buenos Aires and New York.[44] Many of his works re-create panoramic views of specific dance halls and the ambience of specific milongas. His piece *After Hopper* from 2007 (figure 3.16) was painted after Kaplan received a Fulbright scholarship in 2005 that helped him deepen his knowledge and further perfect his technique. The nearly square oil painting recalls many characteristics of Edward Hopper's works, particularly the emphasis on architecture, the careful use of lighting, and the placement of the human subjects in their everyday urban environment. Kaplan chose as his setting the yellowing Confitería Ideal, a revered classic dance hall in the center of Buenos Aires with soaring ceilings, aging grandeur, and a floor danced on by thousands of local and international milongueros. His waist-up focus on a single couple that occupies only a small portion of the canvas frames the tango as ordinary—even mundane (no dramatic fishnet-clad legs flying here)—but the work also conveys the *entrega* (surrender) of a specific, unrepeatable dance moment. The light reflected on the dancers' heads illuminates their age and creates an effect of divine inspiration or heightened reverie. The other couples in the painting, reflected in the glass panes in the background, literally fade into the background in the face of the main couple's concentration on each other. The loudspeaker situated in the convergence of columns in the upper center of the painting reveals the interplay of technology with the patina of the past and functions as a mouth or voice for the music as well as a second eye that looks down at the dancers and back at the artist or viewer. Kaplan's naturalist vision of contemporary tango shows it to reside in the same fundamental experience of connection and communion that characterized it a century earlier, despite the physical decline of its venues or the changes instituted by new technologies.

The pronounced dialogic quality of much contemporary tango art reaches new levels in the highly parodic work of the Argentine photographer Marcos López. His photo *Il piccolo vapore* (figure 3.17), from 2007, has a postmodern, baroque style that parodies the marketing of the tango, Carlos Gardel, and other icons of Argentine identity. Destined, like other works in his *Subrealismo criollo* (Creole subrealism) series, to critique "the kitschy detritus of globalised daily life," *Il piccolo vapore* is a layered, even palimpsestic work that references a cantina in the Buenos Aires neighborhood of La Boca where a variety of stock elements are enlisted to create an "authentic" Argentine experience for the locals or tourists who visit.[45] A "live" impersonator of Carlos Gardel and a painting of Carlitos perform tango stereotypes, as do a live musician and a tacky image of a bandoneonist that adorns a side wall. Both the two-dimensional emblems (copies) and three-dimensional (real)

Figure 3.16. Daniel Kaplan, *After Hopper*, 2007, oil on canvas. Used by permission of Daniel Kaplan.

Figure 3.17. Marcos López, *Il piccolo vapore*, 2007. Used by permission of Marcos López.

figures appear equally "posed" or framed, but the haggard or bored demeanor of the "live" performers defies the carefree attitude of the tango couple that adorns the back wall of the cantina. A knife-wielding butcher stands in the doorway of the kitchen next to strings of chorizos and *morcillas* (blood sausages), suggesting camp horror elements, and a disheveled ingénue, draped in a red boa, dips into a viscera-like bowl of pasta in a nod to La Boca's famed Italian immigrant population and influences.

Other elements, such as the cleaning supplies on the floor next to the bandoneon player, and a hose that snakes around the butcher's feet, make us wonder whether the photographer has posed the figures himself or just happened upon this scene after the exhausted performers have finished for the night. *Il piccolo vapore* thus documents the tedium of performing "authentic" tango for consumers ingesting both food and national identity in Buenos Aires's kitschy tourist havens, and it reveals how the symbols and icons enlisted in these simulacra are worn-out, sordid, superficial, and exhausted. "The photograph is an excuse for exorcising pain . . . for transforming in poetry the hangover from a second-class tequila," López has written.[46] Focusing on detritus or remains in the visual evocation of tango, López performs the ironic and contradictory maneuver of "outing" tango as formulaic, melodramatic, and gaudy, while also framing it in the context of camp taste. The latter style, developed in the wake of postmodernism, highlights an aesthetic of artifice rather than nature to comment on the truth of contemporary experience.

Undoubtedly, Hermenegildo Sábat (born in Montevideo in 1933) is the rioplatense artist who has sustained the longest and most varied engagement with tango in visual culture throughout the twentieth and early twenty-first centuries. Best known perhaps as a cartoonist for the Buenos Aires daily newspaper *Clarín*, "Menchi" Sábat's love affair with the tango and its creators has flourished for more than five decades and shows no signs of waning. Enormous versions of his drawings of musical greats such as Aníbal Troilo and Astor Piazzolla grace the walls of Buenos Aires's subway stations, and his winged portraits of an angelic Gardel attest to the public's reverence for the singer (and his foremost caricaturist) all over the city. But these beloved images of a beloved icon constitute only a fraction of Sábat's extensive collection. *Tango mío* (1981) and many other catalogs and exhibits testify to his long-term relationship with the tango, not only in homages to legendary figures such as Gardel, Troilo, and Piazzolla but also as a recurring "trace" element in works dedicated to other topics.[47]

Figure 3.18. Hermenegildo Sábat, *Lo que nos queda*, 1997, oil. Used by permission of Hermenegildo Sábat and Walter Santoro.

Informed by his work in journalism and political caricature, Sábat's art conflates the lyrical, felicitous aspects of tango music and dance with grimmer sociopolitical realities.[48] His large work *Lo que nos queda* (What remains) (figure 3.18), completed in 1997, takes on a special resonance in the wake of these lingering absences. In it Maestro Sábat resurrects iconic figures of tango history and suspends them between high art and caricature, between official and popular versions of that history. The dominant figure in the painting is the malevo or thug who incorporates his naked or nearly-naked dance partner in an embrace sharpened and hardened by the daggers he holds in both hands, one of them dripping blood.[49] The malevo and his female partner, the figures behind them, and the repeating face that streams across the top of the piece all appear in profile, contrasting with the face of Jorge Luis Borges, who gazes at the viewer from the bottom right center of the piece, his head supported on a blood-red cane. At Borges's side we find the great bandoneonist Aníbal Troilo, but Pichuco's hands are empty here, perhaps signifying the irretrievable loss of tango's inimitable interpreters.

Lo que nos queda is the simultaneous experience of what is lost and what is retained through memory.

There is also a hidden or submerged element in *Lo que nos queda*, a phantom face that looks up between the woman dancer's open legs on the left side of the painting. Perhaps it is a face of one of the disappeared, but it might just as well be one of the authoritarian *represores* or torturers of the dictatorship who has here receded into the "woodwork" of public memory, where he constitutes a horrific, menacing presence. This singular hidden face is juxtaposed with the feminine face repeated, chorus girl style, along the top edge of the work, a repetition that suggests both mass reproduction of tango-related images as well as a sustained rhythm.

Lo que nos queda, like the works of Sábat's four artist contemporaries profiled here, confirms tango's continuing power at the cusp of the twenty-first century. It references the potent mixture of pleasure and pain that constitutes the experience of tango, past and present, and it reveals how tango serves as a tool or lens with which to read and reread local, national, and international histories. We find that *what remains* and what's still to come in future depictions of tango is the paradoxical past in the present, "a memory incapable of dying," born and sustained in "a region in which Yesterday / Can be the Today, the Still and the Not Yet" (Borges and Bullrich 168–70).

Notes

1. Due to space restrictions, I do not consider performance art or conceptual art in this chapter.

2. Despite its proliferation in painting, drawing, engravings, album and CD covers, sheet music, sculpture, and so on, to my knowledge the prominent role of tango in art and visual culture has not been studied systematically. Ferrer takes up tango-themed art in *El Siglo de Oro del tango* and marks the 1970s as the moment of most intense proliferation (165). In terms of a field or genre of "tango art," my interest here is directed at works that explicitly incorporate tango topically, thematically, or in referential terms or that incorporate tango in a collective project such as an exhibit, catalogue, or single or multiauthor work identified with tango. The brief nature of this chapter prevents me from engaging in a more in-depth study; this is work that I hope art historians will take on in the future.

3. Space limitations, and in one case the refusal of the late painter's family members to authorize reproductions of his work, make it impossible to include many other artists who have worked on tango, including Horacio Butler, Juan Battle Planas, Juan Carlos Liberti, Aldo Severi, Juan Carlos Castagnino, Ricardo Carpani, Carlos Gorriarena, and Sigfredo Pastor.

4. Horacio Ferrer has served as the president of the Academy of Tango since the founding of the institution in 1990. See http://www.anacdeltango.org.ar/.

5. Visitors will find similar offerings in Montevideo, a secondary mecca for tango tourists.

6. The mural is located in the 700 block of Paraná Street in Buenos Aires.

7. In most cases the visual elements of early sheet music were textual rather than figurative, including the name of the composer, the title of the piece, and perhaps a dedication. In the majority of early scores, aesthetic considerations were limited to the font choice and perhaps the addition of a flourish or a small drawing of a music staff, bandoneon, or streetlamp. Nonetheless, many examples of early tango sheet music feature noteworthy illustrations, sometimes by well-known artists and, in a few cases, by the composers themselves. The aesthetic value of these documents has been acknowledged in museum exhibits of early sheet music, such as one held at the Centro Cultural Recoleta in Buenos Aires in 2010, and in handsome volumes, such as Gustavo Varela's *Tango: Una pasión ilustrada*, which reproduces art from dozens of *partituras* and includes essays by Varela and other tango historians on their significance.

8. When the artists Nicolás Rubió, a Catalan painter, and his Argentine wife Esther Barugel, a sculptor, realized that no research on the topic existed, they conducted their own investigation in the late 1960s, taking photos of every example they came across. They concluded that despite its dismissal by the so-called experts of the art world, the *filete porteño* "was a living art" in which new images constantly appeared to seduce the attentive observer (Estenssoro 161).

9. Tango appears in the work of future generations of artists specializing in the *grabado* as well, most notably in the work of Víctor Rebuffo. See Gené and Dolinko 100–102.

10. Iconic images include the emblematic *transbordador* bridge across the Riachuelo from the La Boca neighborhood to Maciel Island, the meatpacking plants that lined the Riachuelo, the ships and railroads that transported this commerce, and the undernourished and poorly paid workers who serviced these lucrative industries.

11. "El Chino" is not necessarily a reference to a person of Chinese or Asian descent in porteño Spanish but more generally refers to someone with features associated with indigenous populations (see Conde, *Diccionario etimológico del lunfardo*, 101).

12. Robert Farris Thompson analyzes Bellocq's illustration as showing "traits of the *canyengue colloquial*: dancers cheek to cheek, arms on high, and a woman falling on a man's chest as she danced" (163).

13. In a short section on tango in art and film in *El Siglo de Oro del tango* (1996), Horacio Ferrer names Figari as the first artist related to the tango (165–67). He also mentions the works of Alberto Ross, Valentín Thibon de Livian, Emilio Centurión, and Guillermo Facio Hébecquer.

14. These details were furnished by Fernando Saavedra Faget, great-grandson of Figari and administrator of a large collection of his works, in a personal interview conducted in his home in Montevideo on June 24, 2010.

15. Figari's show notably coincided with the young writer Jorge Luis Borges's return from Europe. Borges wrote a prologue to Samuel Oliver's study of Figari in which he describes the Uruguayan painter's style as lyric and credits him with a criollo sensibility (9). For Figari and others in his cohort, *lo criollo* refers to the selection of archetypical subjects in a concentrated effort to construct national identities, an effort engaged in by

both Argentines and Uruguayans in the early twentieth century. The criollo project is typically nostalgic, utopian, and linked to local landscapes.

16. Figari's success was further cemented at an exhibit in Paris later that same year in which he reportedly sold forty-six of the sixty works exhibited and was the subject of some twenty articles in the French press (Figari, *Figari* 26).

17. Figari's ideas have since been linked to Cuban revolutionary figure José Martí, whose writings in the late 1880s and early 1890s on the Nuestra América (pan-Latin American) theme were published in the Buenos Aires newspaper *La Nación*, where Figari probably read them (see Sanguinetti and Casasbellas 14–26).

18. Borges published an essay on Figari in *Criterio* that same year (*Figari*, 30).

19. "Pedro Figari y el clasicismo latinoamericano" advanced some of the same ideas Carpentier would later develop as the "marvelous real" in his prologue to *The Kingdom of This World* (1949). Other critics have also noticed the connections between writing and painting in Figari's work. In 1927 Samuel Oliver wrote that "there are writers who carry diaries, others write their memoirs, generally when they have lived out their years and many experiences. Figari painted his memories daily" (11).

20. Figari's inclusion of black subjects in his work contrasts with their exclusion by his most important predecessor in Uruguay, Juan Manuel Blanes (*Figari's Montevideo* 8).

21. Figari and turn-of-the-twentieth-century Uruguayan society in general recognized other categories as well as "black" and "white"; in his painting *Los mulatos*, the dancers execute a slightly more genteel version of what appears to be tango, with a violinist, bandoneonist, and pianist accompanying them in a salon setting (Oliver 29). Figari painted relatively few tangos, although social dance was a recurrent theme, and included representations of *pericones*, *saraos*, *bailes criollos*, as well as works with such titles as *Paso de baile* (Dance step), *Bailando* (Dancing), *Camino al baile* (On the way to the dance), and *Baile en la Estancia* (Dance at the country estate).

22. The second of these scenes also makes use of a curb or bank that bisects the image horizontally, dividing the social space between a background of spectators who gaze both at the dancers and implicitly at the viewer from an elevated plane, and a "streetlevel" foreground of active dancers.

23. For a more comprehensive analysis of *modernismo*, see Malosetti Costa.

24. According to Antonio Berni and other contemporaries, Pettoruti and his modernist cohort were guilty of creating "a world of forms so abstract . . . that they are transformed into frivolous and sentimental decoration" (Sullivan and Perazzo 296).

25. The creation of *La canción del pueblo* coincides with the rise of tango's popularity both at home and abroad, where it was being disseminated through musical and dance performances by famous personalities such as José Ovidio Bianquet, immortalized as "El Cachafaz," and through the relatively "new media" of sound recordings and films.

26. Mario Gradowczyk situates Pettoruti alongside Cézanne, Kandinsky, Klee, and Mondrian, as well as the Latin American artist and writer Torres-García (Sullivan and Perazzo 197). All, he points out, grappled with the paradox that what the image or work of art transmits is inexpressible, yet it is language that we must use to articulate the experience of contemplating or meditating on an image. The cubists and futurists addressed this conundrum directly by incorporating language in their pictorial works in the form

of texts, letters, numbers, words, and typographic styles (Sullivan and Perazzo 198). Besides creating a diverse body of paintings, drawings, collages, and mosaics, Pettoruti wrote on the role of the artist as critic, teacher, and administrator. In 1930 he began a career as an arts administrator, later becoming the director of the Provincial Museum of Fine Arts in the city of La Plata, where he was born. In that capacity Pettoruti made extensive visits to the United States, where he had shows and sold paintings in such cities as San Francisco, Portland, Seattle, St. Louis, and Kansas City, thus contributing to the vanguard of cultural circulation between North and Latin America.

27. Emilio Basaldúa's essay in the *Journal of Decorative and Propaganda Arts* on his father's tenure at the Teatro Colón includes outstanding illustrations of his gouache on hardboard designs for the sets of *Bolero, Le nozze de Figaro,* and *La Traviata,* among others.

28. The *sainete porteño* was a humorous theatrical work inserted between acts of a longer drama and usually focused on the experience of the immigrant population (see Pellarolo). The *grotesco criollo* similarly addressed the conflicts and ambivalence of daily life for the immigrant working class, obliged to "laugh and cry in a single gesture" (Ordaz).

29. Basaldúa's "pictoric interpretation" accompanied the tango "Como nadie," written by Manuel Mujica Láinez with music by Lucio Demare, while Torrallardona interpreted the tango "Sabor de Buenos Aires," written by Carlos Mastronardi with music by Miguel Caló.

30. Molar credited Borges with inspiring *14 con el tango.* José Basso composed the music for "Milonga de Albornoz." A YouTube posting of photos of Borges accompanied by Tata Cedrón's interpretation of the composition is available at http://www.youtube .com/watch?v=PflZWkVdE-U, accessed May 11, 2012.

31. The same verses by Borges also figure in some editions of his collection of milonga poems titled *Para las seis cuerdas,* published a year prior to the release of *14 con el tango,* and illustrated by Héctor Basaldúa.

32. Paradoxically, Borges would also participate in some of these "new tango" ventures, including *El tango* (1965), in which he recorded together with Piazzolla and his quintet and the singers Edmundo Rivera and Luis Medina Castro. The LP included musical versions of several of his milongas and tangos from *Para las seis cuerdas.*

33. For an analysis of Alonso's six works depicting the cadaver of Guevara, see Anreus.

34. Alonso illustrated some forty works of literature, including such formidable and wide-ranging assignments as Dante's *La divina comedia,* four volumes of Pablo Neruda's poetry, and the great Argentine classic *Martín Fierro.*

35. In several paintings from the *Manos anónimas y dirección obligatoria* series, painted in the early 1980s, Alonso himself is a victim of this torture and silencing (Alonso, *Carlos Alonso* 158–59).

36. A wrinkled sheet, cast aside in favor of the male figure's overcoat as the only protection against the bare mattress, adds to a sense of transitory encounter or disconnection to the "love" scene.

37. "Sigo creyendo en el arte y, sobre todo, en su memoria insobornable, no sentimental pero que es capaz de fijar las heridas que la realidad deja en nosotros; no creo que el arte pueda resolver ninguno de los problemas del mundo, máxime cuando la

ambiguedad invade el arte figurativo y la banalidad es consagrada de utilidad pública; los Estados del mundo intentan esterilizarnos con la miseria y el terror, pero es con ese amor aterrorizado con el que podemos construir nuestros cuadros" (n.p.).

38. Personal interview, July 10, 2010.

39. Email from Virginia Patrone, November 2, 2010.

40. Email document, May 31, 2010.

41. The Spanish lyrics can be found at todotango.com. The translation is mine.

42. Email document, November 9, 2010.

43. In 2010 father and son exhibited their works together in shows in La Plata and Buenos Aires, providing yet another intergenerational visual dialogue.

44. Personal interview with Daniel Kaplan, June 3, 2010. Kaplan also commented on his work in an email on May 31, 2010.

45. The series also acknowledges and mocks the criollo aesthetics of Borges, Figari, and other early twentieth-century proponents. See the restaurant's website http://www .ilpiccolovapore.com, accessed May 11, 2012, for images of the cantina. López's comment comes from "Arles Photography Festival Highlights," *Telegraph*, http://www.telegraph .co.uk/culture/photography/7867998/Arles-photography-festival-highlights.html?image =1, accessed May 11, 2012.

46. See "Vuelo de cabotage," http://www.marcoslopez.com/marcostextos.htm, accessed May 11, 2012.

47. In Sábat's *Paisajes* (Landscapes) series, painted in the late 1980s, a dancing couple sometimes hides in highly detailed "wallpaper" dominated by repeating organic forms. We see the same technique in his *Pareja* (Couple) series from the early 1990s. Tango dancers show up again—more predictably, perhaps—in the *Danzas peligrosas* (Dangerous dances) series.

48. In the 1980s Sábat created *Desaparecidos* (The disappeared ones), a series of portraits painted in the wake of the military dictatorship's "removal" of many artists, writers, labor activists, and others deemed subversive or threatening. *Madres,* another of Sábat's portraits from this period, pays tribute to the white scarf–wearing mothers of the Plaza de Mayo, who since the dictatorship have marched every Thursday in Buenos Aires's central public square to protest those disappearances—a practice that still continues with the grandmothers and other family members of these victims.

49. The *malevo*'s exposed penis might signal fear, were it not for its diminutive size: perhaps his bark is stronger than his bite. The element is typical of Sábat's incorporation of humor, even in his works of dark matter.

CHAPTER FOUR

Tango, Politics, and the Musical of Exile

ANTONIO GÓMEZ

Paris is usually considered the second capital of tango. It is obvious to connoisseurs of tango—or even regular consumers of the music—that Paris is the international location most frequently mentioned in tango lyrics and poetry. It is also common to understand the Paris–tango association as a historical occurrence limited to the years between the First and Second World Wars, when tango was absorbed by the porous show business of the French capital—a process most commonly referred to from the Argentine perspective as tango's "conquest" of Paris. It was in that moment of fluid communication between Buenos Aires and Paris (via the port of Marseilles), when singers, dancers, musicians, and tango orchestras would not infrequently relocate to Montmartre and tour Europe, that a repertoire of Parisian images, concepts, stories, and characters were incorporated into the rhetoric of tango. Most mentions of Paris, its neighborhoods, bridges, and streets, or even French characters date back to those years. By the 1940s it had already become a fossilized set of commonplaces, and it is not until the 1970s that the fantasy of tango in Paris was revisited by a new type of Argentine exile, one less concerned with the picturesque characters of the Parisian landscape and more with the city's status as a refuge or safe house in the midst of political (and thus aesthetic) instability.

The early internationalization of tango via Paris had a decisive impact not only in economic terms but also in terms of the critical and social recognition of the genre—especially in Buenos Aires, where tango had until that moment been marginal and sometimes even clandestine. Given that tango is a particularly self-reflexive form, the circulation of artists and tango personalities between Paris and Buenos Aires was immediately seized on by tango composers and soon became a dominant topic. There were two basic approaches to narrating this new scenario: the humorous tone of tangos that stressed the contrasts between the still provincial culture of Buenos Aires and Paris's metropolitan, sophisticated lifestyle, and the pathetic tone of tangos that turned this experience of difference into sentimental tragedies. "Araca París" (Beware of Paris, 1930, music by Ramón Collazo and lyrics by Carlos Lenzi) and "Anclao en París" (Anchor'd in Paris, 1931, music by Guillermo Barbieri and lyrics by Enrique Cadícamo) are, respectively, the most popular and representative examples of each tendency, as well as standards in the repertoire of Carlos Gardel (Barsky and Barsky).[1] From either perspective, tangos about Paris establish a list of common tropes that include the fantasy of the easy, instant success in Paris of any tango-related activity (instrumental performance, singing, dancing, or even sporting a "tango" look); the revelation that this fantasy is usually, if not always, groundless; complaining and whining about failure, in most cases translated into poverty, romantic disappointment, or both; and the hyperbolic representation of distance or separation from and nostalgia for the homeland (centered on Buenos Aires, one of its specific neighborhoods, or even a particular corner of the city).

It is important to underline two privileged mechanisms of representation in this corpus, both of which illustrate the affective investment made in the narrative of the tango experience in Paris. First, the process of appropriation of the symbolic center by a peripheral cultural product was often represented in terms of seduction and romantic conquest of a feminine Paris by a masculine Argentina, as an erotic act regardless of the result of the attempt. The line that most effectively expresses this ideal of erotic domination is "Morocho y argentino, rey de París" (Swarthy and Argentine, the king of Paris) in "Araca París."[2] The eroticization of tango's expansion to new markets signals the affective component mediating the relationship between Argentina and France: entrée into the domains of French culture responds to the logics of desire. Tango lyrics reflect in the language of simple love stories the seductive power of metropolitan institutions and Argentine culture's need to be recognized at a universal level. This desire can be described within many levels and facets of Argentine culture in the late nineteenth and early twentieth century, but the erotic and intimate imprint of tango (manifest in the content of the lyrics and especially in the close contact of the dance) transforms a latent political principle into an overt statement, a socially threatening irruption of the unconscious in the material. Second, even in the euphoric context of success in Paris, the anxiety of separation and distance from the origin (that is, Buenos Aires) takes the form of memento mori. Death—in the form of a fear of dying away from home—is the principle that structures the narration of the experience of dislocation and the paradoxical by-product of the triumphant adventure of tango in Paris.

Even if "La canción de Buenos Aires" (The song of Buenos Aires, 1932, music by Orestes Cufaro and Azucena Maizani and lyrics by Manuel Romero) does not mention Paris, it might be the text that best synthesizes these commonplaces. In this self-reflexive song, a song in which the story of a genre is told, tango is not only the topic but also one of the interlocutors addressed by the speaker. The narrator (or singer) speaks both to "tango" and to the city of Buenos Aires and represents tango as a triumphant peripheral product: "This is tango, the song of Buenos Aires / born in the slums, now reigning in all the world" (Este es el tango, canción de Buenos Aires / nacido en el suburbio, que hoy reina en todo el mundo). Tango operated as a way to overcome the anguish of separation when the speaker was displaced: "When I found myself far away from you, Buenos Aires / my only consolation / was in the notes of a sweet tango" (Buenos Aires, cuando lejos me vi / sólo hallaba consuelo / en las notas de un tango dulzón). Now that the speaker seems to be at home, he or she hopes tango will be a consolation in his final moments: "And I ask of my fate a favor / that at the end of my life / I can hear the weeping of the bandoneon / playing your nostalgic song" (Y le pido a mi destino el favor / de que al fin de mi vida / oiga el llorar del bandoneón / entonando tu nostálgica canción). Distance and death are represented as comparable ordeals, and in both cases tango is given a curative value.

Death finds no place, however, in the cheerful, satiric story told in "Araca París" (1930), which enlists the imaginary of romantic conquest. The anecdote in this song centers on the narrator's illusion of an easy life in Paris, since he is a handsome, exotic Argentine man who can seduce wealthy women with his capacity to dance tango. Tango is assigned a specific economic value: "with three tango steps you will be a millionaire" (con tres cortes de tango sos millonario). Paris is feminized, represented as a resource for male agency. The fact that this is a story of defeat, and that the narrator does not succeed in becoming a gigolo, indicates that this trope was a familiar one in the popular imaginary and was already the object of deconstruction.

All of these topoi, common in tango's depiction of Argentine displacement to Paris, would be recuperated—and sometimes revised—in the films that

I discuss in this chapter, but this is especially true of the Eros–Thanatos axis just delineated. I will analyze the way two films released in 1985, *Tangos, the Exile of Gardel* (*El exilio de Gardel: Tangos*) by Fernando Solanas and *The Pavements of Saturn* (*Les trottoirs de Saturne*) by Hugo Santiago, use tango as a thematic and rhetorical artifice for the cinematic representation of the political in relation to the circulation of Argentine culture between Buenos Aires and Paris. The immediate referents of the stories narrated in these films are the experiences of exiles during the last dictatorship in Argentina (1976–1983), when both Solanas and Santiago were living in Paris. But there is also a conscientious effort to transcend the contingency of the local, individual context and elaborate a generalizing statement that refers to the nation as a whole. We could even say that these two films appear among the last examples of such an effort in the Argentine tradition. This allegorizing impulse does not only consist of a synecdochal procedure by which exiles stand for the Argentine community as a whole but also of the historical, diachronic amplification of this process so that the present (the political) and the past (history) can be read as a unitary phenomenon. We will pay particular attention to the role of tango, the history of tango in Paris, and the way tango registers its own history in this process.

In the 1980s, a period that marked the last years of dictatorship and the first stages of redemocratization in Argentina, two Argentine directors were seemingly shooting the same film in Paris. Each was making a film that told the story of a bandoneon player and a group of Argentine exiles in France, but each was also a fable about tango, history, and national "identity" and a treatise on how Argentine exiles and their culture were perceived in the cultural center of the world, the "capital of all exiles"—to quote the narrator of *Tangos, the Exile of Gardel*. Judging from the varied results of their efforts, it is admittedly difficult to maintain that *Tangos, the Exile of Gardel* by Fernando Solanas and *The Pavements of Saturn* by Hugo Santiago, released in the same year, are in fact the same film. The differences are apparent not only at the formal and aesthetic level but also in the way each approaches the present. Nevertheless, both films respond to a similar impulse and stem from the same basic premises: there is a story to be told of the Argentine exile in Paris, and this story has to be told in the style of tango. However, there is a fundamental difference in what each film understands as *tango* and what the relationship between tango and history should be, a difference that a shallow reading of the films may miss by employing a simplified (and colonizing) notion of tango as merely an expression of national identity, separated from the logics of art in general. At this superficial level, tango belongs to the world of folklore rather than to the world of the arts. I want to argue here that both films use tango as an instrument for the expression of Argentine particularity in terms of affect, art, and politics, and they do so by representing tango not as a commodity for metropolitan consumption or the differential result of Argentine "otherness" but as a structure of thinking, feeling, creating, and resolving historical conflicts.

Since both films were atypical products in the French and Argentine cinematographic industries, they do not fit easily into either history. Financed mainly by French funds, both were conceived as mainstream feature films for commercial exhibition. They were shot on location in Paris and postproduced in France and Argentina, and their casts (especially in the case of Solanas's film) include notable figures of the French and Argentine cinema industry, as well as some iconic actors of the Argentine exile community in Europe. Though both films were successfully released in France and widely reviewed by the press, their circulation since has been rather limited—especially in the case of Santiago's film, which is now a cult object and difficult to obtain. The films' limited circulation and commercial success might be attributed to two factors: first, their linguistic hybridity, as dialogues are spoken in a mix of Argentine Spanish and various levels of French to characterize the speech of the Argentine exiles; second, the unique nature of the late twentieth-century Argentine exile experience, bound by temporal and spatial specificity. To facilitate my exposition here, I will provide short summaries of the plots of both films.

The script for *The Pavements of Saturn* was written by Santiago in collaboration with Juan José Saer and Jorge Semprún over a period of five years.[3] The original version is by Santiago and Saer, while Semprún's role was to revise the text to incorporate a "French tone" (Civale). The setting is the Paris of October 1986 (that is, it is a futuristic piece), but the story is closely related to Santiago's first feature film *Invasion* (*Invasión*, 1969), which he cowrote with Jorge Luis Borges. Based on a plot conceived by Borges and Adolfo Bioy Casares, *Invasion* told the story of a conspiracy to resist an invasion in Aquilea (an imaginary city) in 1957. The exiles that the plot of *The Pavements of Saturn* follows come from Aquilea, a country that has recently suffered a military coup and is shaken by civil unrest. Fabián Cortés—played by the renowned tango musician Rodolfo Mederos—is a successful bandoneon player who has lived in Paris for years, but whose life has been altered by the events in Aquilea, events that have changed him from a "travelling musician" into an "exile."[4] Fabián falls into a sudden state of melancholy and is considering the possibility of returning to Aquilea when his sister Marta comes for a visit. Marta, a guerrilla activist twenty years younger than Fabián who has been forced to flee the country, convinces her brother to return to Aquilea with her and take part in the plans of her militant organization to sneak several activists back into the country. At the same time, Fabián is haunted by the "presence" of Eduardo Arolas, a legendary Argentine bandoneon player who died in Paris in 1924. Cortés is in the process of recording an album of new interpretations of Arolas's compositions. He also claims to meet with Arolas several times a week in the streets of Paris to have conversations with him and even to receive professional advice from him. Cortés's girlfriend, a French lawyer who helps exiles from Aquilea with their political asylum papers, is puzzled by his new mood and makes every effort to "understand" these people and their conflicts, though with limited success. Against the recommendations of his Parisian friends, Fabián Cortés finally decides to return to Aquilea. After meeting with the guerrillas to coordinate travel plans, he receives instructions not to make the trip, which it turns out was a setup, and all those who made it to Aquilea have been killed. In the last sequence of the film, Fabián tries to warn his sister of this ominous turn of events, only to find her dead body before he himself is also killed in the streets of Paris.

Tangos, the Exile of Gardel is Solanas's first strictly fictional feature film. It combines a realist narrative with musical segments, some absurd humor, and a few surreal scenes, but the overall structure is that of a fictional film. The story is narrated by an Argentine teenager exiled in Paris with her mother after the kidnapping of her father, a lawyer who represented the families of the disappeared. She tells the story of a group of musicians, dancers, and actors who are trying to put on a stage show titled *The Exile of Gardel*. This is a musical piece conceived as an instrument for spreading the word about the Argentine situation. Juan Uno, who still resides in Buenos Aires, is writing the text, and Juan Dos, an exiled bandoneon player, is composing the music. After long discussions of how to end the piece, the group previews the show for the French producers, who finally decide that *The Exile of Gardel* is "too Argentine" for the French audience and is doomed to fail on the stage. This plot line is intertwined with the personal experiences of several other members of the group. An aging professor of history whose daughter and granddaughter have been disappeared is writing a text that reflects on the exile of José de San Martín, the hero of Argentine independence who died in Boulogne sur Mer in 1850. The historian's wife travels to Argentina to search for her granddaughter with the collaboration of the Grandmothers of the Plaza de Mayo.[5] The narrator's mother—who is also the central figure in the musical piece and Juan Dos's girlfriend—is dealing with the angst of exile and the need to return home. As with the musical they are trying to stage, there is no real resolution for the narrative plot of the film. Juan Dos apparently returns to Argentina after learning about the death of his mother, and the film tries to end on an optimistic note when the narrator states, facing the camera and the audience, that exile has only taught her that there is still so much of life ahead.

The most significant point of coincidence between these two films, and the reason why I argue that they can be read as *the same film*, is that they both aim to provide an explanation of the Argentine in a context where the Argentine is elusive, confusing, and needs to be explained in order to be understood by a foreign subject. Of course, tango turns out to be, in both cases, the closest and easiest tool at hand for assembling such an explanation. The basic premise in both stories is this: because the French cannot understand the Argentine political conjuncture or the moral ordeal faced by the exiles—who, from the French point of view, are not the only exiles in the world, or even in Paris, and whose country is not the only one going through difficulties—the Argentines must find a way to offer a comprehensible version of their history, culture, and identity, which they do by creating a tango show. Now this notion rests on the institutionalization of a radical difference between the Argentine and the French: Argentine history, politics, and culture do not follow the same rules and logic, so their extreme particularity must be justified.

The recognition of this difference presents a paradox in Argentine discourse, since *The Pavements of Saturn* and *Tangos, the Exile of Gardel* are part of a national tradition that conceives of Argentine culture as a natural continuation of French culture, with no contradiction between the two. This notion had either taken the form of "emancipation," affirming the equal value of peripheral cultures and the right of Argentine cultural production to belong to universal culture—that is, French culture (Borges's lecture "The Argentine Writer and Tradition" offers a good example of this tendency)— or had been framed as neocolonial critique and identified Argentine culture as constrained by the process of colonial imitation (as Solanas has contended, for example, in his film *The Hour of the Furnaces*, released in 1968). In any case this is the ideologeme that sustains the films by making France the natural domain of Argentine exile. It is thus odd, if not incongruous, that these films still insist on the mechanics of difference and explanation.

Using tango as the ideal instrument with which to communicate the peculiarities of Argentine history presents certain contradictions. On the one hand, late twentieth-century tango still retained elements of exoticism and typicality and could be consumed in Paris as an import. During the stages of institutional formation of Argentina in the nineteenth century, the intellectual, economic, and social elites of the emerging nation (especially those from the port of Buenos Aires, but also from other major cities in the provinces, which were by then comparable to Buenos Aires in size and political leadership) regularly visited France. A trip to Europe had become a necessary element in the formation of the well-educated subject, and French was the natural language of culture for the privileged classes (see Viñas, *Literatura argentina y política*; Sarlo, "Victoria Ocampo o el amor de la cita"). By the early twentieth century, the presence of wealthy Argentines in Paris was already a common literary topic—even in French literature (see for example Louis-Ferdinand Céline's *Voyage au bout de la nuit*). Tango played a significant role in the renovation of the Argentine tradition of cultural pilgrimage to the French capital in the 1920s and 1930s. The acceptance of Argentine dance and music in the cosmopolitan circles frequented by intellectuals in Paris was part of the process of integration of an emerging Argentine culture in the international cultural market.

At the same time, tango was a music that the French "felt as their own" (*Paris Tango* 77) and could also be thought of as a Parisian export to the world, since it was from Paris, and not Buenos Aires, that tango began to circulate as a global cultural commodity (Thompson 236; see also Pelinski, *El tango nómade*). As is well known, the experience of tango in the 1920s in Paris had reversed (or at least distorted) the notions of place of origin and place of reception in the case of tango, when the success of tango in Parisian nightclubs and cabarets had in turn allowed this outcast genre to be subsequently accepted in Buenos Aires. Since then, tango has been the privileged vehicle for representing the relations between Argentina and France.[6]

We will address the relationship between Argentine political history, the experience of Argentine otherness in France, and tango in *The Pavements of Saturn* and *Tangos, the Exile of Gardel* by asking the following questions: How do these films articulate the notion of a fundamental lack of understanding of the Argentine in French culture? How do the directors use tango to narrate and explain Argentine history? And finally, how does this use of tango express a particular view of the political?

Understanding Argentina

Danielle, Fabián Cortés's French girlfriend, is the element used to express the disconnect between Argentina and France in *The Pavements of Saturn*. In a conversation (in French) with Pablo, one of the exiles from Aquilea, played by Hugo Santiago himself, Danielle complains that the exiles are overreacting, that their country will eventually move beyond this brutal dictatorship and be a normal country again. Pablo replies: "Aquilea has never been a normal country" (L'Aquilea n'a jamais était un pays normal). Danielle concludes: "You are monsters of pride" (Vous êtes monstres de fierté). So, with conflicting arguments, both characters agree that Aquilea/Argentina is substantially different from other nations. The central narrative impulse in the film is the overwhelming need of the French to understand Argentina, an impulse that necessarily reduces music, stories, and people into nothing more than a signifier of the Argentine.

The Pavements of Saturn opens with Fabián's disappearance. He has not come to the club where he performs every night. Nobody seems to know where to locate him. Some of his friends, especially Danielle, start to worry and consider reporting the case to the police. The situation not only reflects the cases of thousands of missing people in Argentina but also is a prolepsis of the resolution of the film. In the midst of Danielle's search, the viewer learns that Fabián is regularly meeting Arolas, who ostensibly has been dead for over sixty years. This search leads to the overt expression of the inscrutable character of the Argentine. When Danielle discusses the Arolas situation with a French girlfriend, her friend replies: "It looks like he is laughing at you. Or maybe he is talking to you in code. If he says that he just met a colleague who died sixty years ago, he is for sure sending a coded message. All you have to do is decode it" (On dirai qu'il se moque de toi. Ou alors il te parle par énigmes. S'il te dit qu'il vient de rencontrer un collègue mort il y a soixante ans, sans doute te transmet–il un message codé. Il ne te reste qu'à le déchiffrer).

What kind of message can be encoded in the reference to Arolas? It becomes obvious that Cortés and Arolas are "historical" doppelgängers, the same person living in different times, and that their stories are going to follow parallel trajectories as well. In this sense Fabián's exile has been preannounced by Arolas's, and he is forced to live Arolas's fate again. This would be the most obvious hidden message in Fabián's "hallucinations": "you can understand me by following Arolas's life story," which is nothing more than a rephrasing of the commonplace of history as a teacher. Now, there is also the more general reading of this reference: after all, Fabián is claiming to be talking to the dead, and this should not go unnoticed in the context of the immediate postdictatorship period. Not only is there a recognition of the voice of the dead but also the fact that there is something to learn from the dead, and Fabián is there to listen and convey their message. At the same time, there is the denial of death, the proposal that the dead still live. These notions could well represent ideas that Fabián has come to understand in his existence as an exile and that Danielle as an outsider to the Argentine experience cannot yet comprehend.

The gap between French and Argentine culture becomes a generation gap between the new political exiles and the old expatriates who question the validity of violence as a political tool. Mario—a painter who, very much like Fabián (and Hugo Santiago), lived in Paris before becoming an "exile" by virtue of political events—vigorously opposes the methods of the guerrilla groups and has fallen into a non-conflictive nihilism. He is the one who asserts that "the Aquilea we come from no longer exists. They replaced it with a different one. A fake one" (la Aquilea de la que venimos ya no existe. Pusieron otra en su lugar. Una falsa), and he is the one who confronts the young guerrillas with a discourse that somehow echoes the "theory of the two demons."[7] Even though this is a very common opposition in Argentine cultural production and political discourse, space and assimilation seem to play a role in Santiago's particular representation of the conflict: it seems that in this case it is not only a matter of generations but also a matter of location. That is, the clash between the old expatriates and the young activists, represented in the film in very histrionic, cathartic performances, does not stem only from the difference in the political style of the 1950s versus that of the 1970s but also is a reflection concerning the effects of distance on the construction of the political imperative in terms of time, space, and cultural separation.

Solanas's film takes a different stand on the generational issue. In *Tangos, the Exile of Gardel* it is those of the younger generation who do not understand the state of melancholy of their parents and can only relate to the past in terms of affect. María, the narrator, questions her mother's attitudes toward their common situation as exiles and attends the meetings of the committee of solidarity with the Argentine exiles not because of her political convictions but because she sees the sessions as a way to reconnect with her missing father. National history has turned into a family issue for her. Since the film attempts to represent the point of view of the younger generations (in a sort of displacement of Solanas's own perspective), the clash between French and Argentine cultures is replaced by the conflict between a generation of Argentines who took history into their own hands and failed and a generation that does not see politics as an urgent matter. Here in his first film of the 1980s, Solanas clearly alters his position from the earlier, more radical political stance of the Third Cinema.

There is a point in *Tangos, the Exile of Gardel* in which the lack of understanding of Argentine history and identity is crucial. The group has created a new genre for the show they want to present. They call it *tanguedia*, a neologism that combines *tango* as a stem (and the main material for the show) with the suffix that appears in the complementary words *tragedia* (tragedy) and *comedia* (comedy). The new genre is thus a sort of hybrid between comedy and tragedy centered on tango. Tango is always seen as a privileged didactic tool, as the most direct way to represent Argentina, even if this generalization is in fact a fictional construct that eventually fails. The tanguedia's title is also *The Exile of Gardel*. This title is called into question twice in the film. First, when Juan Dos is about to present a preview of the music in a nightclub, an official from the Argentine embassy asks, "*The Exile of Gardel*? As if Gardel had been exiled?" ('El exilio de Gardel,' como si hubiera estado exilado Gardel?). Later in the film, one of the French producers regrets that the title is not more explicitly referential: "It's a shame. Why don't we get to see Gardel?" (C'est dommage! Pour quoi on ne voit pas Gardel?). For the Argentine, the representative of the official point of view at that moment, it is the association of Gardel with anything political that is questionable—tango and politics should not mix. For the French, it is Gardel's absence that is dissatisfying, since Gardel is the only icon that could be recognized by the French audience, the element that would make the play understandable. They also argue that the result is "a bit local," "too Argentine." Juan's response is: "Exile is about us. About the South . . . About the Río de la Plata" (El exilio es nuestro. Es bien sureño . . . del Río de la Plata). His answer identifies *exile* as the point that is difficult to transfer to a different code, when the producer's remark made reference to *tango*. So for Juan, tango and exile are the same thing. I will return to this point later.

As a language for explaining the peculiarities of the Argentine, tango (as music, lyrics, and dance) seems to be insufficient. In the discussion with the producers, the artists need to keep paraphrasing the piece to make its meaning clear—a gesture that implies the complete failure of the programmatic impulse behind the show: to tell the story of what is going on in Buenos Aires.

The genetic process of the piece sheds light on the value of understanding. As mentioned before, Juan Uno is the author of the story and still resides in Buenos Aires, from where he sends the text to Juan Dos, who composes the music. When Pierre, the French general director of the production, visits Juan Dos in his attic to get the text of the play, Juan presents him with an old suitcase that contains a mess of loose papers, stray notes, and drawings. "Is this the show?" asks Pierre, surprised. Juan Dos justifies the disorder: "Uno writes in bars and restaurants with no logic.... We must find the overall logic." That is, Buenos Aires is where history takes place, Paris is where history has to be understood—and explained to others. It is, though, the joint experience of Buenos Aires and Paris on the part of the protagonists that produces both versions of *Tangos, the Exile of Gardel*.

I Only Have a Tango . . .

How does each film construct tango to explain Argentina? *The Pavements of Saturn* focuses on the image of Arolas, and Solanas's film centers on Gardel, two tango names particularly associated with France. This association is due not only to their French origin (Arolas, originally Arola, was the son of French immigrants; Gardel may have been born in Toulouse)[8] but also mainly because of their role in the introduction of tango in Paris. Of course, Arolas is a more obscure figure in the history of tango than Gardel and certainly more suitable for use as an "enigma." When Fabián Cortés makes reference to Arolas and recovers his music, he is taking a part in the writing of tango's history and he is choosing Arolas over an ample assortment of Argentine characters (either real or fictional) who have an important role in the development of tango in Paris, or in the history of Argentine exile in France. Choosing Arolas means not choosing Gardel, who is the triumphant conqueror of the Parisian scene, or the farcical protagonist of "Araca París," the arrogant but likeable morocho who fails to succeed in Paris and returns home after learning his lesson. Arolas is a more tragic figure. His is an unfortunate story, marked by personal failure.[9] Against the legend that he died a premature death in 1924 at age thirty-two as a result of a knife fight over a woman, some historical reconstructions suggest a less romanticized story: Arolas left Buenos Aires to overcome the personal crisis of being left by his wife, only to become an alcoholic and die of tuberculosis in a Parisian hospital. To the viewer (especially those viewers who are not well versed in the history of tango), the enigma of Arolas takes the form of substituting this less publicized musician for the stereotypes of Argentine *tangueros* in Paris, both real and fictional. The experience of Arolas in Paris is not especially picturesque—not even when retouched by popular imagination—so his presence in the film entails the recovery of an aesthetic project: Arolas is presented not so much in the story of his life as in his music. Fabián's recording of Arolas's compositions stages a return to Arolas's expression of the Parisian experience, even if he did not compose all of his tangos in Paris. It is as well a return to the stylization of that expression through the elimination of the lyrics and the role of the singer and through the simplification of the orchestral configuration into the "sexteto."[10] In this sense Santiago's filmic effort to explain Argentina through tango is an act of digging into the past to excavate a nucleus of sense and truth in order to expose it to a new light and reinsert it in the flow of history. Not even the vanguard aesthetic superimposed on Arolas's music by the new players can outshine the ghostly reappearance of the past as the force that can provide the answers for the present ordeal.

In one of the tangos written by Solanas himself for *Tangos, the Exile of Gardel*, the voice of Roberto Goyeneche sings: "I only have a tango with which to tell the story of my exile" (Solo tengo un tango pa' contar mi exilio). The film proposes that tango is the only rhetoric suitable and available for the narration of the present. The tanguedia that the group of exiles is staging is mainly a narrative device, conceived to tell the story of what is happening in Buenos Aires. There is not only a clear awareness of the importance of communicating that story but also of the fact that tango is the only means for doing it. In the preview they stage for the producers, the artists are confronted with the fact that not only are the rhetoric and the narrative instruments considered provincial but also the topic itself. The imaginary of tango and the tango songs themselves are seen by the French producers as being too obscure for the metropolitan audience, not recognizably exotic in the way of early twentieth-century tango. This contrast is stressed by one of the producers: "The music, the characters, even the tangos. It's a little too Argentine for us" (La musique, les personnages, même les tangos. C'est un peut trop argentin pour nous).

There is a significant displacement in the translation during this conversation taking place in French. In the urge to justify his view, Juan Dos switches to Spanish and claims: "El exilio es nuestro. Es bien sureño . . . del Río de la Plata," (Exile is about us, about the South . . . about the Río de la Plata), which is translated into French as "Il dit que la tanguedie c'est vraiment du sud, que ça vient de Río de la Plata" (He's saying that the tanguedia is really from the South, that it comes from Río de la Plata). In the passage from Spanish to French, the concept of "exile" has disappeared, as well as the notion of belonging to or being intrinsically about the group of Argentines, since the French translation also discards the possessive adjective. "Exile" is not really the topic of the piece (which, according to the purposes described by Juan Dos and the fragments that we see on screen, is actually about the events that are taking place in Buenos Aires), but the historical process that makes it possible, its condition of possibility. That is the reason why not understanding exile as a historical (or even ontological) process preempts the French from understanding the show, including the music, the characters, and the tangos. But the translation also proves that exile and tango bear equal value. The word *exilio* has actually been translated as "tanguedie." This transposition suggests, on the one hand, that exile as a historical process only exists in its output, in the cultural production that it can generate. On the other hand, it also insinuates that history has been replaced by its representation, that the spectacle of tango has taken the place of exile.

Now, why do the film and the artists in exile candidly trust the expressive potential of tango to convey *argentinidad* to the French audience? Most probably, because of the historical pressure exerted by the previous triumph of tango in Paris, the fact that tango *did* work once as a rhetorical device to incorporate Argentine autochthony into the metropolitan imaginary. Historical change might thus be the force behind the fact that tango, and the traits that made it attractive in the past, such as exoticism, uninhibited sensuality, and an overexposed sentimentality, no longer serve as a language of communication between center and periphery. Both Paris and Argentina are not in the 1980s what they were in the 1920s, and the same goes for tango.[11] The dysphoric resolution of the project of staging the tanguedia indicates that Solanas's premise diametrically differs from Santiago's proposal of stylized repetition. *Tangos, the Exile of Gardel* contends that for Argentines living in Parisian exile in the 1980s, tango is an exercise of double nostalgia: for Argentina and for the Paris of the 1920s, a predisposition to evasion that, in the narrative, is punished with failure.

The Lesson of Tango

We return finally to our last question, that of what each of these narrative uses of tango as difference reveals concerning the political. This, I argue, is where the crucial difference between Santiago and Solanas resides. Both directors rescue from tango a lesson on history: tango has, in the past, represented the experience of displacement. There is something to be learned from tango if we use it as an archive of Argentine history. Tango, like a history book, can provide us with answers for performing Argentine identity in France, for explaining Argentine particularities to the French. The use of tango as a didactic instrument is thus legitimized by history: we can find in tango a discourse and an affective structure that somehow resolves the conflict of dislocation—either physical or symbolic. "Anclao en París" serves as the key example of this dynamic. It accompanies one of the surreal sequences of Solanas's film in which the characters of the 1980s interact with personalities of Argentine history such as the military general José de San Martín, the singer Carlos Gardel, and the musician Enrique Discépolo. The incorporation of this tango number in the film resolves the search for a finale to the show: it is in Gardel's appearance and performance of this song that Juan Dos and Mariana experience an epiphany related to the finale.[12] "Anclao en París" tells a story that diverges so significantly from the experiences of these exiles that it is certainly puzzling as a dramatic resolution, unless we are aware that it is not the story told by the song but Carlos Gardel's presence that is being proposed as a dramatic resolution—much in the way that *The Pavements of Saturn* uses Eduardo Arolas to recover and actualize a particular zeitgeist.

The difference between the two films stems, though, from the capacity of tango to interpolate history, to erupt as a creative possibility in a context in which tango has only been assigned a role that has to do with tradition. Can tango be used as a language to narrate new experiences? As we have already mentioned, Santiago stages a situation in which tango is the re-creation of experience. The relationship between Cortés and Arolas entails an intervention only at the level of execution. Cortés's agency is limited to the interpretation of the music scores composed by Arolas. Replaying his music and reliving his life become two sides of the same experience. But Cortés resists seeing Arolas's story as a mere warning and intends to take an active role in the writing of history. When Danielle takes Fabián to Arolas's gravesite and urges him to accept the fact that Arolas indeed died sixty years earlier, she is also telling him the truth regarding Arolas's stay in Paris—that is, that he was defeated by exile, that he never made it back home (not even as a corpse, since he is still buried in Paris), that the dramatic version of his death is only the product of popular imagination. Fabián stubbornly refuses to accept this rational explanation and insists: "He is alive. I saw him yesterday. I talked to him. He talked to me" (Il es vivant. Je l'ai vu hier. Je l'ai parlé. Il m'a parlé). There seems to be in Fabián a will not so much to write history but to "rewrite" it, to correct Arolas's ineffective life by resuscitating not only his music but also the figure himself. If his life mirrors Arolas's own life in the 1920s, his return to the homeland will serve the purpose of redeeming Arolas, tango, his generation, and himself of the sin of not assuming a role in history. Within the logic of the film, Fabián understands his return to Aquilea as a form of political agency.

That it all ends with Fabián's death is not really a sign of defeat. If there is the pessimistic implication that the repressive forces in control of Aquilea are unquestionably stronger and more efficient than the forces of resistance, there is also the realization that Fabián did succeed in rewriting Arolas's life and in investing the figure of the bandoneon player in Paris with a heroic death.[13] The narrative has granted success to Fabián's impulse toward agency in two ways: he gets to correct Arolas's experience, and he gets to escape from a predetermined life, limited to an imitation of the past. His death also overwrites his earlier remark about the political tone of a conversation with friends: "Politics again! What a drag! Not my problem: I play the bandoneon" (Otra vez la política. ¡Que opio! Yo no tengo problema: yo soy bandoneonista). Even if, however, Fabián has taken steps toward political redemption, we still have the problem of originality: tango remains a territory for reiteration, a domain where the only intervention of new generations can be through rectification but never creation. Cortés is recognized as a very original and genuine artist—there is a significant investment in the construction of the character as an inspired creator, a romantic genius, and even an "artiste maudit": lonely and moody; misunderstood by his epoch, his friends, and his peers; lost in his inner world; but with the capacity to move an audience and generate a profound aesthetic experience. He achieves this not by producing his own music but by interpreting music that someone else has composed. The difference between his activity and that of any other musician who is not a composer, though, stems from the fact that Cortés's agenda resembles that of an archeologist who excavates the past to recover something that is lost and to expose it to a new light. This is the only function the film seems to assign to tango: to serve as an exhibit of the past.

Solanas's film, on the other hand, works hard to construct an image of tango as a vigorous, active cultural space that embodies Argentina as a whole—albeit in a simplification that, first, omits the generational conflicts that from the 1960s forward limited the representational value of tango as the main product of Argentine popular culture, and second, does not reflect the regional diversity of the country's many forms of popular music. In this film tango is characterized as a living form of art, as the natural arena for the expression of current social and political conflicts. It is the privileged form of expression for the communication of Argentine reality, but it is as well an art form not bound by the constraints of tradition. In Solanas's tango, innovation is a major force capable of inventing new genres (the tanguedia), and composition is strictly an act of the present—so much so that the piece that the group is rehearsing is still in the making. Tango's relation with history differs substantially from Santiago's proposal of redemptive reiteration. In Solanas's reasoning, as we have already explained, tango and history are homologues. Tango is just the name assigned in this narrative to history, exile, and reality. For him there is no space outside of tango in the Argentine experience. The sequence that visually condenses this notion is the segment titled "Volver," one of the last chapters of the film. It takes place in the public building where Gerardo, the exiled professor, works as a night guard. Both San Martín and Gardel come for a visit. The three figures represent, respectively, three different moments of possibility: San Martín stands for the Argentina that was still only a project, since he died in 1850, before the government of the new republic was fully consolidated; Gardel, who died in 1935, is the embodiment of the Argentina that had already celebrated its centennial and was at the peak of its economic prosperity; finally, our 1970s exile protagonist, the father of a child who has been "disappeared" and the grandfather of an appropriated child, is the human face of the Argentina that was then disintegrating.[14] The actor who plays the exiled professor, Lautaro Murúa, was also an icon of exiled intellectuals and artists. The three men drink *mate*, chat about returning home, and listen to Gardel's recording of his tango "Volver" (Return). The scene, which mimics the sentimental tone of much tango poetry, proposes a summary of Argentine history in which tango plays the fundamental role of synthesizing past and present in a universalizing text and gesture. As Argentine history can be reduced to a tale of exile, this tale finds its perfect expression in tango and particularly the lyrics of "Volver," a recurring signifier that is presented as timeless. Even though "Volver" is not a song about tango, its use in this segment of the film can be interpreted as a call for the recuperation of the role of tango as a cultural system that can represent that particular moment (and any moment) of Argentine history. As much as the song tells the story of a return in space, it also speaks of a return in time, of the reemergence of the past. But unlike Fabián Cortes's recovery of past tangos as "objects," Solanas stages in his film the wish for the rebirth of tango as a system of cultural production. In this context the line in "Volver" that describes the "fear of the encounter / with the past that returns / to confront my life" reveals the intention of the film to endow tango with a political agency it apparently did not have during almost a century of history.

Tango after the End of History

So Hugo Santiago conceptualizes political action and the commitment to the present as a practice of rewriting, and tango becomes a metaphor for his own artistic endeavor—that is, the film itself. What his character Fabián Cortés achieves in relation to the history of tango, *The Pavements of Saturn* does in Santiago's filmography. Solanas and Santiago—born only three years apart, raised in the turbulence of the rise and fall of Peronism, and thus representatives of the same generation—use these films to reflect on their own impact on national cultural production. *The Pavements of Saturn* and *Tangos, the Exile of Gardel* are the result of revisionism. If these films from the 1980s disguise behind their many similarities a fundamentally disparate political stance, their relationship parallels, in one of those bizarre coincidences of history, the correlation between the landmark films that each director made in the late 1960s: Solanas's *The Hour of the Furnaces* and Santiago's *Invasion*. Were these two antipodal representations of political resistance also the same film? There are so many ways to argue for the irreconcilability of these films that it would be superfluous to point out here the aesthetic and political differences between them or to refer to their respective places in the history of cinema.[15] It is instructive, however, to focus on one particular correspondence between these earlier films, which can only be applied in a very general sense: both pictures materialize a moment of peril. Even if they identify a different source for the danger that threatens society, or if that source is not identified at all, *The Hour of the Furnaces* and *Invasion* acknowledge the fact that a destructive force threatens Argentine experience. Similarly, in their direct or metaphorical systems of referentiality, *Tangos, the Exile of Gardel* and *The Pavements of Saturn* represent the moment *after* the emergence of that threat and its direct consequences.

The lines traced from *The Hour of the Furnaces* to *Tangos, the Exile of Gardel* and from *Invasion* to *The Pavements of Saturn* indicate the evolution of two different versions of the relationship between culture and politics as it was conceived and practiced by the Argentine generation that came of age in the 1960s. In 1985 in the wake of the defining experience of state terrorism and the complete disarticulation of the Left, both Solanas and Santiago reworked from abroad their perception of the most brutal years of Argentine history. The circumstances of their stays in Paris during those years were different

(Santiago's situation, as well as Saer's, who cowrote the script, was the basis for Fabián Cortés's remark on his sudden and unexpected conversion into an exile after many years of living in Paris), as was their inscription into Argentine culture in the 1960s. Solanas had come to cinema from the advertising industry, he identified politically with the Peronist resistance and Ernesto "Che" Guevara's *foquismo*, and he proposed creating a Third Cinema aimed at destroying bourgeois cultural institutions.[16] Santiago, on the other hand, was an outstanding product of those same institutions Solanas explicitly rejected: he had relocated to Paris in 1959 to attend courses at the Sorbonne and work with Cocteau and Bresson, and he believed in the political power of high culture but had no concrete political affiliations.[17]

And yet both directors resorted to tango when they wanted to stage a narrative analysis of the experience of Argentine displacement and exile. Tango turned out to be the appropriate language for this undertaking because the political game in those years had turned national history into an intimate, personal story—the political had become private. The affective proximity of tango, and the affectivity of its rhetoric and poetics, made it the natural vehicle not only for the act of explaining Argentine specificity to a foreign audience (as we discussed earlier) but also for the act of withdrawing into oneself at a personal or social level and reviewing the decisions that resulted in the current state of affairs. I am not advocating for the curative properties of tango or any other highly sentimental form of expression here, but I am trying to ascertain the relationship between the self-reflexive, revisionist spirit of these films (even their solemn and funerary tone at times) and the canonizing use of tango as the essential form of Argentine culture, in an absolute reduction of Argentina to the opposition tango versus politics.

It would be facile and misleading to attribute this coincidence between diverging ideologies in the 1980s, years that marked the beginning of a quick and superficial revisionism that would culminate in the total demobilization of Argentine civil society in the subsequent decade, to a universal quality of tango as the language capable of expressing anything Argentine. It would be more productive to entertain the idea that tango was in that moment emptied of specific content and turned into a new *desert*, an empty signifier available for various uses and misuses and the space for the projection of the most diverse national fantasies. In his study of the imaginary construction of the Argentine national space, Jens Andermann points out that the exiled intellectuals who created the nation as a text and through their texts in mid-nineteenth century Argentina (Echeverría, Mármol, Alberdi, and Sarmiento, to name a few prominent examples) conceived the notion of the desert as the tool to reappropriate the space lost: "The desert is not just the name given to a still precarious and fuzzy [national] space, but also, as a moral signifier, the name of the contradictory relationship between this space and the text that advances and retreats over it in a constant back-and-forth. It is also a political name, the flip side of the exile from where it is uttered; a name for the precariousness of the claim over a space that has banished the author, but which the author can finally define because of his extraterritoriality" (40).[18] In a similar fashion, I want to argue that because of its affective proximity, popular typicality, transnational history, and protean nature, the tango of the 1980s represented on the one hand the image of a forbidden territory and a lost culture and on the other the promise of just restitution. The final song of *Tangos, the Exile of Gardel* (also composed by Solanas) expresses this extremely versatile (and vacuous) meaning of *tango* by repeating the word insistently and using it as the direct object for unlikely verbs, as in "soñando tango" (dreaming tango), "buscando tango" (searching for tango), or "curtiendo tango" (sharing tango in an intimate way—a very particular expression of urban Argentine Spanish, untranslatable into English).

The contrastive analysis of these two films from the sixties and the two films from the eighties results, once again, in the substitution of tango for politics. Politics, especially in the form of collective resistance, had been the common terrain of the sixties, the lingua franca for the representation of the national conjuncture, even if expressed in the radically different forms of a Borgesian tale of bravery and treason and a social documentary intended to foster armed struggle in the proletarian audience. Politics in this sense is absent from the movies of the eighties, which overtly represent political association as a lost cause, and make of individual ethics the new way to politically justify the subject. Despite radically different political positions, these protagonists' new commonality is tango.

Were it not for the continuity of the ideological proposals in each pair of films, we might have felt inclined to celebrate the final and definitive politicization of tango and the affective structures of popular culture in a specifically popular art form, cinema, even if in films quite close to the elitist form of second cinema, to use Solanas and Getino's taxonomy. But this process would only take place in the novel, that is, as a subsidiary gesture to politicize the popular in a non-popular art form.[19] Instead, Hugo Santiago's film raised the stakes for the salvific value of culture, for the special capacity of culture to redeem the subject, and Solanas's film insisted, almost twenty years after the groundbreaking denunciation of the complicity between high culture and neocolonialism, that the mobilization of culture is the only way to subvert structures of domination.

Notes

1. The lyrics of all the songs referred to in this study are compiled in Russo and Marpegán but can also be consulted at http://www.todotango.com.

2. In Argentine Spanish the adjective *morocho* can either indicate fair skin and dark hair (as in Gardel's nickname "el morocho del Abasto") or darkish skin.

3. The title plays with the name of a very popular tango club in Paris in the late 1970s and early 1980s, Trottoirs de Buenos Aires, and the traditional attribution of melancholy to the influence of Saturn. For the history of Trottoirs de Buenos Aires, see *Paris Tango* 76–85.

4. "Yo era un músico viajero, Mario, desde hace mil años que era un músico que estaba de paso. De repente una banda de tipos me hacen volar la Aquilea en pedazos y de la mañana a la noche soy un exilado. Cambió todo."

5. For basic information on the Abuelas de Plaza de Mayo, see Arditti or the organization's website, http://abuelas.org.ar.

6. On the introduction of tango in Paris, see Cadícamo, *La historia del tango en París*; Pujol.

7. On the proposal to understand the dictatorial years as a war between two equally pervasive forces, known as the "theory of the two demons," see Vezzetti.

8. Regarding Gardel's nationality, see Barsky and Barsky; Ruffié de Saint-Blancat et al.

9. The story and the myth of Eduardo Arolas's stay in France are referred to in the film. See also Gálvez and Espina Rawson, 21–33.

10. The elimination of lyrics and the role of the singer is a gesture usually associated with Piazzolla. See Monjeau and Filippelli.

11. Despite the risk of oversimplifying, it is worth pointing out the obvious differences in the historical contexts of the 1920s and the 1980s. On the one hand, if the importance of Paris in the map of Western culture had not diminished, its position was certainly not as central as in the early part of the century. On the other hand, Argentina had experienced radical changes in its short history, moving through the irruption of the masses into public life, Peronism, and state terrorism. Finally, tango represented in the 1980s some sort of a burden from the past, a residue of a provincial Buenos Aires, an image of the never completed process of modernization.

12. We are to believe, though, that this is not directly incorporated as the finale for the show or the producer would not be complaining about Gardel's absence.

13. In this sense *The Pavements of Saturn* reinscribes itself in the Borgesian imaginary of its "prequel" *Invasion*, written by Borges: cowards who overcome their fear, death as the defining moment that reveals the sense of what has happened to that subject until that moment; tango as one of the cultural products that best represents these motives.

14. On the disappeared children of Argentina who were adopted or "appropriated" by families identified with the dictatorship, see Arditti or visit the website of the Grandmothers of the Plaza de Mayo, http://abuelas.org.ar.

15. On the relationship between *Invasion* and *The Hour of the Furnaces*, see Aguilar, *Otros mundos*.

16. On Solanas's proposal for a Third Cinema, see Solanas and Getino; Gabriel; Stam. For a brief comprehensive study of Solanas's work until the early 1990s that includes biographical references, see Monteagudo.

17. The most comprehensive studies of Santiago's work are the book compiled by Oubiña, and the special dossier prepared by *El Amante* 3, 26 (April 1994): 10–25.

18. "El desierto no es, pues, sólo el nombre que se le da a ese espacio todavía precario y borroso, sino que también es, en su carácter de significante moral, el de la relación contradictoria que éste mantiene con una letra que avanza y retrocede en constantes vaivenes sobre él. Es también un nombre político en cuyo revés está el destierro desde donde se lo emite, un nombre para la precariedad del reclamo sobre un espacio donde el autor se encuentra proscripto, pero al que puede, por fin, definir gracias a su posición de extraterritorialidad."

19. Here we are thinking of Manuel Puig's interventions on the issue.

CHAPTER FIVE

The Return of the Tango in Documentary Film

FERNANDO ROSENBERG

In order to understand the significance of the growing corpus of tango-related documentaries by Argentine filmmakers produced in the last few years (particularly after the economic debacle of 2001), it is important to read them against the background of the multiple, rich lives of tango in twentieth-century Argentine and international films.[1] Whereas tango has been featured in many American films as an exotic dance existing in a historical vacuum, invoked to process varied if often entangled passions and anxieties along gender, class, and cultural divisions, for these Argentine documentaries of the last decade or so, tango entails addressing a national history that is inaccessible as a straightforward, continuous temporality.[2] The status of what these films set out to document is placed into question at the outset by the films themselves, as tango's manifestation, its being there, is somewhat ghostly—thus complicating the documentary genre's traditional reliance on the indexical.[3]

Contemporary tango musicians inevitably draw on and emulate the canon of tango music produced and solidified during the first half of the twentieth century, but nothing parallel occurs in filmmakers' search for styles and themes of the same era. That is, these documentaries do not posit a fundamental continuity with the earlier development of the Argentine film industry that accompanies the ascent of tango itself into mainstream middle-class culture. The vast majority of Argentine dramas and comedies from the first half of the twentieth century featuring tango music intricately woven into the plot, and starring tango singers, neither established themselves as "classics" that provided filmic models to follow nor presented a tradition to be challenged.[4] Even though these films might follow melodramatic formulas, they came to represent retrospectively a mythical era when tango coincided with its surroundings. The fact that Argentine filmic production of the last two decades has not continued this lineage suggests that tango might have lost its argumentative thrust or that its ability to reveal the social fabric has diminished. Certainly, earlier tango dramas and comedies contributed to the establishment of a mythology, a repository of tropes and a fictional world that current tango expressions cannot help but interrogate. While addressing a cultural expression that might have only a residual or monumental value, such documentaries are haunted by the gravitational force of a past time when tango appeared to have been one with its present. These documentaries do not continue a filmic legacy as such but instead incorporate it as embedded footage, pointing to a discontinuity while interrogating the current, albeit allegorical, significance of the tango film archive. The remnant of an era of national cultural production, this integrated footage functions in every sense to ground such projects, but it cannot help but reveal at the same time that this ground is undermined, its ties to the present threadbare—and that it wasn't very stable in the first place.

More than the language and narratives developed in early tango film, it is the whole era of tango production, which included the advent of the *orquestas típicas* and the dissemination of this music through mass media (radio, recording industry, and film), that these documentaries cannot escape and that exerts a constant pressure upon the present and on the imagination of contemporary filmmakers. As they strive to document tango's persistent significance following the disappearance of both the universe it portrayed and the cultural apparatus through which it developed, these documentaries cannot avoid being self-reflective, signaling a present moment when tango is no longer produced and consumed in a state of distraction but in one of heightened awareness.

In the face of tango's current incarnation as a world-cultural commodity supplying a trace of remote authenticity, the documentaries I will discuss eschew the never-ending dispute of what deserves to be sanctioned as real or authentic tango—a claim inherent to tango as it has anxiously redefined itself against the current of international flows that have been its condition of production and circulation. Instead, these films point to the current presence of tango within the order of *the real*. What I call the real is the postulation of an extemporary, dislocated presence bearing the traces of inaccessible history, an aural manifestation with no visible reference in the very material that the documentary sets itself to represent.

It is therefore not surprising that the documentarians' search for something more primary and less subject to objectification and commodification in the current state of tango often falls back onto the body as the ultimate dwelling place of the real; or that from there, it leads to an autobiographical exploration of the tango maker, also mirroring the filmmaker, to confront the question of mythical beginnings, the intersection at which tango bites and touches the subject, a fleeting moment holding the secret of passionate attachments. The encounter portrayed is often one with death itself, with the phantasmagorical presence of what is no longer there. Such films record the search within the self for that mythical encounter that makes the subject what it is, a historical search that transcends both history and the self, marking the irrecoverable condition of life passing.[5]

If the dance has been, in Monjeau and Filipelli's lucid analysis, "tango's conservative force par excellence" (16), it has also been, simultaneously, and perhaps partially just because of its picturesque conservatism, the privileged medium for tango's earlier and current worldwide recognition and celebration. Given that the body is central to these films, it is remarkable that tango dancing has only a peripheral presence, as if the "moving image" wanted to recede from the visually recognizable and readily spectacular. But I would argue that it is because of this very success, with dance as the most visible and global expression of tango, that the documentaries assume a distance from the dance, as they also eschew the all-too-common celebration of tango's renewed recognition in order to interrogate its current significance. Furthermore, if tango's world circulation was always determined by the business of exoticism and self-exoticism (Savigliano, *Tango and the Political Economy of Passion* 2–3, 137–39), and dance was the privileged medium for the performance of this romance, for gendering the coloniality of power, shying away from the dance might be the documentarians' best bet for bypassing the colonial knot at the very apex of global tango consumption.

Rather than a language already *available*, ready to be transferred to film in order to display a mysteriously dangerous attraction across national, generational, or cultural borders (as tango has been incorporated previously on the international screen), these documentaries reestablish tango as a set of *unavoidable* local references and symbolic practices whose present significance, and thus the filmic capacity to document and portray tango's presence, is not taken for granted. Thus the documentaries are troubled by the condition of carrying on a lineage that while historically closed—a residue of past social formations, systems of cultural production, and ways of life—never ceased to exist and to persist.

I will turn first not to a documentary proper but to a drama containing in its plot the possibility of a documentary. The director Daniel Burak's *Bar El Chino* (2003) features a documentary filmmaker as its protagonist and is set against the historical condition of possibility characteristic of all the documentaries I will discuss, but which this particular movie with its pedagogical bent makes explicit. I am referring to the socioeconomic crisis of 2001, which closes a decade of upbeat narratives of financial globalization that advised local institutions to refashion themselves in terms of a market economy or to perish and that not coincidentally saw the global reemergence of tango as the chief Argentine export in the scenario of world-culturalism.[6]

What moves the plot along in *Bar El Chino* is the story of one documentary that's been abandoned and a second documentary that might finally be realized by the movie's end. Both documentaries are about the titular neighborhood bar that doubles as a tango bar at night. That is, the drama is a fictionalization around documenting the existence of a real bar that figures prominently in tango mythology, a bar located on the exact corner of the working-class Pompeya neighborhood mentioned in the movie, remote from any of the trendy sections of Buenos Aires. The bar stands in the film not only as a place for true tango authenticity but also as a shrine for revisiting the values of community and friendship.

The time is the spring of 2001, smack-dab in the middle of the financial crisis that led to the freezing of bank accounts, a strategy with catastrophic consequences for the middle-class existence of the main characters and that indeed will prompt, in the movie and in reality, the collapse of the government structure. The protagonist Jorge is a middle-aged filmmaker whose current line of work entails making promotional videos for Spanish companies with investments in Argentina (foreign investment being the line of economic growth favored by neoliberal policies of the 1990s). Jorge's life is divided between work and his passionate, personal filmic project, a split that perfectly mirrors the contrast of a new world order against the primary attachment of surviving local structures.[7] He had been developing a documentary about his beloved bar but had abandoned the project after El Chino, the owner and spirit of the bar, dies.

Although he had been living in exile in Spain, Jorge had come back to Argentina after the return of democracy in 1986, leaving behind in Madrid a son, now in his mid-twenties, and an ex-wife. He never stopped missing Buenos Aires and this bar, and at the beginning of the movie, that's where we find him, on his birthday, singing tangos along with his two male best friends and the rest of the bar's regulars. His story will intertwine with that of the young and beautiful Martina, who shows up at the bar as part of a TV crew covering tango night. Inspired by the humble venue, with its contrast to the glittering tango circuit catering to foreigners, Martina plans to shoot a documentary. She contacts Jorge to discuss the possibility of including his treasured footage, most importantly the conversations shot with the late Chino. Initially ambivalent because Martina, a hip young woman in the TV industry, doesn't seem to have any tango credentials, Jorge and Martina start collaborating, and once Jorge realizes her sincerity, romance predictably ensues.

Many elements of the movie, such as the romantic plot and its frustrating finale prompted by the economic crisis and Martina's sudden departure for Spain, as well as the topic of male friendship, lend themselves to a national allegorical reading, but I will leave them aside here to concentrate on the interdependent role of documentaries and tango bars in the Argentina of the 2000s. By now we realize that the two connected documentaries within this film will ultimately find the authenticity they seek in a place that has remained unencumbered, faithful to its spirit, and unmoved from its rightful spot within the humble peripheral barrio. In contrast to the visibility and flashy surfaces of renowned tango bars favored by TV cameras and tourists, the marginal and unassuming El Chino bar and its late owner are revealed as the secret center of the *porteño* universe. The place is filled with tango iconography, as it is tango that allows for the expression of genuine emotions and for the ethics of hospitality articulated at one point by the late owner. The footage included at the end of the film suggests that tango is not something primarily visible or audible but instead the name of a generous spirit that opens itself to the other, in the same way that this drama provides a space in which the failed documentary can be resurrected.

Bar El Chino thus postulates two roles for the documentary genre, first as a personal exploration of intimate attachments and then as a quest for and redemption of posthumous remains. The documentary register of this drama is relevant not only because documentary making moves the plot forward but also most significantly because we get to see and hear the "real" late Chino philosophizing about life and death behind the bar's counter—real but ultra-mediatized, as he can only be present in the unedited footage rescued from oblivion within a not-yet finished documentary, within a feature film. But by the same token, the drama stands as the recognition that documenting might be a way of declaring time as having run out, a testimony to a slow but certain death—a suspicion that might have stopped Jorge short of finishing on his first (failed) attempt. Indeed, these fictional documentaries deal with the magic of resurrecting what is dead (tango, local attachments, and el Chino himself), or at the very least, they ponder the conditions of a kind of survival in animated suspension.

It might be argued that Buenos Aires's shifting character, or what might be regarded as its de-characterization, bound up with new cultural and economic constellations that have transformed antiquated cafés into glossy pizzerias and storied theaters into discotheques or mega-churches for TV pastors, is precisely what remains unspoken, even as it drives the search for a place of a "pure" or untouched memory. One modernizing wave (that of the neoliberal 1990s) appears to have erased the traces of an earlier modernity from which tango emerged. But after the financial crisis of 2001 marked the dramatic end of a model in which the free market promised to pave the road for Argentina's positioning in the First World, the march of history reaches a standstill in which discarded and recycled pasts are again resignified. Thus, the real-life Bar El Chino, which ceased to function as a neighborhood bar after the death of its owner, both attracts and resists mediatic interventions, and following renovations of the building that aim to both halt and freeze the march of time, it sporadically opens for occasional tango shows as the reincarnation of itself.

Perhaps as a gesture of eschewing this historical drama altogether by challenging the obsession with the relic and the shrine, thus disseminating tango's powerful allure everywhere, a nondescript neighborhood restaurant becomes the setting for another movie, El tango de mi vida (The tango of my life, directed by Hernán Belón, 2007). Far from the mythical café of many tango lyrics in which male attachments are primary (assumed in Bar El Chino but also in the documentary Café de los maestros which I discuss below), here what pulls men and women from different socioeconomic backgrounds together on four consecutive Mondays is an organized talent show and competition for amateurs and semiprofessional tango aficionados.

Presenting the performances and successive elimination of the contestants along with the details of the jury members' deliberations, the film offers an evolving drama of artistic consecration, albeit on a modest scale commensurate with the reduced horizon of expectations of the struggling middle class. Thus, far from the dramatic buildup predictable in talent show formats in which the prize opens the door to fame and perhaps fortune, here the prospect of mediatic success never casts its bright light—perhaps because no TV channel or record company hopes to create a profit machine out of the performances, but more importantly because the movie suggests an intimate association of tango with the simple, everyday life of the title. Indeed, the decision process is not imbued with pathos, and there is no display of anticipatory emotional extremes, as if the "tango of my life," the entanglement of tango and life, were more subtle, intimate, and intricate than what the contest format can allow.

Drawing on another template for a contemporary conception of popularity and stardom, the film is also peppered with "daily life" segments akin to reality TV. The camera follows the contestants for a casual survey of the material of their daily existence; it finds them at work and in public spaces and communes with them at their homes as they carry on with their lives, lives that are neither organized around the pursuit of artistic heights nor particularly imbued with tango mythology or iconicity. Although the subjects produce some "natural" behavior for a camera eager to capture the quotidian, the film also approaches its subjects lightly, with a playful, forgiving, compassionate look that seems to put them at ease. The more casual the evocation, the more mysterious the link between the daily reality of jobs, schools, family, homes, and so on and a tango that seems to simultaneously dwell and persist deep within, nowhere and everywhere. The film thus projects flows of affect that are revealed to act independently of the film: they do not await cinematic redemption, and they are not organized in relation to the achievement of fame, recognition, or professional careers.

All of this amounts to a reclamation of that aspect of tango most neglected in its metropolitan circulation and appropriation, the untranslatable singing practice of emotionally charged lyrics narrating an intimate drama and worldview that are, by convention, performed with a studied sense of personal involvement. The title of the movie makes an explicit allusion to tango singing as something not learned but lived, and the voice is here the material ground on which the lyrics and the body become one. But even as tango lyrics and singing style seem to be the matter of melodrama, the general tone of the film is one of a celebration, albeit in a mellow key. Tango dwells not so much in what the lyrics express, often referring to a world no longer visible, but in the emotional charge of the voice, which has remained. What is celebrated? Perhaps the sheer survival of this middle class and its aspirations, despite decades of political and economic violence; perhaps tango as a gift, a bonus, a leftover that history—the iteration of interrupted projects of modern-ization—failed to wipe out.[8] Removed from the passionate entanglements channeled by tango in international film, remote from the camera-ready visual plasticity of the dance, this tango film is clearly more interested in looking at the fabric of the contemporary Argentine urban middle class. These are lives that, rather than defined or justified by tango drama, are sweetened by tango's faithful company.

Contrary to the collage composition of *El tango de mi vida*, the documentary *Yo no sé qué me han hecho tus ojos* (I don't know what your eyes have done to me, directed by Sergio Wolf and Lorena Muñoz, 2003) provides a stage for the single-minded search of one ghostly female voice, that of singer Ada Falcón—a singer and tango film performer of the 1920s and 1930s who vanished suddenly from public view under rather mysterious circumstances. It was for her that the maestro Francisco Canaro is said to have written the song resurrected in the film's title. In a tango world dominated by male personalities, the eyes of the young rising star acquire legendary status as the object of clashing desires—the latest of which seems to be the directorial eye reconstructing, through glimpses, the star system that surrounded Falcón's public persona. If the culture industry had the power to create through tango "a mythology in the present tense" (as the director voice-over puts it), this documentary proposes a meditation on what is absent and what remains once that present is no more.

The fact that the diva vanished in the early 1940s functions as an allegory of tango's destiny, its mythological allure, its interrupted trajectory. Photographs, film footage, and music recordings are included in the movie not as historical records but as phantasmagoria, like haphazard glimpses of a dream world, a tango legend surviving only in the echo of a voice, the glitter of a gaze. The documentarian appears before the camera personally carrying out the investigation, conducting interviews, tracking down documents, and so forth, as the fragments of tango culture are reduced to a leftover. This use of the archival runs counter to a traditional documentarian incorporation of historical sources, as when a resort to footage naturalizes a perception of progressive time.[9] The futile search for a lost early movie featuring Falcón (*El festín de los caranchos*, 1919) exemplifies this legendary aspect of an early culture industry that, rather than laying the groundwork for steady accumulative progress, survives only in mythical or fragmentary form, perhaps only as a projection of present fantasies.

The film proposes to fill this void at which it teeters by aggressively pursuing Ada's presence. The documentary thus follows the thread of rumors and legends to the hills of Córdoba, to Salsipuedes (meaning "leave if you can," a town with a name of intriguing significance), to the cloister where Ada is said to have been living, and finally to the retirement home where Ada will ultimately be discovered. There she is—an aged ingénue at the end of her life, lost and found. When the documentarian-narrator shows her a tape of her performance and recordings of her voice, she seems to recall those moments; she sings along, albeit quietly, some phrases; she remembers, or so it seems, intermittently, with a sense of wonder or detachment. The camera is fixated on Ada's profile while she listens and looks at her former recorded self, but her face expresses uncertainty regarding the location of these memories—not "hers" but memories of her held by others or by mere recording technology. "Poor Ada! Poor Canaro! Is that me?," she utters, as if her frail body preserved a secretly senile mind, an obscure secret, or both: she is the perfect allegory for tango's vanishing but insistent presence. The intangible presence of a vanished past is made possible by reproduction technologies that, far from cancelling them out, reconstituted, re-created, and disseminated the aura of the voice and the image—modern technologies of reproduction alongside which tango was born and raised and without which no mythological "Ada" could ever have existed.

While the celebratory tango industry of recent years often glosses over historical discontinuities and erasures by way of tracking down aging tango personalities of mythical stature and humble existence, *Yo no sé qué me han hecho tus ojos* follows the same formula only to lead it to unsettling results because the diva is not available for redemption. She is, in different ways, not entirely present but instead "absent" or at least absent-minded in the way that people suffering from dementia might be. In a more radical sense, it was her conscious decision to cut herself off from the symbolic and institutional matrix of tango, to withdraw her body from the record of mediated social memory that makes her presence phantasmagoric. This doesn't prevent the former star and the documentarian from listening to music together and singing along in a pure celebration of the encounter, setting free the enjoyment of the art from the entangled matrix of tango history and its systems of consecration.

If tango in international film is conveniently detached from history—an already prepackaged and shelf-ready cultural product picked up from the counter of available dramatic resources—this film is an exemplary performance of tango as a kind of aborted, traumatic history that keeps haunting the memory of the present.[10] In searching for clues, the film takes us to places that are no more, to significant sites that were the stuff of tango's frayed material fabric, but that bear no traces of their past, as legendary theaters and radio stations were converted into so many McDonalds, banks, and department stores. The renovated façades are shown in fixed shots, the director silently confronting the buildings in their sleek non-concern, staging only a stubborn indifference toward bygone times. Certainly, this move attempts to overcome the logic of the crypt—the trope of a place where the object of desire, tango, is shown to be buried but magically preserved, awaiting routine visitors, like those of Bar El Chino, to fulfill the fantasy of an unchanged condition. Recourse to an actual crypt paradoxically furthers this point by revealing that there is nothing but death there: one of the final scenes of *Yo no sé qué me han hecho tus ojos* depicts the narrow, empty alleys of Buenos Aires's Chacarita cemetery where Ada is buried in the pantheon of the SADAIC, the Argentine Society of Authors and Composers, along with many other faded figures from tango's yesteryear.

It is not surprising that other documentaries such as *Por la Vuelta* (directed by Cristian Pauls, 2005) and *Café de los Maestros* (directed by Miguel Kohan, 2008) also postulate the continuity of tango through appeals to its aging icons. In *Por la Vuelta* the filmmaker Cristian Pauls officiates as the curious middle-aged tango amateur exploring the personal significance of the bandoneon maestro Leopoldo Federico's music, as he pays a close look at Federico's life. The titular *vuelta*, or return, is not an operation that the film itself seeks to produce by rescuing the subject from anonymity (as in *El tango de mi vida*) or from oblivion (as in *Café de los maestros*). We see Federico in his daily routine, the camera focused on his home and his body as the material base that would make the titular "return" possible. We encounter the musician in various stages of a tentative plan to return to the music scene—a very uncertain revival, both because of the maestro's failing health and because of his insistence on making such a comeback only if he is accompanied by his full orchestra. The film seems open to its own incompletion, to the possibility of its own failure, particularly when its meandering progress is halted by the health crises of the musician. Rather than progressing, the movie becomes a meditation on time and aging, on the unpredictability of life, in terms of the very physicality that defines for all of us, but for musicians in a very specific way, the limits of who we are. A testimony of what continues on through time and beyond time, the documentary treats the subject of remains as a fleeting category, much like time and music themselves.

Por la vuelta seems to share with *Yo no sé qué me han hecho tus ojos* the tendency to dwell in the severed connection between a vanished past of tango halls, whose grand names remain only as empty echoes, and the concrete present of a city that seems unforgiving, ready to dispose of its past and possibly its very identity. The many silent passages where we see the directorial camera-eye skimming through a book of old photographs of Buenos Aires (by Horacio Coppola) or contemplating Federico's own childhood pictures or wandering around the city are not offered as a natural referent for tango music but rather as a set of incidental images reluctant to coalesce into a narrative.[11] The constant recurrence of images of traffic, from inside or outside a car or a train, suggest a city in constant flow, a city that is itself a metaphor for the passage of time—where no return is possible.

The meditation on what is passed on, what constitutes a legacy, is expressed explicitly in the language of quasi-filial ties; the filmmaker shows open concern for Federico's failing health and even attends his medical checkups. The movie closes with a revelatory exchange between the filmmaker and the musician who stops chatting, as if struck by a sudden realization, inquiring of Pauls, "You don't know much about tango, do you?" to which the filmmaker, some thirty years younger than Federico, replies, "Not really; that's the reason I am making this film"—a testimony to a generational breach intensified by a historical discontinuity. The only bridge across time is the authoritative, ghostly presence of Astor Piazzolla, who placed Federico in the pantheon of the chosen few great bandoneonists and whose tenderly quarrelsome letters to Federico are read aloud in the film. But discursive authority is absent, an absence reflected in the documentary's reluctance to include even a single interview. The traditional didactic components of documentary genre are interrogated from a stance of awareness of the impossibility of transmission or of the mere remedial aspect of a transmission whose would-be recipient lacks what only experience, a personal involvement with the sound of tango, might have provided. Thus the term *vueltas* points not only to Federico's returns (to the stage, to fame, to renewed health) but also to the destiny of the narrator-filmmaker whose relation to tango is uncertain except when he identifies it as the sound that "saw me growing up and that was now coming back to tell me 'Here I am. And now what? It is impossible to keep going without me.'" That is, we witness a return that is neither conjured nor welcome, the violence of its obstinacy, its stubborn insistence, confronting the filmmaker unexpectedly and condemning him to a never-ending game of catch-up.

Maybe because this film focuses on a bandoneon player who is often seen playing solo (such that the documentarian-narrator says at one point that

"*Portrait of a solo artist* could have been the title of this film"), it shares with the docudrama *El último bandoneón* (The last bandoneon, directed by Alejandro Saderman, 2003) the sense that there is something arcane about tango, that it contains a knowledge accessed and transmitted only by a chosen few. Here, tango is distant from its populist celebration in the talent show, or the picturesque collective sing-along in Bar El Chino. In *El último bandoneón* the drama of survival doesn't pertain only to tango's aging figures but to the bandoneon itself, threatened by the growing rarity of the instrument, by the increasing lack of experienced luthiers trained to repair and maintain it, and by the very world popularity of tango as it converts the bandoneon into a curiosity, a prized commodity, and a cult artifact in the global market of enthusiasts and collectors.

The fictional thread that drives the plot of *El último bandoneón* is the plight of Marina Gayotto, a young and struggling single mother and bandoneonist whose artistic talents are challenged by the lethal combination of a dire economic situation and a crippled instrument in need of urgent repairs. In the early chapters, she awaits an audition with the famous bandoneonist Rodolfo Mederos, who is forming a young tango orchestra in order "to bring tango orchestras back to the world, and also as a social program," as he claims in the film. The meeting between a representative of a new generation of musicians, who is nevertheless stalled in her development by the lack of networks of support (she is seen playing in *colectivos*, public buses, for donations from the passengers), and the acclaimed Mederos points to yet another attempt to reconstitute a broken lineage. The fact that she is a woman is of course indicative of an epochal change, since the overwhelming majority of bandoneon players are and have been men. The film moves constantly between the older generation and the youth, with Mederos mediating between them (born in 1940, he appears to be one of the few members of his age group).[12] The film projects him as a stable, reassuring presence, connecting not only the old and the young but also the old guard and the innovators, tango tourists and locals, collectors, instrument tuners, dancers, and musicians.

Beginning with its title, the film is haunted by the pathos of endings. The movie sets itself up to deny the titular acknowledgment by displaying counterexamples that build to a crescendo. The peripatetic trajectory of the young bandoneonist takes her to different neighborhoods, where, led by word-of-mouth referrals, she knocks upon doors of possible bandoneon sellers, aficionados ready to elaborate on the instrument's special character and on their own relationship to it. After her ailing, irreparable bandoneon is sold to a well-known Japanese dealer, Mederos helps Marina buy an instrument in working condition at an auction.[13] Marina starts rehearsing with the young orchestra. So the last bandoneon might not be the last bandoneon after all, the movie is ready to assure us, provided the magic revival works at all those different levels.

But what will this (pen)ultimate bandoneon play? The old classics? Because despite Marina's hip looks, the only compositions she rehearses are classics from the 1930s and 1940s. Implicitly, tango is doomed if its composition indeed stopped some time in the early 1950s—as if a bandoneon might remain, but the key to any creative impulse has been lost. In a couple of revelatory moments, Marina asks maestro Rodolfo (and she repeats this question to another older musician as well) if he is currently composing and if so, what. This suggestion gestures at what one of the interviewed mature dancers openly declares: that from 1955 (the year of the so-called Revolución Libertadora that toppled Juan Perón's government, banned public meetings, and made expressions of popular culture suspect) to the mid-1980s, tango was virtually dead, pure and simple, with the only supply of air provided by those few dancers who kept it alive against all odds by continuing the tradition of the milonga, in which the same old tunes were (and still are) played over and over again. Though the comment disregards Piazzolla because his music is seldom played in dance halls, the question remains of whether the musician's unsurpassed musical genius has left any direct musical descendents. Mederos is in fact a prolific, talented composer, but none of his compositions have achieved the recognition reserved for the closed repertoire of the classics. And when he listens to Marina in the first audition, playing with her original bandoneon, he comments in private to the bassist that the girl is "struggling with a dead elephant" (peleando con un elefante muerto), faulting not only a lack of air—and this in the wielding of an instrument whose sound originates in compressing and absorbing air—but also invoking a presence of something heavy, exotic, and threatened with extinction. Despite its narrative of overcoming difficulties, this documentary is haunted by imminent death.

To close the cycle of legacy and elegy, we should mention *Café de los maestros* (Café of the masters, directed by Miguel Kohan, 2008), an ambitious, monumental reunion of surviving tango maestros organized by Gustavo Santaolalla.[14] *Café de los maestros* attempts to solve the historical conundrum through production grandiosity (including an audio CD boxed set, a concert in the Teatro Colón, and the movie itself): it recalls tango history and creates a new series of enhanced auditory, visual, and stage performances that can leave no doubt as to tango's lasting legacy. The documentary registers the project leading up to the concert and the recording of the CD, constructing a narrative that assumes the filmmaking process itself and not only its final results will be significant and worthy of celebration. We witness the musician and producer Santaolalla aboard an airplane as it lands in Buenos Aires, where he will visit the studios, and then watch as the old masters warmly greet each other, play, sing, record, and share their musical knowledge before the camera, first in the privacy of their homes and finally on stage, in a continuity that proceeds toward the final performance and recording event that crown the project: this is not just a musical album but a document and a monument. By the time of its release, three of the musicians had already died (Lágrima Ríos, Carlos García, and José 'Pepe' Libertella), and the film ends with a dedication to them. Like Wim Wenders's *Buena Vista Social Club*, with which it shares many features but chiefly an epochal anxiety, the movie seems to purposely regain for the maestros their iconic status, to widen their reach, to bring them from semiretirement to grand stage recognition, and to promise them the remembrance they deserve once they have passed on.[15] This is probably the most unabashedly celebratory of the documentaries, with many scenes imbued with the flavor of a class reunion; the present is shown as charged with a rich past, but its projection into the future is fragile. This fragility is perhaps the very reason to celebrate tango's presence, to indulge in an urgent, overdue homage.

Café de los maestros points to a larger phenomenon of tango orchestra revival that deserves a full-fledged treatment; I will limit myself to consider its filmic representation.[16] Tango revival or survival is, as we see, often presented as an overdue act of recognition of some aging masters, complemented in some cases by a ritual of transmission, with tango officiating as the missing link between a glorious past and the disjointed present. Nonetheless, it is the young who possess the necessary components for mending the wounds of broken history. Recuperation and restoration are accomplished by the young and talented in films such as *Orquesta típica* (Typical orchestra, directed by Nicolás Entel, 2006) and *Si sos brujo* (If you are a sorcerer, directed by Caroline Neal, 2005),[17] which although different in many regards—the former irreverent in its attitude, the latter more didactic and academic—both center on the formation of new tango orchestras (Orquesta Típica Fernández Fierro and El Arranque, respectively).[18] Forming new orchestras in a "typical" configuration becomes a remarkable feat when considered against the background of the virtual disappearance of these orchestras and the environment that sustained them, in part due to financial reasons, after the 1950s ebb of tango culture. Successive generations of urban youth whose musical education was built on the sounds of Argentine rock—a powerful cultural movement from the 1960s onward, which gained strength even during the dictatorship, diversifying and developing amid political and economic turmoil—had been mostly indifferent to or disdainful of what tango represented (nostalgia, tradition, lament, failure, old age, resentment, and so on). The preeminence of the orchestra formation is tied to a particular aspect of tango's greatness: its Apollonian era, as Rafael Flores calls it, marked by the 1940s explosion of orchestras that codified tango for their players, creating a school of musicians "who knew how to read a score" (69). Thus it is not only tango glory that is recuperated by the contemporary orchestras but also a certain sense of order and continuity. Indeed, it might be argued that the two orchestras, despite their radically different sound, bring together the old and the new, both of them integrating new compositions among the old classics. And if Fernández Fierro plays the classics irreverently while El Arranque interprets them literally, it is in any case the innovative spirit of these classics, their untamable force, that remains as the object of desire.

While *Si sos brujo* portrays institutional indifference and a lack of official support for the incipient El Arranque orchestra, in *Orquesta típica* day-to-day improvisation becomes a method of survival and enjoyment for the members of the Fernández Fierro. In both films precariousness only adds to the realization of destiny, in which each orchestra's formation, originating in a leap of faith, is at last led home by fate. *Si sos brujo* rescues an academic model of apprenticeship that the movie suggests fortified the traditional orchestras of the 1940s and that the orchestra El Arranque (named after a Julio de Caro tango) intends to revive. The orchestra embarks upon the project of bringing back to life the style of the canonical orchestras (Gobi, de Caro, Troilo, Pugliese, D'Arienzo, and so on), heeding that legacy to the point of mimicking the sound of each one of them, in order to pass that legacy on, not only through the media of music scores and records but also through the very physicality of playing styles. Thus emerges an orchestra able to conjure up not one sanctified member of tango royalty but the whole hall of fame, a band of ventriloquists, a monster of sorts, since it needs (as is stated in the movie) to be a contemporary orchestra as well, one that is able to yield up the sounds of new tango to a city that has witnessed a profound transformation since the old masters populated the theaters and dance halls.

At the beginning of *Si sos brujo*, we see the bassist and orchestra director Ignacio Varchausky tracking down the retired maestro Emilio Balcarce (former arranger, composer, violinist, and bandoneonist for some of the most important orchestras and one of the maestros featured in *Café de los maestros*) to see if he is willing to collaborate with firsthand knowledge of the golden age orchestras' techniques. *Firsthand* must be read literally, since it is the body involved in playing an instrument in a particular way that is impossible to recover in absentia; thus, semiretired maestros are invited to rehearsal to pass on their unique ways of playing. Urgent action is called for, as Varchausky clearly states at the outset: "We are in a constant race against time . . . trying to codify what the maestros who played in these orchestras know." A tension emerges here, since the codification intended by the project, the handbook for orchestras that Varchausky declares he is planning to compile, cannot stand in for the physical presence of those musicians who had already codified and expanded tango vocabulary through their performances with the great orchestras. When media, from records to scores that Varchausky digs up from dusty antique stores and Balcarce's drawers, is pored through exhaustively, its limits become apparent. The limits to cultural mediation ultimately yield to a desire for the real, for a presence, an actual apprenticeship to the evanescent element of the "style" to be re-created, which can never be codified.

Thus, the most insistent question in the movie is about *arranques*, jump starts, (new) beginnings: how to start a tango orchestra, how to recommence and connect with what is no longer there, how to break through the isolation of aficionados, how to imbue disseminated treasures with present, physical thrust. Whereas the film tracks the musicians to their homes to portray their domestic lives, it also includes 1930s and 1940s tango movie footage to strategically contrast the disseminated, individual efforts of the present with the populated orchestras and halls of the golden age. While the orchestra school is the answer to the *tangueros'* isolation, it also attempts to sublimate the anxiety of beginnings with the progressive narrative of growth and transmission of the legacy. What appeared implausible then becomes not only possible but ultimately highly successful, as confirmed by an impromptu invitation for El Arranque to perform in Europe and taste there the same Parisian acclaim the great orchestras enjoyed in years past. The film also establishes tango's mythical trajectory by comparing it to similar developments in jazz. The master trumpeter Wynton Marsalis is interviewed and describes his visit to an Arranque rehearsal, comparing the methods he sees and hears there to the intergenerational transmission of jazz knowledge in New Orleans.[19] As in *Café de los maestros*, a performance in the Teatro Colón, Buenos Aires's consecratory stage par excellence, signals another apex at the end of the movie. The successive creation of new orchestras comprised of young musicians ascertains the academic quality of the project, granting its continuation.

This narrative of renewal is countered, however, by the aging maestro Balcarce, whose progressive hearing loss becomes part of the story line when he shares his concerns for his growing limitations with some of the young musicians—thus making material the significance of physicality in their enterprise. The film is able to tie together homage to the glorious past (of the soon to be re-retired maestro, composer of the film title's "Si sos brujo," among other tango classics) with regeneration against all odds. If Varchausky was initially discouraged from attempting a quixotic project in a country lacking continuous institutional support for the arts, with naysayers warning him in classical cynical Argentinean style that he could only put this kind of orchestra together *si sos brujo* (only "if you are a sorcerer"), the movie affirms by the end that he and other members of the orchestra indeed possess such sorcery and that such magic does exist. So, too, does tango succeed commercially, expanding its energy, marketing itself to the rest of the world—thus re-creating one of its central narratives of (humble) origins and (worldly) transcendence. Despite the infamy of its low-class breeding at the margins, tango survives against all odds, and its poor (arrogant, some would say) but dignified spirit remains a central tenet of its international status and success. This is the other, complementary sorcery: the art form survives not only against time and death but also through space, projecting a narrative of social ascent onto a world scale—a fantasy fitting for the poor European immigrants to the South American metropolis: a venture abroad that is also a triumphant comeback. The extent to which this narrative privileges the European connection, re-animating parts of tango's legacy but also obfuscating other elements that have been lost or ignored (such as the African components in the form's origins or its capacity to articulate popular elements as it once did), is material ripe for debate—but not one in which this film engages directly.

While *Si sos brujo* posits the orchestra as the institutionalization or academization that would supplement and remedy this broken continuity, the film *Orquesta típica* is invested in rogue tango: a surprising, untamed vitality—a different scene of revival. Although the renowned bandoneon master Daniel Binelli (who played with the legendary orchestra of Osvaldo Pugliese) is at one point called upon to perform the necessary ritual of transmission and approval (which, interestingly enough, he is shown delivering somewhat reluctantly), the film is much more invested in playing up young musicians' irreverence and energy.

The movie opens with a scene of the musicians transporting a piano on a cart through the streets of the San Telmo neighborhood in order to play a traditional tango formation for an enthusiastic crowd that has assembled on the sidewalk. But the police show up, call for order, ask for permits, and insist on keeping the street clear; the young musicians argue that they have no official permit but that they had made previous arrangements with the shop owners, who were accommodating. The placement of this scene at the outset of *Orquesta típica* is designed to underline the creative rebelliousness of the young musicians, their respectful but innovative spirit, and the lack of support of government institutions, which they didn't seek anyway—all of which translates musically into a heterodox embrace of a form that had been viewed both as mainstream and old-fashioned but that under their interpretation unleashes its wild energy, its street cred. The impromptu audience follows suit by spontaneously rebelling against the men in uniform, whose call for order culminates in a heated debate, articulated by members of the crowd in terms of a repressive authority versus expressive enjoyment of culture. No arrests or further enforcement of public order follow, a détente that might be attributed to the presence of the camera, to the atmosphere of a leisurely and tourist friendly sunny day in San Telmo, to personal arrangements made with the officers off camera, or to the sheer ritualistic aspect of this discussion constructed of ready-made antagonisms (the people versus the men in uniform).

In any case this initial scene seems designed to conjure up a vision of a tango renaissance not reduced to an articulation of local expression in tune with the demands of world-culturalism but showing instead its unruly, untamed thrust. Still, in what might be the most novel and revealing turn in the debate, one neighbor defends tango on the streets as an alternative to *cumbia villera*, the music identified with the inhabitants of the slums of Buenos Aires (many of them migrants from poorer neighborhood countries, cumbia itself containing influences from Peru, Bolivia, and Colombia) and associated with drug addiction and criminality. This redefines the discussion in terms of clashing cultures and social classes, in which tango's local credentials are solidly grounded on core middle-class values, in opposition to the global flow of the poor and displaced. One member of the audience even interpolates a policeman with a challenge that he stand by the authentic local music of the city against the reprehensible cumbia—a demand that leaves the police officer visibly startled.

If tango in its origins was an illegitimate offspring, it might be mobilized in its resurgence as a cultural heir and bastion for the defense of legitimacy, an element of a core identity that retracts from new social actors and popular articulations. And that, among other things, is what these documentaries accomplish. That is, if *Orquesta típica* postulates that tango tradition might be carried quite unexpectedly to a new level of realization, that the "typical" is alive and well in the hands of these studiously untidy young musicians assembling an orthodox formation to revive tango's nonconformist spirit, then the contemporary resurgence is perhaps enabled by the social abjection of the new urban poor and the new immigrant. In a silent acknowledgment of what they largely leave to the side, *Orquesta típica* includes short sections in which street kids and other homeless city inhabitants are seen from a distance, a camera glance akin to a fleeting thought, granting filmic existence to what falls outside the scope of the main narrative. If tango grew out of early twentieth-century class and gender oppression and radical changes in the constitution of the social body, these scenes are perhaps harbingers of new tango art forms, the movies showing what tango is not prepared to express, signaling how the real will be confronted anew if tango is to remain as more than a token of sweetened postmodern nostalgia for elite consumption.[20]

Against the usual resort to stock images of Buenos Aires set to a tango soundtrack, *Orquesta típica* offers images of *cartoneros* (cardboard gatherers) and others processing the city's daily production of garbage, accompanied by the sounds of the Latin American pop fusion group El Portón, of which one of the bandoneon players is also a member. The visual-sound semantics are open but seem to suggest a city redefined by its improvised economy, equating not only old and new tango, and new tango spliced with other rhythms, but also the creative irreverence of the musicians with the ever-changing survival techniques of the destitute. The film leaves it at that, however, not going any further down this muddy path. And once again it is the European tour that confirms tango's artistic credentials, as if implicitly accepting that the form's current success is predicated on its incapacity or reluctance to express new social formations or history in the making.

Indeed, *Orquesta típica* also reenacts the legend of modest beginnings, transcending *el barro del suburbio* (the mud of the outskirts), where tango is said to have been imbued with its spirit, and traveling to the center and abroad to become a celebrated world music. The documentary accompanies the band in the peripatetic wanderings of its European tour. The lifestyle of the band, its laid-back attitude of mischievous, playful, and somewhat unpolished but charming boyishness, is the signature of this film. We see the band members inside the van they are driving, getting lost and excited in the course of their trotting about Europe, being hosted in private homes, borrowing a piano from a stranger and pushing it on a cart, putting together impromptu meals, and enjoying their quotidian wanderings in cities, towns, and on the road, admiring the scenery and always having lots of fun, with energetic music-making peppering their every adventure. Pushing a piano might be read as the image allegorizing the intended emotional climate of the movie: obstacles are happily overcome through passionate work, and precarious arrangements are pulled together by artistic magic. The movie concludes with an intriguingly cathartic scene, showing members of the band, once they've returned to Argentina, again pushing a piano, only this time it's toward a run-down or perhaps unfinished pedestrian bridge, where they proceed to push the instrument over into a free fall, punctuated by a sonorous crash to the ground. We are left with an image of urban Third World cool that reinforces a sense of an irreverent but charming youth, of those mischievous but artistic South Americans self-consciously displaying their cultural difference with a light, joyful spirit. The trick seems to work nicely, for they are welcomed to the world-culturalist table where they bridge the cultural gap while performing the enfant terrible. If, as Pedro Ochoa argues, early Hollywood and European films portrayed tango as a barbarian dance when performed by natives or in South American settings but as sophisticated and sexy when performed in Europe and by Europeans, *Orquesta típica* suggests the possibility of a remapped geography of passions, one in which tango is the sophisticated cultural capital flaunted by sexy new barbarians who happily enact their own self-exoticization.

Certainly, one single hypothesis won't do justice to this varied documentary film production, much less to the vast background of the long and complex deployment of tango in films against which it is set. Nevertheless, an epochal character becomes clear in the refusal of these films to treat tango as a self-transparent, available form of cultural expression to be mobilized for negotiating otherness (on the international screen) or dramatizing the same (in Argentine films). Tango's pull toward the closed era of its glory doesn't induce nostalgia, but it exerts pressure as if demanding new recognition and resignification while questioning whether the primary ties to its place of enunciation have been irredeemably lost. If nostalgia and authenticity are prevalent in the promotion of tango as cultural commodity, these documentaries approach tango with a sense of innocence lost and occasionally recovered. Tango, a remnant from another modernity, remains present as a pending assignment, imbued with guilt and remorse but also with desire, guiding yet another historical adventure.

Notes

1. One could argue that this impetus is energized by a global boom in documentary production, which responds to concurrent demands for the testimonial, the (auto)biographical, and the (post)memorial. But more specifically this documentary production is part of a larger boom of Argentine cinema that occurred before and after the economic crisis of 2001, particularly after 1995. New laws protecting national cinema, the organization of new festivals, the emergence of young directors and film critics coming out of different film schools, and the inception of advanced and more economically accessible video technologies all have been cited as relevant factors in bringing about unprecedented growth in the number and diversity of films produced (Aguilar, *Otros mundos* 7–10). Many of those feature films, some of which are considered representative of the new wave of Argentine cinema, include a documentary register and borrow from styles developed by or generally associated with documentary genres, thus interrogating the relationship between fictional film and the indexical (Aguilar, *Otros mundos* 64–66). Paradoxically, the documentaries I will discuss in this chapter do not subscribe to the same neo-realist ethos of this new cinema wave practiced by such prominent directors as Pablo Trapero, Lisandro Alonso, and Adrián Caetano. Among the critical surveys of the rich last two decades of Argentine film, see also Emilio Bernini, "Un proyecto inconcluso."

2. I mention U.S. film production because of its obvious influence and worldwide circulation, but tango has appeared more or less regularly (as a dance form or in diegetic or extradiegetic music) in many world cinemas. Pedro Ochoa's encyclopedic book is to my knowledge the best study of the variety of films of different origins (from Japan, Europe, the Middle East, and beyond) that incorporates tango in these different ways. A good survey of tango in Euro-American movies can be found in Thompson (13–24). Hollywood's early fascination with tango begins, as is well-known, with Rudolph Valentino's ur-performance in *The Four Horsemen of the Apocalypse* (directed by Rex Ingram, 1921), includes Paramount Studios' casting of Carlos Gardel for the Spanish-speaking market in the early 1930s, and arguably closes with the tango number of an aging diva in *Sunset Boulevard* (directed by Billy Wilder, 1950). But a new cycle opens in the 1990s, at a time when the performance of difference functions paradoxically as symbolic glue for times of upbeat globalization, and tango's gendered enactment becomes a medium to choreographically conjure up and make visible a powerful if ambivalent attraction. Blockbuster films featuring tango or tangoesque dance and music numbers include *Scent of a Woman* (directed by Martin Brest, 1992), *Schindler's List* (directed by Steven Spielberg, 1993), *True Lies* (directed by James Cameron, 1994), *Evita* (directed by Alan Parker, 1996), *Moulin Rouge* (directed by Baz Luhrmann, 2001), *Chicago* (directed by

Rob Marshall, 2002), *Shall We Dance* (directed by Peter Chelsom, 2004), *Rent* (directed by Chris Columbus, 2005), and *Take the Lead* (directed by Liz Friedlander, 2006). Notably, some of these films are retrospective pastiches of an era, the first half of the twentieth century, when tango mythology is established internationally through film; this feature is in itself telling in terms of the kind of intercultural fantasies that remained attached to "tango" through the arc of the twentieth century. Tango is mobilized for these exercises of postmodern nostalgia to signal lost authenticity in the age of the purported end of history. Some art-house films such as *Tango Lesson* (directed by Sally Potter, 1997) and *Assassination Tango* (directed by Robert Duvall, 2002) also display the ambivalence of an exotic attraction for tango culture that becomes a pedagogic adventure for a metropolitan subject.

3. The category of the "indexical" is widely used in film and photography studies and in particular in reference to the documentary genre, in which we assume that "the sound we hear and the image we behold seem to bear the trace of what produced them" (Nichols 35). The terminology (icon, index, and symbol) borrows from C. S. Peirce's early semiotics. See also Mitchell.

4. Much has been written about this early development. See Couselo (1291–328) and Garramuño. There are also some early documentaries focused on tango culture and/or featuring tango figures. In his survey of tango in Argentine film, Jorge Miguel Couselo mentions "the organic contribution of Mauricio Berú, to which category we must add two films by Edmundo Valladares about *Homero Manzi* (1964) and *Discepolín* (1967), and the imaginative *Gotán* (1965) with a script by Ernesto Sábato" (1325). Among Berú's filmography, the author mentions *Filiberto* (1964) and *Fuelle Querido* (1965).

5. This autobiographical tendency has been criticized as a shortcut intended to bypass the epochal questions currently raised by the documentary genre (see Beceyro, 2008 and Bernini, 2004).

6. Whereas multiculturalism is a U.S.–specific way of negotiating cultural difference with ties to foundational national narratives, I define *world-culturalism* as the celebratory vision of planetary cultural variety for the ultimate reaffirmation of a liberal globalizing agenda in which visual media plays a fundamental role.

7. Perhaps the alienated labor of this fictional filmmaker is already a factor of the lack of political thrust of his double enterprise. The most relevant documentary practices in Latin America have been until recently those with a political agenda, either testimonial, denunciatory, or propagandistic. The Argentine contribution to this lineage is prominent. The planned documentary on the tango bar stands as a sort of autobiographical project with lofty spiritual intentions, devoid of the political imperative, the necessity, the programmatic quality that lends force to the genre in many of its most important Latin American manifestations. Although the documentaries I explore here can't be directly ascribed to any of these agendas, one particular filmmakers collective with a strong political edge founded in the 1980s, Grupo Cine-Ojo, is responsible for one of the documentaries I discuss, *Yo no sé qué me han hecho tus ojos*.

8. The expression "economic violence," as related to the history of tango, is introduced by Julie Taylor (*Paper Tangos* 61), who identifies this violence with tango's moment of conception.

9. We might contrast this use of footage with the use of archival material in an earlier documentary, *El tango es una historia* (Tango is a history, directed by Humberto Ríos, 1983), in which an impressive amount of historical material is used only as naturalistic illustration of a rather linear, unproblematic narrative of tango's origin and evolution.

10. It is possible—though I have chosen to leave this argument unexplored in this chapter—to open up the truncated temporalities at the core of this and other tango films, their logic of oblivion and return, in reference to an altogether different site of Argentine cultural production. If the problems of complicated, discontinuous filiations are prevalent in these tango stories, they are also present in a seemingly very different body of aesthetic pursuits. I am referring to numerous artistic practices, ranging from documentaries to novels and from plays to street interventions that have emerged in the last decade, in which the personal and the political intersect in the viewpoint of those who were children during the last dictatorship. Even when the tango documentaries make no direct reference to these issues, a search for some form of continuity that has been violated, violently broken, or silenced points to a common thread in these heterogeneous loci of artistic enunciation, signaling a history marked with violent disruptions and posterior restorative efforts. Following the film critic and director Sergio Wolf, the golden age of Argentine film to which tango film belongs (especially in the 1940s) achieves an "abolition of time" (173), or perhaps historicity, through the creation of a mythical, self-enclosed world with recognizable types. If we keep in mind that film production during the last dictatorship (1976–1983) also proposed a time freeze of a different kind (Wolf 174), it is remarkable that Fernando Solanas's films of the democratic transition (*El exilio de Gardel: Tangos*, 1985, and *Sur*, 1988) resort to tango as the expressive language that would conjure up and amend historic discontinuities produced by symbolic and physical repression and disappearance. Editor's note: See Antonio Gómez's discussion of these films in this edited volume.

11. Horacio Coppola's book *Buenos Aires—1936* (published that year to celebrate the four hundredth anniversary of the city's founding) is a stand-alone classic. His clean style is considered Bauhaus-influenced.

12. Mederos has had a prolific filmic career as a fictional bandoneonist, most prominently in *Las Veredas de Saturno* (directed by Hugo Santiago, 1986) and in *El exilio de Gardel: Tangos* (directed by Pino Solanas, 1985). Mederos's music and his reflections on music are the main subject of another documentary, *El otro camino* (A different way, directed by Szollosy, 2008), which I will not discuss in this chapter, since it adds little to the sample of works I have chosen. Another famous bandoneonist of his generation is Daniel Binelli, who is seen at the end of *Orquesta típica*, supervising and approving the young musicians' work.

13. While the local tango scene has benefited from the worldwide hype around tango and its repackaging of itself for a constant influx of new audiences and dance aficionados, this same trend triggers anxiety and the need to protect tango's borders and original heritage. The long-standing Japanese taste for tango is exemplary in this regard: though not as flattering for the Argentine mind as the European obsession, it is much more threatening. A triple threat, the Japanese: successful capitalists, unbeatable tourists, and insatiable tango fans. The topic of cultural survival addressed in these movies thus takes a

new turn in *El último bandoneón,* which might be seen as an argument for protectionist measures in effective policing of bandoneons as material heritage. See Savigliano's chapter "Exotic Encounters," in *Tango and the Political Economy of Passion.*

14. Santaolalla's interesting career deserves mention. A former indie-rock performer, the Argentine musician went on to become a leading Los Angeles–based music producer, electronic tango band leader (with Bajofondo), and two-time Oscar Award–winning film music composer (for *Babel* and *Brokeback Mountain*).

15. The comparison with *Buena Vista Social Club* is intended to highlight a resonance that expresses an epochal drive; it is not a remark on Santaolalla's originality or lack thereof. In fact, the versatile musician was involved in a comparable project long before Ry Cooder's successful promotion of Cuban musicians, when he embarked, along with the Argentine musician León Gieco, on a two-year-long rescue operation of Argentina's folk musicians. Together they traveled to the most remote corners of the country to record *De Ushuaia a la Quiaca* (1985), the title cut from which Santaolalla later used in the soundtrack of *The Motorcycle Diaries.*

16. For a rather pessimistic approach to this orchestra revival, see Monjeau and Filipelli, who argue that tango is basically stagnant despite its current boom and that the orchestras return to the deadlock that Piazzolla had already broken. The article also illustrates the evolution of the instrumental configuration of the orquesta típica.

17. It is perhaps worth noting that film director Caroline Neal is an American who moved to Buenos Aires in order to film this documentary. She subsequently married the director of El Arranque, Ignacio Varchausky.

18. Although it doesn't feature an orchestra, the film *Tango, un giro extraño* (Tango, a strange turn, directed by Mercedes García Guevara, 2004) could have been part of this discussion for its focus on the young tango scene.

19. Jazz was tango's rival in foreign scenarios (see Savigliano, *Tango and the Political Economy of Passion* 170–71). Marsalis's support is significant, among other reasons because he represents jazz's most conservatively academic lineage.

20. To my mind, the most illuminating account of tango's historical breeding ground, and the kind of class and gender issues it tackles or contains, is Adriana Bergero's *Intersecting Tango.*

CHAPTER SIX

"Manejame como un auto"

Drive Me Like a Car, or What's So New about *Tango Nuevo*?

CAROLYN MERRITT

The role of women? Minimum. They were like our tools to have fun. We cannot dance between ourselves, so we should call women. Yeah, that's the first thing that was really obvious in nuevo. Well, not nuevo but the thing we were doing—that it wasn't feminine. Yeah, we were creating steps like kids, and we didn't ask the women for anything. We didn't care about their opinions. (ε)
—Javier (Argentine), tango professional, on the role of women in the late 1990s investigation sessions that many cite as the breeding ground for *tango nuevo*

Some girls get fed up with following, and they want to dance like a man because they say it's more entertaining. But I say you don't have enough time in your lifetime to learn how to follow well. So I would recommend to these girls to really learn how to follow.
—Carlos Gavito (Argentine), tango professional, quoted in Quiroga

Sex and Gender in a "Very Passionate Dance"

In this chapter I examine how notions of gender and sexuality often play out in contemporary Argentine tango dance. Focusing on a contested trend referred to as *tango nuevo*, I map the intersection of local and global norms and desires in tango dance classes, *prácticas*, and milongas in Buenos Aires.[1] Alternately portrayed as a threat to the cultural grounding and essential "Argentine-ness" of the form, a showmanship-oriented nuisance on the dance floor, an empty term imported from abroad and utilized solely as a marketing tool, an overly scientific approach to the dance that disallows feeling, or the next step in the evolution of tango in the twenty-first century, these myriad interpretations of tango nuevo point at once to the difficulty in defining human movement practice and to the many and varied players with a vested interest in doing so. Moreover, earlier incarnations of *nuevo*—Carlos Alberto "Petróleo" Estévez employed the term to describe his dance more than half a century ago, and the term was associated with the music of Astor Piazzolla as early as 1960[2]—reveal the deficiency of the modifier in describing a moment within a tradition still very much alive and therefore inevitably, though not quietly or easily, evolving. I contend that this tension between preservation and evolution extends to gender politics and performances in contemporary tango and, further, that this tension is heightened by the forces of globalization, the tendency to romanticize tradition, and both local and global desires to consume authenticity.

Whether or not there exists another new tango remains to be seen, for there continues to be heated debate over its very definition. Such ambivalence with the term is reflected in Javier's opening quote. Simply put, many Argentines reject the term for the division it implies between the tango of today and that of before and for what they perceive as its fundamental misuse to denote a new style of tango. Countering that the tango of today is evolved rather than new, they object to its reduction to style and/or surface factors, including clothing, music, and acrobatic dance moves. One point that dancers across the board tend to agree on, however, is that the investigation sessions initiated by Gustavo Naveira and Fabián Salas in the 1990s greatly changed tango at the level of conceptualization and instruction; while they might object to the term itself, many would agree that something *new* in tango began here.[3] Also, undeniably new developments are evident in the entry of increasing ranks of younger practitioners to tango communities around the globe and the concurrent growth of a veritable tango industry that is centered in Buenos Aires yet thrives on global interest and circulation. Further, a new práctica scene has exploded in Buenos Aires since the mid-2000s in the form of social dance events that function as young or nuevo alternatives to the traditional milongas.[4] In employing the term *nuevo*, I reference these myriad developments, while also acknowledging that other factors, including the clothing people wear, the music they dance to, their dance vocabulary, and who they dance with in social settings, have evolved in contemporary tango as well.

In the pages that follow, I differentiate between traditional and contemporary veins of Argentine tango, drawing distinctions and pointing to areas of intersection in the performance of gender and sexuality in the practices associated with each. At the heart of this chapter lies an argument that I dance around, speak back to, and question through a series of vignettes, observations, and voices from near and far: that the growth of new venues, a new generation of practitioners, and an increasingly fluid and interconnected global community have freed the dance and its codes from the hold of place and tradition. The following questions guide my investigation: To what extent has the growth of tango nuevo and/or the growing global community of younger practitioners facilitated a more autonomous position for women in the dance? Are there specific elements within the dance vocabulary or among the attendant social codes that encourage practitioners to break from the tango's all-consuming image of heterosexual passion and male domination?[5] Where have these ideas and practices originated, and what does that mean for the future of a dance whose propagation and growth have historically been tied to its evocation of place?

Central to the investigation sessions in the 1990s that for many mark the moment of inception of tango nuevo was an extensive analysis of the physical possibilities in the dance, which many argue yielded a simplification in the teaching and explanation of tango. One significant result of this process was a classroom focus on giving all students the tools with which to deconstruct and re-create their own dance, thus initiating a sort of democratization of information.[6] Female dancers of many different ages cited increased access to information as the primary factor encouraging greater autonomy in the dance, while foreign women have spoken of the further emancipation of the *tanguera* outside of Buenos Aires due to distance from the hold of tradition. Increased autonomy for the woman dancer is referenced at a number of levels: in the embrace—tangueras and *tangueros* frame the dance in tango nuevo as an equal exchange and note that the broadening movement vocabulary requires an agile, active follower; within the social ambient, as a loosening of stringent social codes that has freed women to invite men to dance and to lead other women or men;[7] and professionally, as evident in the rise of women's technique classes, classes for "women who lead," and in the growing number of female professionals who attract students on their own.[8] Finally, dancers trace the relaxation of social codes and the growth of global influences to the emerging gay-friendly tango scene. Nonetheless, gender identities are challenged by larger norms related to place, presenting a complex situation for the global tango community that feeds from, circulates around, and eventually meets in the dance's birthplace, where cosmopolitanism and machismo—already coexisting in an often contentious relationship—are pushed closer together in an often uncomfortable embrace.

Following earlier studies of gender in tango, including Archetti, Castro ("Carlos Gardel and the Argentine Tango"), Saikin, Salessi ("Medics, Crooks, and Tango Queens"), Savigliano (*Angorra Matta* and *Tango and the Political Economy of Passion*), Taylor (*Paper Tangos*), and Tobin, I examine the potential and desire for resistance to clichéd yet still powerful narratives of heteronormative passion, female manipulation, and male domination. More specifically, in turning my lens on the myriad developments associated with nuevo, I question whether these are yielding truly new narratives of gender and sexuality in the embrace. Building on studies that portray movement as a means of both reflecting and constructing the larger societal context (Browning; Collier, Cooper, Azzi, and Martin; Desmond; Ness; Novack; Sklar; Savigliano, *Angorra Matta* and *Tango and the Political Economy of Passion*; Taylor, *Paper Tangos*; Thomas and Miller), I argue that manifestations of gender and sexuality in contemporary tango rise from the heightened circulation of global norms and desires that mark modern life.[9] These norms and desires are informed by disparate, fluid notions of self and other, influenced by narratives of authenticity and exoticism that evolve in reaction to place. In situating my study at the center of these global flows, I hope to produce a snapshot that is true to contemporary tango—a space where young and old, local and foreign, new and traditional, preservation and innovation meet, and where the future of a dance once described and more often pigeonholed as the "vertical expression of a horizontal desire" (Rippon) is negotiated, both on and off the dance floor.

Performing Tradition: *El Piropo*

For the tango pilgrim who travels to the mecca of Buenos Aires, the *piropo* is one of those local customs that immediately raises awareness of one's displacement from home.[10] In the *porteño* tango world, sweet talk on the dance floor has achieved the status of an art form in the piropo, in which one-liners the likes of "what beautiful eyes you have" stand at the tame end of the scale. A compliment that might also be a pick-up line, uttered without necessarily serious intentions or expectations, piropos are the *juego* de jure in many of the more traditional dance venues. With piropos, male dancers fulfill their partners' expectation of the porteño male, on the one hand conforming to the (admittedly clichéd) notion of what it means to be Latin, macho, a *seductor*, and on the other seeking to convince the tanguera of her singularity, to more fully extend the illusion of communion on a crowded dance floor. One wonders, of course, if the *milonguero* is indeed defenseless in the presence of countless beautiful young women, many of whom hail from abroad, many in desperate search of a "true tango moment" assumed to be achieved only in the dance's birthplace, in the arms of a real porteño.[11] More than simply generational, piropos are one of the many practices around which notions of style or community are constructed. As a game, piropos render the milonga a site for a theatrical enactment of traditional notions of masculinity and femininity, employed alternately to intimidate, entertain, define roles, fulfill the sexually charged promise of the dance's reputation, and test the boundaries of possibility.

However, a part of the steady growth of a younger community of dancers and the creation of new venues represents an interest in approaching the dance and the larger social milieu in a more contemporary fashion, including relinquishing gestures such as the piropo. Buenos Aires's "laid-back" práctica scene offers relief from such ritual theatrics sometimes deemed an annoyance or hindrance to simply enjoying the dance itself:

> If you go to the milongas, you don't want to look at the milongueros if you don't want to be felt up, or if you don't want to be told how beautiful your eyes are, and "if only they were younger." And then they would mention that their last girlfriend was younger than you! There's this cropping up of prácticas, and a lot of people trying to get away from that—not necessarily the milonguero style but more so the milonguero attitude—"el juego de la seducción" . . . all of the old guys trying to seduce the girls, and the younger people are more interested in the dancing and having fun, and they're not analyzing it in this way that's so sexist. (Ginger [American expatriate], chef)

Emphasizing this distinction between age and style, Ginger pointed out that "even some of the younger guys will do that in the context of the milonga," thus framing the milonga as a site to play, to try on postures associated with a notion of tanguero identity informed by exaggerated representations of tango from the stage, screen, and visual media, as well as a form of apprenticeship in the milongas themselves. Of course, these exaggerated postures could be the milonguero's response to what he perceives as the foreign woman's expectations on her tango pilgrimage. Nonetheless, such reactions to this type of playing as "sexist" or "macho" (if ultimately harmless) are not uncommon among younger female tangueras from abroad, even long-term residents like Ginger.

Imagining places as experiential containers, housing and imparting memories to those who would claim them (see Basso 1996; Samuels, "The Whole and the Sum of the Parts" and *Putting a Song on Top of It*), I argue that cultural practice facilitates the expansion of community across spatial and temporal bounds. Drawing on the national obsession with remembrance in sites constructed around and drowned in a sense of nostalgia,[12] such posturing feeds from a sort of collective unconscious that is nourished at home and abroad through films, stage shows, images, and tango lore. Further, tango dancers insert themselves within a cultural tradition through a shared movement practice that doesn't merely reference but in fact pays homage to a worldview that emerged at a specific place in time. In manifesting such postures out of time, however, a degree of kitsch and caricature may color the behaviors of the milongueros, their protégés, and the foreign dancers whose presence serves to encourage their perpetuation. According to Luciana Valle, organizer of the popular El Motivo práctica, the new social dance venues grew from a desire to escape an *onda* (vibe) approaching circus and to create a scene accessible to dancers who had lives to attend to outside of tango: "The night is weird. We were girls who lived in the daylight, we got up at 9:00 to go to yoga, so why I can't dance until 1:00 AM, why I have to go to a place that is packed . . . have all that smoke, and be in a place where everybody is like . . . in a mise en scène. Why?!" (ε). As Valle frames it, the milonga is situated in the life of the night, an otherworldly realm that encourages behaviors that don't make sense in the light of day.

To be fair, the piropo finds expression off the dance floor as well. At times it may be as simple as a cheerful "que linda" (how pretty), while at others a barely audible comment muttered under a challenging glance by the porteño who catches you on a crowded sidewalk. For women moving through the Argentine capital, piropos quickly become one more element in an already overloaded soundscape, blending in with the noise of too many *colectivos* (buses) and the incessant drone of the drilling, banging, and sawing, slowly extending the reach of the city several stories higher, wider, or, for those with money, closer to a notion of First World comfort and amenities. Generally framed as a representation of traditional gender norms, it is also plausible that the piropo functions as a reaction to so much noise.[13]

Female writers from abroad have produced varying takes on the piropo. For instance, Miranda France reports relinquishing control over her most intimate possession while living in the Argentine capital, where piropos are a constant reminder that one's body (if one is female, that is) is at the mercy of porteño scrutiny and commentary. Kaitlin Quistgaard, on the other hand, describes the charm of the piropo as "refined machismo." Unlike its vulgar North American cousin, the "white-trash catcall," the piropo is subtle, romantic, and ultimately private, delivered like a quiet "gift" intended only for the recipient, the goal being tribute rather than shame (Quistgaard). Through the eyes of an enchanted outsider, the piropo also becomes a sign of inclusion, and Quistgaard takes these gifts as an indication that she is perceived as having arrived, capable of handling piropos like a real porteña.

While the foreign woman in Buenos Aires may arm herself against such comments by cultivating a healthy degree of haughtiness or an acute ability to ignore, the porteña abroad may acclimate herself to their absence. For the writer Alicia Dujovne Ortiz, born in Buenos Aires and exiled to France in the late 1970s, the piropo is at the root of a decidedly porteña mode of existence. Just as the larger country of Argentina has historically sought outside approval to confirm its existence, Dujovne Ortiz argues that it is under the reassuring gaze of the porteño male, reinforced through the piropo, that the porteña draws her strength and her very sense of identity. Without this gaze, or "when away from the Mediterranean countries," her sense of self is blunted: "she is seen in an extremely modest manner that makes her feel invisible" (Dujovne Ortiz, "Etre Porteño (in Buenos Aires)" 74). Like Dujovne Ortiz, a young porteña who had relocated to Germany for several years confessed to exasperation over the lack of attention she received there. On her first day, she ran home five minutes after leaving the house, convinced she had made a catastrophic fashion blunder, for what other possible excuse could there be for the lack of male commentary? In conversations with porteñas, I found that rather than disrespectful or threatening, such comments are viewed ambivalently at worst. One of the many customs that allow the two sexes to revel in their separateness, piropos are generally perceived as harmless and, although unacknowledged, often secretly appreciated.

Beyond the informality and anonymity of the streets, the piropo is also at home in the realm of the professional. In my own experience conducting research in the tango world, I grew accustomed to comments I would have deemed inappropriate, infantilizing, and sexist away from Argentine soil— like the teacher who told me he had "never met such a beautiful woman with so many problems" after asking about my research. Such flattery and flirtation are arguably central to the business of tango itself. It isn't just that these

Argentine tangueros never learned to filter their thoughts, something Kaitlin Quistgaard attests to with humorous effect in describing the special attention she received from "fawning men in suits" (government officials and corporate executives) as a foreign correspondent in Buenos Aires. In the porteño tango world, such posturing is expected, especially by foreign tangueras who take piropos as confirmation of the cultural difference that makes the dance in its birthplace so enticing, regardless of how they might ultimately feel about their propriety. Further, this posturing is frivolous, of the moment, and transparently hyperbolic; although by no means meaningless, the weight of its meaning is decidedly light. More importantly, the piropo warrants analysis that looks beyond the message itself.[14] As Matthias points out, foreign attitudes in the face of such commentary reveal just as much about the recipient of the piropo as of the local who delivers it:

> This subject comes up again and again if you talk to foreigners. Women in general start judging that way of playing because we experience it as threatening, or sometimes without any respect, but for Argentineans it's a game. So asking a woman home is just their way of saying goodbye. And the other extreme—I have had experiences where if you don't ask a woman this question, it doesn't mean that she would follow you, but it's almost "Am I not worth this? I'm not attractive enough to deserve this invitation?" As much as you perceive with your American values, they perceive with their values. (ε) (Matthias Kroug [German expatriate], scientist)

In this context, if the foreign tanguera is unable to read such flattery as a game, she may be judged as unwilling to fully give herself to the experience of tango in Buenos Aires, and there is a chance that she will miss out on more than just piropos.

Leading and Following: The Gendered Division of (Tango) Labor

"The dance portrays an encounter between the powerful and completely dominant male and the passive, docile, completely submissive female," writes Julie Taylor ("Tango" 485). Further along in her essay, Taylor comments on the fact that the classic image of tango dance (of male domination and female submission) is at odds with that presented in many tango lyrics, in which men are quite often portrayed as suffering at the hands of willful, cunning, heartless women.[15] Pablo Verón's famous outburst in The Tango Lesson (Potter), that tango partner and film director Sally Potter "follow, JUST follow!" mirrors Taylor's description of sexual domination in the dance. But the tango has long since evolved beyond this initial, chauvinistic signification. Farris Thompson notes that the female partners of the 1940s Club Nelson dancers "rebelled against men who bossed them around with peremptory hand motions" (257). While he roots the origins of a fifty-fifty tango partnership in the 1940s, Juan Carlos Copes and María Nieves, international stars of stage and screen and virtual ambassadors of tango dance from the 1960s, are often credited with fully breaking with the image of male domination and placing the man and woman on equal footing (Del Mazo and D'Amore 56; personal communication with Juan Carlos Copes, March 2006). Gloria and Rodolfo Dinzel, who gained fame alongside Copes and Nieves in the stage show *Tango Argentino,* characterize this parity as "communion": "in tango, one and one make one. . . . When tango is being danced well it is simply impossible to observe either one of the individuals. . . . To effect this image of oneness means to be in a constant quest of communion between these two bodies into one dynamic structure. In the very instant that the development of the form turns into an individual effort, the couple disappears, and when this happens, tango vanishes as well" (9). Dancers continue to make personal and generational claims to female autonomy and to equality in the embrace to this day.[16] Nonetheless, culture impacts the way dancers conceive of, approach, and enact the roles of leading and following, and the modern implications of this (largely) gendered division of roles are anything but straightforward.[17]

The title of this chapter comes from a friend's initiation into tango in Buenos Aires. In an effort to get him comfortable with the concept and practice of leading, his female instructor told him to "drive her like a car" as they walked through the space in a practice embrace. This wording might seem a terrible step backward to some, but the metaphor is not entirely uncommon among Argentine instructors. Nonetheless, it stands in contrast to the generally more nuanced and egalitarian explications of the sexual and physical mechanics of the dance commonly invoked by U.S. instructors. Framing the dance as a conversation, a back and forth exchange based upon the equal participation of each, many U.S. teachers position the woman as an autonomous partner through the language they employ to teach and conceptualize the dance, problematizing this image of male domination. For instance, the dance historian and Stanford professor Richard Powers speaks of "great partnering" on his website, rejecting an outdated approach to the roles of leader and follower that hails from an intense period of formalization in ballroom dance beginning in the 1930s:

After centuries of ballroom emphasis on dancing for the pleasure of one's partner, the 1930s saw the emergence of a particularly disagreeable phase of social dance, when the term "lead" came to mean "command" and "follow" meant "obey." . . . The main reason I don't like the term 'following' is that it doesn't accurately describe the role. Women do not "follow," they *interpret* signals they're given, with a keen responsiveness that is not passive. . . . The follow role is mentally and physically active, like the flow state in sports.

And Powers describes the leader's role as "tracking," complicating a simplistic division between the two roles and pointing to the leader's responsibility to respond to the follower's cues as well.

Despite an advanced approach to the concept of partnering, it is worth noting that Powers still divides the roles according to gender. This brings to mind a conversation with an Argentine professional who confessed to feeling exasperated, at times even angry, when he first went abroad to teach and was asked time and again to explain why the man leads and the woman follows. Surely this most basic principle of tango, of social dance in general (and by extension in life as well), was only natural. Indeed, implicit to the dance's functioning is a naturalization of this division (Benarós; Collier, Cooper, Azzi, and Martin; Dínzel and Dínzel; Pujol; Saikin; Savigliano, *Tango and the Political Economy of Passion*; Taylor, *Paper Tangos*).

This has interesting implications in the United States, Europe, and elsewhere, where instructors employ images, metaphors, and values from their various cultures to communicate the mechanics and meaning of the dance. The same dance can be imagined quite differently, and the relation of leader to follower can play out and be experienced distinctly. In an interview with Kevin, a dancer from the United States, he noted that one popular teacher explains the role of the follower through a post-feminist, American lens, encouraging a masculine energy in following. Arguing that this would be considered inappropriate in Argentina, Kevin distinguished the intention with which he perceives Argentine and American women enact the role of follower:

He'll tell followers that they need to step with a leader's energy, especially in the forward step; that they need to step as if they were leading, using his intention but with that kind of certainty, that masculine energy. This is something that I don't think you would hear in Argentina—they would never tell a woman to step like a man, you know? . . . I think the active voice of a follower in Argentina is more like what she can add in her own kind of monologue running on the side, and that the active voice of a follower say in the Northwest is challenging or responding or provoking the dialogue between the two. It's not a sideline, it's essential to the conversation, and for me that's much more interesting.

According to this description, "active following" implies not only a subversion of gender but also a certain devaluation of femininity, where it is "masculine energy" that renders the follower an equal protagonist in the embrace.[18] The ambivalence expressed by foreign tangueras to traditions like the piropo and to the terms *lead* and *follow* may also be a reaction to such thinking, for despite the gains of feminism, we have yet to fully reconcile empowerment and femininity. Indeed, Argentine tango is a practice par excellence for confronting and negotiating what many foreign tangueras experience as profound contradictions.

Building on Powers's "tracking" and "interpreting," another U.S. teacher cites *The Tao of Tango* (Siegmann) on his website to portray the interplay of masculine (yang) and feminine (yin) qualities in each of the roles. In an effort to dissuade American resistance to the male-leader and female-follower dichotomy, Jay Rabe draws on Asian philosophy, separating and overlapping the masculine and feminine roles and energies under the guise of an ancient, exotic, and decidedly less macho worldview. In conversation with an Argentine professional, he used the same image to free the tango from its image of strict heterosexuality, speaking of the dance as an experience where the idea of two sexes is lost, and gender distinctions are muddied or dissolved. At the same time, several foreigners employed the yin-yang image to frame tango as a dance that frees practitioners to embrace a separation of the sexes often discounted in the wake of feminism: "The primary thing for me is that you've got the connection of the male-female, masculine-feminine energy, which for me can create synergy and it's fantastic for people to get through their prejudices" (Sarah Bonnar [Australia], tango professional).

"In Europe we always look for the equality, while here it's more obvious that the man and the woman have different roles. . . . You could say there's the feminine and masculine qualities that meet each other and do something together. It sounds maybe philosophical but I think every experience where opposites in a way unite is something we strive for. And it's for me one explanation why this dance fascinates people all over the world" (ε) (Matthias Kroug [German expatriate], scientist).

In *Tango: Un baile bien porteño* (Tango: A very porteño dance) the German native and tanguera Nicole Nau-Klapwijk describes a similar quest for balance in her life, attained through her discovery of tango in Argentina, an activity and culture that together teach her to be a woman and to allow herself partnership with a man. A common theme in conversations with foreigners was that of the tango as a realm within which sexual difference is accepted and celebrated. A dancer and choreographer from the United States, Michele Kadison described how tango had released her from her dynamic, external, almost masculine body, freeing her to explore another dimension of her being through movement: "I was always a tough-ass—whatever the role was that did the most jumps and turns, that was me. So when I came to tango all of the sudden I could really explore my truly feminine side.... Tango is unraveling all of these neurological pathways to my muscular system to get me to be soft and listening and acquiescent, and really appreciate the goddess side of being female." Foreigners also contrasted the experience of tango in Buenos Aires with that in their home community, where notions of gender equality pervade nearly all aspects of life. Like Michele, Nancy underscored the femininity of tango in Buenos Aires, while she described her first year of tango in the United States as a nearly genderless experience: "I didn't feel the dance at all, which means I wasn't in touch with my femininity. It was just, I'm a person and I'm dancing with this person and we're creating something, and it was creative, but I didn't feel feminine" (Nancy [American expatriate], actress).

I argue that this reembracing of a separation of the sexes is connected to notions of place that play out in the representation, enactment, and conceptualization of the dance. Here I borrow from Dempster's notion of visual kinesthesia, in which she frames the skin as a surface that perceives visually and kinesthetically, that is inspired to thought through both touch and images (and, I would add, evocative, image-producing words). Stage shows, films, and promotional materials have traditionally been geared toward reinforcing romantic notions of the essential "Argentine-ness" of the dance, represented through a passionate, heterosexual embrace and references to late nineteenth- and early twentieth-century porteño society symbols and characters, such as the *farol* or gas lamp, the *conventillo* (tenement house), the port slum of La Boca, the *compadrito* (hoodlum) with his fedora and knife, and the prostitute in high heels and fishnets (Duvall; Orezzoli and Segovia; Romay; Saura; Zotto). Though male-male partnering was crucial to tango's development and the spectacle of two compadritos dancing on a street corner is a fixture of the tango stage show, this practice is consistently attributed to the demographics of Buenos Aires at the turn of the twentieth century, when men greatly outnumbered women. As Tobin points out, such same-sex partnering is regularly defined as "practice" and distinguished from "dancing," so that, both in tango histories and in porteño tango classes and prácticas, the story of gender transgression is clarified and the possibility of homosexual desire is frequently dismissed.

While the tango has evolved beyond its bordello, slum, and tenement house origins, this narrative—of its dangerous, lower-class origins and its connection to a licentious heterosexual embrace—lingers. It is carried in movement vocabulary passed down through generations, lifted from historic images, and transferred from the stage performer's theatrical reenactment to the dance class. Much like Browning's "survivals" in samba—gestural references to a colonial or precolonial past—the plethora of tango movements developed since the dance's inception serve as a window onto its past.[19] The Argentine professionals who took the dance abroad in stage shows, training locals and planting the seeds of global communities in their wake, carried these narratives as memories, a sort of embodied cultural heritage. Furthermore, these narratives play out in classroom exercises[20]—whether to mock and discount as clichéd or essentialist or to elicit heightened performances from students through poetic and theatrical anecdotes that get at one particular aspect of the dance's history (where tango equals passion and drama), often at the expense of any other. In turn this image of the tango is deeply embedded in the global imaginary.

Outside of Argentina the tango is a safe space to explore the separation of masculine and feminine because it is "other," "exotic," and "Latin." Indeed, part of the dance's appeal for the non-native may be its perceived "dangerousness," which is subverted and cleansed through its very performance; it is safe for foreign tangueras and tangueros to dress and dance suggestively, for there remains a degree of cultural appropriation or a sense that one is playing a character. This performance of a more traditional gender identity often involves a sense of theater, where throwbacks to the past and to a notion of "otherness" may relieve the self of any discomfort in the present-day implications of one's role (for example, when women don fishnet stockings and slit skirts and men fedoras and scarves). Furthermore, behaviors prohibited by notions of propriety enter a state of limbo or experimentation when abroad, when thrown into contact with a culture or subculture where a separation of the genders and their roles is quite firmly embraced, and the notion of equal rights does not yield an erasure of male-female difference. So it is that tough, independent foreign tangueras find themselves accumulating corsets and stiletto heels in Buenos Aires and dreaming of a *tanda* or entire song set spent in the arms of a *viejo milonguero*.

While the embrace sanctions a performance of gender that many non-Argentines described as freeing in contrast to that experienced in their everyday lives,[21] others framed these gendered posturings in a negative light. Distinguishing between the relaxed codes of the emerging nuevo or práctica scene and the codes of the more traditional milongas in Buenos Aires, they highlighted an emptiness in the theatrics of the latter: "You have to get dressed up in fishnet stockings and a short skirt to dance tango. It's like, no—more of that stuff we don't need. You know, more of that fakery and all that stuff on the surface. The world is already enough about that and it's not helping. You know, the facelifts and the lies and the bullshit" (Sarah Bonnar [Australia], tango professional).

Underscoring the difference she experienced on her first visit to Buenos Aires, Pia, a painter from Sweden, noted an emphasis on appearance in some of the more traditional milongas, where women are especially subject to all manner of discrimination and one's ability is often the least important factor in securing dances: "Just sitting here and thinking maybe my dress is not nice enough.... And all of these beautiful girls. That's another thing I don't like about Buenos Aires. The macho culture and the idea that you have to be beautiful to dance, and if you're not beautiful you're not worth anything. And there's no old women in the milongas—if they're not so beautiful they can just sit at home" (ε). As these two foreign women perceive it, the culture in some of the traditional milongas is not only superficial but also places disproportionate demands upon men and women.

Savigliano describes the milonga as a site where such external factors dissolve, where the dance comes first. For Savigliano, no matter how young, old, short, tall, fat, thin, or in whatever manner aesthetically endowed or challenged the participant, it is skill that determines whether and how much one will dance (*Angorra Matta* 153–55). This is still the case in many venues; moreover, I would argue that this logic operates to a degree, or among certain dancers, in most venues. But the sentiments expressed by Sarah and Pia also ring true. It is important to note here that Argentine tango stands out among dance forms for its acceptance of the aging body; in a realm that generally celebrates youth, tango is considered an appropriate activity for people of all ages. Moreover, there are plenty of traditional milongas where one will encounter a largely mature crowd. At the same time, however, there is a milonga circuit that has grown alongside the city's ever-expanding tango tourism,[22] where the absence of older women is often striking.[23] In these famed *confiterías*, dance halls, bars, and social clubs—attended by a mix of foreigners and Argentines, the percentage of each shifting throughout the year according to foreign holidays, porteño festivals, and international demands on Argentine teachers—the clichéd yet defining image of this particular milonga scene is the famed milongueros' table. It is here that the male old-timers hold court, drinking champagne, watching the floor with an alternating mix of amusement and disdain, and occasionally emerging to grace one of the beautiful young milonguitas with a song or, if lucky, an entire tanda. The young women wait patiently on the sidelines, maybe stopping at the table to say hello, but never to stay and certainly never to invite the revered male *bailarines* to dance.[24]

The above speaks to the cultivation of fantasy within this particular milonga circuit, inspired at once by historic anecdotes and images that favor the dance's male forebears, traditionalist arguments that link age to authenticity, and global desires to experience the "authentic." The further they decline, the more the male milongueros are celebrated and rewarded with the adulation of the young and beautiful women, while the young and beautiful act out an exaggerated notion of femininity inaccessible to them in the light of day.[25] Conversations with foreign men did not reveal a parallel desire to encounter the tango in the arms of elder porteñas. Perhaps this reflects the absence of inspiration in the social scene or the larger imaginary created in films, media images, lyrics, and promotional materials. (On the other hand, perhaps these foreign men wouldn't divulge such a desire to me for the simple fact that I don't fit that profile.)

At the same time, this subworld serves as a window onto the larger, fantastical values embraced in porteño society, where "true beauty" does not preclude surgical intervention, in turn encouraged and heightened by global desires.[26] Home to a growing plastic surgery industry,[27] Buenos Aires's medical tourism market has thrived in the wake of the economic crisis of 2001 and the ensuing peso devaluation, which made tourist consumption of the city available at a fraction of its former price for those with foreign currency (Balch; Dodes).[28]

The importance accorded physical appearance in the tango world is reinforced in the city's tango guides. Glossy, full-color, magazine-style pamphlets and other publications include information on classes, milongas, shoe and clothing outlets, tourist excursions, interviews with dancers, photos of milongas, and ads for aesthetic surgery clinics (Caserón Porteño; Palumbo). Speaking about the connection between tango and the city's booming aesthetic surgery industry, a native tanguera rooted the precedence accorded physical appearance in tango within the larger porteño culture:[29]

> If you like to dance tango, you're going to like to look good. . . . Buenos Aires was a city and it still is a city where everybody really takes care of themselves. The ladies like to be elegant. They really want to look the best that they can. . . . The beauty and cosmetic clinics are all full, and the prices are much better than in the United States. So I think it is one of the reasons that a lot of people come here right now—because of the exchange. (ε) (Linda [Argentine], doctor)

Despite this cross-promotion of aesthetic surgery and tango, there is no question that the cult of good appearance exists outside of the tango world as well. Moreover, many tango venues *do* offer older women refuge from a media-saturated culture that favors youth and beauty above all else and that places higher demands upon women in this respect. There are plenty of traditional milongas where older women are evaluated for qualities other than their appearance, and in tango communities around the world, older women are accorded license to express their sexuality in ways that are generally at odds with society's expectations of women over a certain age (see Savigliano, *Angorra Matta*).[30] Nonetheless, the pairing of beautiful young women with elderly milongueros speaks to the fact that men still wield greater power in the tango world and to the sexist ageism women face, both in the tango world and at large.

In the nuevo or práctica scene, on the other hand, dancers noted more flexibility in carving out gender identities, arguing that practitioners are free to dress as they like. In the prácticas fishnets and high heels are traded in for dance sneakers and bell bottoms, the suit jacket and tie for T-shirt and tattoos. (Of course, one might counter that the rules of looking good are simply different in these spaces and reflect the aesthetic values of their attendees.) Aside from dress, in the prácticas the music is generally not programmed into tandas (musical sets of three to four songs),[31] freeing tangueras and tangueros to dance as many or as few songs with each partner as they choose. Free of the *cabeceo*—that silent invitation to dance performed by establishing and maintaining eye contact—in the prácticas dancers may walk right up to the partner of their choice, making the invitation unmistakably clear (if not potentially coercive, as the act of declining such an invitation is equally clear and undeniably public). Further, women are (theoretically) free to invite men, and same-sex partnering is more widely accepted than in the traditional milongas, though as I discuss below, this is generally enacted as a practice technique or as a last resort, outside of the specifically sanctioned "gay" spaces.

"Women Who Lead" and Tango Queer

Deconstructing the leader-follower dichotomy, many dancers argue that learning the second role helps them better understand their partners' position and feedback, and thus it serves to further refine their overall dance. With the entrance of growing numbers of younger practitioners to the dance and the creation of social and practice spaces in which experimentation is encouraged, the division of roles according to gender has relaxed in tango communities the world over. At times responding to a lack of male partners, but also often framed as an interest in more fully understanding the mechanics of the dance, more and more women are learning to lead. And they are leading in social dance settings, though this is occurring chiefly outside of Buenos Aires. No longer just a classroom or practice endeavor, women are increasingly dancing with other women in milongas around the world. The gender balance outside of Buenos Aires may discourage the reverse among men, where they are often outnumbered by women, and thus less often at a loss for a partner. Still, the man who wishes to follow is offered comfort in the generally accepted notion that knowledge of the second role will assist one in execution of the first, as well as in tango lore and historic images that trace the dance's origins and development to male-male practice (figure 6.1) (Benarós; Collier, Cooper, Azzi, and Martin; Thompson; Savigliano, *Tango and the Political Economy of Passion*; Salessi, "Medics, Crooks, and Tango Queens"; Tobin).[32] Indeed, some Argentines have argued that the tradition of male-male practice produces sensitive and understanding leaders *because they have first learned to follow*, and they question the potential for female autonomy with the loss of that tradition today.

In the wake of La Marshall, Buenos Aires's first and most popular "milonga gay" that opened in 2002, several gay-friendly venues have emerged in the city. Among the more successful is Tango Queer (figure 6.2), relocated on at least three occasions due to its growing popularity. Like La Marshall, Tango Queer is open to all regardless of sexual orientation and founded on the desire to create a space where everyone feels free to dance the role of her

Figure 6.1. *Un Tango en el Agua* (1912). Image courtesy of the Archivo General de la Nación, Dto. Doc. Fotográficos.

or his choice. In weekly classes students learn both to lead and to follow, switching back and forth throughout the hour-and-a-half lesson. And gender is not necessarily the best indicator of a dancer's role in the post-lesson milonga, where the exchange of leading and following, oftentimes within a single song, is a common sight. Further, beyond the weekly class and milonga, Tango Queer has a decidedly political bent. The founder Mariana Docampo advocates tango as a platform to engage larger questions of inclusion and exclusion grounded in the relationship between gender and power, and she frames tango an ideal form for this project, specifically because of its historically macho profile. Through events, including scholarly conferences and the annual international Queer Tango Festival (inaugurated in 2007), Tango Queer aims to link dancers, researchers, writers, and artists interested in the role of gender in tango to the larger fields of gender and queer studies.

Outside of these specifically advertised gay spaces, however, the absence of women leading and men following in the práctica scene is striking. On those rare occasions when women dance together outside the classroom, it is likely that one (if not both) is from abroad, while few men appear to dance together outside of La Marshall and practice venues. And in Buenos Aires's more traditional venues, same-sex partnering could elicit outright hostility. Dancing with a woman one night at Confitería Ideal, I was unnerved by the attention my partner and I received from an elderly tanguero. A famed

Figure 6.2. *Tango Queer*. Photo by Karina Maccioli. Used by permission of Mariana Docampo of Tango Queer.

tango institution, Ideal is classic porteño-faded elegance, bestowing a sense of nostalgia on those who never even knew its better days. Popular to the point of being a museum, in Ideal traditional milonga codes were respected one moment and tossed aside the next: twenty-year-olds struggled with the subtleties of the cabeceo, while retirees would cockily cross the floor and walk straight up to the table to invite women to dance. But the hall remains a beloved bastion of the dance, and in such sites traditionalists often made it their business to keep transgressors in line. On this occasion it was a sep-tuagenarian tanguero who crossed into the line of dance from the sidelines, invading our space mid-song—this a crime in and of itself. Smirking from beneath his fedora, he clapped in our faces and muttered "que bueno, que bueno, que bueno," his voice dripping with condescension and disgust, the intention crystal clear for us: In Argentine tango, women follow men.

While it is essentially required that today's female tango professionals un-derstand the lead, this capacity does not appear to have a voice in the social realm in Buenos Aires comparable to that in the United States and Europe. When I have broached this topic with local professionals, they have framed the milonga and the práctica as social events designed to bring men and women together: "It's a social thing—why I don't dance with girls in the milonga. When I go out to a milonga or a práctica, the dance is no longer about investigating. . . . When I go to dance in the milonga, it's an outing, it's a social encounter. I'm going out to have fun and dance, and if I'm going to have fun and dance, I want to have fun with a boy" (τ) (Marcía [Argentine], tango professional). Simultaneously, some foreign women have described Buenos Aires as a sort of "follower's candy store," where the unimaginably large pool of male dancers renders leading unnecessary or even uninteresting:

> In the United States tons of women are leading, but here there aren't many women leading, really. There are women who know how to lead but women don't lead socially. I was leading more than I was following in the United States, and I don't know if I've led two songs in the past six months. I have no interest right now. I feel like leading for women also has a feeling of last resort, like "I want to dance tango and there's no one to follow. Okay, I'll lead." If you get to follow, for a lot of people it doesn't seem to be that important. (Miriam [American expatriate], tango professional)

Inherent in Miriam's comment is a naturalization of the division of roles according to gender and, further, an acknowledgment that women tend to lead more out of necessity than desire. As Marcía noted, leading falls under the realm of "investigation"—arising from her need to understand the dance in a more complete fashion, in order to transfer that knowledge to students. While one might argue that women lead more in the United States and Europe because women enact a different notion of what it is to be female in those societies, many foreign tangueras described their entry into leading as a way to keep the tango interesting when there weren't enough skilled men for them to follow or as a necessary step toward professionalization, rather than as an expression of feminist ideals.

A Nuevo Machismo?

I think it's very clear in tango that the man leads and the woman follows. But that doesn't mean that the woman is passive, nor does it mean that the man is the boss, that he commands the woman. Because the tango is a dialogue, it's a conversation. One proposes the topic, and the other continues the conversation, and the content and the form of the dialogue is constructed by each. . . . The man who dances tango well dances smoothly, clearly, piecing together the dialogue one step at a time. And this isn't a new idea. If you look at the old dancers, and the true milongueros, the really good milongueros don't have that arrogant attitude in their dance. On the contrary, the man who dances like that doesn't know how to dance.— Olga Besio (Argentine), tango professional

En route to the milonga one night, I got into a discussion about the role of the woman in tango with Jorge, an Argentine expatriate living in the United States. He argued that what characterizes "traditional" tango are the pauses, and that it is the woman who signals and makes these pauses happen. Contrasting this to nuevo, where the man manipulates the woman through complicated, acrobatic figures that grant her no voice in what is happening, he suggested that the woman exerts much greater control in traditional tango. Dancers who identify with nuevo may disagree, contending that rather than acrobatics, the tango being danced by young people is grounded in a whole new manner of thinking about the dance, that an expansion in vocabulary accompanied this, and finally that calling it acrobatics reduces contemporary tango to one element—and not a necessary one by any means—that ignores the conceptual and pedagogic revolution at its heart. Still, such manipulation (or "manhandling" for some) and acrobatics do have their place in contemporary tango, complicating the link between nuevo and female autonomy.

Discussions of the meaning of *nuevo* at the level of movement vocabulary have yielded a wide range of observations. In response to the question of changes in the woman's role in nuevo or contemporary tango, I encountered a few recurring themes. First, many dancers noted that the woman dances on her own axis, rather than leaning or depending upon the man. Also common was the idea that the dance's increasingly complex vocabulary requires a more skilled and active follower. Describing increasing flexibility in the embrace—the embrace may open and close and there is more *disociación* or torsion (the spine is allowed to spiral, the torso may break from the hips, creating a more circular and less rigid dance) (figure 6.3)—many dancers argued that this grants the follower more freedom. Finally, many pointed to the introduction of movements "off-axis," where one or both partners lean into or away from one another, as a recent development necessitating both a more skilled follower and a more sensitive leader.[33]

Many of these dancers would likely argue that women are just as free to introduce pauses in contemporary tango as they are in traditional tango. With the opening and loosening of the embrace, the follower is free to comment on the lead throughout her entire body, thus increasing her role in defining the dance. Moreover, I contend that the possibilities within the embrace have

Figure 6.3. *Disociación* (Torsion). José Halfon and Virginia Cutillo, "El Tango en la Piel." Body art by Alfredo Genovese. Used by permission of José Halfon and Virginia Cutillo.

expanded greatly, and I trace this directly to the increasing entry of dancers from other disciplines such as modern dance, classical ballet, contact improvisation, martial arts, and partner dances, including salsa, zouk, swing, and rock 'n' roll, among others, and deliberate efforts on the part of these dancers, both professional and social, to expand the vocabulary of the dance through the integration of non-tango elements. The contributions of followers with training in other disciplines have allowed the tango to stretch beyond the bounds of the embrace. Now the woman does not remain rigidly upright or constantly pegged to the leader. Her legs, torso, and hips are relaxed and free to explore the space away from her partner, and the timing with which her limbs fly, explore, and rebound through space may slow down or speed up the lead, thus shaping the conversation. Finally, in moving the follower onto her own axis (as opposed to the milonguero or "close" style of embrace, which often encourages the follower to give weight to the leader), the leader grants her greater control over her movement.[34]

Many young dancers from Buenos Aires and abroad connect the emancipation of the follower to the evolution of the dance that began in the 1990s. Further, as Luciana Valle suggests, changes in the gender politics of the dance are rooted in larger social shifts that have empowered women in other aspects of their lives:

> The tango changed a lot; it evolved a lot and the last big change in the past ten years is that of the woman. . . . The woman has a much more active role, but not in the sense of stealing the lead. Not active in leading, but active in dancing, because the woman is more active in life. Women carried on with men differently, and they lived life differently. Today women are much more active in general; they're much more free in general, and so we dance differently. (ε) (Luciana Valle [Argentine], tango professional)

Many also spoke of the evolution at the level of conceptualization and instruction and of the democratization of information in the classroom. Rather than demonstrating entire figures for reproduction, the system developed by Naveira and Salas broke the dance down to its simplest elements—front, side, and back step—providing both leader and follower the basics with which to deconstruct, improvise, and re-create their own dance. This facilitated the development of female teachers who command the classroom on their own. Graciela González was considered revolutionary when she began teaching classes in women's technique in the 1980s. Such classes geared toward and instructed by women are now quite popular; however, they generally address walking, balance, or the aesthetic contribution of the woman through adornments or embellishments. Female instructors noted that to move beyond women's technique classes and to broaden their professional possibilities, they had to take responsibility for understanding the mechanics of both leading and following: "Until we'd studied enough to know what happens in the dance in its totality, and not only how to follow the man, there wasn't work for women alone. But having studied a bit more profoundly, now we're able to travel and work on our own" (τ) (Cecilia González [Argentine], tango professional).

Moreover, such knowledge provides security in a market where women are viewed as plentiful and more easily replaced than men: "You need to teach, to be the one speaking in order to have an independent reputation. Your dancing isn't enough. And like we've all said a million times, there are more women who can dance at the level that they could partner with any of the top dancers than there are those top dancers, so the women are quite changeable" (Miriam [American expatriate], tango professional).

While the advances acknowledged above are noteworthy, resistance to women leading still exists among male tangueros. In one illuminating interview with a young porteño, he rejected the notion that a woman could hold her own as a leader in an advanced class. He then admitted that even if a woman could lead at the level of a male teacher, it made him uncomfortable:

> Female instructors can't teach advanced classes, aside from a women's technique class. But they can't demonstrate sequences that are long or difficult, because they can't lead them. I don't know of any girl. . . . There are some that lead well, but I don't know of any who is at the level of a man. And if she is I don't like it. It's ugly. I don't like how it looks. *Because it's a woman acting like a man.* Maybe she can do it—lead the sequence—but I don't like the way it looks, it turns me off. (τ) (Orlando [Argentine], tango professional; emphasis added)

While the image of the conversation might be the ideal, the fact remains that it is the leader who retains responsibility for initiating. With the position of lead comes the job of choreographing, on the spot, what will happen. In line with the quote opening this chapter, where women are "tools to have fun,"[35] manipulation of the follower occurs among dancers of all ages, at times approaching something along the lines of manhandling. For instance, at an *investigación* (or investigation session, a closed practice session where a small group of dancers gather to work on steps) one night, I observed as three young Argentine men tried to execute a complicated figure with two foreign women. Tossing the women back and forth like dolls, they shouted over them in Spanish, talking much too quickly for the women to keep up as they discussed the mechanics of the step. It was only when they determined what the followers needed to do (without their input) that the men either spoke in English or more slowly and clearly in Spanish. This pattern continued for most of the night: the woman was relegated to the role of follower in every sense, her input in deconstructing the movement was deemed unnecessary, and the men dictated to her what she should do once they'd determined that among themselves. While there was arguably a problem of translation, and perhaps a differential in the skill level of the women versus the men, this scene bespoke a fundamental asymmetry, where the follower was largely at the mercy of the leader.

Promotional images are often no less ambiguous in their take on gender relations. Veritable entrepreneurs who share equal footing with their male counterparts, female dancers are heavy hitters in today's tango industry. Nonetheless, many contemporary tango ads tell a more complicated story, walking a fine line between celebrating and exploiting the female form (figure 6.4), linking the tango to sex through nudity and even references to domination. In these ads women may at once be the dominators and the protected, "tools to have fun" and acrobatic innovators, anonymous seductresses and savvy businesswomen, proudly flaunting and quite strategically trading on their feminine assets.

The nude male form is less often utilized as a promotional tool. However, a handful of ads in recent years point to a potential shift in this regard, most notably with the billboards and DVD cover image for Bocca Tango, in which we see almost all of Julio Bocca's naked body. Of course, Bocca is famed for his long career as a ballet dancer, not as a tanguero, and the nude or partially nude male form has a long history in ballet. While shirtless men have appeared in a few tango ads of late (figure 6.3, for example), the message in this case has tended more toward male strength or even prowess. In general these images have appeared to reinforce the role of the male as protector and/or protagonist, in contrast to the ambivalence suggested by many representations of the tanguera's body.

El Tango del Futuro

Contemporary tango continues to evolve. By 2010 a handful of new prácticas had emerged in Buenos Aires, more than one situated somewhere in between the traditional and the nuevo. Like the previously mentioned prácticas, these new spaces are organized by and cater to younger dancers. However, there is a palpable feeling in these sites that something new is occurring yet again. Many dancers frame this latest shift as a return to the "essence" of tango.[36] In these spaces one can see a return to this essence in the closeness of the couple (as opposed to the more open embrace that had become common in prácticas), in the return to the tradition of dancing in tandas, in the relatively ordered look of the floor, and in the decidedly classic costumes donned by some of the city's hottest young tango stars during their exhibitions.

The term nuevo is still tossed about and debated, and the reinvigoration of tradition has not yielded a rejection of innovation by any means. The "return

Figure 6.4.
Tanguera. The
tango musical
produced by Diego
Romay (2007).
Used by permission
of Diego Romay.

to the embrace" so evident on my most recent trip to Buenos Aires is not
a mere reversion to a former image. Rather, young tangueros appear to be
integrating the creativity and experimentation of so many years of "investigation" within the frame of a more closed embrace. Situating themselves
in a hundred-year-old lineage, they are the most recent protagonists of the
tango's continued evolutions, recognizing El Cachafaz, Petróleo, and Naveira
as their forebears. In these newer prácticas, as well as in their predecessors,
there is a maturity and assuredness on the floor that contrasts with the rebelliousness (and occasional chaos) of only a few years earlier.

Flesh and blood evidence of yet another "new" era, Ariadna and Federico Naveira, the children of Gustavo Naveira and Olga Besio, are today's
rising tango stars. An exquisite dancer who blends femininity and power to

stunning effect, and who dances both roles flawlessly, Ariadna is known to exchange lead and follow on the social dance floor and in exhibitions with partner Fernando Sánchez.

At the same time, young dancers continue to wrestle with the tango's fundamental contradictions. For instance, the organizers of the Estilo Parque Patricios festival of 2010 evoked in their promotional materials a simpler time, when groups of men met on street corners to practice steps, while a promotional flyer for a new práctica featured an anonymous woman's torso, her crotch barely concealed by a dangerously low-cut *bombacha* (panty) from which a tattoo of revered composer and orchestra leader Osvaldo Pugliese emerges. In this image a return to the essence of tango does not preclude a more modern aesthetic when it comes to marketing, and the tanguera appears not necessarily as a dancer but as an object to be gazed upon or a body part to be fetishized.

Tango and machismo have become so intertwined in the global imaginary that their connection may (mistakenly) appear to be somehow causal. But machismo is not an element of the dance itself, and this linking of the two ignores the fact that the essence of the dance depends upon a social connection. The threat of machismo lies in the practices of individuals themselves, and in the relationship they must establish within the embrace. As one porteño teacher reminded me, this relationship is fraught with the potential for misunderstanding—especially in Buenos Aires, where the two dancers are often communicating across linguistic, cultural, and generational divides. While the foreign tanguera might ascribe her porteño partner's behaviors to the macho culture of tango, machismo is not a problem specific to the dance. Ultimately, each exchange on the dance floor, and any problem that may arise within it, is the product of the two individuals who meet in an embrace.

The notion that meaning is dependent upon context is hardly revolutionary, but I would take this idea further to suggest that place in its larger sense—including its history, mythology, and the metaphysical traces it imparts upon people and things—impacts our actions, our interpretation of and response to behaviors. Following Michael Jackson's notion of intersubjectivity, I suggest that activities that engage the self and other(s) offer participants an opportunity to confront difference. In tango this experience of being with others is heightened by the physically intimate, nonverbal nature of the dance itself. The differences that separate us—language, culture, worldview—are subsumed in the moment of the dance, and this ability to converse through tango may facilitate communication outside of the embrace. In short tango may have something to teach us about accepting difference, about allowing—even enjoying—contradiction, about honoring the existence of self and other.

This aptitude for playfulness—the capacity to receive and go with what you're given, to advance and retreat, to perceive exactly when it's your turn, which over time one hopes will blend into an almost seamless whole—is the gem at the heart of tango's mystery and allure. And these skills that are so desired in the dance spill over into the social context. In Buenos Aires, where an increasing number of dancers seeking to carve out some kind of existence through the dance meet with the ever-growing barrage of tourists and expatriates seeking to experience the dance in its birthplace, the result is a dizzying but ultimately energizing clash of contradictory norms and desires. While a loosening of rigid social codes is inherent to the philosophy of nuevo, such new trends are subject to more intense scrutiny in the dance's birthplace. I argue that the future of the dance lies in the ability of practitioners young and old, local and global, to transcend the romance and exoticism of the tango's often consuming macho imaginary.

Notes

1. A milonga is a social event where people dance Argentine tango. Somewhere between a class and a milonga, a *práctica* is a space in which to practice without the strict codes of the milonga (which regulate the line of dance, musical programming and dancing in sets, the invitation to dance, clothing, and more). Buenos Aires's práctica scene functions both as a supplement and an alternative to the milongas, but with codes deemed more appropriate for younger practitioners.

The bulk of data informing this chapter was gathered over two years in Buenos Aires (2005–2007), during which I conducted participant observation in tango classes, milongas, and prácticas; attended tango festivals, theatrical and dinner show productions, music concerts, and museums; conducted research at institutions, including the National Archives and the Academia Porteña de Lunfardo; and interviewed social and professional dancers from Argentina and abroad, milonga and práctica organizers, tango tour organizers, local and foreign festival organizers, local tango entrepreneurs, and officials from the Ministry of Culture. I also draw on experiences and observations from my early tango education in the United States (2002–2005), two preliminary trips to Buenos Aires in 2003 and 2005, my return to the United States in 2007, and a follow-up visit to Buenos Aires in 2010. Aside from two noted exceptions, interviews with Argentines were conducted in Spanish and I provide English translation of their words throughout. These quotations are noted either (τ): translation by the author from Spanish, or (ε): an English response from a non-native English speaker.

2. Decades before young, hip dancers coined the phrase, Astor Piazzolla called his

music *tango nuevo* in 1960. A classically trained musician, Piazzolla was famous for creating complex compositions rejected as "undanceable" by traditionalists, for bringing the tango into contact with other music, and for importing ideas from other genres into the tango. Largely responsible for keeping the tango alive among international audiences, his music inspired rancorous debate at home, where the most common criticism, "eso no es tango" (that is not tango), can still be heard today. The term has been traced back even further in tango dance to the famed Club Nelson men who instigated a period of rich choreographic innovation in their all-male practice groups in the 1940s (Thompson 257).

3. Dancers are divided as to whether the results of these investigations, both in the dance classroom and on the floor, have been good or bad, however.

4. Prácticas have long existed in tango. Transcending the implications of their name, these new prácticas are social venues for dancing tango (not really for practice), attended primarily by dancers in their twenties and thirties, where an entirely new set of codes has arisen to create a space more befitting younger bodies and minds. One of the longest-running and most important of these new spaces is El Motivo, an all-female run práctica, tango academy, and teacher training program inaugurated in 2004 by Luciana Valle, Valeria Batiuk, and Dina Martínez. A favorite among young dancers, El Motivo is also a powerful symbol of the expanding role of female professionals in the tango world. Luciana Valle, in particular, was a crucial figure in the early dissemination of nuevo principles in the United States, where she began touring and teaching in 1999, following her participation in the Naveira and Salas sessions.

5. Taylor points out that what appears the dominant and oppressive vocabulary of the male lead directly contradicts tango lyrics that portray the natural state of man to be suffering at the hands of women. See also Archetti on the "doubting masculinity" of tango lyrics (157) and Castro ("Carlos Gardel and the Argentine Tango") on tango as the "song of male defeat" (70).

6. Sources include personal communication with Mario Consiglieri and Anabella Díaz-Hojman (March 2006), Luciana Valle (June 2006), Cecilia González (July 2006), Javier (January 2006). Websites referencing the 1990s investigation sessions and their results include http://www.andresamarilla.com/bio.htm, accessed June 1, 2012; an interview with Mariano "Chicho" Frumboli (Plebs); and an interview with Fabián Salas at http://www.totango.net/salas.html, accessed June 1, 2012.

7. More than one dancer pointed out that it is the woman who controls the invitation to dance in traditional milongas through the *cabeceo*, the nonverbal invitation to dance secured through maintained eye contact, because it is only when she returns and holds the gaze directed at her that the invitation is accepted and the two leave their seats and make their way to the dance floor. In many tango communities in the United States and in Buenos Aires's prácticas, it is not uncommon to see a woman physically approach and verbally invite a man to dance.

8. Graciela González (http://www.tangoweek.com/bios/old/gracielabio.html, accessed June 1, 2012) is often cited as the founder of "women's technique" classes. Luciana Valle, Valeria Batiuk, and Dina Martínez are key figures in the resurgence of the práctica in Buenos Aires (http://www.elmotivotango.com/quienes.html, accessed June 1, 2012). Olga Besio, former partner of Gustavo Naveira, has had a long solo career and

has brought tango to children since 2000 through her Tango con Niños program. Susana Miller (http://www.susanamiller.com.ar/, accessed June 1, 2012) is largely responsible for bringing tango milonguero to students in the United States and Europe. Ana Maria Schapira (http://www.tangopulse.net/interviews/ana_maria_schapira.php, accessed June 1, 2012) has run her own tango milonguero academy in Buenos Aires since 1999. Cecilia González (http://www.tangomotion.com/vision.php, accessed June 1, 2012) and Carla Marano (http://sites.google.com/site/carlamarano/, accessed June 1, 2012) are among the newer generation of female dancers who teach both on their own and with different male partners, in addition to teaching women's technique classes.

9. Globalization is nothing new in tango—indeed it was central to its early development and to the more recent renaissance of tango dance beginning in the mid-1980s—but I argue here that the degree and intensity of global interconnections that marks our modern lives distinguishes such processes today from those of the past.

10. The *piropo* is widely documented in many Spanish-speaking cultures. Here, I draw attention to its use in marking space and defining dance style and community in the Buenos Aires tango scene.

11. A *milonguero* is someone who attends the milongas frequently, sometimes every night. Historically, the term often carried negative connotations, to refer to a man who "lives" in the milongas, is unemployed or barely holds down a job, and in many cases, is supported by a woman or family. The term was appropriated by a sector of porteño dancers and organizers in the 1990s to brand a style of tango danced in a close or "chest-to-chest" embrace, featuring a simple vocabulary that stresses rhythmic complexity, and that was quite successfully marketed locally and abroad as the "real" tango danced in Buenos Aires's milongas, where the crowded dance floors often do not permit a more open frame.

12. See France. Memory is particularly politicized in Argentina as regards the horrific events of the Dirty War or the *proceso*, the "process of national reorganization" carried out by the military dictatorship that ruled from 1976 to 1983, during which it is estimated that up to thirty thousand Argentine citizens were "disappeared" under a program of state-sponsored terrorism aimed at ridding the country of subversives. Sites dedicated to remembering these events in Buenos Aires include the Parque de la Memoria, the Paseo de los Derechos Humanos, and the ESMA museum (un espacio para la Memoria y para la Promoción y Defensa de los Derechos Humanos) on the site of the naval school that served as a torture center. The Madres de la Plaza de Mayo (http://www.madres.org/navegar/nav.php, accessed June 1, 2012) and the Abuelas de la Plaza de Mayo (http://www.abuelas.org.ar/, accessed June 1, 2012) have long devoted themselves to uncovering the truth regarding those who were disappeared and to recovering the children of the disappeared, respectively, and for many years the Mothers attracted international attention to the plight of Argentines through public performances in which they "remembered" the disappeared by marching before the Casa Rosada, their heads covered under white kerchiefs embroidered with the names of the missing. Also, see Memoria Abierta (http://www.memoriaabierta.org.ar, accessed June 1, 2012), an organization dedicated to preserving the memory of events that occurred under this period of state terrorism.

13. While Sebreli cites Buenos Aires as the world's third noisiest city (280), a World Health Organization report in 2006 ranks it the noisiest city in Latin America. Sergio Avello's "Volumen," which ranks the city's ever-changing decibel level via a system of noise-sensitive lights installed on the front steps of the MALBA, speaks to the often oppressive character of the city's noise (http://volumenurbano.blogspot.com/, accessed June 1, 2012).

14. See also Jacques-Alain Miller on the piropo as an indication of lack of interest, an attempt to connect with one's object of desire (where that object is represented by any unknown woman), and a form of aggression in which the recipient is a "fiction," a woman who represents all women for the piropeador.

15. Taylor explores gender roles in greater depth in Paper Tangos; in particular, see her discussion of a scene from a tango class in which dancers reversed roles only to have the professor relegate such an exercise to the classroom, specifically to assist the male to better understand his role as leader (86–87).

16. See Plebs.

17. Fabiano notes that Argentines often use the terms marcar ("mark" or "show the way") and responder ("respond") to describe the mechanics of the dance, while Tobin suggests that "el hombre propone y la mujer dispone" (the man proposes and the woman decides) is a common expression in the porteño tango world. During my time in Buenos Aires and in my interviews with Argentine dancers, I found that llevar and seguir ("lead" and "follow") were more frequently used. Tobin suggests this reflects foreign influence, especially during the early 1900s, when tango was codified and tamed by European dance masters who transformed the dance into a bourgeois commodity to be consumed by an international elite schooled in the heterosexist politics of leading and following (94). One young porteño professional suggested that llevar and seguir were the preferred terms in verb form and that la marca ("the lead") might be the preferred term for the noun form.

18. Salessi, "Medics, Crooks, and Tango Queens"; Savigliano, Tango and the Political Economy of Passion; and Tobin all draw attention to the "masculine" character of the women who were involved in tango's early development.

19. See also Garramuño's discussion of the cultural processes that have facilitated the integration of "primitive" elements into "modern" tango and samba, as a means of both amplifying understandings of the modern and demonstrating how once primitive cultural products have transformed themselves to become acceptable national symbols.

20. Tango is not always learned in a classroom setting. Writings and interviews left by the tangueros of yore and the milongueros of today speak to the survival of the dance through "acquisition" (see Del Mazo and D'Amore; Thompson; and Savigliano, Tango and the Political Economy of Passion). A typically nonacademic process, tango was passed down from one generation to the next through contact with the dance itself, through practice with family, neighbors, and friends. No longer a dance of the masses, such "acquisition" is increasingly being replaced by more formal classroom education in Buenos Aires, which is also the most common path for dancers outside of Argentina. Many point to the tango's transformation into industry and the growing emphasis upon the consumption of classes as evidence of the demise of "traditional" tango.

21. In contrast with its humble origins and general association with lower-class porteños (despite a lengthy period of widespread popular appeal between 1920 and 1950), tango communities around the globe are decidedly middle- and upper-class enclaves, where the majority of practitioners are degree-holding members of the professional class and thus generally educated, successful, and financially stable. In particular foreign women spoke to the initial distance they perceived between their assertive, independent, egalitarian selves and the tango self who "surrenders," "follows," and "listens."

22. According to Barco, four out of every ten visitors mention tango as a reason to visit Buenos Aires, a $400 million a year global industry. In 2000 a report by the *International Herald Tribune* (F. Ortiz) sets the number of tango tourists at twenty-five thousand per year. In 2009 the *Observer* reported that the tango industry brings $100 million annually to Buenos Aires (Carroll and Balch).

23. As tango communities have grown around the world and Buenos Aires has situated itself as the center of the global tango industry, the milongas have become sites for the city's growing class of tango professionals to promote themselves. This shift toward the milonga as both marketplace and spectacle, as opposed to merely social gathering, incurred greater demands upon women to look good, as well as the growth of "exhibitions," or short performances by professional couples at the milongas. The growth of exhibitions has been accompanied by a general shift toward more elaborate and showy choreography, in particular for the woman, and an image of professional tango that favors a young and agile female body (often capable of executing balletic and acrobatic movements), while the man may be of any age.

24. See the late Gavito's explanation of being a milonguero and the "men's table" in Trotta.

25. See Tobin on "phallic displays," or the pairing of elder male dancers with *nenas* (girls) in exhibitions as evidence of the "homosocial desire" that marks tango, evidenced in the milongueros' verbal exchanges of praise in response to their displays of young women.

26. "Get your true beauty in the city of tango," proclaimed a text from an advertisement for Plenitas, an aesthetic surgery clinic, that was published in the Buenos Aires Tango Guide in 2006.

27. The United States currently ranks highest in the number of cosmetic procedures, Argentina in eleventh place, according to a survey of 2011 by the International Society of Aesthetic Plastic Surgery, but the growth of "destination" cosmetic and medical industries suggests the intensifying triangular relationship of economics, aesthetics, and health. While economic inequities are surely driving the commodification of medical care, they may also be encouraging aesthetic surgery among locals in the postcolonial sites where many middle-class First World clients go for such procedures, unable to afford such luxuries at home.

28. Under the presidency of Carlos Menem, Argentina passed the Convertibility Law in April 1991, which converted the peso to a one-to-one fixed rate in relationship to the U.S. dollar. A host of factors in the late 1990s precipitated the country's economic crisis and a series of currency devaluations and adjustments in late 2001 and early 2002, including rising unemployment, the appreciation of the peso (alongside the U.S. dollar)

in relation to its trading partners' currencies, Brazil's economic crisis (which also hurt Argentine exports), the devaluation of the peso for foreign trade, a series of debt restructurings, and bank runs (widespread efforts to withdraw funds from bank accounts) with declining confidence in the peso and rumors of default. Following a 29 percent devaluation in early 2002 for major foreign commercial transactions, and the institution of a floating rate for all other transactions, the peso quickly fell to 2.05 (to the dollar) in active trading (Hornbeck). By early 2003, the peso had stabilized in a nearly 3:1 relation to the dollar (BBC "Q&A"). While the peso moved toward a 4:1 relationship in the late 2000s, and was officially at 5.44:1 in July of 2013, this has been accompanied by rising inflation. However, the combined impact of these trends is hard to gauge in the face of declining trust in INDEC, the government statistics bureau, since a host of analysts were let go or resigned following the institution of a new method for calculating inflation, introduced by a government appointee (Gabino; Barrionuevo).

29. In relation to the growing aesthetic surgery industry, a Renfrew Center report of 2003 estimates that the rate of eating disorders in Argentina is three times that of the United States (Renfrew Center Foundation).

30. For instance, in 2010 Google declared the CougarLife dating website (for women seeking younger men) "non-family safe" and prohibited ads for such sites from displaying on their content pages, yet they did not extend the same categorization to websites geared toward older men seeking younger women (Kershaw).

31. A *tanda* is a musical set of three to four songs, all either waltzes, tangos, or milongas, in which dancers remain with the same partner until a *cortina* (thirty-second fragment of non-tango music) indicates the end of the set.

32. Tobin and Salessi ("Medics, Crooks, and Tango Queens") highlight tango's homosexual and gender transgressive roots, noting public discourse surrounding male transvestite prostitutes in the brothels that gave birth to the tango, as well as shifting gender roles in early twentieth-century Buenos Aires, exemplified by "masculine" women entering the public domain (whether prostitutes, artists, including early tango singers, or working-class women) and the "feminine" tango pimp, a vain character who depended upon a woman to support him.

33. More than one dancer argued that these themes could be used to describe expert "traditional" training for women as well. An arguable change in the look of tango when one travels from the milonga to the práctica is the increased distance that may separate the partners, the more frequent rupture of the embrace, and the increasing integration of non-tango vocabulary on the social dance floor. That such themes are championed by tangueras with "traditional" training underscores the difficulty in defining nuevo; furthermore, it demonstrates the tendency to assert independence from predecessors through a linking of style, generation, and culture.

34. This last point perhaps reflects the growing popularity of close embrace or milonguero style tango from the 1990s. While this image is not representative of traditional tango in a more general sense, nuevo and/or younger dancers might frame the woman standing on her own axis as something "new" because they had earlier been schooled in milonguero style or because the milonguero embrace had become popular in certain locales. Foreign influence may play a role here as well, for close embrace tango is often

promoted through the language of "authenticity" and sold as the "real tango of Buenos Aires," danced in a tight embrace to accommodate the city's small and crowded dance floors.

35. The reverse may also be true. For instance, I once heard men referred to as "dance-able objects" by a traditional tanguera, the point being that both male and female dancers are capable of manipulating their partners or using their partners for entirely self-serving purposes.

36. Also, see a December 2009 interview with Mariano "Chicho" Frumboli (star pupil of Naveira and Salas, renowned for his unparalleled inventiveness and musicality, and generally cited as a global ambassador of *tango nuevo*, though like Naveira and Salas he has long rejected the title), in which he discusses how many younger dancers have lost touch with the essence and depth of the dance following years in which investigation and an obsession with creativity reigned (Plebs).

CHAPTER SEVEN

Contemporary Tango and the Cultural Politics of *Música Popular*

MORGAN JAMES LUKER

As the chapters in this edited volume attest, tango is a rich and diverse cultural phenomenon. Global audiences have been familiar with tango from its circulation in films, television, musical recordings, and other media going back at least to the Parisian tango "craze" of 1917 if not earlier (Matsuda). In these circulatory contexts, tango has served as a conduit for the creative misunderstandings and cross-cultural fantasies that are at the heart of cultural globalization as it is envisioned today (Tsing). At the same time, such global circulations have not eroded the deep meanings the genre has in local contexts. In Argentina, for instance, tango has been drawn upon as a potent symbol of the nation throughout modern Argentine history, contributing at different times to the project of national consolidation (Bergero), the projection of the nation within global politics and economies (Goertzen and Azzi), the local rearticulation of musical modernism, and current efforts to promote Argentina as a destination for cultural tourism (Marchini).

This complex narrative of cultural production and creativity was turned on its head by the devastating Argentine economic crisis of late 2001. The economic crisis caused tremendous hardship in Argentina, the severity of which is difficult to overstate: during the crisis the nation's GDP rapidly dropped 15 percent, the open unemployment rate rose to 25 percent, and the number of households living in poverty reached nearly 50 percent (Felix 2002). In the context of the widespread human suffering represented in these statistics, music might not seem particularly important. But debates going on within tango nevertheless engage the crisis and the broader contours of

Argentine history in ways that cannot be reduced to a symbolic function. In other words, contemporary tango not only reflects the impact the economic crisis of the early twenty-first century had on Argentine society, culture, and history, but is also an integral and productive part of those contexts.

In particular tango has become a focus of the many "managerial regimes" that shape how music and the arts are produced and consumed in post-crisis Buenos Aires. By managerial regime I mean any entity that aims to channel cultural practices into resources for social and/or economic development. In the case of tango, these regimes include the cultural industries and other media corporations, nonprofit and nongovernmental arts organizations, and, especially, the cultural policies of the city government of Buenos Aires. Similar trends can be observed at the global level, with governments the world over increasingly framing local cultures as a natural or renewable resource in need of management like any other (see Yúdice, *The Expediency of Culture*). The two quintessential examples of this are, on the one hand, the traditional cultural knowledge of indigenous and other place-based ethnic groups (Escobar) and, on the other, *culture* with a capital *C*, that is, philharmonic orchestras, art museums, and other high-art institutions that are promoted as the engines of urban renewal and economic development above and beyond whatever aesthetic value the "content" they contain or produce might have (Miller and Yúdice).

What does not fit this managerial model so well—and what I want to focus on here—is the category of so-called popular arts, especially popular music, which are neither traditional culture nor high art in the way those domains have tended to be conceived by governmental cultural agencies, nongovernmental arts organizations, and other managerial regimes. This incongruity is even more acute in the context of Latin America, where the idea of the popular as it is used in discussions of *música popular* is particularly nuanced. In Latin America the term *música popular* not only describes specific forms of musical style and mediation (as does the English term *popular music*) but also lingering hierarchies of musical value that are closely correlated with macro-patterns of social exclusion and inclusion (Capellano). That is, in Latin America the idea of música popular is associated not only with the relations between tradition and mass mediation but also with the social definitions of inclusion and exclusion centered on *the popular* or *the people* as a social and political category (Martín-Barbero). These patterns map directly onto musical concerns, such that socially popular genres of music have been largely excluded from most support programs for the arts in Argentina, that is, from the sphere of official cultural politics (Luker, "The Managers, the Managed and the Unmanageable").[1]

Tango occupies a curious position within this larger discussion. On the one hand, it is clearly *popular music* as that term is usually understood in English: it is considered by some to be of inferior quality to other musics, it is neither folk nor art music, it has been and remains fully entrenched within the mass media and cultural industries, and so on (see Middleton). On the other hand, it is no longer *música popular* as that term is deployed in Spanish. Indeed, one of the key facts of tango's life as a genre in contemporary Buenos Aires is that it no longer functions as a música popular—a cultural practice that both expresses and articulates the people as a lived social and political category—as it very much had in previous historical moments. Tango's break from the popular experience led to a steep decline of the genre in Argentina, despite its continued salience as a potent symbol of Argentine culture within the national imaginary and global representations. And it is precisely this dual trend of detachment and connection that makes tango such a productive resource for so many different projects in Buenos Aires today—not so much a national genre (that is, a sonic icon of the nation state) as a national brand, something used to bolster a wide variety of developmental projects, the value of which clearly extends beyond the aesthetic domain. At the same time, these tensions have also made the genre a highly charged zone of engagement for alternative musical practices and cultural politics of the popular in contemporary Argentina.

I want to ground this discussion in an analytic and ethnographic examination of Astillero,[2] a contemporary tango ensemble whose work is based on remaking tango as a música popular, that is, on rearticulating the genre's relationship to a specifically Latin American notion of the popular.[3] For the members of Astillero, tango must operate as música popular in order to be socially meaningful and aesthetically effective, despite the fact that tango has not functioned in this particular way for some fifty years in Argentina.[4] I will discuss the formal details of Astillero's music and the social milieu in which it circulates and is made meaningful. Each of these domains is framed by the contested musical and social histories of tango as a popular genre in Argentina, as well as the larger challenges posed by the economic crisis of 2001 and its aftermath. Taken together, I will show how Astillero's project of remaking tango as a música popular must be understood as taking into account both a musical style and a social movement, an aesthetic ideology and an embodied social practice.[5] This example—like the popular as such—allows us to question the managerial impulse to productivity that is increasingly determining cultural life in Buenos Aires and beyond, while also helping us to better understand the changing role of music and the arts within the global context of crisis.

Música Popular in Tango History and Memory

Formed in May 2005, Astillero is a sextet of two bandoneonists,[6] a violinist, a cellist, a bassist, and a pianist, plus a singer. Brought together by the pianist and composer Julián Peralta—who is one of the key figures within the contemporary tango scene in Buenos Aires—the group is dedicated exclusively to the composition and performance of original tango music. While this focus on original composition may seem unexceptional, the group operates in a historical juncture that has made the very act of composing original tangos—and perhaps the performance of tango in itself—a highly charged domain of musical activity. On the one hand, there is the repetition of memory on the part of Argentine tango audiences nostalgic for times and musics past, making them notoriously unreceptive to new, original work. On the other hand, I would argue that the majority of Argentines—especially those who came of age during and following the last military dictatorship (1976–1983)—have generally ignored tango if not rejected it outright, despite its influence on some early forms of Argentine rock music (Vila, "Argentina's 'Rock Nacional'").

Claiming this position has therefore required that the group both break from and recommit to tango as a musical genre, a stance that they have theorized as the "tango of rupture." As Patricio "Tripa" Bonfiglio, the group's first bandoneonist, explained to me in an interview: "We talk about the tango of rupture precisely because it is not classic tango—it is a new tango, with new elements, but it comes from tango itself. It breaks with the classic scheme without falling into fusion, because it does not incorporate elements taken from other genres. It's not that we break with tango by using jazz harmonies, but by developing the extreme gestures that are in tango but have never been interpreted in this way. So it breaks with the classic scheme but from within the genre" (Bonfiglio). While Astillero's musical style is a sharp departure from that of previous tango groups, their tango of rupture in fact represents a break with tango's recent musical history more than a break in musical sound per se. Understanding the stakes in this statement and in the group's musical project as a whole therefore requires an (admittedly broad-stroked) overview of the history of tango music in Argentina.

The history of tango music is generally divided into three periods, to which I would like to add a fourth. First is *La guardia vieja* or the Old Guard period, which began with the genre's initial formation on the outskirts of Buenos Aires (and Montevideo, Uruguay) in the late nineteenth century and ended with its codification as a national genre during and after the First World War. Significant parts of the classic tango repertoire were composed and published during this period, and many of the core stylistic features of the genre were consolidated at this time. Furthermore, many of the key aesthetic tropes and social sensibilities still associated with tango—such as passion, sexuality, loss, nostalgia, violence, and the ruptures of urban modernization—derive from and conjure the guardia vieja moment, though I think it is also important to acknowledge the mythologizing role that works of literature such as Jorge Luis Borges's "Hombre de la esquina rosada" (1935; "Man on Pink Corner," 1998) and others retroactively played in cementing these associations. Highlighting this back and forth between the musical history of tango and the history of thinking, writing, and talking about tango is significant because, in general, the documented history and historic material culture of tango is rather limited.[7] As such, many historical claims about the genre, including those presented here, are arguably better understood, at least partially, as narratives of musical memory rather than music history per se.

Second is the golden age period, which dates from roughly the mid-1920s to 1955, during which tango reached its peak as both a popular music and a *música popular* in Argentina. At the height of the golden age, in the 1940s into the 1950s, tango was a massively *popular music* in the broadest sense of the term. There were innumerable large-scale tango ensembles known as *orquestas típicas*, both professional and amateur, that performed for large dancing audiences in venues ranging from the most refined and lavish dancehalls of the city center to the most humble social clubs in the suburban outskirts and beyond into the provinces (Sierra). Social tango dancing was a widespread phenomenon, enjoyed by all but the very highest strata of society, and the top bandleaders were stars who would come to have corners, streets, and subway stations named for them. At the same time, domestic cultural industries produced and promoted an array of tango media, from radio broadcasts to records, starting with 78s and then LP recordings, and from tango-themed magazines and books to tango film and, later, television production (Castro, *The Argentine Tango as Social History*).

Following the golden age is what is known as the "vanguard" period, which roughly covers the years from the late 1950s to the early 1990s, though in many ways the vanguard movement is still very much alive and well today. The vanguard period was defined in part by a self-conscious attempt to transform tango into what could be described as an alternative art music. These efforts are most famously associated with the composer, bandoneonist, and bandleader Astor Piazzolla (1921–1992), whose *nuevo tango* or new tango style deliberately fused tango gestures with forms and techniques drawn from Western art music and jazz. These included utilizing specific compositional techniques such as fugal counterpoint, developing a more extensive (though not necessarily improvisatory) role for virtuosic instrumental soloists, drawing upon larger-scale compositional structures such as suites and other extended forms, utilizing smaller instrumental forces such as quartets or quintets (versus the ten to twelve members of a golden age orquesta típica), and cultivating performance contexts—such as genre-specific nightclubs and formal concert settings—that encouraged focused listening over social dancing (Azzi and Collier).

Along with these and other musical innovations, the vanguard period was also defined by the precipitous decline of tango as a popular form in Argentina, which happened for a number of specific musical, historical, and political reasons. In particular the members of Astillero trace the decline of tango as a música popular to the violent ouster of the populist president Juan Perón in September 1955. Upon taking power, the new provisional government declared a state of siege that, among other things, banned large public gatherings of any kind, including the innumerable formal and informal tango dances that were then taking place throughout the city (James). While the new regime was probably not anti-tango in any meaningful way—despite the fact that many prominent golden age tango musicians were ardent Peronists (Azzi, "The Tango, Peronism and Astor Piazzolla")—its generalized fear of oppositional organizing outweighed whatever value tango dances and other ostensibly harmless social activities may have had, and they were swept away as collateral damage, if only temporarily. Nevertheless, the state of siege effectively drained the financial, social, and cultural lifeblood of the golden age orquestas típicas, if not the genre as a whole, marking what the members of Astillero considered the beginning of the end of tango as a música popular in Argentina.[8]

In the wake of these and other political ruptures and aesthetic upheavals, post–golden age tango came to be perceived, in the words of Julián Peralta, as "more and more conservative, more reactionary," eventually taking on entrenched negative associations with the vast majority of Argentines who came of age during and following this transitional period, despite the real (though generally singular) successes of certain tango-related cultural productions and representations (Peralta, Interview).[9] Over time, however, tango came to have a renewed significance for many Argentines, especially those who are active in the current musical "renovation" of tango taking place in Buenos Aires today, including the members of Astillero and many of their peers. This renovation of tango, which I would suggest as a fourth period of tango history, began in the mid- to late 1990s. It is defined less by a dominant musical style than by a self-conscious return to tango as a means of reexamining and rearticulating the genre's historical tropes and meanings against contemporary experiences and concerns (Luker, "Tango Renovación"). It is crucial to recognize that these artists have not taken up tango because it somehow inherently speaks to them or their concerns in ways that other musical forms or genres do not. On the contrary, it is the temporal distance between these artists and the more reactionary elements of post–golden age tango—along with the unique semantic flexibility of music as an expressive practice (Meintjes)—that has allowed those renovating tango to approach the genre in ways that are influenced but not overdetermined by the broader sweep of music history. As Julián Peralta explained in an interview: "Forty years have passed, and in those forty years we appeared, a generation for which tango has lost some of its bad connotations. . . . For us tango was nothing more than music, it returned to being nothing more than music, because when we listened to it tango was beyond all that other stuff. It was just records, which we approached with other connotations, . . . able to say 'hey, there is some good music here'" (Peralta, Interview).

When considered within this historical context, Astillero's tango of rupture can be heard as a fundamental critique of the previous vanguard movement and what they perceived as the broader decline of post–golden age tango. For instance, where the tango of rupture is based on transforming tango from within the genre itself, the vanguard movement deliberately looked outside of tango for new techniques and inspiration. As such, Astillero's tango of rupture is a musical style that is essentially about music history. At the same time, the members of Astillero have been drawn to "classic tango"—by which they mean golden age tango of the pre-vanguard period—not only because of its rich musicality but also because tango then operated as música popular. The group incorporates and exaggerates features of golden age tango in their original compositions in order to create a contemporary music that can sonically claim the historic legacy of tango as a popular form. Thus, despite Astillero's modernist discourse of rupture with the tango tradition, their project in fact marks a return to concerns with cultural history and local musical meanings. The stakes in this project go beyond those of musical revivalism to matters of social and historical renewal via new forms of artistic synthesis within a context of profound crisis, with musical form itself operating as the privileged site of historical and artistic intervention. It is therefore crucial to examine how this process operates at the level of musical gesture.

Música Popular as Music

The utilization of a set of standard accompaniment patterns is, in many ways, what defines tango as a genre. The most basic and fundamental of these patterns is the marcato, in which the accompanying instruments articulate all four downbeats in a 4/4 measure. There are two general ways of playing marcatos, one giving an equal emphasis to all four beats of the bar and the other placing accents on the first and third beats. These differences may seem minimal, but they have strikingly different effects in practice. Another fundamental accompaniment pattern is the *síncopa*, the basic rhythmic form of which, in a 4/4 bar, is: eighth note, eighth note, eighth note rest, eighth note, quarter note, quarter note rest (see figure 7.1).

Like the marcato, the síncopa can also be varied depending on how it is accented. These variations can be expanded even further by applying different sorts of accented or unaccented *arrastres*—rhythmic anticipations of as much as a half of a beat—to the basic pattern. These variations provide tango with much of its rhythmic liveliness. Indeed, while the Spanish term *síncopa* could be translated as "syncopation," without *arrastres* and various other forms of accentuation the basic síncopa accompaniment pattern does not actually produce any musical syncopation.[10] Julián Peralta and other members of Astillero believed that the pattern's seemingly inappropriate name was a holdover from its origin in the fusion of what were (and are) two truly syncopated accompaniment patterns found in the *bordoneo* texture (see figure 7.2) of the *milonga campera*, a genre of folkloric music from Buenos Aires province.

While the bordoneo itself is occasionally heard in tango (as one of several more standardized accompaniment patterns), perhaps the clearest folkloric influence in tango is the 3–3–2 eighth note rhythmic division that is derived from the bass accompaniment figure of the milonga campera (seen in the downward facing stems in figure 7.2). However, formal links between specific aspects of folkloric practice and fundamental features of tango like the

Figure 7.1. The basic *síncopa* accompaniment pattern.

Figure 7.2. The *bordoneo* pattern from the *milonga campera*, as notated for guitar.

síncopa and the 3–3–2—as clearly as they might be heard—tend to be un-derappreciated if not rejected outright by many of the genre's aficionados, who imagine tango as a deeply if not exclusively cosmopolitan genre in con-gruence with broader trends in Argentine modernism. Still, the members of Astillero consider such connections between tango and Argentine folk music to be a core component of what makes tango compelling to their generation of Argentines. For if nothing else, folkloric music is another form of música popular, the acceptance or rejection of which parallels tropes of inclusion and exclusion that are at the heart of Argentine cultural politics, musical and otherwise. Therefore musical features such as the marcato, the síncopa, and the 3–3–2 are not just generic stylistic features of tango but also the sonic foundation upon which coherent readings of musical and social history can be constructed.

While the deliberate use of accompaniment patterns from golden age tango can be used to emphasize the popular roots of tango, other features of Astillero's music connect their work to different types of values. A partic-ular use of musical motives, for instance, links Astillero's music to popular ideologies of musical sophistication and compositional rigor. In tango, as in other forms of music, a motive functions as the smallest unit recognizable as a distinct musical idea, with specific melodic, rhythmic, and harmonic char-acteristics. Usually no more than one or two measures in length, motives are used as the fundamental unit of melodic development in tango, the building blocks of larger musical ideas. Complete melodic phrases, for example, are often made up of a sequence of imitative and/or contrastive motives; units of two or more phrases, in turn, can be arranged into larger parts; parts can be paired to create a complete song and so on. Motivic constructions of this sort can be heard throughout the repertory of golden age tango. Therefore, however formulaic such motive-oriented music might be, adhering to these types of melodic constructions also operates as a way for contemporary composers to maintain their allegiance to the genre's traditional compositional processes.

At the same time, some golden age tango composers used motivic development in a more extensive fashion, creating compositions that are today exalted as something akin to a popular art music. The tango composer, pianist, and bandleader Osvaldo Pugliese's (1905–1995) piece "La Yumba" (1943) is emblematic in this regard. Based on the elaborate development of a single motivic cell that is varied and expounded upon throughout the course of the piece, it has been described on numerous occasions as "the Beethoven's Fifth of tango." The compositional rigor of this piece, alongside its undisputable position at the core of the popular tango tradition,[11] has served as a key inspiration for Astillero's project of creating original tangos that can be both musically rich and socially popular. As Julián Peralta observed: "One does not need to make bad music in order for it have reach. Pugliese demonstrated that [with "La Yumba."] . . . It shows that one can make a song . . . with an almost Schubert-like structure, but in a certain moment it can become música popular because . . . it transcends conscious enjoyment and just hits you in the gut" (Peralta, Interview). While these and other compositional techniques can be and are valorously compared to those found in Western art music, my interlocutors repeatedly emphasized their development within tango itself. Therefore, while many contemporary tango composers are familiar with Western art music and its techniques, the motivic orientation of golden age tango predisposes them to compositional practices that might appear borrowed from Western art music but in fact emerged from the common practice of tango as a popular form. Utilizing such techniques does not add value to tango by raising it to the so-called higher level of an external art music, but instead it marks the inherent sophistication and artistic merit of tango as a música popular.

Given this emphasis on composition, it is perhaps not surprising that tango, in general, is not a highly improvisatory music. The golden age orquestas típicas, for instance, played from written parts in which most aspects of a given composition and/or arrangement were notated, including instrumental solos. However, there was and is a significant amount of interpretive space between what is notated on the page and what an ensemble or individual performer is at liberty and indeed expected to play. This is especially true

regarding overall rhythmic interpretation, which, in tango, is based on ex-
aggerating the perceived pull that the notes that fall on the "strong" beats of
the bar (one and three) exert on those that fall on the "weak" beats (two and
four). When executed effectively, this interpretive style creates a rhythmic
tension that makes it sound as if the strong beats of the bar are being rushed,
when in fact the strong beats remain metrically steady as the rest of the musical material is slightly delayed, thereby creating a rhythmic swing that is
essentially the opposite of that heard in straight ahead jazz.

The members of Astillero believed that the rhythmic tension created by
this performance practice was central to tango's appeal as popular dance
music, and therefore learning how to interpret pieces according to these
principles was considered a key component of performing tango "correctly."
Patricio "Tripa" Bonfiglio took these associations even further in my beginning bandoneon lessons with him, explaining to me that tango's particular
rhythmic feel could be understood as a musical embodiment of the tension,
toughness, and looming violence that is at the heart of popular identity and
experience in Argentina—in tango and beyond—both past and present. For
example, in teaching me what he considered an acceptable rhythmic interpretation for the opening phrase of Jesús Ventura's composition "A la gran
muñeca" (1920; famously recorded by Carlos Di Sarli in 1951), Patricio constantly reminded me that tango was a popular form, that it was what he called
"bien italiano." He illustrated the musical implications of this by setting the
piece's rhythmically simple melodic line to a common but very vulgar set of
Argentine curse words, creating heavy accents on the strong beats and their
corresponding rhythmic drag on the rest of the measure: "CON-cha de tu
MA-dre."[12] Though he used it only to illustrate the larger rhythmic concept,
setting the line to these curse words made for a good interpretation not only
because it highlighted the kind of rhythmic tension any version of the piece
would need in order to be heard as tango but also because it established the
stakes of remaking tango música popular.

By incorporating these and other features of golden age tango into their
contemporary compositions, Astillero aligns its music with historical practices that its members believe to be essential components of what once made
tango a música popular. These features are, in a way, what tango as a popular
form is, and using them is what makes music tango. That said, the group has
by no means embraced all the musical features of golden age tango, and those
that they do draw upon are often exaggerated in an extreme way.[13] Taken as
a whole, Astillero's music breaks with some of the most reified stereotypes of

tango without rejecting—or indeed radically altering—the musical funda-
mentals of the genre as it was practiced during the golden age, again suggesting a new concern for cultural synthesis on the part of these artists despite
their modernist discourse of rupture. This, coupled with their rejection of the
vanguard's impulse toward fusion, is ultimately what the tango of rupture is
about: reaffirming the genre's roots in popular practice while reinvigorating
it as a newly relevant form, something capable of speaking to a wider range of
contemporary experiences in a way that golden age tango no longer could. As
Mariano Caló, the group's second bandoneonist, observed in an interview:

> Tango was originally born from nostalgia, from the "lost world" [of the
> immigrants], but now that nostalgia is not there. I don't miss any lost world
> because I was born here, my parents were born here. But there are other
> things that happen, this is a messed up country, a lot of things happen.
> … So it's not that we just have a style: if you sit down to compose a tango
> today this is what comes out: something violent, with strong rhythms, in-
> fluenced by a lot of things that have happened. There just aren't many more
> ways of making tango today, making tango as a música popular. (Caló)

Música Popular as Social Practice

These formal features and compositional techniques are part of what makes
Astillero's tango of rupture popular music, but they are not everything that
make it música popular. In Buenos Aires, as in the rest of Latin America,
música popular is defined less by matters of musical style and mediation
than by specific types of popular social institutions and networks, including, in the case of golden age tango, the large milieu of professional and
amateur musicians who performed in the orquestas típicas, the social network of tango dancers and other audience members, and the institutional
structures of neighborhood social clubs and other performance spaces. In
other words, golden age tango was not música popular because it had a mass
audience and was distributed through the mass media, it was música popular because it served as the center of gravity around which a specific type of
participatory popular culture could coalesce, creating a literal golden age of
live performance and participation that had a near-magical effect on social
reality (Turino). But because tango has not mobilized popular participation
and sociability of this type since the end of the golden age, Astillero has had
to build, largely from the ground up, the participatory networks and institutional structures required to remake tango a música popular. These include

an underground tango school and a weekly tango dance and performance event.

Astillero's tango school operates entirely underground, that is, outside of any official regulation or accreditation. It does not grant any degrees and has no real curriculum or sequence of courses, though students of all skill levels—many with extensive backgrounds in Western art music—take classes there. These include lessons on tango instruments, student performance ensembles, and private or group classes in tango music theory, arranging, and composition. I took weekly bandoneon lessons at the school and played with two different student ensembles that rehearsed there as part of my ethnographic fieldwork. The primary goal of the school, which had about fifty active students at the time I attended it, is to make tango musicians, to create a critical mass of performers who would want and be able to participate in tango as a newly popular form. As Mariano Caló explained:

> The school is necessary so that there can be more groups like Astillero,
> . . . so that the friends of the people who are in each group like Astillero
> begin to listen to tango. After they listen to Astillero, and after they listen
> to other groups, they will want to create another group. And there will be
> more and more groups, like it was during the golden age of tango. That is
> it: tango as música popular. Having tango as música popular means that
> there are forty orchestras, playing tangos from one another's groups. That
> is what happened before, and that is the logic of what we are looking for
> now. (Caló)

The training project of the school is paired with a weekly tango dance event or milonga, which is produced, organized, and staffed by members of Astillero and some of their students. The milonga as I participated in it opened with an hour-long dance lesson that began around ten or eleven PM.[14] The lesson was followed by several hours of formalized tango dancing to historic audio recordings of golden age tango orchestras, as is typical at contemporary milongas in Buenos Aires and elsewhere. Sometime between two and four in the morning, a short set of live music would be performed by Astillero, one of the student ensembles from the school, or another invited group. These musical performances served at least two specific purposes. On the one hand, they helped build an audience for Astillero, the other groups, and live tango music in general. This is important because there is no necessary affinity between an interest in tango as dance and an interest in tango as music— much less ostensibly new types of music—among tango audiences in Buenos

Aires today. However, because tango's popular roots are firmly grounded in the genre's historical function as a music made for social dancing, systematically reconnecting live performance with the dance-oriented sociability of the milongas—if not creating dance music outright—was considered a crucial component of Astillero's project. On the other hand, the milonga also provides a readily available and relatively supportive venue for the school's student ensembles or other emerging groups to present themselves before an audience. This is important because however pleasurable it might be to arrange or compose tangos in private, or to practice an instrument or even rehearse with an ensemble of friends, the members of Astillero believed that making tango música popular was ultimately about creating a back and forth dialogue with the audience in performance. The dancing continued following these live performances, eventually shifting to a variety of popular folkloric genres—such as *chacarera*, *chamamé*, and *zamba*—each of which is danced to a relatively elaborate set of steps (though none as involved as tango itself). Even later, the music would shift to cumbia, a massively popular and somewhat polemical genre of contemporary urban dance music (Cragnolini). The more informal style of cumbia dancing went on well into the daylight hours.

In the course of this particular milonga, Astillero mapped a specific narrative of the popular, sonically tracing connections not only between the contemporary tango of rupture and the genre's popular past but also between tango and the popular folk music of the Argentine provinces as well as the hugely popular music of the peripheral urban "masses." At the same time, the school and the milonga also created the space needed for the participatory sociability of tango as a música poplar to be experienced by these musicians and their peers. As Mariano Caló observed:

> The only way we have access to the public is by generating spaces, there is no other way to do it. This is not a genre that you can sell on the radio. The first thing you need to do is create a space where you feel like you belong. Where you can bring your friends and where they like it. I go to the milonga and I feel it, I go to the school and I feel like I am a part of it. . . . It is really a necessity for everyone that this kind of movement exists, because we need the tango, and we also need a space in which we belong. It is a thing that feeds itself, a movement. (Caló)

As suggested in this quote, Astillero's inspiration for building alternative networks and institutions came not only from the group's vision of tango's popular past but also from the many social movements that emerged in Argentina following the economic crisis of 2001, including unemployed workers movements, neighborhood assemblies, local, regional, and national barter networks, and community soup kitchens, among others. A key feature of these movements was a set of radically democratic organizational strategies that managed resources and institutions in such a way that they would belong to everyone and to no one at the same time (Sitrin). Astillero's tango school and milonga both operated in strict adherence to these ideas and ideals. As Mariano Caló observed:

> For example, when we first put together the milonga, I put in around a thousand pesos, all of us put in about that much, and we bought the piano, we bought lights, we bought a few speakers, glasses, and the first round of drinks to sell. That was returned to us in about two months, from the entrance fee, from the bar, and we were left without any debts. So, who does this all belong to? We all pitched in and helped, but we have already been repaid, so it is no longer ours. It isn't anyone's, it just is. It exists. The same goes with the movement. It is. It is everyone's. So this is the crazy part of the aesthetic, of being collective like that. We all do things because it is good, not because it is a favor to anyone. You do it for yourself, because you like that it exists. This is the movement. (Caló)

But as inspirational as these post-crisis social movements have been for local participants and outside observers alike (Lewis and Klein; Klein), it is important to emphasize that they emerged from a context of desperate need. They were (and are) mobilized to address the state's abject failure to provide even the most basic provisions and services in the wake of the economic crisis of 2001, essentially denying many Argentines full recourse to citizenship. These failures—or refusals, really—long predate the crisis (Auyero), and they are in many ways what define the popular experience in Argentina in the last quarter century.

Such uneven "modes of citizenship" (Lomnitz) have direct implications for music and the arts. In this particular case, Astillero's project of remaking tango a música popular has been entirely excluded from official efforts to promote or develop tango as an emblematic component of Argentine culture, especially those of the city government of Buenos Aires.[15] This is all the more striking given the sheer extent of those efforts: the city government is by far the largest producer of cultural events in Buenos Aires, having, for instance, produced more than 1,500 mostly free performances throughout their network of city owned venues in 2006, the year I conducted my field-work (Ministerio de Cultura). The city has also mobilized an elaborate set of cultural policies designed to promote tango and the city's historical connection to it as a cultural and/or economic resource, including two large-scale tango dance and music festivals that take place annually, though Astillero and many of their peers have been excluded from these projects. As Julián Peralta observed: "The city government has cultural policies [for tango]. They say, quote unquote, 'we promote,' 'we develop,' . . . but everything that is new they throw out like garbage, and in the end it is development without development. So you eventually begin to generate your own way of developing things, so that they work the way you want, because you have already been dismissed by the state. You already know that they are not going to help you" (Peralta, Interview).

The Cultural Politics of Música Popular

Here we can begin to see the real impasse that the popular as such represents in post-crisis Buenos Aires. On the one hand, the post-crisis popular social movements and those inspired by them have had to create alternative spaces and institutions because they have been excluded from the realm of official politics, cultural and otherwise. On the other hand, they have been excluded precisely because their "popularity" places them outside of what is considered acceptable or supportable by the government and other official institutions, with the popular here conjuring a complex amalgamation of longstanding racial, ethnic, gender, and, especially, class differences and prejudices, each of which has a specific genealogy within Argentina and other Latin American contexts (Grimson and Jelin; Wade).

At the same time, the popular points less to overt discrimination based on racial, ethnic, gendered, or class differences than to the social logic of systematic inequalities that are largely defined by patterns of cultural production and consumption. As the anthropologist Néstor García Canclini notes: "The popular is the excluded: those who have no patrimony or who do not succeed in being acknowledged and conserved; artisans who do not become artists, who do not become individuals or participate in the market for 'legitimate' symbolic goods; spectators of the mass media who remain outside the universities and museums, 'incapable' of reading and looking at high culture because they do not know the history of knowledge and styles" (145). Such exclusions have only been exacerbated by the spectacular series of failures on the part of international political-economic ideologies that have successively intended to "develop," "modernize," "integrate," or "globalize" Latin American economies, political policies, and cultures, of which the Argentine economic crisis of 2001 is but one recent example. Far from achieving their stated goals, these policies have succeeded only in compounding exclusions of all sorts—from economic opportunity, social integration, political participation, or cultural legitimacy—to the point that the region as a whole has been mired in what has been identified as a more or less permanent state of "crisis" (Yúdice, Flores, and Franco; Richard; Grimson). Within such a context, the popular has come to operate as a key component of Latin American politics (Laclau), social movements (Eckstein; Alvarez, Dagnino, and Escobar), culture (Míguez and Semán), the arts, and, of course, música popular.

Such divisions are reinforced—not reduced—by state cultural policies and other managerial regimes that aim to channel the multitude of local cultural practices and aesthetic meanings into a manageable, productive resource: in this case circumscribing what is or is not acceptable as tango. Astillero's project of remaking tango a música popular highlights how these divisions are reinscribed on and through musical sound and style within the context of social practice. Indeed, música popular is worth talking about in part because it fits so uncomfortably within these processes, because it is at once irreducibly aesthetic and social, artistic and political, such that the most minutely artistic and aesthetic concerns are immediately implicated in a much broader cultural politics.

Recognizing this, however, does not represent a further invitation to depart from the serious consideration of specifically musical materials in favor of a more contextual and/or interpretive analysis. Indeed, as I hope to have demonstrated in the preceding discussion, both the political claims and material consequences of debates regarding tango as a música popular in contemporary Buenos Aires are embedded precisely within the sonic details of musical style itself—specific accompaniment figures, particular melodic gestures, modes of rhythmic interpretation, and so on—such that musical style, at least in this particular case, can and does serve as an aural icon of an alternative social universe. But this is not an instance of sound structure somehow representing social structure (Lomax; Feld) or even sound structure representing social sensibilities (Turino). Astillero's tango of rupture is nothing more than a partisan reading of tango's historic legacy as a música popular qua music, through which the alternative social sensibilities and institutional structures envisioned by Astillero and their peers can be imagined and called forth in social practice.

At the same time, it should be stressed that the aesthetic project of Astillero and the broader musical and social movement they have attempted to cultivate does not, in the last analysis, represent a radical alternative to the hegemonic forms against which they define themselves, particularly those of the city government. It could instead be argued that Astillero represents something of a "loyal opposition" that ultimately accepts tango as the privileged genre of the city's aural public sphere. From this perspective the musicians of Astillero and their peers have not re-created tango as a música popular as much as they have convincingly engaged and animated the idea of the popular as it is imagined to have existed in the historical experience and legacy of tango by this particular demographic of musicians and their audiences (many of whom, it should be said, come from genuinely disenfranchised backgrounds among the so-called popular classes in Argentina). In this sense Astillero's project—despite its real alterity—can ultimately be seen as broadly congruent with the broader narrative of purification and transculturation that Ana María Ochoa has located at the heart of the Latin American aural public sphere.

These debates, in turn, are framed by the new place of local musics within the transnational arena, which has reconfigured how these types of social and aesthetic divisions are experienced and lived in local contexts. For instance, while Astillero's efforts to remake tango a música popular have been largely excluded from the aural public sphere of tango in Buenos Aires, it is very much in demand in places like Europe and East Asia, where the group regularly tours. In May 2010, as I was drafting this chapter, Astillero was in London rehearsing for a new production of *Romeo and Juliet* by the Mercury Theatre Company, which reenvisioned the star-crossed lovers as a pair of tango dancers. The production's publicity brochure stated, in part, that "through the power and passion of the evocative tango the decline of the lovers is seen not as fate, but an act of orchestration. The musicians intertwine with the actors creating their world, their love, and ultimately their fate" (Mercury Theatre 4). Astillero's participation in the play was made possible by financial support from the British Council, the international cultural relations organization of the British government, as well as other funding sources.

This production should be considered as a specific instance of engagement within a much larger and broadly shifting terrain of musical circulation, cultural policy making, and global commerce, perhaps the ultimate expression of which is the United Nations Education Scientific and Cultural Organization's (UNESCO) declaration of 2009 that named tango an "intangible cultural heritage of humanity." As defined in the proposal submitted to and approved by UNESCO regarding tango's status as intangible heritage:

> Tango is a genre that originally involved dance, music, poetry and singing. Tango expresses a way of conceiving the world and life and it nourishes the cultural imagery of the inhabitants of the capital cities of the Río de la Plata [Buenos Aires and Montevideo, Uruguay]. Tango was born among the lower urban classes in both cities as an expression originated in the fusion of elements from Argentine and Uruguayan's African culture, authentic criollos (natives of this region) and European immigrants. As the artistic and cultural result of hybridization's processes, Tango is considered nowadays one of the fundamental signs of the Río de la Plata's identity (UNESCO).[16]

The UNESCO declaration, one of the first to acknowledge a genre of popular music with this distinction, has had many important consequences within Argentina and Uruguay, which jointly submitted tango for UNESCO's consideration. On the one hand, and as can be seen even in the short passage cited above, it reinscribed tango within highly prestigious international networks of musical production and consumption while simultaneously reframing local musical and cultural histories within revisionist narratives of multicultural transnationalism. On the other hand, it gave a significant boost to already robust efforts on the part of local and national governments to promote tango as an engine for economic development via international cultural tourism and the exportation of music and other cultural goods abroad. It also (perhaps unwittingly) transcended the terms of the debate regarding tango as a música popular in Buenos Aires and the broader patterns of inclusion and exclusion that it represents by including a photograph of Astillero among the visual materials announcing tango's new status as an intangible cultural heritage.[17] Does the UNESCO declaration therefore represent a new path toward cultural legitimacy for these artists and their peers, or is it just another instance of the dual fetishization and gloss of local cultural difference on the part of cosmopolitan aesthetic and economic ideologies? Either way, it is clear that tango's life as an object of cross-cultural fantasy and desire, now channeled by these and other managerial regimes, continues on.

Notes

I would like to express my profound gratitude to Julián Peralta and the other members of Astillero—Patricio "Tripa" Bonfiglio, Mariano Caló, Osiris Rodríguez, Leonhard Bartussek, Félix Archangeli, and Peyo—for their participation and engagement with this project at the time of my fieldwork. Working with them taught me so much more than can be represented in these or any pages. I would also like to thank Oscar Fischer and all the musicians of the Orquesta Típica Piel de Mono and the Orquesta Típica Mario Baracus. Portions of this project were presented at the meeting of the International Association for the Study of Popular Music (IASPM) in 2007, a session of the EthNoise! Ethnomusicology Workshop at the University of Chicago in 2010, and the meeting of the Latin American Studies Association (LASA) in 2010; I would like to thank the organizers of these events for the opportunity to present my work and those who participated in them for their valuable feedback. Previous drafts of this piece received careful scrutiny from many colleagues and friends, especially Ana María Ochoa and David Novak. I would also like to thank Marilyn G. Miller for her rigorous editorial work and continuous support of this project since its inception. Finally, and as always, thanks to Ruth Wikler-Luker for her love and support of this and so many other projects.

1. This is not to say that the popular arts and popular music have not been the object of these managerial regimes. Instead, I highlight the longstanding disconnect between governmental and nonprofit modes of promoting the arts and culture as a means of addressing the "ethical incompleteness" of the modern political subject (T. Miller) and/or the uneven distribution of state services and protections (Yúdice, "Afro Reggae") and for-profit models that define music and the arts as nothing more and nothing less than consumable entertainment. Socially popular genres of music fall somewhere between these two poles: on the one hand, they are often considered unsupportable by governmental and nonprofit organizations that take them to be aesthetically suspect, while, on the other hand, they are increasingly implicated in large-scale music piracy operations that significantly undermine the profit motives of the transnational cultural industries (Ochoa and Yúdice), which, by definition, are not invested in the social meanings of music and the arts in local contexts.

2. The name Astillero translates as "shipyard." The name was chosen in homage to the shipyard unions of Argentina, which, according to the band's members, were among the groups that most fiercely resisted the atrocities of the last military dictatorship (1976–1983).

3. The material presented here is part of a larger research project on the cultural politics of music in post-crisis Buenos Aires. Data for this project were gathered over eighteen months of fieldwork in Argentina between 2004 and 2007, including participant observation, "bi-musical" training and performance (Hood), and interviews with members of Astillero and others in their orbit (including tango musicians, dancers, journalists, audience members, and governmental policy makers, among others), only some of whom are directly represented in the text.

4. Tango has, of course, remained salient in certain sectors of Argentine society over the past half century. However, there is an undeniable gap between the continued enthusiasm of those who grew up with tango as the *música popular* of their youth and the vast majority of the subsequent generations, including Astillero and their peers, for whom tango has at best been a self-referential caricature and at worst an embarrassment to be explained away. Beyond these two poles, tango has continually attracted a significant though ultimately niche audience of dance enthusiasts and music aficionados, who have generally not been committed to or invested in the genre's historic legacy as a música popular.

5. As such, Astillero's efforts should be distinguished from those of other contemporary engagements with the genre on the part of the city government of Buenos Aires or nonprofit arts institutions such as TangoVia Buenos Aires, which have focused on the aesthetic and economic revalorization of tango over its potential life as a popular practice.

6. The bandoneon is a button squeeze-box instrument of German origin that by the early 1920s had become a standard component of tango ensembles.

7. Only now are we seeing systematic efforts to preserve tango's historic material culture, and these efforts are being undertaken by nonprofit arts organizations such as TangoVia Buenos Aires rather than by any exclusively public entity (see http://www .tangovia.org).

8. While Julie Taylor has described how, for her, "some of the weight of past terror was borne by the tango" (*Paper Tangos* 22), tango was never, to my knowledge, the direct target of organized repression on the part of any government, military or otherwise.

9. Included in the tango-related cultural productions and representations are, among others, Fernando Solanas's film *El exilio de Gardel: Tangos* (1985) and Claudio Segovia's stage production *Tango argentino*. The latter premiered first in Paris (1983) and then on Broadway (1984) and is widely credited with rekindling interest in tango at the international level.

10. *Syncopation* is defined as "the regular shifting of each beat in a measured pattern by the same amount ahead of or behind its normal position in that pattern" (Oxford Music Online).

11. The significance of this piece is also due to Pugliese's sociopolitical beliefs and positions, including his deep commitment to radical political causes. A dedicated communist, Pugliese ran his *orquesta* as a collective, distributing income equally among himself and his musicians and coming to collective decisions regarding repertoire. He articulated a particular aesthetic philosophy that saw composing and performing tango less as a personalized or individualistic artistic pursuit than a response to the collective needs of audiences and the larger genre as a whole (Liska, *Sembrando al viento*). As such, Pugliese has come to represent the musical, social, and political epitome of tango's historic legacy as a música popular, serving as a model figure for the members of Astillero and their peers.

12. Literally, "your mother's cunt."

13. The members of Astillero have also created several ostensibly "new" elements, including a deliberately less florid approach to composing and interpreting melodic lines,

especially in vocal pieces; the use of some original instrumental and vocal effects; the use of modern studio recording techniques such as overdubbing; and the use of projected visual material during live performances.

14. I attended Astillero's milonga on an almost weekly basis throughout my primary research period.

15. This is not to say that individual policy makers or governmental cultural agencies are homogeneously opposed to Astillero's specific project, though the notion of música popular is undeniably problematic for the city. As one government functionary involved in programming cultural festivals explained to me in an interview, the city did not program truly popular genres such as cumbia "because of the people who would come, because of prejudice. Maybe because the city government still has a conception of culture in which the popular does not have a place."

16. This description was available in the English-language version of the nomination form found under the "Documents" tab at http://www.unesco.org/culture/ich/index .php?RL=00258, accessed July 8, 2013.

17. The image of Astillero is the fourth image in the series of thirteen that is accessible under the "slideshow" tab at http://www.unesco.org/culture/ich/index.php?RL=00258, accessed July 8, 2013. It shows two bandoneon players with a violin player in the background; the foregrounded bandoneonist is wearing a black muscle shirt.

CHAPTER EIGHT

Gotan Project's Tango Project

ESTEBAN BUCH

Translated by Michael Wiedorn

FOR SILVIA

The Olympia Music Hall in Paris, May 17, 2010: The concert launch for *Tango 3.0,* the third album from the Parisian group Gotan Project, begins to take shape with an acoustic song, played in the dark by a quartet consisting of a bandoneon, a violin, a guitar, and a piano. The song is "Cuesta abajo" (Downhill), the famous tango by Carlos Gardel, composed in 1934 with Alfredo Le Pera for the film of the same title, shot in New York by Paramount Pictures: "Las ilusiones perdidas / Yo no las puedo arrancar" (Lost illusions / I cannot tear them away). It is played in a conventional arrangement, except for the fact that at the end, instead of the typical dominant and tonic *chan-chan* rhythm, electronic percussion emanating from a mixing board weaves its way in, as it moves on to the second piece, which will be played in full light. The second piece is "Época," one of the band's hits released in Paris in 2001 with their first album *La Revancha del Tango* (The revenge of the tango), whose lyrics allude elliptically to the era of the *desaparecidos,* that is, to the dictatorship of 1976–83, its sad procession of disappeared people, and to the Mothers of the Plaza de Mayo: "Si desapareció / En mi aparecerá" (If he disappeared / He will reappear in me).

It is tempting to see in this beginning, which was repeated at each concert of the tour, a sort of manifesto or at the very least a commentary on the history of the tango genre. One might gloss the initial scene of the concert thus: the electronic tango was born of the classic tango, which lives on in its own venerable history, connecting it to recent and tragic historical experience.

This thread drawn between different periods in Argentine culture, which found in large cities like Paris or New York an auspicious location to resume its quest for sensuality and for richness, would therefore project the music of Buenos Aires into the future and into glory. Such a scenario has the merit of clarity. In addition to being the band's third album and the technical term indicating the future of the web, *Tango 3.0* thus announces a third life for the genre, after the traditional tango and the *tango nuevo* of Astor Piazzolla. That is, unless we take "Cuesta abajo" at its word and see the downward slope of Gardel's tango (the star died in 1935 in a plane crash in Medellín) as an allegory of the melancholic heart of the genre itself. Tango in this sense becomes like a phoenix, always dying, being reborn from the ashes of each of its countless declines. Nevertheless, the conclusion would remain the same; Gotan Project's tango project is nothing less than the future of tango.

What we have here is, to say the least, something of a risky bet, and no one knows what the outcome will be in the next few years—historiographical consecration, pure and simple forgetting, or, rather, something in between. In any case the members of Gotan Project are not the only ones concerned with these efforts. They implicate all of the groups who, in France, Argentina, and elsewhere, make up the phenomenon of electronic tango, which is emblematic of the creative renewal within the tango of the last ten years.[1] It must, however, be pointed out that for the moment, the global socialization of this music expresses more a generic instability than a clear inscription in the tango milieu. At the same time, there is no doubt that we are dealing with a massive phenomenon. Shortly after its release in April 2010, *Tango 3.0* reached the spot of the fourth best-selling album in France, where it remained for two weeks before beginning to drop slowly, not to mention first place in Belgium and second in Italy.[2] Even more significantly, six weeks after its release the album was still in second place overall in the world music category and fourteenth in the dance/electronic slot on Billboard.com, the main indicator of the record market in the United States.[3] If one adds to these partial figures an ambitious international tour, extensive radio airplay, and an unknown number of pirated copies on peer-to-peer sites, and if one notes that YouTube in January 2012 showed "Época" as having nearly nine million views after four years online and that at the same time "Mi Confesión" was approaching three million, one must conclude that from a purely quantitative point of view the career of Gotan Project, and of its founders Eduardo Makaroff, Philippe Cohen-Solal, and Christoph Müller, has no equal in the history of the tango.

That is, of course, if we are speaking of "real" tango. The aforementioned chart rankings betray the generic ambivalence of this music, one that lies most prominently in its technical features. Indeed, from the basic eurhythmics to the melodic profile and by way of the secondary role of instrumental virtuosity, the pieces' open form or the brevity of the lyrics, not to mention the invisible, powerful percussion triggered by computers that contrasts sharply with the absence of a drum set characteristic of the tango, all this is distant from the family resemblance that established until now any minimal belonging to the genre, even in non-prototypical cases. It is of course true that any attempt whatsoever to renew a genre cannot emerge as a novelty except at the price of a certain distance from the genre's conventional forms. For this reason the proposition's aesthetic validity cannot be decided solely on the basis of its initial strangeness. And while it may be unorthodox, the electronic tango maintains enough in common with the tango that even specialists cannot easily rule out the *question* of what relationships might link them.

In the case of Gotan Project, the presence of traditional instruments played by musicians of incontestable tango skills—the bandoneonist Niní Flores and Facundo Torres, the singers Cristina Vilallonga and Claudia Pannone, the arranger and pianist Gustavo Beytelmann, among others—tends to align their experiment with other reforming currents that the genre has witnessed throughout its history.[4] And the farther we move from the networks of specialists, the greater the chances that what distinguishes the electronic tango from the traditional tango tout court becomes blurred, and what we might call a *tangotude* or, stated otherwise, the global presence of the tango signifier in the public space, prevails.

In this sense the electronic tango—the latest example of what Ramón Pelinski, taking up a phrase of Mauricio Kagel, has called the "nomadic tango" (*El tango nómade*)—seems to summon up a number of ideological polarities that have become incontrovertible in the contemporary context. It is anchored in local heritage as well as a worldwide context via a technological crossover, that of the venerable German bandoneon vulgarized in the suburbs of Buenos Aires in the early twentieth century with the computer freshly arrived from Silicon Valley. In this crossover, the rhythmic sex appeal of the old, languorous *dos por cuatro* and of the metronomical regularity of electronic percussion combine. The phrases built into periods of four bars in accordance with the legacy of nineteenth-century dances are unhinged as they become minimalist, circular sequences, and all of it is reflected in the double, localized rootedness of the tango hall's location and the dance floors of this local globality that has become, or so we're told, the world. And with it we find everywhere a revisited eroticism, with girls in fishnet stockings cleverly "cross-dressed" with hats perched at a jaunty tilt. The conventions here rediscover that which can always be indexed in relation to the law of desire, as Pedro Almodóvar would say, even if it means being left to wonder what remains of desire once it has become a law.

Until now, all of this seems to have worked quite well. The extensive list of uses of the Parisian band's music in cinema and on television—here in a movie with Jennifer Lopez and Richard Gere, there in a gymnastics sequence at the Olympics in Beijing, or there again as a jingle for a brand of soap, or in a soundtrack for a documentary denouncing consumerism[5]—is an ambiguous indicator of its prestige and its influence, once we realize that any, or almost any, sign of success can invite critique.[6] Reactions to this music can take various forms. For example, one could advance an apology for innovative music whose progressive perspective proclaims the black roots of tango. One might celebrate the fact that this is music whose international success has heretofore only been paralleled by the brilliant career of Carlos Gardel. On the other hand, there are critiques that perceive in electronic tango a commercial product based on nationalist clichés, and one that is subject to the standard procedures of the culture industry. Between these two extremes, the spectrum of reactions and responses to this phenomenon is remarkably broad. That is why the gamble of integrating the electronic tango with the history of the tango, which is just as much a narrative construction for specialists as an international form of sociability, is in reality primarily a question of the definition of the tango genre and—which is to say the same—of its limits. And any question concerning the limits of a genre is also a question of values, those of the genre and those of the limit itself.

Biographical Trajectories

The origin of electronic tango's ambivalences is first and foremost to be found in the story of its protagonists, a story that is nothing like those of tango musicians in the traditional sense. Eduardo Makaroff's career before Gotan Project was that of an eclectic artist, and one whose principal strength would perhaps be his ability to circulate not only among different genres but also between different spaces of production, from the underground to mass media via the café concert and advertising. According to his autobiographical narrative, he began as a rock musician before breaking into advertising and television, which explains why his first tango, "El Tango de los pebetes"

(Tango for kids), was actually a children's song. The very fact of claiming to *compose* tangos, whereas in that genre it is the interpreter who reigns, is drawn from rock and roll, as was the decision to use Gotan Project's success to promote the revival of tango innovation through his label Mañana.[7]

Born in Buenos Aires in 1954 to a secular Jewish family, Makaroff's parents combined a bourgeois domestic status—an engineer father, a chemist mother—with activism in the Communist Party. His adolescent years were marked by his closeness to his brother Sergio, born in 1951. The rebel of the family, Sergio would land, in those hippy years, a part in the local version of *Hair*. With him, Eduardo formed a rock duo in 1972 called Los Hermanos Makaroff.[8] One of their songs, "Rock del Ascensor," has remained in the popular memory thanks to its saucy image of a couple making love in an elevator: "Hagámoslo de parado / hagámoslo de pie" (Let's do it standing up / let's do it on our feet).

In the duo Eduardo played the guitar, which he had begun studying at age fourteen with Juan Tata Cedrón. The latter incarnated, well before his years of Parisian exile, a reforming current in the music of Buenos Aires, one that was sensitive to tango and to modern poetry. Cedrón was also a politically active person, most notably in left-wing Peronism. Makaroff's apprenticeship with Cedrón, who would soon encourage him to diversify his knowledge of musical styles by taking bossa nova and classical guitar classes, was until that moment his sole contact with tango. He remained distant, however, from the repertory's figures and the institutions of the genre that, in those days under pressure from "youth music," had become set in a decadent and often bitter conservatism. It was in this context that he discovered Piazzolla's music, though without dwelling upon it. At that point in time his identity seemed clear: "Fui rockero" (I was a rocker), he would later say, describing an Argentina colored by the "contrast between being a rocker and what the tango represented, such as well-groomed fascists":

> [I] didn't have any contact with the true tango, I knew nothing about the tango. In reality my training was primarily that of an Argentine rocker. But because I knew music and I could read it, because I could play classical guitar and all that, my training was a little more extensive than my brother's, for example, or than that of some guy who would pick up an electric guitar and an amp and who would try to do solos from Jimi Hendrix or whoever, or the blues. . . . I never had the prejudice or the close-mindedness of the rocker against the tango. (Makaroff)[9]

A dispute with his brother and the latter's departure for Spain in 1977 would mark a new stage in Makaroff's career. Argentina had been, since March of the previous year, under the repressive boot of General Jorge Rafael Videla, and some of Makaroff's friends from the revolutionary Left, who happened not to be communists, found themselves pursued by the regime. At that time he became associated with a friend who would become his artistic partner for nearly twenty years: Daniel Mactas, better known as El Pollo, who, eight years older than Makaroff, had a true *tanguero* background that he had inherited from his father, "a character of the night, a friend of the showbiz people and the racecourse people" (Amuchastegui; un personaje de la noche amigo de la gente del espectáculo y del turf). The Mactas-Makaroff duo soon became Edu y el Pollo, and then Mano a Mano, the title of a Gardel tango. At Mactas's side, Makaroff began something of a long march toward the tango, one that nonetheless took a rather humorous turn from its beginnings—a *tango joyeux* (cheerful tango), in sum, an oxymoron, one that would become the album's title as well as the theme of the duo's tour after their arrival in Paris in 1990. Indeed, their first tango, "The Typical One," was a parody of the genre's platitudes (Amuchastegui).

Around 1985, at the invitation of a live music venue called Café Mozart, the duo produced their first tango show, leading Makaroff to take lessons with professional tango guitarists. But rather than being tango musicians, the two friends were then artists who navigated between musical genres and various professional milieus. Even before the end of the dictatorship in 1983, they started to write music for advertising, such as a government campaign against tobacco that included a famous *Ohrwurm*, or earworm, as the Germans say, that played obsessively in one's head: *Chau chau chau pucho*.[10] Then, beginning in 1984 under the democratic presidency of Raúl Alfonsín, they would have access to radio and to television with a children's show on the state-run channel ATC. The next year they made their incursion into cinema, as interpreters of the songs from the Fernando Solanas film *El Exilio de Gardel: Tangos*, which was set in Paris during the dictatorship and portrayed the world of Argentine exiles living there.[11] Aside from the songs composed by Solanas and José Luis Castiñeira de Dios, which musically have very little to do with the tango, the film includes several original pieces by Astor Piazzolla, thus sketching out a perimeter of hybridizations that anticipates, in certain aspects, Gotan Project's future project.

In 1990 the two left for Paris at the invitation of their friend Silvia Yako-McCloskey, an Argentine psychoanalyst who had recently arrived in France herself. In the next six years, after France's Radio Latina gave them their start, they appeared under the name Mano a Mano and not without success. This was despite the vagaries of the immigrant artist's life, one that invariably included problems with papers or difficulties with official status as cultural workers. Mactas's return to Argentina in 1996 would mark the end of their long collaboration. Makaroff then became MC at the Coupole dance hall in Montparnasse, which marked a turning point in the rediscovery of the tango by Parisians. He met Philippe Cohen-Solal, a producer at Virgin, in 1998 and proposed a collaboration that would become a hit during the World Cup soccer competition: "La Ola Dance," in which the sound of the bandoneon can be heard over a milonga rhythm. Shortly thereafter he made another move, this time with the folk dancer José Castro. For Makaroff this amounted to holding on to an old idea, one that in 1995 had already furnished the theme song for the French television program *Droit de regard*: "The electronic tango, we had tried that with El Pollo plenty of times, already in the eighties. We even wrote a jingle called 'Tecnotango'" (Makaroff; Y con el tango electrónico ya con el Pollo habíamos intentado muchas veces, incluso en los años 80. Habíamos hecho hasta un jingle que se llamaba tecnotango). But Cohen-Solal did not agree to this new suggestion: "I told Eduardo that the project he wanted to do didn't interest me, but that rather than doing a . . . 'commercial' project, I said to him, let's do just the opposite, let's do a project that we like and if we like it, maybe other people will too" (Cohen-Solal).

Setting aside the debate over the "commercial," with or without quotation marks, this early sketch of Gotan Project's undertakings would find in Philippe Cohen-Solal an ear as if made to hear it. Born in France of a Tunisian father and a Dutch mother, he had drawn from his family background a real taste for music from "far away," particularly from Latin America. He also acquired a sort of generic nomadism that led him to have difficulty understanding people who, as he put it, "spend their lives in one kind of music" (Cohen-Solal). This upbringing, and in particular the strong left-wing bent of his parents, gave him a certain idea of the historical experience of Latin American countries and would eventually translate into his borrowing of the name of his record label, Ya basta! (We've had enough!) from the Zapatista leader Subcomandante Marcos.[12] The same can be said of the fragments of political speeches that can be heard in Gotan Project's songs. In fact, it is Cohen-Solal, and not the Argentine Makaroff, who is behind the loops of Evita Perón that can be heard in "El Capitalismo Foráneo," or those of Che Guevara in "Queremos Paz." It is also Cohen-Solal who records, in Buenos

Aires in 2000, the *cacerolazos*, the noises of citizens banging on cooking pots that became symbols of revolt there and that can be heard in the live version of "La Revancha del Tango." And it is, once again, he who, after reading in the French newspaper *Libération* the story of the poet Juan Gelman and his granddaughter Macarena, who was born in captivity after her parents were kidnapped by the military, imagined a song dedicated to those who were disappeared during the dictatorship of 1976–1983 and asked Makaroff to write the words: whence the song "Época."

Cohen-Solal distinguishes this sensibility from political engagement, preferring perhaps the more modest notion of an aesthetic perception of politics. At any rate, when he met with Makaroff in 1998, this "great nostalgia for [his] childhood" was connected to diversified professional experiences in advertising, in the record industry, and in media. During the eighties he was successively a booking agent and the host of a radio show, helping to bring house music as well as other "new sounds" to France.[13] He next became a producer, first at Polydor and then at Virgin, where he worked mainly on film soundtracks alongside Arnaud Depleschin, Nikhita Mikhalkov, and Bertrand Travernier. He soon came to write music himself, notably for Tonie Marshall. At the same time he pursued a career as a DJ and musician with the group Boyz from Brazil, which was named after the thriller of 1978 based on the story of Josef Mengele's blonde and blue-eyed clones in Amazonia. Cohen-Solal created this latter duo in 1997 with Christoph H. Müller, who had been collaborating with him for the previous two years. With the occasional participation of a Brazilian musician from the transvestite group Les Étoiles, Rolando Faría, he blended house music and Brazilian popular music for the dance floor.

Müller, who was born in Germany and raised in Switzerland and who had studied in London and Paris, experimented with hybrids of electronic music and non-Western musical forms, beginning with the song "Muhammar," something of a techno fantasy piece featuring samples in Arabic and produced by a group called Touch el Arab. The track made it to the Swiss top five in 1987.[14] More recently, besides collaborating with Makaroff on the film *El Gaucho* (2008), Müller ventured into Afro-Peruvian music with Rodolfo Muñoz and the group Radiokijada, releasing an album titled *Nuevos Sonidos Afro-Peruanos* (2009).

Thus met the members of this eclectic trio with varied skills and experiences in the winter of 1999, in a studio on Rue Martel in the tenth arrondissement in Paris, to produce the first creations of what had yet to be named

Gotan Project—a name that came up in their first gatherings, and one that links the utopian dimension of rock groups such as the Alan Parsons Project or the Jimi Hendrix Experience with the *vesre* or reverse term for *tango* in Argentine slang (see Oscar Conde's description of this term and the *lunfardo* phenomenon in this edited volume).

The Making of the Project

The first fruit of this collaboration was a version of "Vuelvo al Sur," a song that Piazzolla had composed for the Pino Solanas film *Sur* (1987) and that the famous singer Roberto Goyeneche had interpreted for the film. It reads in the screenplay for the picture:

> Vuelvo al Sur,
> como se vuelve siempre al amor,
> vuelvo a vos,
> con mi deseo, con mi temor.
>
> Llevo el Sur,
> como un destino del corazón,
> soy del Sur,
> como los aires del bandoneón.
>
> Sueño el Sur,
> inmensa luna, cielo al revés,
> busco el Sur,
> el tiempo abierto, y su después.
> Quiero al Sur,
> su buena gente, su dignidad,
> siento el Sur,
> como tu cuerpo en la intimidad.
>
> Te quiero Sur,
> Te quiero Sur,
> Te quiero Sur.[15]
>
> [I'm returning to the South
> just as one always returns to love,
> returning to you,
> with my desire, with my fear.

I carry the South,
like a destiny of the heart,
I am from the South,
like airs from the bandoneon.

I dream the South,
immense moon, backwards sky,
I seek the South,
open time, and its afterward.
I love the South,
its good people, its dignity,
I feel the South,
like your body in intimacy.

I love you, South,
I love you, South,
I love you, South.]

In its original form, this piece is not a classic tango but rather a sort of *nuevo tango*. Even though Piazzolla is as close as he can be to traditional forms here, the text diverges from the proverbial pessimism of the tango as it expresses a communitarian ideal. These "good people," united in dignity, would later find themselves at the heart of the filmmaker's political program. For the filmmaker would later become the leader of an important current of the Argentine Left: a presidential candidate in 2007, and later a candidate for mayor of Buenos Aires, Solanas was elected deputy in 2009 under the banner of a movement called, in fact, Proyecto Sur. It is perhaps in the combination of a nostalgic, sentimental tone and political activism oriented toward the future, where "the South" becomes a true object of love, that we find the explanation for the success of this piece and the covers of it by such diverse artists as Mercedes Sosa, Caetano Veloso, and Florent Pagny. In any event the spirit of the song is not without its links to the "revenge of the tango" proclaimed by Gotan Project's album, where the piece would find its place once the time was right.

That said, the piece in question was also simply one of the only musical references common to Makaroff, Cohen-Solal, and Müller, and it is primarily for this reason that they held onto it. From a musical point of view as well, "Vuelvo al Sur" allowed generic and stylistic interactions that cannot be reduced to a simple meeting of tango and electronic music. The 3–3–2 rhythm structuring the piece, typical of Piazzolla, is also characteristic of the *milonga campera*, a traditional rural form. When added to a percussive background inspired by the Argentine folklorist Domingo Cura, a musical universe begins to take shape that, as far as solely Argentine elements are concerned, remains almost as close to folklore as to the tango. Whereas the initial bandoneon solo proclaims a representation of Buenos Aires and the milonga background for the guitar alludes to the image of the pampa, the percussion, inspired by pop/rock, corresponds to the metric demands of the contemporary dance floor.

It is on this principle, proper to house music, that the solo bandoneon deploys the tanguero phrasing and, later—as in the traditional tangos where the lyrics don't appear before the refrain—the warm voice of Cristina Vilallonga, whose Catalan origins in no way diminished her *porteño* evocations. Within seven minutes, "Vuelvo al Sur" sets forth a vessel of signifiers organized around a rhythmic formula with a fetishized value for Argentine music, one that in turn is projected into the international arena as a sonorous symbol of a South that is to varying degrees mythical.

Reconstructing the collective production of "Vuelvo al Sur" using interviews with Makaroff and Cohen-Solal provides a clear idea of the creative process that unfolded in early 1999 and also offers a more general take on the group's method of working. Once made, the choice of the piece launched a period of exchange of musical references between the Argentine and the two Europeans, with each member admitting his ignorance of the other's favorite genre. Next came the first direct interventions into the song, which were guided by precise stylistic orientations. Third, other musicians were called in—a singer, a bandoneon player—who reinforced the tango's generic markers while seeking to avoid certain melodramatic commonplaces. Last, the material that came out of the sound recordings was subjected to a process of *abstraction*, to use the musicians' term.

First, it is worth returning to Makaroff's narrative of events, told with a Spanish guitar in hand:

> "Alright, let's do a version of... so, what do you know? Piazzolla? OK." I like singing, you know. I'm neither Piazzollian nor neo-Piazzollian, not when I play or anywhere else. I love it, but no. So, "Vuelvo al Sur," Piazzolla and Solanas. OK.... And I began playing a milonga on the guitar, the same one that Cedrón had taught me early on in my lessons. Here's how it goes: in A minor... I'll show you, there's a method to it. To do rock, this is what you

do [he plays a rock scheme]. And this A minor sixth, the sixth minor in 3–3–2, that is to say, in rhythm [he begins to play a milonga with a *bordoneo* or melodic bass in 3–3–2 rhythm]. And I said to the girl who was singing with me: sing the same thing, but with a *canchero* [casual] style. Not like this: [he sings in an exaggerated, whiny tone]. I began to imagine what would happen with a rhythm like that in the background, instead of doing it like Piazzolla, I mean, [he plays some chords with a 3–3–2 rhythm,] even if Piazzolla is very good, what he does is great and all the versions that have been done of it are great. And then I told Christophe: put in a clip, instead of putting in 1–2–3–4 put in 3–3–2. . . . We recorded the song two times, and then I said "for me it's ok like that, now it's your turn to work, see you later." No, sorry, I mean I said: "Now we have to put in a bandoneon." . . . I said, "I'm going to introduce you to a country boy, he doesn't speak much French, what's more he doesn't speak at all, in general." . . . [Niní Flores] played to that, to the song, and I told him: "Good, play here, left hand, right hand. Record it another time." You know, you can record eighty thousand times with these machines. . . . You no longer have to get the arrangement right and play right, otherwise you're screwed. You can play well, badly, however you like. "Now, improvise, play along. Now we'll just give you the middle part, the milonga part, and you improv," etc. . . . Nothing was written in that version. Afterward, yes, we started to write certain melodies down more precisely, but the song was already written. . . . And that's how we made the song "Vuelvo al Sur." Because afterward, they [Cohen-Solal and Müller] were left alone with this recording, they started to experiment with it, and what you hear is what they did at the end of what I played. (Makaroff)[16]

Makaroff's story will be corroborated by Cohen-Solal point by point and notably with regard to the principle of a real division of labor within the group, one that translated into their way of connecting themselves in the circuit of the creative process. Once the choice of the Piazzolla piece was made together, we can perceive a first stage where the Argentine of the band contributes his technical awareness of the original genres (tango and milonga) and the social and artistic resources of his network of friends (that is, the tango musicians). In the next stage, the two Europeans, left alone to their computer, subject these materials to a process of abstraction. This process consists of attenuating, via electronic manipulations, the generic connections to origins, with the goal of bringing the material closer to dance floor music. Here is Cohen-Solal's story:

We had to start somewhere and I proposed a Piazzolla piece that came from the movie *El Sur.* . . . So we started to do a cover of "Vuelvo al Sur" and at first it wasn't working so well, not quite conclusively. And then, along with Christophe, I remember . . . you know when you don't really know what to do in the studio . . . we began to go a little crazy and add effects, echoes to the bandoneon, to Domingo Cura's percussion, to all kinds of things, you know . . . and we started to make it a little more free, and a little more irreverent most of all. And it started to sound really good. . . . I think Eduardo did the guitar chords first, then Niní added the bandoneon; it was really great, he made more tracks than you can count, each more beautiful than the other, which became useful later for "El Capitalismo Foráneo" but anyway . . . it was very . . . the skeleton of it was very simple, guitar, we added a bass, a bass line on the keyboard, and the percussion. We sampled little bits of percussion from Domingo Cura and made some more along the same lines. But the problem in the beginning, I'd say, was that we hadn't yet gotten into the sound of the bandoneon. Those are two kinds of music that are a little bit incompatible, in a way, that is, on a rhythmical level it's very different, it's a very mechanical music, one that's really . . . there's no movement between one time or another, and the very principle is to dance to something rather repetitive, very sequenced, and the tango is kind of the opposite, lots of accents, lots of halts, things . . . they're really not kinds of music that share enough for them to get along. But I think that what provided the connection, what made the connection was the dub part, the dub element, a music that Christophe and I listened to a ton at the time, and that influenced us enormously in our production. And I think that the difference . . . I think that the acoustic tango that we had with us . . . was something very concrete, very realistic, what you hear is what was played, whereas in electronic music what you hear isn't exactly what was played, it's what was transformed, tampered with. And from the point where you start to make tango more abstract, in a certain way, less concrete, less realistic, that's where it begins to become interesting for us. (Cohen-Solal)

These two stories of the genesis of "Vuelvo al Sur" give us insight into the internal dynamics proper to a project constructed from a universe whose elements are "a little incompatible," to use Cohen-Solal's expression. At least in this particular case, the group's work seems to start right where the artist stopped. The relationship of complementarity is clear here, and one could even go so far as to describe it as a meeting between a man from the South, a provider of techniques and materials from a cluster of types of music from his heritage, with men from the North who put these techniques and materials together with a know-how that is at once technological and aesthetic. This schema must have some truth to it, a truth that can offer a solid grounding to a number of critiques. At the same time, we must not draw parallels too quickly based on a suspect notion of economic and geopolitical contrast between a South that gives raw materials and a North that is the sole power capable of transforming them. On the one hand, it would be erroneous to reduce the entirety of the electronic tango phenomenon to this framework, given that the majority of musicians, in Argentina and elsewhere, combine an awareness of both generic registers and the technologies that make it possible to manipulate them. On the other hand, the mode of production behind Gotan Project's very first song in 1999 did not define their roles once and for all. From one album to the next, the group would modify their discourse and their aesthetics. To give only one example: while the tracks of *La Revancha del Tango* lasted around 6 minutes and 12 seconds, on *Tango 3.0* this figure was 3 minutes and 54 seconds, clearly much closer to the song format than to the vinyl format used by DJs. And the stories of other moments of production allow a glimpse into the more complex and interactive exchanges between Makaroff and his friends Cohen-Solal and Müller (whose much lengthier collaboration would itself merit a special examination). Also, one can note that "Vuelvo al Sur" is a rather atypical piece of their repertoire, comparable in this light to "Chunga's Revenge" by Frank Zappa or to "Last Tango in Paris" by Gato Barbieri, also covered by Gotan Project.

That said, it would be wrong to see arrangement and composition as being in opposition. The arrangement of pieces that are to various degrees well known holds a vital place in the history of the tango, somewhat similarly to how in the history of jazz an artist's originality comes into play through his or her approach to the standards.[17] In the framework of electronic music too there is no creation that, with its pre-recorded samples, loops, and colors, does not presuppose preexisting elements. Moreover, one could say the same for any piece that is taken to exemplify a genre, whether a waltz, a symphony, or reggae.

To return to the pieces created by Gotan Project, their original creations are based on rhythmic or harmonic formulas typical of folkloric Argentine genres such as the *chacarera* ("El Mensajero"), milonga ("La Vigüela") or *baguala* ("Paris, Texas"). There are also many musical gestures typical of tango itself, omnipresent albeit often reduced to a cadence, a color, or a repeated melodic motif. At times it can also be a matter of working with sounds that are invested with a strong symbolic content, as are the speeches of Che Guevara or Evita, with a cultural reference value, as with the voice of Julio Cortázar reading one of his own texts ("Rayuela"), with a fragment of an old Argentine film soundtrack ("Desilusión"), or with sounds that have a documentary function, such as railroad noises ("Mil millones").

The project would thus appear to be a way of coming to terms with the tango genre and its history—otherwise put, with the twentieth century. It attends to the national territory just as much as it does to its inverse, which is to say, the world. The paradox of the electronic tango is that its roots—in the sense of a stable relationship between a past, a practice, and a territory—are, strictly speaking, nowhere, yet the phenomenon unfolds in an international space thanks to a systematic return to a place that is quite clearly fixed on the map while remaining ontologically in motion. This is of course Argentina, but an Argentina that is less a particular country in South America than a theoretical vision or rather a repertory of symbols: the tango of Gardel and Piazzolla, dancing couples in red and black, the neighborhoods of La Boca or San Telmo, the mounted gauchos on the horizontal vertigo of the pampa, Evita, Che Guevara, Maradona and soccer, the writers Borges and Cortázar, Videla's dictatorship and the Mothers of the Plaza de Mayo, and so on. All these signifiers are associated not only in the music but also in the assemblage of images, since in the case of Gotan Project, all the song videos bear the signature of director Prisca Lobjoy—and they are infinitely recycled, in a sort of kaleidoscope of identity.

Revenge of the Tango?

At its start the project undertaken by Gotan Project was not aimed at the tanguero public but rather at the world of electronic music. According to Philippe Cohen-Solal, "the first 'Vuelvo al Sur' came out on vinyl [in 1999], and it was for DJs, and we had no desire to add our stone to the edifice that is the tango" (Cohen-Solal). That said, retrospectively one might think that the ambition to bring a "stone to the edifice that is the tango" was indeed already inscribed, under the surface, in the title of Gotan Project's first album, which came out in 2001, *La Revancha del Tango*. With, of course, the nuance that this "revenge of the tango" was played out in a space that was not its own, neither stylistically nor geographically. The first maxi-single vinyls had quick success via the BBC, notably thanks to Gilles Peterson, an influential taste maker. At this stage the trio's music became part of the world of dance music that, in

England in particular, was characterized by an ideological rejection of the star system.[18] This often brought about a quasi-anonymity on the part of the artists concerned, as well as a voluntarily marginal status. The shift to CD format quickly capitalized on this burgeoning fad, reorienting the group's circulation toward larger circuits, but not without modifying the cultural references. Ya Basta! worked from then on in a partnership with Barclay/ Universal—in other words, an alliance between a major and a smaller label that, as David Hesmondhalgh puts it, inevitably requires the former to try to preserve the "subcultural reputation" of the latter, without necessarily guaranteeing success (244). At any rate this turning point emphasized the group members' identification with rock and perhaps their "starification" following the rock model: it is no coincidence that in 2001 the concerts for the tour of *La Revancha del Tango* began with the musicians playing behind a veil that would drop away while they performed.

It would nonetheless appear that it was the dissemination of Gotan Project in certain milongas or tango dances frequented by amateur dancers and sprinkled throughout the entire world that precipitated their introduction into the world of the tangueros. This is the moment when the electronic tango came to be inscribed in the transformations then underway, transformations that would come to raise generational, stylistic, and ideological questions. Indeed, for the men and women who believe that the practice of tango implies an eternal return to the repertory of large orchestras, from Firpo to Pugliese via Troilo or Di Sarli, the fact of dancing to electronic music was itself a major deviation. And the dancing was done more often than not with an *abrazo abierto* or open embrace, that is, with two dancers at a distance from each other, rather than pressed together chest to chest as in the classic *milonguero* style. This open embrace is one of the characteristics of the style called *nuevo tango*. The latter, which is not without its debts to Piazzolla and which began without waiting for the electronic tango to develop itself, shares with the open embrace a number of sociological and technical traits. These overlaps can be summarized as a potential questioning of traditional gender roles and as a spatial autonomy accrued by each individual. This explains the fact that at times the new dance and the new music crossed paths, for example, when certain groups integrated dancers into their concerts.[19]

Beyond this micro-sociological anchorage, it was the perception of tango as a historical loser that gave meaning to the idea of a moment of revenge. Indeed, the word's presence in this title by Gotan Project can resonate as a sort of rallying cry for the whole of the phenomenon. In the interwar period in Europe, the tango competed with jazz for the role of the "exotic" musical product, whether by the intermediary of Argentine musicians on tour or thanks to local orchestras for whom playing jazz and/or tango was part of their daily work.[20] And after the first fruits of the prewar period, the 1920s featured what we might call tango's first globalization, where the launch of disks and radio were to define its guiding role within the "political economy of passion," to take up Marta Savigliano's expression (*Tango and the Political Economy of Passion*). Moreover, it is worth noting that commercial success and blending with other genres had always been at the heart of tango's socialization, particularly since the record companies Pathé and later Paramount Pictures appropriated the Gardel phenomenon and made a worldwide multimedia icon of it.[21]

The paths of jazz and tango did not take long to diverge: while the former would become a protean source of all that the twentieth century would label "popular music," from the most standardized and "commercial" products to the most deviant and confidential, the tango would take on the role of a subaltern genre within the world economy of entertainment, following in that regard the turns of fortune of its home countries, Argentina and Uruguay. It is true that the golden age of Argentine tango, the age of the big orchestras of the forties and fifties, was yet to come. But this glory would bypass and exclude the "nomadic tango" from the ensemble of representations of the genre in favor of the *typical*, in the narrowest sense of the term. Here we can witness the downward journey of a South American genre that, sharing the advantages and the prestige of the great European trend of "American dances" with North American music, quite simply lost the battle. Hence the resonances between the narratives on the decline of tango and the more recent denunciation of the economic and stylistic hegemony of the international pop and rock "system" governed by Anglo-Saxon music.

It is from this perspective that the notion of revenge becomes the key to a historical problem. For in the album of 2001 the word *revenge* is drawn not from a *tanguera* allusion but rather from the Frank Zappa song "Chunga's Revenge." It sports not only a bandoneon but also lyrics that proclaim the various genealogies that the Parisian group claims: "Piazzolla, Troilo, Cura / Mad Professor Zappa / Kruder Dorfmeister Pugliese / Es la revancha del tango." All these names are strung together, juxtaposing the glories of the tango, of dub, and of house music (with the latter being represented by the Austrian duo Kruder and Dorfmeister who, moreover, in 1996 produced a track titled "The Revenge of the Bomberclad Joint"). The message becomes clear: salvation comes not from the tradition in its purity but rather from the blending of all of these genres.

If we are to believe this story's principal characters and their accounts, what is at issue here is a return to the prehistoric sources of the genre, in the strictest sense of a period before history and historical documents. That is, a return to the black origins of the tango as described by the theory of the *tango negro*, a theory making black musicians and dancers of the Río de la Plata region the primary actors in the genre's birth. According to this view, which can be traced back to Vicente Rossi's book *Cosa de Negros*, published in 1926, and which has recently been articulated in the writings of Michel Plisson, Gustavo Goldman, and Juan Carlos Cáceres (as well as in the latter's musical oeuvre), tango's black origins are a truth that was systematically hidden by a historiography indentured to the dominant, white culture. Indeed, "negationist" is the adjective that Cáceres (13) unhesitatingly brandishes against this historiography in order to proclaim these black origins.[22] According to this perspective, adopted by the founding trio of Gotan Project and transmitted to their fans via the abundant media attention that they enjoyed, the group's electronic percussion is the heir of the immemorial African drums that resonated in the primitive form of tango negro, just as they resonate in the pulsating rhythms of jazz, rock, house, or techno. The revenge of the tango is therefore, in this view, a revenge of Afro-descendant peoples and their histories. Indeed, Cáceres himself echoes this view as he marries virtual drums and real percussion in the song "Notas" from Gotan Project's album *Lunático*: "Africanos en las pampas argentinas / Toques y llamadas de tambores / Candombe, tango . . ." (Africans in the Argentine pampas/ Sounds and calls of the drums/ Candombe, tango . . .).

Given that what is at issue here is, rather than a historiographical position, an aesthetic proposition formulated in mythological terms, the ensuing debate promises to be endless. That said, a skeptic might note that the aforementioned affirmation of the oppressed is a privileged point of entry into the mainstream of the globalized pop/rock system that the world music genre has contributed to for twenty years. That fact furnishes the grounds for many negative reactions to electronic tango. It is nonetheless far from easy to separate a purely conservative criticism limiting itself to proclaiming devotion to heritage from the concerns around a renewal of cultural hegemony in the guise of modernization. Rodolfo Mederos, a pioneer in the fusion of tango and rock in the seventies, could thus reply with the following to a journalist who envisioned in electronic tango a renewal of the genre by the new generation: "That is no doubt a form of ignorance. It seems like a good thing to me that they're looking for their own path, but they're taking the wrong direction. Electronic tango is nothing more than a mechanism of domestication, of the unification of cultures. Is electronic tango modern tango? What is the modern?" (Jemio).[23]

Such a charge, which might appear strange coming from a tanguero skilled in crossover, nonetheless summarizes other public and private statements made by historical figures in the world of tango. It should be read alongside Cohen-Solal's cutting remark that "we detest world music" (Cohen-Solal). Indeed, the intensity of this hatred corresponds to the risks inherent in an international success that was achieved thanks to icons of the anti-globalization movement. The term *electronic tango* itself, which would at first glance appear to be relatively neutral, is far from being unanimously accepted by those who practice the form. Cohen-Solal, for example, rejects it outright, along with the notion of "genre fusion" and suspicions as to any "commercial" aims in their project: "I find the very principle of electronic tango to be garbage."

It is significant that everything in Cohen-Solal's language revolves around a term that Walter Benjamin placed at the heart of the aesthetics of modernity: *collage*. As Cohen-Solal puts it, "I find that what was done a lot, in what is called electrotango or *tango electrónico*, is a collage of a techno track with a guy playing the bandoneon over it or every now and then, a little sample of tango. But that's not techno and that's not tango, it's really not electronic music. That's nothing more than a collage, it doesn't stick together." These claims remind us of the diversity of styles and, no doubt, of qualities of electronic tango when taken as a whole. Electronic tango runs the gamut from the mechanism of the beat box superimposed onto a fragment of classic tango to more complex and creative ways of tying and untying the musical knots of the musical heritage. Temptations to simplify in this domain can be strong. Once the sounds of a bandoneon are all it takes in order to "do tango" in another stylistic context, the aforementioned bandoneon need not play anything interesting. By the same token, when a phrase of Gardel is enough to evoke Buenos Aires, the phrase need not be elaborated upon in order to be significant. On the contrary, repeating it infinitely is a lovely way to kill two birds with one stone. Setting aside the pleasure produced by repetition itself, an already predetermined verbal content is here exploited through the simple fact of transposing it into another aesthetic framework.

With this in mind, it must be pointed out that Gotan Project scrupulously avoids laying percussion over fragments of tango singing. In what probably constitutes the most sophisticated example of electronic tango in general, the band's composing work is not limited to the simple operations made possible by sound-editing software. Rather, their compositions combine varied electronic sources with professional musicians playing complex arrangements live and displaying the virtuosity that is the hallmark of solo performances. But is the notion of collage enough to distinguish between the good and the god-awful? It would be better to say that there are collages and there are collages, and collages are only one gesture among others within the panoply of resources proper to the craft of a music producer in a globalized world. Here, once again we must avoid simplification, in research as in composition. As the story of the first meeting of Gotan Project's founders shows, it was Makaroff who had the idea that the exotic and erotic image of the tango, the evolution of its technological resources, and the legitimacy of hybrid forms of music produced for dance would come together to make the project of a *tecnotango* possible. Here we can locate one argument against the simplistic North-South scheme. And at the time when these new partners agreed to attempt the experiment, even as they sought to modify its terms in order to distance it from the overly "commercial" dimension, they had already undertaken similar *mélanges*, with Brazilian music in particular. Coming from different horizons, the three were, so to speak, on the same wavelength.

This wavelength did not result from the habits that one customarily associates with artistic creation, at least according to the cliché of the inspired and solitary artist. Rather, it can be traced to an ability to anticipate stylistic trends, one that is essential in the contexts of the advertising, media, and recording industries. It is no accident that these domains of cultural production can all be found on the CVs of our three protagonists, alongside their experience in the domain of musical creation in the proper sense. And all these resources, insofar as their very essence is relational, are made to be shared and can be seen to emerge together in a certain conjuncture. Gotan Project launched an idea that was, quite literally, in the air at that time, just before others did the same. Makaroff mentions a telephone call from Gustavo Santaolalla, a musician and producer that he knew from his time as a rocker. Santaolalla had called from Los Angeles with congratulations on Gotan Project's first vinyls, sharing his idea "to do something like that" (*hacer algo así*) with his group Bajofondo. Makaroff then reportedly said to Cohen-Solal: "Let's get to it now because soon there will be tons of groups like this. The Argentines have seen that they can do this" (Makaroff; Metámosle pata porque van a empezar a salir muchos grupos así. Vieron los argentinos que se puede hacer eso). The album *La Revancha del Tango* should be dated to that day in 2000. In fact, the creation of the principal electronic tango groups would be spread out over the next few years or even the next few months. The takeoff of electronic tango was rapid and exponential, so much so that in November 2007 an Argentine journalist could call the category a "saturated" market (E. Castillo). And yet that in no way explains why this Parisian group had more success than all the other electronic tango groups combined. On the other hand, it does explain the fact that, looking beyond a micro-chronology of events, the same idea surfaced nearly simultaneously in different places across the planet.

Notes

This chapter is a contribution to research on contemporary creation in the tango milieu in Paris and Buenos Aires, conducted with Marina Cañardo, Camila Juárez, and Federico Monjeau under the auspices of the Music and Globalization ANR (*Agence nationale de la recherche*), which is directed by Emmanuelle Olivier of the Centre de Recherches sur les Arts et le Langage (Center for Research on the Arts and Language), CRAL, UMR 8566 EHESS / CNRS. See http://www.globalmus.net.

1. I am focusing on Gotan Project here and purposely setting aside their relationships and differences with other electronic tango groups such as Bajofondo, Narcotango, Ultratango, Tango Crash, Electrocutango, Tangodrims, Tanghetto, Otros Aires, Debayres, San Telmo Lounge, and so on.

2. The rankings for France come from the Pure Charts website, http://www.charts infrance.net/charts/, accessed June 8, 2010.

3. The rankings for the United States come from Billboard's website, http://www .billboard.com/charts/, accessed June 8, 2010.

4. See Buch. Also among the musicians who participated in Gotan Project's activities are the singer Veronika Silva, the bandoneonist Víctor Villena, Juan José Mosalini Jr., Olivier Manoury, Serge Amico, and Matías González, the violinists Line Kruse and Ananta Roosens (also a trumpeter), and the pianist Lalo Zanelli.

5. I refer to, respectively, the film *Shall We Dance?* (2004); the American gymnast Alicia Sacramone; Jet Dry, the Finnish dish soap; and the Swedish documentary *Surplus* (2003). See the article "Gotan Project," *Wikipedia*, English version, http://en.wikipedia .org/wiki/Gotan_Project, accessed June 22, 2010.

6. See T. Taylor.

7. See Bazely.

8. See the "Biography" section on Sergio Makaroff's personal website, http://www .sergiomakaroff.com/biografia/, accessed April 27, 2010.

9. "Una contraposición entre ser rockero y lo que representaba el tango, como los fachos con el peluquín. . . . Pero yo no tenía contacto con el verdadero tango, ni la tenía la del tango. En realidad, me hice una formación musical que fue principalmente de rockero

argentino, pero gracias a saber música y poder leer música, y poder interpretar guitarra clásica y todo, tenía una formación un poquito más extensa que mi propio hermano, por ejemplo, o de lo que puede tener el tipo que agarra una guitarra eléctrica y pone el amplificador y trata de hacer solos de Jimi Hendrix o no sé quién, o blues.... Nunca tuve el prejuicio o la cerrazón mental del rockero contra el tango."

10. See Szendy.

11. On Argentine exiles in Paris, see Franco.

12. See Marcos.

13. On techno in France, see Smith; Jouvenet.

14. See "Christoph H. Müller's Discography," *Discogs,* http://www.discogs.com /artist/Christoph+H.+Müller, accessed April 28, 2010.

15. While these lyrics come directly from the text of Gotan Project's version of the song, the original lyrics to "Vuelvo al sur" by Pino Solanas can also be found at http://www.todotango.com/english/las_obras/letra.aspx?idletra=1880, accessed July 10, 2013.

16. "Bueno, hagamos una versión de ... ¿cuál? ¿qué conocés? Piazzolla. Bueno." Yo soy canción, eh. No soy piazzollero ni neo piazzollero, ni tocando ni nada. Me encanta, pero no. Entonces Vuelvo al Sur, Piazzolla y Solanas. OK.... Y empecé a tocar con la guitarra una milonga que era la misma que me enseñó Cedrón al principio de mis clases, que es así: ponés la menor ... te voy a mostrar porque es un plan. Como hacer así para tocar rock [toca una base de rock], es la sexta, la sexta menor en tres/tres/dos, es decir, en ritmo [toca una base de milonga]. Y le dije a la piba que cantaba conmigo: esto mismo cantalo pero con una onda canchera. O sea, no es [canta en tono quejoso exagerado]. Me imaginé cómo podría ser con un ritmo atrás, en vez de hacerlo como Piazzolla que realmente era [toca acordes en ritmo 3–3–2], que está bueno lo de Piazzolla, pero ... es una super versión todo lo de Piazzolla y todas las versiones que se hicieron. Y le dije a Christophe: poné un clip, en vez de poner 1–2–3–4 poné 3–3–2.... Grabamos dos veces las canciones, dije "para mí esto ya está. Trabajen. Chau." Me fui. Ah, no, perdón, dije "ahora a esto hay que agregarle un bandoneón."... Dije, "bueno, ahora les voy a presentar un flaco, este flaco no es ... viene de una provincia, no habla mucho francés, ni nada en general.... [Nini Flores] tocó encima de eso, tocó encima de la canción y yo le dije "bueno, tocá acá. Tomá mano izquierda, mano derecha." Volvé a grabar. Viste que se puede grabar 80 mil veces en esas máquinas, la música ya no es hay que hacer bien un arreglo y tocar bien una vez porque sino cagaste. Podés tocar mal, bien, lo que quieras: "ahora zapá, improvisá, tocá por encima. Ahora te ponemos solamente la parte del medio, la parte de la milonga, y hacete una improvisación," y qué se yo.... No había nada escrito en esa versión. Después sí empezamos a escribir más precisamente ciertas melodías, pero para esa ya estaba escrita la canción.... Y así salió la canción Vuelvo al Sur porque ... entonces ellos se quedaron solos con esa grabación y empezaron a hacer experiencias diversas y lo que escuchás es lo que les salió a ellos después de lo que toqué. Pusieron un ritmo atrás."

17. See in particular Monjeau and Filipelli; Kohan, *Estudios sobre los estilos compositivos del tango* 12–15.

18. See Hesmondhalgh.

19. See in particular Liska, "El cuerpo en la música"; Plebs.

20. See Jacotot; Matallana.

21. See in particular Barsky and Barsky.

22. On the *tango negro* see also Rossi; Plisson; Goldman; Ortiz Oderigo; and Rafael Mandressi, unpublished talk from the seminar "Musique et politique au vingtième siècle," Ecole des Hautes Etudes en Sciences Sociales, Paris, May 21, 2010.

23. "Es, sin duda, una forma de ignorancia. Me parece bien que busquen su camino, pero lo hacen por la ruta equivocada. El tango electrónico no es otra cosa que un mecanismo de domesticación, de unificación de culturas. ¿El tango electrónico es el tango moderno? ¿Qué es lo moderno?"

GLOSSARY

Arrabal: A slum or sketchy neighborhood.

Bajo: The area of Buenos Aires where the city meets the Río de la Plata.

Bajofondo: underground, lumpen

Bandoneón: A small box-shaped button accordion or concertina popularized in the early twentieth century in relation to the growth of tango music in Argentina and Uruguay.

La Boca del Riachuelo (or simply La Boca): A working-class Italian immigrant neighborhood in the southern outskirts of Buenos Aires, located along the banks of the Riachuelo, where it meets the Río de la Plata.

Boedo-Florida: The names of two different streets in Buenos Aires, each used to identify a different aesthetic or literary tendency in the vanguard period of the 1920s. Left-leaning writers were identified with Boedo, a main street and name of a working-class neighborhood in which they published a magazine titled *Extrema izquierda* (Extreme left). Cosmopolitan writers became identified with Calle Florida, a more upscale, commercial avenue in the city center where their favorite café was located.

Candombe: Afro-Uruguayan drum music and dance form that contributed to the formation of tango.

Canyengue: 1. Low-class, related to the slums. 2. Expressive style of tango dance developed in the early twentieth century, characterized by a close embrace in which the couple does not directly face each other but forms an inverted *V*, both dancers maintain bent knees, and the steps are typically short.

Compadre: A man who acts in an arrogant, provocative, or presumptuous way, ready for a fight.

Compadrito: A street thug or pimp, known for his strut or forward-bent gait as well as a signature style that included a hat, specific hairstyle, and high-heeled shoes.

Conventillo: Tenement or boarding house that typically catered to poor or immigrant renters and was characterized by overcrowding, substandard sanitary conditions, and lack of privacy. Most had an interior patio, associated with the development of early tango dance.

Corte: A pause, break, or embellishment in tango dance.

Cortina: Literally, curtain. Used in tango to refer to a short musical interlude that separates *tandas* during a milonga.

Criollismo: In Argentina and Uruguay, the valorization of autochthonous cultural expression in literature and other arts. Despite the focus on local cultural production, criollismo was significantly influenced by European cosmopolitan values and preferences.

Criollo, criolla: Noun: A person born in the Americas of "pure" Old World blood, whether European or in some cases African. In the Río de la Plata region, criollos distinguished themselves both from indigenous peoples and from anyone not born in Argentina. Adjective: Aesthetic style privileging local elements over European or other foreign influences.

Farol: A streetlamp or gaslight, an iconic symbol of early tango danced on the street.

Filete, fileteadores: The art and artists of a decorative style of painting used for commercial purposes in early twentieth-century Buenos Aires and now associated with tango. Fileteadores typically portray flowers, leaves, ribbons, flags, and lettering in their works.

Gardel, Carlos (1890?–1935): The most famous tango singer of all time, generally credited with inventing the *tango canción* or tango song.

Gaucho: A native cowboy of the South American pampas or Patagonian grasslands, a symbol of criollo identity.

Golden age of tango (roughly 1935–1950): The period of the twentieth century during which tango enjoyed its greatest popularity in the Río de la Plata region. Characterized by the proliferation of the *orquestas típicas*, especially those of Juan D'Arienzo, Aníbal Troilo, and Francisco Canaro. The popularity of the *orquestas* of Osvaldo Pugliese and Carlos di Sarlo continued on into the post–golden age period.

Guardia vieja (1900–1925): Literally, Old Guard, the period in which tango developed a recognizable form in dance and music. The most famous figures from the period are Eduardo Arolas and Ángel Villoldo.

Gringo: In the context of the Río de la Plata, a disparaging term for a foreigner or immigrant, very commonly used to refer to Italians.

Habanera: Dance rhythm developed and popularized in Cuba in the nineteenth century, considered an antecedent to tango.

Lunfardo: Colloquial vocabulary or language that developed in the Río de la Plata region in the late nineteenth and early twentieth centuries that borrows from several immigrant influences and indigenous terms, as well as various kinds of word play including *vesre*, in which the syllables of words are used *al revés* or backward, for example, *gotan* for tango.

Malevo: A low-life character or troublemaker, skilled with a knife.

Manzi, Homero (1907–1951): Revered Argentine poet, tango lyricist, and screenwriter.

Milonga: 1. A *rioplatense* style of music and dance that preceded and contributed to the formation of the tango. 2. The fastest of three basic rhythms that constitute traditional tango dance music (the others being *vals* and tango). 3. The places or events where the tango is danced.

Milonguero, milonguera: 1. A person whose life revolves around tango dance and tango philosophy 2. The most skilled dancers in a milonga, able to negotiate within the reduced spaces of a crowded dance floor 3. A dance style characterized by a close embrace and short steps.

Murga: In Uruguay and Argentina, a collective of street musicians or troubadours, usually identified with a specific neighborhood.

Nuevo tango: 1. A style of music associated with Astor Piazzolla and the incorporation of jazz and classical elements with traditional tango, popularized from the 1950s on. 2. A style of tango dance popularized from the 1990s on that breaks with the traditions of *tango de salon, tango canyengue,* or *tango milonguero* by opening the embrace, dancing off-axis, and avoiding the rigid social codes of the milonga. 3. A style of electronic music influenced by hip-hop and other contemporary world musics, popularized from 2000 on.

Oriental: Uruguayan, someone or something from the east side of the Río de la Plata.

Orilla: Literally, water's edge; metaphorically refers to a fringe or marginal area.

Orquesta típica: The ensemble of instrumental musicians associated with the popularization of tango and tango dance during the golden age of tango. Usually included at least three bandoneons, a string section with violins, viola, and sometimes cello, and a rhythm section with piano and upright bass.

Payador: Itinerate poet and musician or minstrel associated with the pampas and later the outlying urban areas, famous for engaging in verbal-musical duels.

Piazzolla, Astor (1921–1992): Composer, arranger, and bandondeón player who revolutionized the sound of instrumental tango by introducing new rhythms, jazz and classical orchestration, and untraditional instruments such as saxophone and electric guitar. Considered the primary architect of *nuevo tango* music.

Piringundín or peringundín: Low-end bar or dance hall that caters to the riffraff or *orillero* population.

Porteño, porteña: Adjective used to describe a person, thing, or quality of Buenos Aires.

Práctica: Dance "practice" session in which the social codes typical of the milonga are relaxed and dancers are free to experiment. Musical accompaniment is generally constant, instead of being divided into *tandas.*

Pugliese, Osvaldo (1905–1995): Legendary tango composer and musician known for his rhythmically intense style beloved by dancers. A leftist, Pugliese has been adopted as a popular saint by *tangueros,* who invoke his name as a talisman for good luck.

Quilombo: 1. Brothel. 2. Mess, disorder, upset. 3. In Brazil a maroon settlement of escaped or fugitive slaves.

Río de la Plata: River Plate, the river and estuary formed by the confluence of the Uruguay and Paraná rivers that serves as a border between Argentina and Uruguay.

Rioplatense: From the Río de la Plata region, especially the primary port cities of Buenos Aires and Montevideo.

Sainete: A short theater piece, often a farce, important in early twentieth-century theater in Argentina and Uruguay. Sainetes often dealt with popular and vernacular topics and provided an early forum for tango.

Suburbio: A poor, outlying neighborhood.

Tanda: In a milonga a set of three to five songs, usually all tango, vals, or milonga.

Tango de salón: A dance style generally built on an eight-count basic sequence of *salida, cruzada,* and *resolución,* modified or embellished with *sandwiches, calesitas, sacadas, barridas,* and other adornments. The embrace is often open, and steps may be longer than in *tango milonguero.* Outside of Argentina salon style tango often erroneously refers to stage performance tango, in which *ganchos* (leg hooks), *boleos* (leg swings), and other large movements are more frequent than in the traditional milonga setting.

Tango milonguero: A dance style designed for the limited maneuverability of a crowded milonga, in contrast to *tango de salón* or other styles used in performance. Characteristics include a close or closed embrace, chest-to-chest contact, a straight spine inclined slightly forward, allowing for free movement from the waist down, with the *marca* proceeding from the chest of the leader.

Tango rioplatense: A term that recognizes tango's origins and development in both Argentina and Uruguay, especially in the principal port cities of Buenos Aires and Montevideo.

Troilo, Aníbal "Pichuco" (1914–1975): Legendary Argentine bandoneón player, composer, arranger, and bandleader.

WORKS CITED

Aguilar, Gonzalo. *Otros mundos: Un ensayo sobre el nuevo cine argentino.* Buenos Aires: Santiago Arcos, 2006.

———. "La salvación por la violencia." *Invasión* y *La hora de los hornos: Episodios cosmopolitas en la cultura argentina.* Buenos Aires: Santiago Arcos, 2009. 85–120.

Alonso, Carlos. *Carlos Alonso.* Buenos Aires: Ediciones de Arte Gaglianone, 1986.

———. *Carlos Alonso: (Auto)Biografía en imágenes.* Buenos Aires: RO Ediciones, 2003.

———. *Hay que comer.* Valencia: Institut Valencià d'Art Modern, Generalitat Valenciana, 2005.

———. *Mal de amores y otros males.* Exhibit catalog. Buenos Aires: Centro Cultural Recoleta, May 2011. Accessed July 8, 2013, http://www.fundacionalon.org/?p=901.

Alvarez, Sonia E., Evelina Dagnino, and Arturo Escobar, eds. *Cultures of Politics, Politics of Cultures: Re-Envisioning Latin American Social Movements.* Boulder: Westview Press, 1998.

Amuchastegui, Irene. "Un pollo para el tango," interview with Daniel Mactas. *Clarín*, April 4, 1997. Accessed April 27, 2010, http://entrevistasdolina.blogspot.com/2008_03_01_archive.html.

Andermann, Jens. *Mapas de poder: Una arqueología literaria del espacio argentino.* Rosario: Beatriz Viterbo, 2000.

Andermann, Jens, and William Rowe, eds. *Images of Power: Iconography, Culture, and State in Latin America.* New York: Berghahn Books, 2005.

Anreus, Alejandro. "Carlos Alonso's Anatomy Lesson." *Third Text* 24.3 (2010): 353–60.

Antoniotti, Daniel. *Lenguajes Cruzados: Estudios culturales sobre tango y lunfardo.* Buenos Aires: Corregidor, 2003.

Archetti, Eduardo P. *Masculinities: Football, Polo, and the Tango in Argentina.* Oxford: Berg, 1999.

Archivo General de la Nación. *Un tango en el agua.* Buenos Aires, 1912.

Arditti, Rita. *Searching for Life: The Grandmothers of the Plaza de Mayo and the Disappeared Children of Argentina.* Berkeley: University of California Press, 1999.

Auyero, Javier. *Poor People's Politics: Peronist Networks and the Legacy of Evita.* Durham: Duke University Press, 2001.

Azzi, María Susana. *Antropología del tango: Los protagonistas.* Buenos Aires: Ediciones de Olivarria, 1991.

———. "La inmigración y las letras de tango en la Argentina." *Tango tuyo, mío y nuestro.* Edited by Ercilia Moreno Chá. Buenos Aires: Instituto Nacional de Antropología y Pensamiento Latinoamericano, 1995. 81–90.

———. "The Tango, Peronism and Astor Piazzolla during the 1940s and 1950s." *From Tejano to Tango: Latin American Popular Music.* Edited by Walter Aaron Clark. New York: Routledge, 2002. 25–41.

Azzi, María Susana, and Simon Collier. *Le Grand Tango: The Life and Music of Astor Piazzolla.* Oxford: Oxford University Press, 2000.

Balch, Oliver. "Buenos Aires or Bust." *Guardian Unlimited,* October 24, 2006.

Barco, Gustavo. "Los Turistas Llegan Atraídos por el Tango." *La Nación,* May 8, 2005.

Barnitz, Jacqueline. *Twentieth-Century Art of Latin America.* Austin: University of Texas Press, 2001.

Barrett, Terry. *Why Is That Art? Aesthetics and Criticism of Contemporary Art.* New York: Oxford University Press, 2008.

Barrionuevo, Alexei. "Top Official on Economy Steps Down in Argentina." *New York Times,* April 26, 2008.

Barsky, Julián, and Osvaldo Barsky. *Gardel: La biografía.* Buenos Aires: Taurus, 2004.

Basaldúa, Emilio. "Héctor Basaldúa and the Colón Theater: Thirty Years of Stage Design." *Journal of Decorative and Propaganda Arts* 18 (1992): 32–53.

Basso, Keith. *Wisdom Sits in Places.* Albuquerque: University of New Mexico Press, 1996.

Bates, Héctor, and Luis Bates. *La historia del tango.* Buenos Aires: Talleres Gráficos Compañía General Fabril Financiera, 1936.

Bazely, Solange. Interview with Eduardo Makaroff. October 14, 2004. Accessed April 28, 2010, http://www.musicargentina.com.

BBC. "Q&A: Argentina's Economic Crisis." *BBC News World Edition,* February 12, 2003. Accessed October 1, 2010, http://news.bbc.co.uk/2/hi/business/1721061.stm.

Beceyro, Raúl. "El Documental Hoy." *Punto de Vista* 90 (2008): 33–37.

Benarós, León. "El Tango y los Lugares y Casas de Baile." *La Historia del Tango vol 2: Primera Época.* Buenos Aires: Corregidor, 1977. 205–87.

Benjamin, Walter. "La obra de arte en la época de su reproductibilidad técnica." *Discursos interrumpidos I.* Madrid: Taurus, 1989. 15–60.

Bergero, Adriana J. *Intersecting Tango: Cultural Geographies of Buenos Aires, 1900–1930.* Pittsburgh: University of Pittsburgh Press, 2008.

Bernes, Jean-Pierre. "Cortes y quebradas. Borges généalogiste du Tango." *Europe: Revue littéraire mensuelle* 637–39 (1982): 84–91.

Bernini, Emilio. "Un estado (contemporáneo) del documental. Sobre algunos films argentinos recientes." *Kilómetro 111: Ensayos sobre cine* 5 (2004): 41–57.

———. "Un proyecto inconcluso. Aspectos del cine contemporáneo argentino." *Kilómetro 111: Ensayos sobre cine* 4 (2003): 87–106.

Bertin, Celia. *Marie Bonaparte: A Life.* New Haven: Yale University Press, 1982.

Bianco, Eduardo. "Plegaria." Todotango.com. Accessed July 13, 2013, http://www.todotango.com/Spanish/las_obras/Tema.aspx?id=UUPUSyhwUOM=.

Bonfiglio, Patricio. Interview with Morgan Luker. Buenos Aires, April 10, 2007.

Borges, Jorge Luis. *On Argentina*. Edited by Alfred MacAdam. New York: Penguin, 2010.

———. "El escritor argentino y la tradición." *Obras completas I (1923–1949)*. Edición crítica. Buenos Aires: Emecé, 2009. 438–44.

———. "Historia del tango." *Evaristo Carriego*, second ed. Buenos Aires: Emecé, 1955. 141–64.

———. *Jorge Luis Borges: Selected Non-Fictions*. Edited by Eliot Wienberger. New York: Penguin, 2000.

———. *Jorge Luis Borges: Selected Poems*. Edited by Alexander Coleman. New York: Viking, 1999.

———. "Man on Pink Corner." *Collected Fictions*. Translated by Andrew Hurley. New York: Penguin, 1998. 45–52.

———. *Obra poética, 1923–1977*. Buenos Aires: Emecé Editores, 1984.

———. *Other Inquisitions, 1937–1952*. Translated by Ruth L. C. Simms. Austin: University of Texas Press, 1965.

———. *A Personal Anthology*. New York: Grove Press, 1967.

———. *Prosa completa*, vol. 1, *Evaristo Carriego: Discusión; Historia universal de la Infamia*. Barcelona: Bruguera, 1985.

———. *Prosa completa*, vol. 3, *Otras inquisiciones: El hacedor; Elogio de la sombra*. Barcelona: Bruguera, 1985.

———. *Selected poems, 1923–1967*. Edited, with an introd. and notes, by Norman Thomas di Giovanni. New York: Delacorte Press, 1972.

———. *El tamaño de mi esperanza*. Buenos Aires: Seix Barral, 1993.

Borges, Jorge Luis, and Silvina Bullrich. *El compadrito*. Buenos Aires: Emecé, 2000.

Borges, Jorge Luis, and José E. Clemente. *El idioma de los argentinos*. Buenos Aires: Emecé, 1968.

———. *El lenguaje de Buenos Aires*. Buenos Aires: Emecé, 1968.

Bourdieu, Pierre. "Notas provisionales sobre la percepción social del cuerpo." *Materiales de sociología crítica*. Edited by C. Wright. Madrid: La Piqueta, 1982. 183–94.

Browning, Barbara. *Samba: Resistance in Motion*. Bloomington: Indiana University Press, 1995.

Buch, Esteban. "Trayectorias de Gustavo Beytelmann. Lo cercano se aleja." *Tangos cultos. Kagel, JJ Castro, Mastropiero y otros cruces musicales*. Edited by E. Buch. Buenos Aires: Gourmet Musical, 2012. 146–75.

Cáceres, Juan Carlos. *Tango negro: La historia negada: orígenes, desarrollo y actualidad del tango*. Buenos Aires: Planeta, 2010.

Cadícamo, Enrique. *La historia del tango en París*. Buenos Aires: Corregidor, 1975.

———. *La luna del bajo fondo / Abierto toda la noche*. Buenos Aires: Freeland, 1964 [1940].

———. *Viento que lleva y trae. Poesías*. Buenos Aires: Editorial Fermata, 1945.

Caló, Mariano. Interview with Morgan Luker. Buenos Aires, June 13, 2007.

Cámara de Landa, Enrique. "Recepción del tango rioplatense en Italia." *Trans, Revista Transcultural de Música 2*. Accessed October 15, 2009, http://www.sibetrans.com/trans/trans2/camara.htm.

Camnitzer, Luis. *On Art, Artists, Latin America, and Other Utopias*. Edited by Rachel Weiss. Austin: University of Texas Press, 2009.

"Canyengue, Candombe and Tango Orillero: Extinct or Non-existent Tango Styles?" Accessed July 8, 2013, http://tangovoice.wordpress.com/2010/03/19/canyengue -candombe-and-tango-orillero-extinct-or-non-existent-tango-styles/.

Capellano, Ricardo. *Música Popular: Acontecimientos y confluencias*. Buenos Aires: Editorial Atuel, 2004.

Cara-Walker, Ana. "Borges' Milongas: The Chords of Argentine Verbal Art." *Borges the Poet*. Edited by Carlos Cortínez. Fayetteville: University of Arkansas Press, 1986. 280–95.

"Carlos Alonso. El horror y la memoria." Universidad Tres de Febrero, 2005. Accessed July 8, 2013, http://www.elortiba.org/pdf/carlos_alonso_el_horror_y_la _memoria.pdf.

Carpani, Ricardo. *Tango: 20 Dibujos de Ricardo Carpani presentados por Daniel Moyano*. Catalog. Maqueta de Jorge Mennella. Buenos Aires, n.d.

Carpentier, Alejo. "Pedro Figari y el clasicismo latinoamericano." Figari, *Figari* 19–22.

Carrascal, María Laura. "Marcia Schvartz, 'El arte es un mundo para vivir.'" *La Capital*, December 14, 2008. Accessed July 8, 2013, http://www.lacapital.com.ar/ed _senales/2008/12/edicion_8/contenidos/noticia_5051.htm.

Carretero, Andrés M. *Tango: Testigo Social*. Buenos Aires: Peña Lillo Ediciones Continente, 1999.

Carriego, Evaristo. *La canción del barrio*. Buenos Aires: Ediciones de Aquí a la Vuelta, 1990.

Carroll, Rory, and Oliver Balch. "Latin Rivals Learn it Takes Two to Tango." *Observer*, January 25, 2009.

Caserón Porteño. *Tango Map Guide*. Buenos Aires, 2006–2007.

Castillo, Edgardo Pérez. "Cada vez más cercanos al tango." *Página/12*, November 30, 2007.

Castillo, Jorge. "Pedro Figari. Conformación de un estilo." Figari, *Figari* 5–17.

Castro, Donald. *The Argentine Tango as Social History, 1880–1955: The Soul of the People*. Lewiston: Edwin Mellen Press, 1991.

———. "Carlos Gardel and the Argentine Tango: The Lyric of Social Irresponsibility and Male Inadequacy." *The Passion of Music and Dance: Body, Gender, and Sexuality*. Edited by William Washabaugh. Oxford, New York: Berg, 1998. 63–78.

———. "Popular Culture as a Source for the Historian: The Tango in Its Época de Oro, 1917–1943." *Journal of Popular Culture* 20 (1986): 45–71.

———. "Popular Culture as a Source for the Historian: The Tango in Its Era of La Guardia Vieja." *Studies in Latin American Culture* 3 (1984): 70–85.

Cecconi, Sofía. "Tango Queer: territorio y performance de una apropiación divergente." *Trans. Revista Transcultural de Música* 13 (2009). Accessed July 10, 2013, http://www.redalyc.org/articulo.oa?id=82220946008.

Chasteen, John Charles. *National Rhythms, African Roots: The Deep History of Latin American Popular Dance*. Albuquerque: University of New Mexico Press, 2004.

Cirio, Norberto Pablo. "La presencia del negro en grabaciones de tango y géneros afines." *Temas de Patrimonio Cultural* 16 (2006): 25–59.

Civale, Cristina. "El exilio sin Gardel." *El Periodista* 234 (March 1989): 43.

Cohen-Solal, Philippe. Interview with Esteban Buch. Paris, April 29, 2008.

Collier, Simon. *The Life, Music, and Times of Carlos Gardel.* Pittsburgh: University of Pittsburgh Press, 1986.

Collier, Simon, Artemis Cooper, María Susana Azzi, and Richard Martin. *¡Tango!: The Dance, the Song, the Story.* London: Thames and Hudson, 1995.

Conde, Oscar. *Diccionario etimológico del Tango.* Buenos Aires: Taurus, 2004.

———. *Poéticas del rock*, vol. 1. Buenos Aires: Marcelo Héctor Oliveri Editor, 2007.

———. *Lunfardo.* Buenos Aires: Santillana Argentina, 2011.

Connerton, Paul. *How Societies Remember.* Cambridge: Cambridge University Press, 1989.

Copes, Juan Carlos. *Bailemos Tango: Let's Dance Tango.* Buenos Aires: Ricordi, 1989.

Couselo, Jorge Miguel. "El tango en el cine." *Historia del Tango Vol. 8.* Edited by Luis Alposta, Luis Ordaz, and Jorge Miguel Couselo. Buenos Aires: Corregidor, 1977.

Cozarinsky, Edgardo. *Milongas.* Photos by Sebastián Freire. Buenos Aires: Edhasa, 2007.

Cragnolini, Alejandra. "Articulaciones entre violencia social, significante sonoro y subjetividad: la cumbia 'villera' en Buenos Aires." *Trans. Revista Transcultural de Música* 10 (2006). Accessed July 10, 2013, http://www.redalyc.org/articulo.oa?id =82201006.

Dávila, Arlene. *Culture Works: Space, Value, and Mobility across the Neoliberal Americas.* New York: NYU Press, 2012.

De la Púa, Carlos. *La crencha engrasada.* Buenos Aires: Schapire Editor, 1978 [1928].

De Lara, Tomás. *El tema del tango en la literatura argentina.* Buenos Aires: Ediciones Culturales Argentinas Ministerio de Educacion y Justicia, 1961.

Del Barco, Mandalit. "Carlos Gardel. Argentina's Tango Maestro." *National Public Radio*, September 13, 2010. Accessed July 8, 2013, http://www.npr.org/templates /story/story.php?storyId=129783483.

Del Mazo, Mariano, and Adrián D'Amore. *Quién Me Quita lo Bailado: Juan Carlos Copes: Una Vida de Tango.* Buenos Aires: Corregidor, 2001.

Dempster, Elizabeth. "Touching Light." *Performance Research* 8.4 (2003): 46–52.

Desmond, Jane C., ed. *Meaning in Motion: New Cultural Studies of Dance.* Durham: Duke University Press, 1997.

Die Tango-Idee: Künstlergruppe Talleres del Mercado. Catalogue for the collective exhibit from October 31 to November 28, 2002, Bankhaus Lübbecke & Co., München, Sociedad Hispano-Alemana. Montevideo: Talleres del Mercado, 2002.

Dínzel, Gloria, and Rodolfo Dínzel. *Tango: An Anxious Quest for Freedom.* Translated by Martin Harvey. Stuttgart: Editorial Abrazos, 2000.

Dínzel, Rodolfo. *El tango, una danza: Esa ansiosa búsqueda de la libertad.* Buenos Aires: Corregidor, 2008.

Dodes, Rachel. "Going To: Buenos Aires." *New York Times*, December 12, 2004.

Dos Santos, Estela. *Las Cantantes: Historia del Tango.* Vol. 13. Buenos Aires: Corregidor, 1994. 2225–455.

———. "La Mujer en el Tango: Tango Magia y Realidad." *20 Miradas Sobre una Aventura que no Cesa.* Buenos Aires: Corregidor, 1998. 241–77.

Dujovne Ortiz, Alicia. "Buenos Aires." *Critical Fictions: The Politics of Imaginative Writing.* Edited by Philomena Mariani. Translated by Caren Kaplan and Aurora Wolfgang. Seattle: Bay Press, 1991. 115–30.

———. "Etre Porteño (in Buenos Aires)." *Discourse* 8 (Fall/Winter 1986–1987): 73–83.

Duvall, Robert. *Assassination Tango.* Metro-Goldwyn-Mayer, 2002.

Eckstein, Susan, ed. *Power and Popular Protest: Latin American Social Movements.* Berkeley: University of California Press, 2001.

Escobar, Arturo. *Territories of Difference: Place, Movements, Life, Redes.* Durham: Duke University Press, 2008.

Estenssoro, María. "Rediscovering the Master *Fileteadores* of Buenos Aires." *Journal of Decorative and Propaganda Arts* 18 (1992): 154–69.

Fabiano, Sharna. "Essential Tango: Dancing in the Moment." 2002. Accessed June 24, 2013, http://www.sharnafabiano.com/.

Falcoff, Laura. "Elegí gente que a mi juicio era la más auténtica." *Clarín,* November 21, 2003. Accessed July 10, 2013, http://edant.clarin.com/diario/2003/11/21/c-00611.htm.

Falicov, Tamara. *Cinematic Tango.* London: Wallflower Press, 2007.

Farías, Víctor. *La metafísica del arrabal. El tamaño de mi esperanza: un libro desconocido de Jorge Luis Borges.* Madrid: Anaya and Mario Muchnik, 1992.

Featherstone, Mike. "Estilo de vida y cultura de consumo." *Cultura de consumo y posmodernidad.* Buenos Aires: Amorrortu, 2000. 142–59.

Feld, Steven. "Sound Structure as Social Structure." *Ethnomusicology* 28.3 (1984): 383–409.

"Felipe de la Fuente." *Arteargentino.com.* Accessed July 10, 2013, http://www.arteargentino.com/dic/d/delafuente,f1.htm.

Felix, David. 2002. "After the Fall: The Argentine Crisis and Repercussions." *Foreign Policy in Focus* (August 2002): 1–6.

Ferrer, Horacio. *El Siglo de Oro del tango.* Buenos Aires: Editorial El Mate, 1996.

———. *El tango: Su historia y evolución.* Buenos Aires: Peña Lillo, 1999.

Ferrer, Horacio, and Oscar del Priore. *Inventario del Tango. Tomo I (1849–1939).* Buenos Aires: Fondo Nacional de Las Artes, 1999.

———. *Inventario del Tango. Tomo II (1940–1998).* Buenos Aires: Fondo Nacional de Las Artes, 1999.

Figari, Pedro. *Arte, estética, ideal.* Prólogo de Arturo Ardao. Montevideo: Biblioteca Artigas, 1960 [1912].

———. *Figari: XXIII Bienal de San Pablo.* Jorge Castillo, curator. Martín Castillo, coordination. Buenos Aires: Banco Velox, 1996.

———. *Intimate Recollections of the Río de la Plata. Recuerdos íntimos del Río de la Plata.* Paintings by Pedro Figari. Marianne Manley, curator. New York: Center for Inter-American Relations, March 5–May 19, 1986.

Figari's Montevideo (1861–1938) = *El Montevideo de Figari (1861–1938).* Washington, DC: International Development Bank, Cultural Center, 1995.

Fischerman, Diego, and Abel Gilbert. *Piazzolla. El mal entendido.* Buenos Aires: Edhasa, 2009.

Flores, Celedonio. *Cuando pase el organito.* Buenos Aires: sin editorial, 1965 [1935].

———. *Antología poética.* Buenos Aires: Ediciones del Sol, 1975.

Flores, Rafael. *El tango desde el umbral hacia dentro.* Madrid: Euroliceo, 1993.

Fontanella de Weinberg, María Beatriz. "El lunfardo: de lengua delictiva a polo de un continuo lingüístico." *Primeras Jornadas Nacionales de Dialectología (1977).* Tucumán: Facultad de Filosofía y Letras, Universidad Nacional de Tucumán, 1983. 129–38.

Ford, Aníbal. *Homero Manzi.* La Plata: Editorial de la Universidad Nacional de la Plata, 2005.

Foucault, Michel. *Historia de la Sexualidad I. La voluntad del saber.* Buenos Aires: Siglo Veintiuno Editores, 1995.

———. *Historia de la Sexualidad II. El uso de los placeres.* Mexico City: Siglo Veintiuno Editores, 1996.

———. *Historia de la Sexualidad III. La inquietud de sí.* Mexico City: Siglo Veintiuno Editores, 1997.

———. *Vigilar y Castigar. Nacimiento de la prisión.* Buenos Aires: Siglo Veintiuno Editores, 1991 [1976].

France, Miranda. *Bad Times in Buenos Aires: A Writer's Adventures in Argentina.* New York: Ecco, 1999.

Franco, Marina. *El exilio: Argentinos en Francia durante la dictadura.* Buenos Aires: Siglo XXI, 2008.

Frank, Patrick. *Los Artistas del Pueblo. Prints and Workers' Culture in Buenos Aires, 1917–1935.* Albuquerque: University of New Mexico Press, 2006.

———. "Xilografías de escenas urbanas e industrials de Buenos Aires, 1922." Accessed July 10, 2013, http://grabados.org/bellocq/intro.htm.

Frank, Waldo. *América Hispana, a Portrait and a Prospect.* New York: Scribner's, 1931.

Frith, Simon. "Hacia una estética de la música popular." *Las culturas musicales. Lecturas de etnomusicología.* Edited by Francisco Cruces et al. Madrid: Editorial Trotta, 2001. 413–36.

Fuentes, Carlos. *The Buried Mirror: Reflections on Spain and the New World.* New York: Houghton Mifflin, 1999.

Fumagalli, Mónica. *Jorge Luis Borges y el Tango.* Buenos Aires: Abrazos Books, 2004.

Furlan, Luis Ricardo. *Esquema de la poesía lunfardesca.* Buenos Aires: Torres Agüero Editor, 1995.

———. *La poesía lunfarda.* Buenos Aires: CEAL, 1971.

"Gabino Ezeiza." Ensantelmo.com.ar. Accessed July 1, 2013, http://www.ensantelmo.com.ar/Cultura/Mitos%20y%20Bohemia/gezeiza.htm.

Gabino, Rosario. "Argentina: Cifras en Duda." *BBCMundo.com.* October 3, 2007.

Accessed July 8, 2013, http://news.bbc.co.uk/hi/spanish/business/newsid_7023000
/7023806.stm.

Gabriel, Teshome H. *Third Cinema in the Third World: The Aesthetics of Liberation.*
Ann Arbor: UMI Research Press, 1982.

Gallego, Mariano. "Identidad y Hegemonía: el tango y la cumbia como 'constructores'
de la nación." Papers of the CEIC, September 2007. Accessed July 10, 2013, http://
www.identidadcolectiva.es/pdf/32.pdf.

Gálvez, Lucía, and Enrique Espina Rawson. *Romances de tango.* Buenos Aires: Norma,
2002.

Gálvez, Manuel. Hisotria de arrabal. Buenos Aires, 1927.

Gambarotta, Lisandro. "Jorge Muscia: El Fileteador del Tango," interview with Jorge
Muscia. *El Tangauta,* April 2009.

Garbatsky, Irina. "Marcia Schvartz: 'El mundo del arte está muy banalizado.'" *La Capital,* December 20, 2009. Accessed July 10, 2013, http://www.lacapital.com.ar
/ed_senales/2009/12/edicion_61/contenidos/noticia_5031.html.

García Blaya, Ricardo. "Idas y vueltas con 'El tango de la muerte'." Todotango.com. Accessed July 13, 2013, http://www.todotango.com/spanish/biblioteca/CRONICAS
/el_tango_de_la_muerte.asp.

García Canclini, Néstor. *Hybrid Cultures: Strategies for Entering and Leaving Modernity.*
Translated by Christopher L. Chippari and Silvia L. López. Minneapolis: University of Minnesota Press, 1995.

Garramuño, Florencia. *Modernidades primitivas: Tango, samba y nación.* Buenos Aires:
Fondo de Cultura Económica de Argentina, 2007.

Gasio, Guillermo. *Jean Richepin y el tango argentino en París en 1913.* Buenos Aires:
Corregidor, 1999.

Gelman, Juan. "Semblanza." Accessed July 13, 2013, http://www.diariomardeajo.com
.ar/semblanzadejuangelman.htm.

Gené, Marcela, and Silvia Dolinko. *Víctor Rebuffo y el grabado moderno.* Buenos Aires:
Fundación Mundo Nuevo, 2008.

Gewurtz, Ken. "It Takes 200 (or More) to Tango." *Harvard Gazette,* November 1,
2007. Accessed July 8, 2013, http://news.harvard.edu/gazette/story/2007/11/it
-takes-200-or-more-to-tango/.

Gift, Virginia. *Tango: A History of an Obsession.* Charleston: BookSurge, 2009.

Girondo, Oliverio. "Manifiesto de Martín Fierro." *Martín Fierro* (May 15, 1924): 1–2.

Glusberg, Jorge, and Ángel Kalenberg. *Pedro Figari en el Museo Nacional de Bellas Artes.*
Buenos Aires: Museo Nacional de Bellas Artes, 1996.

Gobello, José. *Aproximación al lunfardo.* Buenos Aires: EDUCA, 1996.

———. *Crónica general del tango.* Buenos Aires: Editorial Fraterna, 1980.

———. "Gardel en la evolución del tango." *Tres estudios gardelianos.* Buenos Aires:
Academia Porteña del Lunfardo, 1991.

———. *La historia del tango.* Buenos Aires: Corregidor, 1976.

———. *El lunfardo.* Buenos Aires: Academia Porteña del Lunfardo, 1989.

———. *Vieja y nueva lunfardía.* Buenos Aires: Editorial Freeland, 1963.

Gobello, José, ed. *Letras de tango: Selección (1897–1981)*. 3 vols. Buenos Aires: Ediciones Centro Editor, 1997.

Gobello, José, and Jorge Bossio. *Tangos, letras y letristas*. 3 vols. Buenos Aires: Plus Ultra, 1993.

Gobello, José, and Marcelo Oliveri. *Diccionario del habla de Buenos Aires*. Buenos Aires: Carpe noctem, 2006.

Goertzen, Chris, and María Susana Azzi. "Globalization and the Tango." *Yearbook for Traditional Music* 31 (1999): 67–76.

Goldman, Gustavo. *Lucamba. Herencia Africana en el tango 1870–1890*. Montevideo: Perro Andaluz Ediciones, 2008.

Grimson, Alejandro, ed. *La cultura en las crisis latinoamericanas*. Buenos Aires: CLASCO, 2004.

Grimson, Alejandro, and Elizabeth Jelin, eds. *Migraciones regionales hacia la Argentina*. Buenos Aires: Prometeo, 2006.

Groppa, Carlos. *The Tango in the United States: A History*. Jefferson, NC: McFarland, 2004.

Guido, Walter, and Clara Redy de Guido. *Cancionero Rioplatense (1880–1925)*. Caracas: Biblioteca Ayacucho, 1989.

Hall, Stuart. "Notas sobre la reconstrucción de lo popular." *Historia Popular y teoría socialista*. Edited by R. Samuels. Barcelona: Crítica, 1984. 93–110.

Harris, Wendell V. "La canonicidad." *El canon literario*. Edited by Enric Sullá. Madrid: Arco/Libros, 1998. 37–60.

Hesmondhalgh, David. "The British Dance Music Industry: A Case Study of Independent Cultural Production." *British Journal of Sociology* 49 (1998): 234–51.

Hood, Mantle. "The Challenge of Bi-Musicality." *Ethnomusicology* 4.2 (1960): 55–59.

Hora, Roy. *The Landowners of the Argentine Pampas: A Social and Political History, 1860–1945*. New York: Oxford University Press, 2001.

Hornbeck, J. F. *The Argentine Financial Crisis: A Chronology of Events*. U.S. Library of Congress: Congressional Research Service, 2002. Accessed October 1, 2010, http://fpc.state.gov/documents/organization/8040.pdf.

Horvath, Ricardo. *Esos malditos tangos*. Prólogo de Norberto Galasso. Buenos Aires: Editorial Biblos, 2006.

"Hugo Santiago." *El Amante* 3.26 (Buenos Aires, April 1994): 10–25.

Isola, Laura. "Arte que me hacés bien." *Pagina/12*. Accessed July 10, 2013, http://www.pagina12.com.ar/diario/suplementos/las12/13-1679-2004-12-31.html.

Jackson, Josh. "Gustavo Santaolalla: A Film Composer Finds His Roots." *National Public Radio*, October 30, 2008. Accessed July 10, 2013, http://www.npr.org/templates/story/story.php?storyId=96273922.

Jackson, Michael. "Introduction: Phenomenology, Radical Empiricism and Anthropological Critique." *Things as They Are: New Directions in Phenomenological Anthropology*. Bloomington: Indiana University Press, 1996. 1–50.

Jacotot, Sophie. "Entre deux guerres, entre deux rives, entre deux corps. Imaginaires et appropriations des danses de société des Amériques à Paris (1919–1939)." Doctoral Thesis, Paris I, Adv. Pascal Ory, Paris, 2008.

James, Daniel. *Resistance and Integration: Peronism and the Argentine Working Class, 1946–1976*. New York: Cambridge University Press, 1988.

Jemio, Diego. "El regreso a la tradición," interview with Rodolfo Mederos. *Clarín*, March 5, 2004.

Jiménez, José. *Teoría del arte*. Madrid: Tecnos, 2002.

Jouvenet, Morgan. *Rap, techno, électro . . . Le musicien entre travail artistique et critique sociale*. Paris: Éd. de la Maison des sciences de l'homme, 2006.

Juárez, Camila, and Martín Virgili. "Contrapunto y enunciación en la Orquesta Típica Fernández Fierro." Paper presented at the VI Congreso de la Rama Latinoamericana de la Asociación Internacional para el estudio de la Música Popular (IASPM-AL). Buenos Aires, August 23–25, 2005.

Judkovski, José. *Buenos Aires, fervor y—tango: una historia con judíos*. Buenos Aires: Fundación IWO, 2003.

Kershaw, Sarah. "Google Tells Sites for 'Cougars' to Go Prowl Elsewhere." *New York Times*, May 15, 2010.

Klein, Naomi. *The Shock Doctrine: The Rise of Disaster Capitalism*. New York: Metropolitan Books, 2007.

Kohan, Pablo. "Carlos Vega y la teoría hispanista del origin del tango." *Espacios* 34 (June 2007): 74–85.

———. *Estudios sobre los estilos compositivos del tango (1920–1935)*. Buenos Aires: Gourmet Musical Ediciones, 2010.

Kramer, Lawrence. "Dangerous Liaisons. The Literary Text in Musical Criticism." *Nineteenth-Century Music* 13 (1989): 159–67.

———. *Music as Cultural Practice, 1800–1900*. Berkeley: University of California Press, 1990.

Kuri, Carlos. *Piazzolla. La música límite*. Third ed. Buenos Aires: Corregidor, 2008.

Lacalle, Carlos. "Evocación de Pedro Figari, Pintor / An Evocation of Pedro Figari, Painter." *Evocación de Pedro Figari, Pintor*. Montevideo, 1938. 7–20.

Laclau, Ernesto. *On Populist Reason*. London: Verso, 2005.

Lash, Scott, and John Urry. *Economías de signo y espacio. Sobre el capitalismo de la posorganización*. Buenos Aires: Amorrortu Editories, 1998.

Lavandera, Beatriz. "Lunfardo." *Grupo de Trabajo de Desarrollo Cultural: Términos latinoamericanos para el Diccionario de Ciencias Sociales*. Buenos Aires: CLACSO, 1976. 86–88.

Lewis, Avi, and Naomi Klein. *The Take*. New York: First Run/Icarus Films, 2004.

Lima, Nicanor. *El tango argentino de salón: Método de baile teórico y práctico. 1ra. Parte*. Buenos Aires: Edición de autor, 1916.

Liska, María Mercedes. "Cultura popular y nuevas tecnologías: El baile del Neotango." *La revista del CCC* 2 (2008). Accessed July 10, 2013, http://www.centro cultural.coop/revista/articulo/32/.

———. "La renovación de los valores de autenticidad o el tango electrónico como producto del mercado." Actas del VIII Congreso IASPM-AL: "Alma, corazón y vida. La canción popular y sus discursos analíticos." Lima, June 18–20, 2008. Accessed June 15, 2010, http://www.iaspm-al.org/uploads/file/cdocDocumentos/836326821 c46fa1eca165af670fd232c.pdf.

————. *Sembrando al viento. El estilo de Osvaldo Pugliese y la construcción de subjetividad desde el interior del tango*. Buenos Aires: Ediciones del Instituto Movilizador de Fondos Cooperativos, 2005.

————. "'Vos sos milonguera.' La percepción sonora en la contemplación generacional de una bailarina de tango." VII Congreso de estudios de Música Popular (IASPM-Rama Latinoamericana). La Habana: Casa de las Américas, 2006. Accessed July 10, 2013, www.iaspmal.net/wp-content/ . . . /MercedesLiska.pdf.

Lomax, Alan. "Song Structure and Social Structure." *Readings in Ethnomusicology*. Edited by David McAllester. New York: Johnson Reprint Corporation, 1962. 227–52.

Lomnitz, Claudio. *Deep Mexico, Silent Mexico: An Anthropology of Nationalism*. Minneapolis: University of Minnesota Press, 2001.

López, Marcos. *Pop Latino plus*. Buenos Aires: La Marca Editora, 2007.

————. "Vuelo de cabotaje, 2009." Accessed July 10, 2013, http://www.marcoslopez .com/marcostextos.htm.

Lugones, Benigno B. "Los beduinos urbanos." *La Nación*, March 18, 1879.

————. "Los caballeros de industria." *La Nación*, April 6, 1879.

Luker, Morgan James. "The Managers, the Managed, and the Unmanageable: Negotiating Values at the Buenos Aires International Music Fair." *Ethnomusicology Forum* 15.1 (2010): 89–113.

————. "Tango Renovación: On the Uses of Music History in Post-Crisis Argentina." *Latin American Music Review* 28.1 (2007): 68–93.

Makaroff, Eduardo. Interview with Esteban Buch. Paris, January 10, 2008.

Malosetti Costa, Laura. *Los primeros modernos: arte y sociedad en Buenos Aires a fines del siglo XIX*. Buenos Aires: Fondo de Cultura Económica, 2001.

Manzi, Homero. *Sur: Barrio de Tango*. Edited by Acho Manzi. Buenos Aires: Corregidor, 2000.

Marchini, Jorge. *El tango en la Economía de la Ciudad de Buenos Aires*. Buenos Aires: Subsecretaria de Industrias culturales, Ministerio de Producción, 2007.

Marcos, Subcomandante. *Ya Basta! Ten Years of the Zapatista Uprising*. Oakland: AK Press, 2004.

Martín-Barbero, Jesús. *Communication, Culture, and Hegemony: From the Media to Mediations*. New York: Sage, 1993.

Martorell de Laconi, Susana. "Hacia una definición del lunfardo." Paper presented at the Jornadas "Hacia una redefinición de *lunfardo*," organizadas por la Academia Porteña del Lunfardo, December 3–5, 2002.

————. "El lunfardo en la nueva edición (2001) del diccionario de la Real Academia Española." *Estudios sobre Tango y Lunfardo ofrecidos a José Gobello*. Edited by Oscar Conde and Marcelo Oliveri. Buenos Aires: Carpe noctem, 2002. 69–80.

————. *Salta lunfa: El lunfardo en Salta*. Salta: Instituto Salteño de Investigaciones Dialectológicas "Berta Vidal de Battini," 2000.

Mascia, Alfredo A. *Política y tango*. Buenos Aires: Paidos, 1970.

Matallana, Andrea. *Qué saben los patucos. La experiencia del tango entre 1910 y 1940.* Buenos Aires: Prometeo, 2008.

Matamoro, Blas. "Orígenes musicales." *Autores Varios: La historia del tango*, vol. 1. Buenos Aires: Corregidor, 1976. 55–98.

———. *El tango.* Madrid: Acento, 1996.

Matsuda, Matt K. "Desires: Last Tango at the *Académie.*" *The Memory of the Modern.* New York: Oxford University Press, 1996. 185–204.

Mazzucchelli, Aldo. "El modernismo en el tango." *Revista de Crítica Literaria Latinoamericana* 32 (2006): 25–45.

Megenney, William W. "The River Plate *Tango*: Etymology and Origins." *Afro-Hispanic Review* 20.2 (2003): 39–45.

Meintjes, Louise. "Paul Simon's Graceland, South Africa, and the Mediation of Musical Meaning." *Ethnomusicology* 34.1 (1990): 37–73.

Mercury Theatre. "February–July 2010." Colchester: Mercury Theatre, 2010.

Middleton, Richard. *Studying Popular Music.* Milton Keynes: Open University Press, 1990.

Mignolo, Walter. 2002. "Las geopolíticas del conocimiento y la colonialidad del poder." Interview with Catherine Walsh, 2002. Accessed July 10, 2013, http://www.oei.es/salactsi/walsh.htm.

Míguez, Daniel, and Pablo Semán, eds. *Entre santos, cumbias y piquetes: Las culturas populares en la Argentina reciente.* Buenos Aires: Biblos, 2006.

Miller, Jacques-Alain. "El piropo." *Quehacer del Psicoanalista: Recorrido de Lacan—ocho conferencias.* Buenos Aires: J.A. Miller y Ediciones Manantial, 1986. 25–40.

Miller, Marilyn G. *Rise and Fall of the Cosmic Race.* Austin: University of Texas Press, 2004.

Miller, Toby. *The Well-Tempered Self: Citizenship, Culture, and the Postmodern Subject.* Baltimore: Johns Hopkins University Press, 1993.

Miller, Toby, and George Yúdice. *Cultural Policy.* New York: Sage Publications, 2002.

Mina, Carlos. *Tango. La mezcla milagrosa (1917–1956).* Buenos Aires: Sudamericana, 2007.

Ministerio de Cultura. *Balance de la Gestión 2006.* Buenos Aires: Gobierno de la Ciudad de Buenos Aires, 2007.

Mitchell, W. T. J. "Iconology and Ideology: Panofsky, Althusser, and the Scene of Recognition." *Image and Ideology in Modern/Postmodern Discourse.* Edited by David B. Downing and Susan Bazargan. Albany: State University of New York Press, 1991. 321–30.

Molar, Ben. *14 con el tango. Poetas-pintores-músicos.* 33 rpm LP with texts and illustrations. Buenos Aires: Discos Fermata 1966.

Monjeau, Federico, and Rafael Filipelli. "Fue lindo mientras duró. Contribuciones a una crítica del tango." *Punto de Vista* 86 (December 2006): 15–22.

Monsalve, Jaime Andrés. *El tango en sus propias palabras.* Bogotá: Icono, 2006.

Monteagudo, Luciano. *Fernando Solanas.* Buenos Aires: Centro Editor de América Latina, 1993.

Morena, Miguel Ángel. *Historia artística de Carlos Gardel.* Buenos Aires: Freeland, 1976.

Morin, Edgar. "¿Sociedad mundo, o Imperio mundo? Más allá de la globalización y el desarrollo." *Gazeta de Antropología* 19 (2003). Accessed July 10, 2013, http://www .ugr.es/~pwlac/G19_01Edgar_Morin.html.

Morin, Edgar, Emilio Roger Ciurana, and Raúl Motta. *Educar en la era planetaria.* Valladolid: Universidad de Valladolid-UNESCO, 2002.

Murillo, Susana, ed. *Sujetos a la incertidumbre. Transformaciones sociales y construcción de subjetividad en la Buenos Aires actual.* Buenos Aires: Ediciones del Instituto Movilizador de Fondos Cooperativos, 2003.

Nau-Klapwijk, Nicole. *Tango: Un baile bien porteño.* Buenos Aires: Corregidor, 2006.

Ness, Sally Ann. *Body, Movement, and Culture: Kinesthetic and Visual Symbolism in Philippine Community.* Philadelphia: University of Pennsylvania Press, 1992.

Nichols, Bill. *Introduction to Documentary.* Bloomington: Indiana University Press, 2001.

Nogués, Germinal. *Buenos Aires, ciudad secreta.* Buenos Aires: Ruy Díaz-Sudamericana, 1993.

Novack, Cynthia J. *Sharing the Dance: Contact Improvisation and American Culture.* Madison: University of Wisconsin Press, 1990.

Novati, Jorge, et al. *Antología del Tango Rioplatense. Desde sus comienzos hasta 1920.* Buenos Aires. Instituto Nacional de Musicología "Carlos Vega," 2002. CD-ROM.

Nudler, Julio. *Tango Judío. Del ghetto a la milonga.* Buenos Aires: Editorial Sudamericana, 1998.

Ochoa, Ana María. "Sonic Transculturation, Epistemologies of Purification and the Aural Public Sphere in Latin America." *Social Identities* 12.6 (2006): 803–25.

Ochoa, Ana María, and George Yúdice. "The Latin American Music Industry in an Era of Crisis." Paper prepared for the Global Alliance for Cultural Diversity, Division of Arts and Cultural Enterprise, UNESCO. Paris, 2002.

Ochoa, Pedro. *Tango y cine mundial.* Buenos Aires: Ediciones del Jilguero, 2003.

Oliver, Samuel. *Pedro Figari.* Buenos Aires: Ediciones de Arte Gaglianone, 1984.

Ordaz, Luis. "Frustraciones y fracasos del período inmigratorio en los 'grotescos criollos' de Armando Discépolo." Teatro del Pueblo. Accessed July 10, 2013, http://www .teatrodelpueblo.org.ar/dramaturgia/ordaz002.htm.

Orezzoli, Hector, and Claudio Segovia. *Tango Argentino.* New York: Mark Hellinger Theater, Gershwin Theater, 1986, 1999–2000.

Orgambide, Pedro. *Cuentos con tangos.* Rosario, Argentina: Ameghino Editora, 1998.

Ortiz, Fiona. "Argentina Sees Comeback of Tango." *International Herald Tribune,* January 31, 2008.

Ortiz, Renato. "Legitimidad y estilos de vida." *Mundialización y Cultura.* Buenos Aires: Editorial Alianza, 1997. 247–89.

Ortiz Nuevo, José Luis, and Faustino Núñez. *La rabia del placer: El origen cubano del tango y su desembarco en España (1823–1923).* Sevilla: Diputación de Sevilla, 1999.

Ortiz Oderigo, Néstor. *Latitudes africanas del tango.* Edited by Norberto Pablo Cirio. Caseros: Eduntref, 2009.

Ostuni, Ricardo. *Borges y el tango*. Buenos Aires: Ediciones Lumiere, 2009.

Oubiña, David, ed. *El cine de Hugo Santiago*. Buenos Aires: Nuevos Tiempos, 2002.

Page, Joanna. *Crisis and Capitalism in Contemporary Argentine Cinema*. Durham: Duke University Press, 2009.

Palermo, Vicente, and Rafael Mantovani. *Batiendo la justa. Manual de jergas argentinas*. Buenos Aires: Capital Intelectual, 2008.

Palumbo, Tito, ed. *Buenos Aires Tango: Guía Trimestral*. Buenos Aires, 2006.

Paoletti, Mario. "Borges y la ciudad del tango." *Revista de Occidente* 69 (1987): 87–100.

Paris Tango. Dirección general, Manrique Zago; dirección editorial, Eduardo Guibourg; textos, Alberto Mario Perrone, Luis Vázquez, Miguel Angel Gutiérrez; fotografías, Patricia Rivolta [et al.]. Buenos Aires: Manrique Zago Ediciones, 1998.

Pelinski, Ramón. "La corporalidad del tango: breve guía de accesos." *Invitación a la etnomusicología. Quince fragmentos y un tango*. Madrid: Akal, 2000. 252–81.

———. "Tango Nómade — Una metáfora de la globalización." *Escritos sobre tango en el Río de la Plata y en la diáspora*. Edited by T. Lencina, O. García Brunelli, and R. Saltón, 65–120. Buenos Aires: Centro Feca Ediciones, 2009.

Pelinski, Ramón, ed. *El tango nómade: Ensayos sobre la diaspora del tango*. Buenos Aires: Corregidor, 2000.

Pellarolo, Sirena. *Sainetes, cabaret, minas y tangos. Una antología*. Buenos Aires: Corregidor, 2010.

Pelletieri, Osvaldo. "Evaristo Carriego y el sistema literario de las letras de tango." *Relieve* 1.1 (1998): 2–14.

Peralta, Julián. Interview with Morgan Luker. Buenos Aires, October 4, 2006.

———. *La orquesta típica: Arreglo y orqestación en el tango*. Buenos Aires: Ediciones Orsai, 2006.

Pessinis, Jorge, and Carlos Kuri. "Astor Piazzolla. Chronology of a Revolution." Accessed July 10, 2013, http://www.piazzolla.org/biography/biography-english.html.

Pinsón, Néstor. "Eduardo Bianco." Todotango.com. Accessed July 13, 2013, http://www.todotango.com/spanish/creadores/ebianco.asp.

Plaza, Gabriel. "Un tango clavado en la yugular del rock." *La Nación,* October 25, 2007. Accessed July 10, 2013, http://www.lanacion.com.ar/nota.asp?nota_id=956150.

Plebs, Milena. "Mariano 'Chicho' Frúmboli. Esencia y enseñanza." *El Tangauta* 182 (December 2009). Accessed July 13, 2010, http://www.eltangauta.com.

Plisson, Michel. *Tango: Du Noir au Blanc*. Arles: Actes Sud, 2001.

Potter, Sally. *The Tango Lesson*. Sony Pictures Classics, 1997.

Powers, Richard. "Great Partnering." 2010. Accessed June 24, 2013, http://socialdance.stanford.edu/syllabi/partnering.htm.

Prieto, Adolfo. *El discurso criollista en la formación de la Argentina moderna*. Buenos Aires: Siglo Veintiuno Editores, 2006 [1988].

Pujol, Sergio. *Historia del baile. De la milonga a la disco*. Buenos Aires: Emecé, 1999.

Quesada, Ernesto. "El 'criollismo' en la literatura argentina." *En torno al criollismo*. Edited by Alfredo Rubione. Colección Capítulo, no. 190. Buenos Aires: CEAL, 1983. 103–230.

Quiroga, Carlos. "Tango Is a Shared Moment," interview with Carlos Gavito.

Reportango (New York), January 2001. Accessed July 3, 2013, http://web.ics.purdue
.edu/~tango/Articles/Gavito.pdf.

Quistgaard, Kaitlin. "The Argentine Art of Flirting." *Salon.com*, 1999. Accessed July 3,
2013, http://www.salon.com/1999/05/07/argentina/.

Rabe, Jay. "Gender Relationships." *TangoMoments.com*. 2004. Accessed January 29,
2012, http://www.tangomoments.com/pages/ATango.htm#gender.

Reinoso, Susana. "La literatura de la Argentina es la mejor del mundo hispánico." *La
Nación*, November 12, 2004. Accessed July 10, 2013, http://www.lanacion.com.ar
/nota.asp?nota_id=653312.

Renfrew Center Foundation. *Eating Disorders 101 Guide: A Summary of Issues, Statistics,
and Resources*. Originally published September 2002, revised October 2003. Accessed October 1, 2010, http://www.renfrew.org.

Renzi, Juan Pablo. "A propósito de la cultura mermelada." *Manifiestos argentinos:
Políticas de lo visual 1900-2000*. Edited by Rafael Cippolini. Buenos Aires: Adriana
Hidalgo, 2003. 350–54.

Richard, Nelly. *The Insubordination of Signs: Political Change, Cultural Transformation,
and the Poetics of the Crisis*. Translated by Alice A. Nelson and Silvia R. Tandeciarz.
Durham: Duke University Press, 2004.

Rippon, Angela. "Vertical Expression of a Horizontal Desire." *Tango Para Dos, Homage
to Carlos Gardel*. Sadler Wells, London, 1993. Concert program.

Rivera, Jorge B., et al. *La historia del tango*, vol. 1. Buenos Aires: Corregidor, 1976.

Romano, Eduardo. "La poética popular de Celedonio Esteban Flores." *Sobre poesía
popular argentina*. Buenos Aires: Centro Editor de América Latina, 1982. 117–53.

Romay, Diego. *Tanguera*. Buenos Aires: Romay Producciones Teatrales, 2002, 2005,
2007.

Romero, Walter. *Ocho claves en la poética de Homero Manzi*. Buenos Aires: Ateneo
popular de la Boca, 2010.

Rosboch, María Eugenia. *La rebelión de los abrazos. Tango, milonga y danza*. La Plata:
Editorial de la Universidad Nacional de la Plata, 2006.

Rossi, Vicente. *Cosas de negros. Los oríjenes del tango y otros aportes al folklore rioplatense. Rectificaciones históricas*. Río de la Plata: Imprenta argentina, 1926.

Rossner, Michael, ed. *"Bailá! Vení! Volá!": El fenómeno tanguero y la literatura: actas del
coloquio de Berlín, 13–15 de febrero de 1997*. Madrid: Iberoamericana, 2000.

Ruffié de Saint-Blancat, Monique, Juan Carlos Esteban, and Georges Galopa. *Carlos
Gardel: Sus antecedentes franceses*. Buenos Aires: Corregidor, 2006.

Russo, Juan Angel, and Santiago D. Marpegán. *Letras de tango*. 3 vols. Buenos Aires:
Basílico, 1999–2000.

Sábat, Hermenegildo. *Hermenegildo Sábat en el Museo Nacional de Bellas Artes*. Buenos
Aires: Museo Nacional de Bellas Artes, 1997.

———. *Tango mío*. Madrid: Editorial Ameris, 1981.

Sábato, Ernesto. *Tango. Canción de Buenos Aires*. Buenos Aires: Ediciones Centro
Arte, 1964.

Saikin, Magali. *Tango y género. Identidades y roles sexuales en el Tango Argentino*.
Stuttgart: Abrazos, 2004.

Salas, Horacio. *Borges: Una biografía*. Buenos Aires: Planeta, 1994.

———. *Homero Manzi y su tiempo*. Buenos Aires: J. Vergara, 2001.

———. *El tango*. La Habana: Casa de las Américas, 2006 [1986].

Salessi, Jorge. *Médicos, maleantes y maricas. Higiene, criminología y homosexualidad en la construcción de la nación Argentina (Buenos Aires 1871–1914)*. Buenos Aires: Beatriz Viterbo Editora, 1995.

———. "Medics, Crooks, and Tango Queens: The National Appropriation of a Gay Tango." *Everynight Life: Culture and Dance in Latin/o America*. Edited by José Esteban Muñoz. Translated by Celeste Fraser Delgado. Durham: Duke University Press, 1997. 141–74.

Salinas Rodríguez, José Luis. *Jazz, Flamenco, Tango: Las orillas de un ancho río*. Madrid: Editorial Catriel, 1994.

Salvador, Nélida. "Mito y realidad de una polémica literaria: Boedo-Florida." *Revista Sur* (1963): 68–72.

Samuels, David. *Putting a Song on Top of It: Expression and Identity on the San Carlos Apache Reservation*. Tucson: University of Arizona Press, 2004.

———. "The Whole and the Sum of the Parts, or, How Cookie and the Cupcakes Told the Story of Apache History in San Carlos." *Journal of American Folklore* 112 (1999): 464–74.

Sandez, Fernanda. "Los artistas tenemos algo de espiritistas." Accessed June 15, 2010, http://www.revista-noticias.com.ar/comun/nota.php?art=2669&ed=1739.

Sanguinetti, Julio María, and Ramiro Casasbellas. *Figari*. Buenos Aires: Fundación Pettoruti, 1992.

Santiago, Hugo, dir. *Invasión*. Argentina, 1969.

———. *Les trottoirs de Saturne*. Argentina-France, 1985.

Sarlo, Beatriz. *Jorge Luis Borges: A Writer on the Edge*. London: Verso, 1993.

———. *Una modernidad periférica: Buenos Aires, 1920 y 1930*. Buenos Aires: Ediciones Nueva Visión, 1988.

———. "Victoria Ocampo o el amor de la cita." *La máquina cultural: Maestras, traductores y vanguardistas*. Buenos Aires: Ariel, 1998. 93–194.

Sarmiento, Facundo. *Civilization and Barbarism*. Berkeley: University of California Press, 2003.

Saura, Carlos. *Tango*. Columbia/Tristar Studios, 1997.

Savigliano, Marta. *Angorra Matta: Fatal Acts of North-South Translation*. Middletown: Wesleyan University Press, 2003.

———. "Nocturnal Ethnographies: Following Cortázar in the Milongas of Buenos Aires." *Trans. Revista Transcultural de Música / Transcultural Music Review* 5 (2000). Accessed July 10, 2013, http://www.redalyc.org/articulo.oa?id=82200508.

———. *Tango and the Political Economy of Passion*. Boulder: Westview Press, 1995.

Scribano, Adrián. "Capitalismo, cuerpo, sensaciones y conocimiento: desafíos de una Latinoamérica interrogada." *Sociedad, cultura y cambio en América Latina*. Edited by Julio Mejía Navarrete. Lima: Universidad Ricardo Palma, 2009. 89–110.

Sebastián, Ana. *Tango, Literatura e Identidad*. Buenos Aires: La rosa blindada, 2006.

Sebreli, Juan José. *Buenos Aires, vida cotidiana y alienación; Buenos Aires, ciudad en Crisis.* Buenos Aires: Editorial Sudamericana, 2003.

Selles, Roberto. *El origen del tango.* Buenos Aires: Academia Porteña del Lunfardo, 1998.

Sessa, Aldo. *Tango.* Buenos Aires: Sessa, 1999.

Siegmann, Johanna. *The Tao of Tango.* Victoria, Canada: Trafford, 2000.

Sierra, Luis Adolfo. *Historia de la orquesta típica. Evolución instrumental del tango.* Buenos Aires: Corregidor, 1985.

Sitrin, Marina, ed. *Horizontalism: Voices of Popular Power in Argentina.* Oakland: AK Press, 2006.

Sklar, Deidre. "Invigorating Dance Ethnology." UCLA *Journal of Dance Ethnology* 15 (1991): 4–16.

Smith, Nigel E. "And the Beat Goes On: An Introduction to French Techno Culture." *French Review* 77 (2004): 730–41.

Solanas, Fernando E., dir. *El exilio de Gardel: Tangos.* Argentina-France, 1985.

Solanas, Fernando E., and Octavio Getino, dirs. *La hora de los hornos.* Argentina, 1968.

Soler Cañas, Luis. *Orígenes de la literatura lunfarda.* Buenos Aires: Ediciones Siglo Veinte, 1965.

Soletic, Antonio. *Cuaderno de Acuarelas Lunfardas.* Buenos Aires: Ateneo Popular de la Boca, 1995.

Sorrentino, Fernando. *Seven Conversations with Jorge Luis Borges.* New York: Whitston, 1982.

Stam, Robert. "*The Hour of the Furnaces* and the Two Avant-Gardes." *The Social Documentary in Latin America.* Edited by Julianne Burton. Pittsburgh: University of Pittsburgh Press, 1990. 251–66.

Sublette, Ned. *The World That Made New Orleans: From Spanish Silver to Congo Square.* Chicago: Lawrence Hill Books, 2008.

Sullivan, Edward J., and Nelly Perazzo. *Pettoruti.* Buenos Aires: Fundación Pettoruti, 2005.

"Syncopation." *Oxford Music Online.* Oxford University Press. Accessed July 8, 2013, http://www.oxfordmusiconline.com/subscriber/article/grove/music/27263.

Szendy, Peter. *Tubes: Le philosophe dans le juke-box.* Paris: Minuit, 2008.

Tango Argentino. Playbill. Mark Hellinger Theater, New York, March 1986.

Taylor, Julie M. *Paper Tangos.* Durham: Duke University Press, 1998.

———. "Tango: Ethos of Melancholy." *Cultural Anthropology* 2.4 (1998): 481–93.

Taylor, Timothy D. "World Music in Television Ads." *American Music* 18 (2000): 162–92.

Teruggi, Mario. *Panorama del lunfardo.* Buenos Aires: Ediciones Cabargón, 1974.

Thomas, Helen, and Nicola Miller. "Ballroom Blitz." *Dance in the City.* Edited by Helen Thomas. New York: St. Martin's Press, 1997. 89–110.

Thompson, Robert Farris. *Tango: The Art History of Love.* New York: Pantheon, 2005.

Tobin, Jeffrey. "Tango and the Scandal of Homosocial Desire." *The Passion of Music and Dance: Body, Gender, and Sexuality.* Edited by William Washabaugh. Oxford: Berg, 1998.

Trotta, Mafalda. *Milonga. El abrazo del tango.* Documentary. Cinematography by Federico Ferrario. Italy: n.p., 2006.

Tsing, Anna. "The Global Situation." *Cultural Anthropology* 15.3 (2000): 327–60.

Turino, Thomas. *Music as Social Life: The Politics of Participation.* Chicago: University of Chicago Press, 2008.

Ulanovsky, Carlos, et al. *Días de radio.* 2 vols. Buenos Aires: Emecé Editores, 2004.

Ulla, Noemí. *Tango, rebelión y nostalgia.* Buenos Aires: Centro Editor de América Latina, 1982 [1966].

UNESCO. "Nomination Form." 2009. Accessed July 8, 2013, http://www.unesco.org /culture/ich/index.php?RL=00258.

Varela, Chuy. "Bajofondo Mixes Latin, Rock, Hip-hop Sounds." *San Francisco Chronicle,* August 3, 2008. Accessed July 22, 2010, http://www.sfgate.com/cgi-bin/article .cgi?f=/c/a/2008/08/01/PK8S11TS6M.DTL.

Varela, Gustavo. *Mal de tango: Historia y genealogía moral de la música ciudadana.* Buenos Aires: Paidós, 2005.

———. *Tango: Una pasión ilustrada.* Buenos Aires: Ediciones Lea, 2010.

Vega, Carlos. *Estudios para los orígenes del Tango Argentino.* Buenos Aires: EDUCA, 2007.

Vezzetti, Hugo. *Pasado y presente: guerra, dictadura y sociedad en la Argentina.* Buenos Aires: Siglo XXI, 2002.

Vidart, Daniel. *El tango y su mundo.* Montevideo: Ediciones de la Banda Oriental, 2007 [1967].

———. *Teoría del tango.* Montevideo: Ediciones de la Banda Oriental, 1964.

Vila, Pablo. "Argentina's 'Rock Nacional': The Struggle for Meaning." *Latin American Music Review* 10.1 (1989): 1–28.

———. "El tango y las identidades étnicas en Argentina." *El tango nómade. Etnografía de la diáspora del tango.* Edited by R. Pelinski. Buenos Aires: Corregidor, 2000. 71–97.

Viladrich, Anahí. "From Shrinks to Urban Shamans: Argentine Immigrants' Therapeutic Eclecticism in New York City." *Culture, Medicine, and Psychiatry* 31 (2007): 307–28.

———. "Neither Virgins nor Whores: Tango Lyrics and Gender Representations in the Tango World." *Journal of Popular Culture* 39.2 (April 2006): 272–93.

———. "Tango Immigrants in New York City: The Value of Social Reciprocities." *Journal of Contemporary Ethnography* 34 (2005): 533–59.

Viñas, David. *Literatura argentina y política.* 2 vols. Buenos Aires: Sudamericana, 1995.

———. Untitled text in Alonso, *Carlos Alonso* 105–9.

Wade, Peter. *Music, Race, and Nation: Música Tropical in Colombia.* Chicago: University of Chicago Press, 1997.

Webster, Susan Verdi. "Emilio Pettoruti. Musicians and Harlequins." *Latin American Art* 3.1 (1991): 18–22.

Whitelow, Guillermo. *Héctor Basaldúa.* Buenos Aires: Academia Nacional de Bellas Artes, 1980.

Williams, Raymond. *Marxismo y literatura.* Barcelona: Editorial Península, 1980.

Wolf, Sergio. "Aspectos Del Problema Del Tiempo En El Cine Argentino." *Pensar el cine. Cuerpo(s), temporalidad y nuevas tecnologías,* vol. 2. Edited by Gerardo Yoel. Buenos Aires: Manantial, 2004. 171–85.

Wortman, Ana, ed. *Pensar las clases medias: Consumos culturales y estilos de vida urbanos en la Argentina de los noventa.* Buenos Aires: La Crujía Ediciones, 2003.

Yúdice, George. 2001. "Afro Reggae: Parlaying Culture into Social Justice." *Social Text* 69 (2001): 53–65.

———. *The Expediency of Culture: Uses of Culture in the Global Era.* Durham: Duke University Press, 2003.

———. "La *funkización* de Río." *La cultura como recurso.* Barcelona: Gedisa, 2003. 137–67.

Yúdice, George, Juan Flores, and Jean Franco, eds. *On Edge: The Crisis of Contemporary Latin American Culture.* Minneapolis: University of Minnesota Press, 1992.

Zito, Carlos Alberto. *El Buenos Aires de Borges.* Buenos Aires: Aguilar, 1998.

Zlotchew, Clark M. "Tango from the Inside: Interview with Enrique Cadícamo." *Journal of Popular Culture* 21 (1987): 131–43.

———. "Tango, Lunfardo and the Popular Culture of Buenos Aires: Interview with José Gobello." *Studies in Latin American Culture* 8 (1989): 271–85.

Zotto, Miguel Angel. *TangoX2 / Tango Para Dos.* Buenos Aires, 1988.

CONTRIBUTORS AND TRANSLATORS

ESTEBAN BUCH, an Argentine musicologist and writer, teaches music history at the Ecole des Hautes Etudes en Sciences Sociales in Paris. He is the editor of *Tangos Cultos: Kagle, J. J. Castro, Pastropiero y otros cruces musicales* (2012) and the author of *The Bomarzo Affair: Ópera, perversión y dictadura* (2003) and *O juremos con gloria morir— Historia de una épica de Estado* (1994). In French he has published *La Neuvième de Beethoven: Une histoire politique* (1999; English edition, 2004) and *Le cas Schönberg: Naissance de l'avant-garde musicale* (2006).

OSCAR CONDE taught at the University of Buenos Aires for twenty-four years and is now a professor at Argentina's UNIPE (Pedagogic University) and UNLa (National University of Lanús). He is the author of *Diccionario etimológico del lunfardo* (1998; second edition 2004) and, most recently, of *Lunfardo: Un estudio sobre el habla popular de los argentinos* (2011). He compiled *Estudios sobre tango y lunfardo ofrecidos a José Gobello* (2002), *Poéticas del tango* (2003), *Poéticas del rock vol. 1* (2007), and *Poéticas del rock vol. 2* (2008). He is also a published poet (*Cáncer de conciencia*, 2007; *Gramática personal*, 2012) and is a named member of the Academia Porteña del Lunfardo.

ANTONIO GÓMEZ is Assistant Professor of Latin American literature and film at Tulane University. His research interests include the discourse of exile in Latin American intellectual history, documentary film, and the writing of recent history—especially the present rewriting of the sixties and new cinematic poetics in Latin America. He is the author of *La escritura del espacio ausente* (2013).

KURT HOFER received a degree from St. Andrews University and is completing a doctorate degree in Spanish at Tulane University. His research interests include articulations of the family and the private sphere in early modern Spain and colonial Latin America.

KATHARINA KEPPEL received her undergraduate degree from the Freie Universitaet in Berlin, Germany, and her master's degree in Latin American studies at Tulane University. Her research interests include nineteenth-century travel narratives, the links between ethnography and literature, and the role of museums in Latin American nation building.

MORGAN JAMES LUKER is Assistant Professor of music at Reed College. His research examines the cultural politics of contemporary tango music in Buenos Aires, focusing on the intersection of musical practice and cultural policy. His work has appeared in the *Latin American Music Review* and *Ethnomusicology Forum*, and he has presented at conferences throughout the United States, Latin America, and Europe.

CAROLYN MERRITT is an anthropologist with a background in dance who has studied tango since 2002. She lived in Buenos Aires from 2005 until 2007, conducting research on *tango nuevo*. She is a Lecturer in Anthropology at Bryn Mawr College, and writes regularly for ThINKingDANCE. Her book *Tango Nuevo* was published in 2012.

MARILYN G. MILLER is Associate Professor of Latin American literature and culture at Tulane University. Her research focuses on inter-American and inter-Latin American influences and the relationship between Latin American cultural production and intellectual and cultural histories. She is the author of *Rise and Fall of the Cosmic Race: The Cult of Mestizaje in Latin America* (2004).

FERNANDO ROSENBERG is Associate Professor of romance and comparative literature at Brandeis University. He taught previously at SUNY-Binghamton and Yale. He is the author of *Avant Garde and Geopolitics in Latin America* (2006) and numerous articles on modernism, avant-gardes, and modernity in Latin America. He coedited with Jill Lane a special issue of *e-misférica* titled *Performance and the Law*. He also contributed to the *Blackwell Companion to Latin American Literature and Culture* (ed. Sara Castro-Klarén, 2008). His current research focuses on issues of justice in contemporary Latin American artistic production.

ALEJANDRO SUSTI completed a doctorate in Hispanic American literature at Johns Hopkins University. After returning to Peru, he published five collections of poems as well as the book-length study *"Seré millones": Eva Perón: Melodrama, cuerpo y simulacro* (2007). He has coauthored *Ciudades ocultas: Lima en el cuento peruano moderno* (2007) and *Umbrales y márgenes: El poema en prosa en el Perú contemporáneo* (2010). He is also a musician and composer. He currently teaches at the University of Lima and the Catholic University in Lima.

MICHAEL WIEDORN is an Assistant Professor of French at the Georgia Institute of Technology. His research focuses on the Martinican novelist and philosopher Edouard Glissant and his engagement with the work of Gilles Deleuze. He has published with *The Society for Francophone Postcolonial Studies* and *Callaloo*, among others. His current work includes a project on Lafcadio Hearn's notion of the Creole. He wrote his doctoral dissertation while living at the Casa Argentina in Paris.

INDEX